The Encyclopedia of the Occult, the Esoteric, and the Supernatural

The Encyclopedia of the Occult, the Esoteric, and the Supernatural

(published in hardcover as *Man and the Beasts Within*)

Benjamin Walker

A SCARBOROUGH BOOK
STEIN AND DAY/*Publishers*/New York

FIRST SCARBOROUGH BOOKS EDITION 1980

The Encyclopedia of the Occult, the Esoteric, and the Supernatural was originally published in hardcover as *Man and the Beasts Within* by Stein and Day/*Publishers.*

Printed in the United States of America
Stein and Day/*Publishers*/Scarborough House,
Briarcliff Manor, N.Y. 10510

LC: 76-42238
ISBN: 0-8128-6051-9

Contents

Contents

Introduction

A large number of books dealing with human anatomy, physiology and psychology are available to those who wish to study these subjects on scientific lines. But there is probably no single work that gives information about the arcane side of these and related branches of knowledge. The need for a comprehensive encyclopedia presenting these topics with special reference to esoteric teachings has prompted the present compilation. As far as I am aware this is the first work of its kind.

Originally the term esoteric meant what was known only to a select few and not available to the common man. In this sense most specialists deal in esoterics, be they neurologists, astronomers or mining engineers. But whereas their specialties are established on concrete facts, the data of esoteric studies remain largely beyond the reach of the physical senses and scientific instruments. Much of this knowledge has been acquired by what might be called subjective research, and handed down by word of mouth.

The esoteric view is based on the aphorism that nothing in this world has only one meaning. The human body is a labyrinth of wonders, and the scientist has so far explored only the antechamber, and that too in part. A purely physical concept of man is bound to be limited. The more significant approach is the hidden or esoteric one. And the esoteric view provides us with an advanced concept of the human entity at all the many levels at which it operates.

A remarkable insight into the human body and its functions, and the human mind and its potentialities, had already been gained long before our own day. The age-old traditions dealing with these matters have their roots in ancient Egypt, Israel, China, India, Greece, Medieval Europe, as well as in the pre-Columbian civilizations of North, Central and South America. Providing as they do a deep understanding of man's total self, these traditions have been with the human family for countless generations, and far from being outmoded, they still form part of customary belief in all parts of the world, and what is more are increasingly attracting the attention of present-day research. Those who have the opportunity of studying these sources are often surprised to discover how many of the ancient theories are being endorsed by modern science.

We are today entering a new phase of understanding about ourselves and our environment. It must be evident to anyone whose interests take him outside the current of orthodox scientific thought, how within the last decade or so the pace of research into such matters has been accelerated. And the growing number of scholars and scientists who risk their reputations by venturing to examine these unorthodox disciplines might be regarded as a sign of increased awareness that many of the ancient beliefs about ourselves are well worth a second and more searching look.

Introduction

Those who are familiar with the prevailing emphasis on mechanistic theories, behaviourist experiments and psycho-pharmacological research in an attempt to understand the human personality, must feel that some essential element in man is being overlooked or ignored in all such investigations. One cannot avoid the impression that the earlier, occult, and in the broad sense, the religious or mystical view of mind and body, and of the human entity as a functioning whole, in reciprocal relationship with the total environment, has a great deal to recommend it, and needs to be given a hearing once more. Even if such a view is as yet scientifically inexplicable, it could usefully supplement the modern outlook. We perhaps need to be reminded that the science of man as taught in our academic institutions is not the only one accepted by thinking people.

In bringing the material of this volume together I have tried to cover the ground as comprehensively as possible, so that no significant aspect of the subject should be excluded. The topics dealt with are presented from the traditional viewpoint, and, where possible, explained in the light of the latest scientific findings.

The book deals with external anatomy and physiology, including the main organs, limbs and parts of the body; it describes the chief functions, processes and products of the body, from the enigmatic ros, which is generated in the subtle system and materializes in the cranium, to the scatological substances that form the egesta of the physical organism. The mystical and magical beliefs connected with respiratory and sexual techniques and other related matters, have been exhaustively treated.

It also covers the chief psychological concepts, again with an esoteric emphasis, including the whole area of what is known as metapsychology, which extends the sphere of investigation outside the field of psychology proper, to speculative considerations relating to the self, personality and mind, the mind-body relationship and similar hypotheses that lie beyond empirical verification. The sphere of the non-physical body such as the astral and etheric vehicles, as well as the borderline phenomena of the bioflux and its attributes, now the subject of intensive study in the USA and USSR, are also considered.

It will be seen that this work covers a considerable area, for the net has been cast wide. The criteria of selection have not debarred any topic that has any prominence in the occult view of man in his totality. Taken as a whole it presents, in reasonable detail, an alternative view of ourselves.

Most of the subjects are interconnected, and may be traced by reference to related topics. An asterisk after a word means that it forms the subject of a separate article.

It must be added that this work summarizes what has been acquired from many mentors, experts and friends over the years. My grateful thanks are due to them as well as to the authors of the many books and articles I have read. The bibliography at the end of each article indicates only the principal and most accessible authorities from whom I have drawn my material, and will be a useful guide to those who want to take their reading further.

B.W.

The Encyclopedia of the Occult, the Esoteric, and the Supernatural

ACCLIVITY

The direction of sexual energy upwards towards the brain for the purpose of enlightenment and power. It is based on the belief that the fluids secreted during sexual excitement have an ethereal essence that can be utilized by special techniques for occult purposes in sex magic.

Many methods of acclivity are possible: exercises such as the headstand; the sublimation of semen through encratism; secret methods of solitary sex; forms of sexuality not involving heterosexual partners. But for the highest kind of acclivity there is need for what both partners of opposite sexes can provide.

In taoist sex-magic the basic aim of acclivity is the utilization of the generative forces of male energy (*yang*), contained in man's semen, combined with the generative forces of the female energy (*yin*), contained in the woman's ova (*hsüeh*). Chinese sex alchemy further teaches that the male represents the watery element, and the female the element of fire, and their union becomes a cosmic event uniting earth and heaven. This is represented in the *I-Ching*, the Chinese classic of divination, by the trigram for water over the trigram for fire, together forming *Chi*, 'completion', the sixty-third hexagram.

In the acclivity process the flow of the combined yang and yin energy is first activated by special sexual stimulus and while it is in movement the glow or effulgence generated by sexual heat is converted into vital energy (*ch'i*). This combined yang-yin energy is picked up by the phallus, enriched and energized by breathing and other methods, and then drawn up along the spinal column to the brain. The semen is not emitted until its subtle essence is absorbed, after which the grosser elements that remain are ejaculated.

Precedent mastery of breath control, coitus prolongatus and upward penile peristalsis, are essential for success in the operation. In their sex magic rites taoists practise intrajaculation, by pressure on the perineum* just before emission, so that the male stream is directed inwards into the body of the adept himself. Expressing its basic feature, the Chinese taoist master, Lieh Hsien Chuan, says, 'The act of commerce with woman lies in refraining from ejaculation, and causing the sperm to return and nourish the brain' (Cakravarti, 1963, p. 89).

Certain refinements are added to the broader pattern of the practice, so that the man might draw benefit from the woman's breath, saliva and other secretions, and receive from her all the pulsations of yin energy that she continues to give off for some time. It is also pointed out that the longer the male can continue with the performance of the sexual act the better for him. A succession of partners is eminently desirable if he can keep up his tumescent state and withhold ejaculation. But on this there is disagreement, as some taoists believe that a woman's vital force, unlike a man's, is inexhaustible.

The object of tantrik sex magic is similar to the taoist, which is to make the semen (*retas*) go upward to the region of the Paramatman, or abode of the Great Soul at the crown of the head. Some authorities believe it may be associated with the ascent of the kundalini* from the base of the spine to the sahasrara at the top of the head. Tantrik adepts claim to have evolved certain methods of sex magic known as *oli* techniques. The word oli is a tantrik cult-word of obscure origin meaning 'womb-fire', referring to the sex-energy given off by women on heat, especially during the throes of sexual activity, and the purpose of oli techniques is the capture and absorption of this energy.

Three separate oli processes are involved in this operation: (1) vajroli (Sanskrit, *vajra*, 'thunderbolt'), where the female seed is drawn to the tip of the vajra, i.e. the erect phallus; (2) sahajoli (Sanskrit, *sahaja*, 'co-born'), in which the male seed moves down and unites with the female seed, which is irresistibly drawn towards it; and (3) amaroli (Sanskrit, *amara*, 'immortal'), when the combined seeds are drawn into the yogi's body, and then made to ascend to the brain.

The disciplines to be undertaken to achieve competence in oli are extremely arduous, and many yogic practitioners have unequivocally condemned these and related practices as futile, dangerous and degrading. Tantrik (and taoist) magicians do not always arouse the woman by intercourse, but sometimes do so by clitoral stimulation and draw her energy direct from her mouth at the end of each orgasm. Whatever the process used, and scores of them are listed, it is said that the female partner always suffers physical and psychic damage. Adepts of the left hand make it a point of getting the services of willing females who are prepared to be the passive vehicles in the ritual, although these women 'wither' and dry up after a few sessions as a result of this psychic vampirism.

Many experts feel that the eastern techniques of acclivity are highly improbable, and are not to be taken literally. Intrajaculation by pressure on the perineum* does not direct the sperm to the brain, but to the bladder. The absorption of the female 'seed', or the reabsorption of the ejaculated semen are merely figurative ways of describing a process in which the male augments the female generative energy during sexual activity, and then appropriates it by 'sipping' it for his own benefit, using various well-established occult methods for doing so.

A number of eleutherian (free-love) sects of the European Middle Ages, such as the Brethren of the Free Spirit, advocated what was known as *acclivitas* (Lat. 'ascent'), which was described as the upward movement of the soul during sexual intercourse. This variation of spiritual eroticism involved the 'direction uphill' of the participants during coitus, and was usually practised in association with coitus reservatus, or sex without emission. Medieval esotericism referred to the ros* or brain fluid as tending to seep downwards and get dissipated, and the objective of acclivity was to make the seminal essence ascend and combine with the ros.

It is to be noted that most forms of mutually satisfactory intercourse are believed to involve an exchange not only of physical substance but of 'spiritual fluids', and this does indeed produce a sense of heightened awareness and exhilaration, and thus constitutes the highest form of sexual sublimation through 'acclivity'.

Books

Blofeld, John, *The Secret and Sublime: Taoist Mysteries and Magic*, Allen & Unwin, London, 1973.

Cakravarti, C., *Sex Life in Ancient India*, Mukhopadhyay, Calcutta, 1963.

Fränger, W., *The Millennium of Hieronymous Bosch*, Faber, London, 1952.

Gulik, R. H. van, *Erotic Colour Prints of the Ming Period, with an Essay on Chinese Sex Life from the Han to the Chhing Dynasty* (206 BC to AD 1644), privately printed, Tokyo, 3 vols, 1951.

Needham, Joseph, *Science and Civilisation in China*, Cambridge University Press, vols 1–3, 1954–9.

Walker, Benjamin, *Hindu World: An Encyclopedic Outline of Hinduism*, Allen & Unwin, London, and Praeger, New York, 2 vols, 1968.

Woodroffe, Sir John, *Principles of Tantra*, 2 vols, Ganesh, Madras, 1914.

ANUS

The outside terminus of the rectum at the lower end of the alimentary canal. In psychoanalytical theory the second stage in the development of the libido* is the anal stage, when the child becomes aware of the pleasure derived from sensations centring around the rectum and the anal sphincter, and in the act of defecation. This leads to coprophilia, 'dirt-love', or interest in faeces and in dirt generally, and to the unconscious cultivation of costiveness, or a tendency to retain faeces as a treasured possession. A fixation at the anal stage manifests in compulsive obstinacy, orderliness, parsimony, a desire to collect and hoard things (stamps, coins, jewels, curios, antiques, works of art, money and other forms of 'filthy lucre') and a general urge to 'wallow in wealth'. There is a connection between anal preoccupation and money-getting, homosexuality and sadism.

The importance of the rectum and anus in the physical and mental well-being of the individual was recognized from very ancient times. The Egyptian physician Irj (c. 2500 BC) is described on his tomb as Shepherd of the Royal Anus. Continued pressure on the anus, as in constipation, can cause toxicity and bring on hallucinations. Until two centuries ago one of the standard methods used by exorcists in Europe to get rid of demons believed to possess the bodies of victims, was to apply the clyster or enema: the invading demons promptly vanished with the clearing of the bowels. It is a well-established medical fact that resentment, fear, anxiety, hatred, affect the functional capacity of the anus.

Situated near the perineum*, which is one of the most important plexuses of the human body, the anus is regarded as an occult plexus in certain forms of left-hand occultism. Chinese taoist magicians use a wooden plug to block the anus, during exercises performed to create the immortal embryonic seed, in order to prevent the vitalized wind from escaping via the rectum. In tantrik meditative exercises wooden pegs are inserted into the anus, and during sex-magical rites a finger is introduced into the rectum of the female partner.

By opening and closing the anal sphincter and exercising the muscles of the belly, yogis can draw water in and out of the rectum for purposes of colonic lavage. This is achieved after long practice. The alternate contraction and dilation of the anal sphincter for several hours is one method of attaining a particular kind of xenophrenia*, which is suddenly reached while the anus is dilated.

A close connection appears to exist between a relaxed anus and trance states. There is also said to be a secret correspondence between the rectal annulus and certain higher centres of the subtle body. Aleister Crowley (d. 1947) believed that anal intercourse with either sex was better for acquiring magical power than normal intercourse.

The nerves of the rectum and genital zone are closely connected. In fact the nerves of this region have wide ramifications, and contractions of the anal sphincter produce contractions in a number of remoter parts of the body, causing an acceleration of the heart and resulting in deeper respiration. Deep breathing can be started in a person in anaesthesia by inserting a finger into the anus.

The aberration known as sodomy or buggery, and some, but not all, forms of male homosexuality, involve coitus *in ano*. This form of sex is sometimes practised between husband and wife during menstruation, late pregnancy and as a means of birth control. Dr Paul Gillette states that recent studies suggest that 'most, if not all, persons are capable of responding erotically to the anus'.

Among the ancient Peruvians the husband did not use his wife vaginally so long as she was nursing a baby, for they believed that the mother's milk would be spoilt and the child would become ill. As lactation lasted for two years the husband had to resort to anal intercourse, and extant Peruvian vases depict couples having intercourse *per anum*. The Hebrews practised it in the belief that it created beneficial conditions in the womb, so that when normal coitus was performed afterwards, a clever child would be born. Hindus used their wives in the same way in emulation of Shiva who never tired of experimenting in new sexual postures with his wife Parvati.

Arabs followed the ancient injunction: 'Your wives are your tillage; go in therefore unto your tillage in what manner soever ye will.' Husbands in Rome are known to have followed the same custom. Gracchus so used Cornelia; Pompey, Julia; Brutus, Portia. Similarly, despite the fact that the Church Fathers strongly condemned intercourse *extra vas naturale*, 'outside the natural vessel', or *per vas nefandum*, 'by the unmentionable receptacle', it was widely practised in Christendom, and openly recommended by the medieval Courts of Love. Geoffrey Chaucer in 'The Parson's Tale' mentions anal intercourse, but likewise condemns it.

The muscular control of the anus and its contraction can promote erection and emission in men, and can help in the achievement of fuller erotic sensibility in women. Pressure on the anus causes excitation of the sexual organs and stimulates sexual desire. The anus and genitals share muscles in common.

The front of the anus is the back of the vagina. Some women can best obtain venereal orgasm with the added stimulus of digital friction of the anal passage during an otherwise normal intercourse. Often the female herself desires this or even anal intercourse, and can reach a climax by no other means.

Books

Crowley, Aleister, *The Magical Record of the Great Beast 666*, ed. J. Symonds and K. Grant, Duckworth, London, 1972.
Davenport, John, *Sexagyma*, p.p., London, 1888.
Edwardes, Allen, *The Jewel in the Lotus*, Lancer, New York, 1965.
Fielding, W. J., *Strange Customs of Courtship and Marriage*, Souvenir Press, London, 1961.
Freud, Sigmund, *New Introductory Lectures on Psychoanalysis*, Hogarth Press, London, 1964.
Gillette, Paul J., *The Complete Sex Dictionary*, Tandem, London, 1969.
Kinsey, Alfred C., *Sexual Behaviour in the Human Female*, Saunders, Philadelphia, 1953.

ARMS

Arms are an indispensable vehicle of complete human expression, by means of which most of the major activities are carried out. They terminate in the two external tools of the cerebral hemispheres, the hands*. With our arms we work, protect, donate, reject, soothe, comfort, embrace; and make the signs of invocation, conjuration and command. All major occult gestures involve the use of the arms, which give them an imperious and magical quality. In Egyptian hieroglyphics, two upraised arms is the sign for the *ka* or human double.

In the study of gesture all wide, outward movements of the arms indicate the extraverted person, one used to giving commands, and easy and confident in his ability and power. The person with folded arms is on the defensive and refuses to be swayed by the influences around him. A subordinate who receives orders from his superior with his arms folded makes a token of resistance and defiance; it is commonly regarded as a naturally insubordinate attitude. The man who walks with his arms swinging easily is relaxed and free; when his hands hang down limply he is defeated and beaten.

Upraised arms signify jubilation and victory. The Bible describes how when the Amalekites attacked the children of Israel at Rephidim, Joshua was deputed to fight against them while Moses stood on a hilltop watching the battle with his arms raised. So long as Moses kept his arms up the Israelites prevailed, but when he grew tired and his hands dropped the Amalekites prevailed. Aaron and Hur therefore stood by the side of the patriarch and kept his arms upraised until sunset, when the Amalekites were finally routed.

The symbolism of the 'stretched out arms', which occurs more than a dozen times in the Bible, is replete with overtones of reverent awe; it is strong to redeem and chastise, to sustain and judge. The blessing of the children of Israel that brings the last book of the Pentateuch to a close contains the famous verse: 'The eternal God is thy refuge, and underneath are the everlasting arms.'

Books

See under hand

ASOMA

(Gk. *a*, 'non', *soma*, 'body'), the non-material elements in man* comprising all the intangible factors that constitute his non-physical self, and contribute to his existence, identity and personality during his life, and, if belief in continued existence is valid, after his death.

There is a great deal of confusion in the vast nomenclature and classification of the asomatic elements, and there exists such a diversity of opinion on the subject that it would be a futile task to attempt to reproduce them all here. No one can hope to give universally acceptable definitions for, or distinguish between: Soul, Spirit, Vital Spirit, Anima, Pneuma, Nous, Psyche, Mind, Self, Superego, Ego, Perispirit, Etheric Double, Astral Body, and the hundreds of other terms in all their variations and shades of meaning, as posited by peoples ancient and modern, the Egyptians, Greeks, Chinese, Jews, Hindus, Moslems, Christians, and other nations, tribes, religions, cultures and cults throughout the world.

Many primitive tribes, for instance, believe in a multiplicity of asomatic elements, localized in different parts of the body, largely variations of the life-concept. The Amerindian tribes of the Menomini assign one soul to the head and another to the heart. The Bagobo of the Philippines distinguish a right-hand soul from a left-hand soul: one soul remains earth-bound as a ghost, the other joins the ancestors. Certain Melanesians believe that a man has seven different kinds of soul. In both primitive and advanced communities ghosts are commonly regarded as bearing the soul of the individual, but the modern tendency is to regard the majority of such apparitions as empty asomatic 'shells', or re-played 'recordings' of some traumatic event of the past.

A number of metaphysical problems arise in any consideration of the asomatic elements: whether they actually exist; whether they are interrelated, and how; whether they are material in any sense; whether they can become tangible, visible or otherwise perceptible; whether they have independent awareness, habits, feelings, individuality; whether they are connected with the physical body, and if so at what points (*see* plexus); whether they can operate apart from the physical body (*see* astral projection); whether they survive the death of the physical body.

Most of the asomatic elements can be reduced to three main groups, namely, the etheric body*, which carries the energy-principles of life and sensation; the astral body*, the vehicle of consciousness and the emotions; and the soul*, or the immortal principle. The following tabulation will indicate the varying designations given to the asomatic elements of the human body as conceived by different peoples through the ages.

	Etheric body associated with physical life; sense impressions; brain or animal consciousness; physical pleasure and pain; nervous energy. Subject to natural law	*Astral body* associated with pathemia* or the emotions; higher intellectual faculties, dreams, intuitions, memory. Subject to moral or ethical law	*Soul* or Spirit, the immortal principle or divine element. The absolute or essential Self. Subject to the spiritual law
Ancient Egyptian	*khaba* or shade	*ka*, protecting genius, or mind	*ba* or soul
Babylonian	*napistu*, animating or life principle	*etimmu*, spirit which on death goes to the underworld or returns as a ghost	*edim* or soul
Zoroastrian	*urvan*, the body-soul	*daēna*, the mind-soul, or conscience	*fravashi*, the immortal soul
Chinese	*p'o*, inferior, material soul, governs the functions of the body and perishes with it	*hun*, heavenly soul, or intelligence	*ch'i*, vital force, which forms part of Universal Reason
Japanese	*tamashii*, body-spirit	*mitama* (or tama), mind-spirit	*seishin*, soul
Tibetan (Bon)	*sems*, consciousness, possessed by men, animals, birds, insects	*yid*, thought	*bla*, spirit
Hindu	*jiva*, life or breath	*prāna*, life-soul, or *para-sharira*, astral body	*ātman*, soul
Voodoo	*loa-maît-tête*, 'loa (or god) master of the head'; vitalic principle that lives on in future generations	*gros-bon-ange*, 'great good angel' or the double. Becomes an ancestral spirit and forms part of the past	*ti-bon-ange*, 'little good angel', the moral guardian which returns to the gods after death
Greek (Aristotelian)	*skia*; 'shadow', *pneuma*, 'breath', *etor*, 'heart', *phrēn*, 'diaphragm'; the nutritive psyche	*eidolon*, 'double', the intellectual psyche	*psyche*, 'soul', creative reason
Greek (Plutarch)	*thymos*, life principle; *pneuma*, breath	*psyche*, partly submerged in the body and tainted by the body's desires	*nous*, the upper, uncorrupted part of man which survives death

Jewish	*nefesh*, lower or animal soul; principle of egotism, which resides in the blood or heart	*ruah*, astral soul, nucleus of man's being. Intellectual or moral part of man	*neshamah*, 'breath', the holy or divine soul, incapable of sin
Moslem	*nafs*, carnal breath and life principle; governs functions of body	*ruh*, intellectual or moral soul; comes from the mind	*sirr*, immortal soul; rises God-ward
Medieval church scholastics	*anima bruta*, the animal soul in man	*anima humana*, the 'human' soul in man	*anima divina*, the divine soul in man

Books

See under astral body *and* soul

ASTRAL BODY

Traditionally the second element of the asoma* or non-physical part of man. It comprises the emotional, mental and psychic basis of the individual, and largely conforms in character and intellect to the man himself. It relates to the domain of the ethical or moral law. Numerous qualities have been ascribed to the astral body and it is accordingly known by names corresponding to these features. It is often erroneously used as a synonym for the etheric body*, but there are clear distinctions between the two.

The astral is the vehicle of the pathemic or feeling (in the sense of emotional) self, and as such is called the *feeling* body. It is the element underlying higher consciousness and memory, and is therefore the *mental* or *memory* body. Because it experiences dreams it is the *dream* body. As the agent experiencing psychic phenomena it is the *psychical* body.

Since it is neither the physical body nor the soul, but forms as it were a sheath for the soul, early spiritualists called it the *perispirit*, 'around the spirit'. Since it has characteristics both of the mortal body (because it perishes) and of the immortal soul (because it houses the soul), it is called the *mortal soul*. Reincarnationists believe that evil actions taint the astral body, which taint is communicated to the soul, and is the cause of the soul's condition. It is thus the *causal* body, or *karmic* body, which is responsible for one's karma. Because it is the body that goes through the experience of death (Gk. *thanatos*, 'death') to emerge on the other side, it is the thanatic body. As the link between body and spirit, it forms a *unifying* body.

Unlike the soul, but like the etheric body, the astral is not immortal. It is a continuing body, which after death continues its existence on the next plane and goes on, along with the soul, to other fields of experience. It has sometimes been described as the containment vessel for the soul, keeping the individual integrated as he moves along the planes of progression in the course of his spiritual evolution. But eventually, after a period of many years, perhaps centuries in terms of terrestrial time, it is cast off by the soul and disintegrates. Reincarnationists maintain that a reincarnated individual has the same soul but a different astral body.

During the lifetime of a person the astral can separate from the physical for short periods (*see* astral projection).

Books

Bendit, Phoebe and Bendit, Laurence, *Man Incarnate: A Study of the Vital Etheric Field*, Theosophical Publishing House, London, 1957.

Besant, Annie, *Man and His Bodies*, Theosophical Publishing House, London, 1911.

Besant, Annie, *The Self and Its Sheaths*, Theosophical Publishing House, London, 1903.

Boirac, Emil, *Our Hidden Forces*, Rider, London, 1918.

Hallock, Charles, *Luminous Bodies: Here and Hereafter*, London, 1921.

Leadbeater, C. W., *The Astral Plane*, Theosophical Publishing House, Adyar, 1933 edn.

Mead, G. R. S., *Doctrine of the Subtle Body in Western Tradition*, Stuart & Watkins, London, 1919.

Powell, A. E., *The Astral Body and Other Astral Phenomena*, Theosophical Publishing House, London, 1927.

Powell, A. E., *The Etheric Double and Allied Phenomena*, Theosophical Publishing House, London, 1925.

Powell, A. E., *The Mental Body*, Theosophical Publishing House, London, 1941.

Shirley, Ralph, *The Mystery of the Human Double*, Rider, London, 1972.

Spiegelberg, F. *et al.*, *The Concept of the Subtle Body*, Esalen Institute, Big Sur, California, 1964.

Walker, Benjamin, *Beyond the Body: The Human Double and the Astral Planes*, Routledge & Kegan Paul, London, 1974.

Watters, R. A., *The Intra-Atomic Quantity*, London, 1933.

ASTRAL CORD

An invisible cable that connects the astral body with the living physical body. In the waking state the two bodies of a human being, the material and the supra-physical, fit together and are 'in coincidence', and the astral cord disappears into the physical body. Where exactly it resides at such a time is not clearly known. Some occultists say that the substance of which the cord is composed is spread all over the body like a thin integument or skin; others variously state that it is concentrated like a knot near the navel, the epigastrium, solar plexus, perineum (between sex organs and anus), the bregma (the part of the skull where the frontal and side bones meet), the medulla oblongata or other part of the brain, the roof of the mouth, a spot on the forehead between the eyes, or one of the plexuses. Some think it may lie just beneath the skin in a circle around the neck like a necklace.

During sleep and other xenophrenic states the astral body 'discoincides', or moves out of alignment with the physical, but the two bodies remain joined together by means of the astral cord, and it is through this cord that contact and communication are maintained between them. The point at which the cord is attached to the physical body is again variously said to be the solar plexus, the top of the head, the navel, and so on. The thickness of the cord depends on the distance between the two bodies during discoincidence; the closer they are the thicker the cord and the stronger the pull. When the physical and astral bodies are only slightly out of coincidence, say approximately two to six inches apart, the cord is about two inches in diameter; when the bodies are six feet apart the cord has the thickness of a sewing thread, but it never gets any thinner than that no matter how great a distance there may be between the two bodies thereafter.

When a sleeper is disturbed there is a tug at the cable which vibrates and draws back the astral body 'with unthinkable and lightning-like speed'. At death the cord is broken, and it is perhaps to this that the Bible refers in the verse: 'When the silver cord is loosed, then shall the dust return to the earth as it was, and the spirit return to God' (Eccles. 12:6).

Occultists and others who have had experience of the astral cord, and claim to have seen it, say that it is extremely elastic and can stretch to any length, so that no matter how far apart the two bodies may be, they are always connected by the cord. The astral body controls the vegetative, respiratory, cardiac and other vital processes of the physical organism, and during discoincidence the astral cord acts like an umbilical cord, providing a line of communication and sending vital currents to the physical body. The cord has a pulsation and its expansions and contractions can be noted along its whole length.

References to the astral cord are found scattered in literature. Plutarch (d. AD 120) in his essay *On the Daimon of Socrates* says that the part of the non-physical body that is submerged in the physical and is tainted by its sins is the psyche (astral body), but the uncorrupted part is the nous (soul). He goes on to say that the nous hangs like a cord above the head, the lower end touching the top of the skull, and thus remains in contact with and guides the astral.

The ectoplasm* exuded by spiritualist mediums is believed to be an identical substance, which emerges from the body often in the form of a cord or rope. One explanation of cryptokinetic phenomena advanced by Dr Julien Ochorowicz (d. 1918) is that ectoplasmic filaments or threads from the medium's body cause movements in the seance room. The explanation of Dr W. J. Crawford, after studying the materializations in the Goliger Circle (1922), was that an invisible and unknown substance emanated from the medium and solidified into 'psychic rods'.

Anthropologists in various parts of the world describe native magicians performing strange feats by means of a cord which emerges from their bodies. One observer, Lucas Bridges, mentions a shaman of the Ona tribe in Tierra del Fuego who had an internal magical rope three metres long which he produced from his mouth, and which he could cause to disappear in the twinkling of an eye by swallowing it.

The most extraordinary recorded instances of their power comes from the aborigines of Australia. The ectoplasmic cord issues from the navel, mouth, head, hand or other part of the magician's body. It is extremely strong and elastic, can move things at a distance, cure diseases by its touch, emit fire and flashes, strike and even kill. With its aid the magician climbs trees and 'ascends to heaven'. Professor Elkin relates how a cleverman once lay on his back at the foot of a tree and sent his cord upwards like a rope and then climbed up it with his head well back, body loose, legs apart and arms at his sides. When he reached the top, about forty feet high, he waved his hands to those below, then descended. On his return he lay quietly on his back and the cord re-entered his body.

Books

Bridges, E. Lucas, *The Uttermost Part of the Earth*, Hodder & Stoughton, London, 1948.
Eliade, Mircea, *The Two and the One*, Harvil Press, London, 1965.
Elkin, A. P., *Aboriginal Men of High Degree*, Angus & Robertson, London, 1944.
Johnson, Raynor C., *The Imprisoned Splendour*, Hodder & Stoughton, London, 1953.
Muldoon, Sylvan J. and Carrington, H., *The Projection of the Astral Body*, Rider, London, 1929.
Walker, Benjamin, *Beyond the Body*, Routledge & Kegan Paul, London, 1974.

ASTRAL PROJECTION

Astral projection is the natural, spontaneous, accidental or deliberate exteriorization of the astral body. During the conscious state of the individual, the astral body coincides with the physical, so the withdrawal of the astral from the physical is spoken of as discoincidence, separation, exteriorization, dissociation, externalization, or an OOB (out-of-the-body) experience.

Since the astral body carries consciousness and feeling, discoincidence results in the temporary unconsciousness of the physical body and the transfer to the astral body of sensation and feeling. But in all cases there is a tenuous rapport between the two bodies through the astral cord by which they are joined. In the case of an accident or surgical operation a person often has the experience of *autoscopy*, 'self-seeing', in which the conscious astral body sees the inert physical body, and is identified not with the normal self, but with the other, viewing body. Astral projection is to be distinguished from *bilocation*, the phenomenon attributed to saints and other holy persons of being bodily in two places at the same time; usually one of the materially duplicated bodies is in a trance.

According to legend, Pythagoras, Empedocles and other sages of ancient Greece were credited with practices that allowed them to enter a state of dissociation at will. The idea that some people have the power of leaving their bodies temporarily was familiar to Europe till well past the Middle Ages. In the east, certain classes of adepts have long been alleged to have the power to project and travel in the astral body while the physical body lay inert. The Bon magicians of Tibet, who belong to this class, have perfected a rite known as *mi-lam*, 'dream-state', in which they learn to control their dreams. In the astral state they are said to enter into their own dreams and those of others and participate in them in full consciousness, and with full remembrance thereafter.

When and how, and in what circumstances, spontaneous astral projection takes place is not clear. Some people have a constitution naturally prone to projection. Hereditary factors possibly also help. It is believed that during infancy and in extreme old age the astral and physical bodies are not completely aligned, and hence are in slight discoincidence. This results in uncoordinated movement and slurred speech, since the astral is not in full control. Again, whenever physical vitality is at a low ebb, as during illness, fasting, asceticism, exhaustion, enforced wakefulness, the astral tends to get loose from its moorings and drift away. Drugs such as ether, chloroform, hashish, alcohol, and especially LSD, are conducive to projection. So also are certain xenophrenic states.

A broken habit, great concentration, strong desire, intense pain, near-death experiences may also lead to instability of the astral–physical coincidence and result in total or partial displacement of the double. Before death and in times of great danger or crisis, the projected double may appear to a loved one. According to psychic researchers the projection of the astral body is not at all unusual; everyone has experienced it at some time in his life, although most people do not remember their experiences except in the distorted version of dreams.

Astral projection in full consciousness from beginning to end is possible but very rare. Experiences of course vary. They include cases of spontaneous exteriorization, when under anaesthesia or during illness or accident, people have had a vivid experience of floating upwards and witnessing what is happening to the physical body below.

In normal circumstances a full-scale projection usually takes place after a person has been asleep for some hours. He finds he is slowly awaking, but remains unaware of his position or orientation. For a time he is cataleptic and immobile. Then, with the body still rigid, the double floats upward horizontally, vibrating rapidly. There is often a feeling of a number of tiny things snapping inside, accompanied by sounds of humming, cracking, zinging. Some can see the cord connecting the physical and astral bodies. Then the astral slowly assumes the vertical, ready to move away. At this point too, catalepsy ends, and consciousness is transferred to the double. In most cases the actual process of projection, and the astral body's return to coincidence afterwards, is preceded by a short period of blackout and unconsciousness.

Everything on the astral plane appears to be very vivid, and even the commonplace is mystically aglow. The objects of the actual world seem dull and unreal shadows in comparison. The mind is alert and crystal clear. Sensory activity is enhanced and one has a feeling of increased understanding. Physical defects vanish. The projected double enters a plane where time, place and matter do not have the same meaning as here. It can pass through closed doors, travel immense distances in the twinkling of an eye, but it cannot move material objects. It is endowed with a degree of paraperception. Except in rare instances it cannot be seen by people in the physical world.

The astral body can be projected experimentally after occult development, and can move along the astral planes and contact the denizens of other dimensions. The astral is naturally fitted to perceive and act in its own sphere, and can have sexual union with others. Occultists have devised methods of causing the separation of the body with full consciousness in order to work magic on the planes.

The interiorization of the double, or its return to coincidence after projection, is marked by the return of consciousness to the physical body. Normally the astral settles into the physical gently and smoothly, and the person continues sleeping or remains in an unconscious state for a little while. But in case of sudden noise or shock, the astral cord receives a sharp tug and the jarring 'repercussion' creates a sense of panic in the physical body and the person sees 'stars' and suffers from violent palpitations as a result. For this reason, in many parts of the world a sleeper is never awakened suddenly in case his spirit returns too violently and kills the body.

Most psychologists of course regard the hypothesis of the astral body as unscientific; and explain the phenomenon of astral projection as an 'autoscopic hallucination', that is, the delusion that one is seeing oneself, or having an experience outside one's own body. Many cases are thus dismissed as self-delusion, when not actually fictitious or fraudulent.

From the occult point of view the hypothesis of astral projection (including etheric extrusion) is a useful one and could perhaps explain certain mental states and paranormal phenomena, including a great deal of folklore. Thus, dreams, mystic visions, clairvoyance and hallucinations could be explained as perception on the astral level, or through astral eyes; déjà vu, as earlier astral experience; wraiths, phantoms and other apparitions, as the visible form of the exteriorized astral or etheric body; insanity and epilepsy as the temporary or permanent dislocation of the astral body; unconscious states, sleep, fainting fits, catalepsy, suspended animation, as the absence of the astral body; mediumship, multiple personality, possession, vampirism, expersonation, as the occupation of the physical body by another entity; the experiences of candidates in the ancient mystery religions, as conscious projection and astral travel, with memory retained; hypnosis as the control over the astral body of the subject; ectoplasm, materialization at seances, telekinesis, poltergeist phenomena, as resulting from the extrusion of etheric substance; psychic vampirism as the feeding on the energy of the etheric system of a victim; werewolves and shape-shifting, as the astral of a living person taking possession of an animal body.

Books

Brennan, J. H., *Astral Doorways*, Aquarian Press, London, 1971.

Crookall, Robert, *The Study and Practice of Astral Projection*, Aquarian Press, London, 1961.

Crookall, Robert, *The Jung-Jaffe View of Out-of-the-Body Experiences*, World Fellowship Press, London, 1970.

Fox, Oliver, *Astral Projection*, University Books, New York, 1962.

Green, Celia, *Out-of-the-Body Experiences*, Hamish Hamilton, London, 1968.

Leadbeater, C. W., *The Astral Plane: Its Scenery, Inhabitants and Phenomena*, Theosophical Publishing, London, reprint, 1968.

Muldoon, Sylvan and Carrington, Hereward, *The Projection of the Astral Body*, Rider, London, 1929.

Oxenham, John, *Out of the Body*, Longmans Green, London, 1941.

Rochas, Albert de, *L'Extériorisation de la Sensibilité*, Paris, 1895.

Rochas, Albert de, *L'Extériorisation de la Motricité*, Paris, 1906.

Smith, Susy, *Out of the Body Travel*, Garrett Publications, New York, 1965.
Walker, Benjamin, *Beyond the Body: The Human Double and the Astral Planes*, Routledge & Kegan Paul, London, 1974.
Yram, *Practical Astral Projection*, Rider, London, 1935.

BEARD

Regarded by the ancients of the middle east as a token of wisdom and a sign of power. So much so that even some of the Great Goddesses of the early Mediterranean cultures were depicted with beards, including a number of Bearded Venuses in Greece. In ancient Egyptian monuments several reigning queens are shown with beards in order to emphasize their authority. The Egyptians, however, were not a hirsute people, so the pharaoh and the higher functionaries resorted to wearing a false beard or postiche, which remained the male fashion from 3000 to 1580 BC.

In ancient Mesopotamia the beard was a mark of virility and manly worth, and was carefully shaped and tended to give it distinction. Assyrian beards were meticulously arranged in tiers of circular curls stiffened with perfumed gum. Even the sacred winged bulls of Assyria were carved with curly beards. But as a rule the lower classes in ancient Mesopotamia were clean shaven, as befitted their lowly status. On the other hand orthodox Jews were enjoined not to 'mar the corners of the beard' (Lev. 19:27), suggesting that the beard was never to be trimmed but allowed to grow untouched.

In Islamic countries too, the beard was considered the supreme badge of male dignity for the faithful. Traditionally all the prophets of old before the time of Muhammad (d. AD 632) were said to have had long flowing beards. Muhammad, who was bearded himself, charged his followers: 'Do the opposite of the polytheists, and let your beard grow long.' Moslems used to swear 'by the beard of the Prophet'. They regarded it as a great insult to have their beard pulled. The Sikhs of India were greatly influenced by the Islamic tradition, and growing a beard became obligatory after one of their leaders made it a mark of their faith.

The Greeks considered shaving entirely a matter of personal preference, until the time of Alexander the Great (d. 323 BC) who forbade his soldiers to grow beards because they provided a convenient handle for the enemy. After that shaving became fashionable in the Macedonian empire, the Roman empire and early Christendom, and for centuries beards were cultivated chiefly by the priesthood and the nobility.

In the reign of Elizabeth I (d. 1603) there was a tax on beards in England, which was levied according to the age and status of the person concerned. In eastern Europe and especially Russia, where beards remained in vogue, travellers frequently described, not without scorn, the massive and none too clean growths of the peasantry. When Peter the Great (d. 1727) decided to reform his country and bring it in line with western Europe, he put a tax on beards, and personally lopped off the beards of anyone he came across.

But men have ever had a regard for the beard, which, if it seems incongruous in youth, adds dignity to the face of an older man. It is said that Sir Thomas More (d. 1535), Lord Chancellor of Henry VIII, when sentenced to death for high treason, showed anxious concern to preserve his beard and keep it out of the way of the executioner's axe.

Besides being a sign of manliness the beard was often regarded as a sign of mature wisdom. It was even believed that stroking the beard, like touching the forehead, assisted thought and deliberation. Hence the gesture of stroking the beard was often satirized to signify an imminent pontifical utterance that turns out to be worthless.

It has been argued that the beard, being the attribute of a mature male, must require a considerable amount of male energy to help its growth. But when the beard is full grown, the energy normally diverted to grow it becomes available for virile purposes. The beard should therefore never be cut by anyone who wishes to preserve his manhood unimpaired.

Books

See under hair

BIOFLUX

In occult theory there is said to be an energy diffused in an uninterrupted continuum throughout the universe, which has properties as yet unknown to science. Aggregations of this cosmic energy in varying degrees of concentration constitute the particles, electrons, atoms and molecules of the physicists, and all the visible units of common observation from tiny grains of sand to the largest galaxies.

The energy in these specialized concentrations actually makes up the ent or unit, be it mineral or man, and every ent has its own pulse or signal which is characteristic both of the species to which the unit belongs, and of the individual unit itself. The term applied to these emanations from ents is *ectenium*, a radiating cosmos of impulses which links everything to everything else in a vast interrelationship.

Metal, leather, cloth, wood, paper, rubber, all have an ectenic 'surround', consisting of their characteristic emanations, but the radiation differs in living and non-living things. The emanation from living entities is specifically known as *bioflux*, and every species, every individual within the species and every part within the individual has different and distinctive patterns. The conclusions arrived at by those who have studied the subject are summarized below.
(1) Bioflux is given out by the living cells, tissues and organs of all plants and animals.

(2) It has certain properties of magnetism and electricity, such as polarity, and can in some measure be affected by these physical energies, but is itself neither magnetism nor electricity.
(3) It can be seen as brilliant colours, auras and rays, felt and registered as heat. Normally it seems to extend from two to eight inches from the living organism.
(4) It is affected by the heavenly bodies including the stars, sun and moon, by seasons, winds, tides, thunderstorms and other cosmobiological factors.
(5) In the human being the bioflux changes with age, health, fatigue, moods and emotions. Changes can also be induced by noise, and other strong sensory impressions, and by drugs and hypnosis.
(6) It is concentrated in such areas as the eyes, brain, spine, sex organs and the plexuses.
(7) It can be projected and transmitted outside the body, to influence the mind and body of animate creatures, as well as plants and inanimate objects. It can also be transmitted from a distance by concentration.

The notion that such a force exists is at least four thousand years old, and the following brief chronology will show that it has always been widely prevalent and is still current.

According to the ancient Egyptians the semen of the god Ra gave forth a mysterious essence called *sa*, which pervaded the universe. By special rites this essence could be drawn down to charge the images of the deity. From time to time the pharaoh, duly prepared, would be made to kneel before such an image and place his head against the idol's hand, in order that the divine efflux might flow into him and renew his strength.

The early Greeks, including Hippocrates (d. 359 BC), held that a mysterious energy (Gk. *dūnamis*, 'power') inhered in certain individuals who had gifts of healing which they exercised by touching the sick. The same idea prevailed among the Romans and was universally held in the ancient middle east. It is in this sense that Christ used the term when the woman with an issue of blood touched the hem of his garment, whereupon, 'Jesus, immediately knowing that virtue (Gk. *dūnamis*) had gone out of him said, Who touched me?' (Mark 5:30).

The ancient Chinese called this energy *ch'ī*, the vital atmosphere that is found everywhere, in minerals, plants, animals, and in special concentrations in men of authority and great spiritual power. A closely related concept is the universally diffused *prāna* or life force of Hindu belief, which in man energizes the body and is sometimes identified with the soul. The *baraka* of the Moslems, the *orenda* of the Iroquois, and the *mana* of the Polynesians are variations of the same belief.

Plutarch (d. AD 120) spoke of the *aura* surrounding the human body which by its varying colours and movements reveals the passions and vices of the soul. In Christian tradition the aura is called the *aureole*, when it surrounds the whole body, and the *halo* or *nimbus* when it encircles the head.

From the belief in powerful impulses arising from embalmed mummies, the medieval physician Paracelsus (d. 1541) conceived his notion of the *mumia*, a magnetic emanation that issues from all things, but in particular from living beings. The mumia was thought of as the double or vital essence of a man that was being constantly sent forth from him and radiated around him like a luminous sphere.

In the following century the Belgian chemist and physician, Jean Baptiste van Helmont (d. 1644), came up with the idea of a magnetic power present in all things which he called *magnale magnum*. Although it infused the whole human system its principal area of concentration was the solar plexus.

The next landmark in the history of the human bioflux is the theory of *animal magnetism*, first systematically enunciated by Franz Anton Mesmer (d. 1815). This too was part of a universal magnetic fluid pervading all things. The human body, said Mesmer, has properties analogous to the magnet, including polarities, and he made use of this magnetism as the medium for his healing sessions, by communicating the energy to the patient.

In Germany the clairvoyant, Frederica Hauffe (d. 1829), became the recipient of certain teachings communicated through spirit entities during trance. Among them was the idea of the *Nervengeist*, 'nerve spirit', an ethereal substance engendered by the body, which it enshrouded as in a garment. It had qualities that resembled the aura, being affected by the presence of others, and in turn affecting them.

In about 1845 the distinguished German chemist, Baron Carl von Reichenbach (d. 1869), carried out a series of experiments in an endeavour to establish on scientific lines the age-old theory of these human emanations. He found evidence that such an energy did exist and could be measured. He named it *od* (odyle or odic force) after the Norse god Odin. It pervades all nature; in varying degrees it radiates from all objects and living tissues, and exhibits physical properties including polarities.

Ten years later, in 1855, the Swiss physicist, Professor Marc Thury (d. 1905) of Geneva University, spoke of a universal ectenium issuing from all objects. The specific emanation from the human body he named *psychode*, coined from psyche, 'spirit', and Reichenbach's odic force. He said it had both physical and etheric attributes and constituted a link between body and soul. Its most substantial manifestation was the ectoplasm* of spiritualist seances.

Since then bioflux has continued to appear in various guises and under various names, being sought with special interest by French investigators. The French writer, Louis Jacolliot (c. 1860), spoke of it as *vril*, a concentration of cosmic ether, which he claimed could be used by those acquainted with its qualities, for the development of individuals and the race as a whole.

The English psychical researcher, Edward William Cox (d. 1879), serjeant-at-law, in a book published in 1872, spoke of *psychic force*, an emanation that seemed to be apparent beyond the periphery of the body, a kind of 'nerve atmosphere of varying intensity enveloping the human structure'.

A variation of this was the *vital force* of the French researcher, Hippolyte Baraduc, who in 1896 conducted experiments with a biometer of his own invention to measure the auric, radiant, biometric, fluidic and vibratory forces of the human body.

Another French investigator, Col. Eugène Rochas (d. 1914), after many experiments in human emanations, magnetic fluids and odic streams, concluded that it was an *undefined force* but of distinct and undoubted power.

In 1895 yet another Frenchman, Dr Paul Joire, gave the name *bio-efflux* to all emanations from biological organisms, both plant and animal. He invented the sthenometer to measure their force and propounded the theory of exteriorization of motricity, by which this force could cause movements outside the body; and exteriorization of sensitivity, by which it could cause a subject to feel things beyond the periphery of the body.

In 1903 Professor Prosper Blondlot, a French scientist, claimed to have discovered radiations which he named *N-rays*, after the town of Nancy where he worked. This human radiation from the brain and nerves could penetrate paper and other opaque material, illuminate objects, register on the thermometer, show sensitivity to electric and magnetic currents as well as chemicals, could be concentrated by a lens and reflected by a mirror. The French Academy awarded the professor a prize for his discovery. The following year an American physicist, Robert Wood, visited Blondlot to have the phenomenon of the N-ray spectrum elucidated. While this was being done he surreptitiously removed a vital prism from the mechanism and noted that it had no effect on the experiment, so that the N-rays, as demonstrated by Blondlot, were in fact non-existent. Wood's exposure so disturbed the unhappy French savant, who was obviously dedicated to his work, that he lost his mind and died soon after.

In 1910 Professor Farny of Zurich coined the term *anthropoflux* for the magnetic effluence believed to radiate from the human body. It was said to be generated from the cells, tissues, nerves and muscles, and was concentrated in the blood, brain, solar plexus, hands (digital effluvium) and sex organs.

Dr Walter Kilner (d. 1920), physician at St Thomas's Hospital, London, in the course of experiments in 1911, observed what he called the *human atmosphere* around men and women when he looked at them through a specially treated glass plate. He found that it was like a coloured aura surrounding the body.

In 1915 Dr W. J. Crawford (d. 1920), while carrying out investigations during seances with the mediumistic Goligher family in Belfast, advanced the theory of the *nerve energy*, emanating from living bodies. This energy was constantly in contact with the nerve energies of other bodies in its environment, all of which mutually reacted on one another. It was this energy that spirit entities drew upon for their manifestations and materializations.

In 1923 the Russian scientist, Dr Alexander Gurvitch, discovered what he called *mitogenetic rays*, invisible radiation from all living plant and animal cells. This consisted of short wave-length rays belonging to the ultra-violet region of the spectrum, and was responsible for stimulating mitosis or cell division. In 1930 Professor Guido Cremonesa, working in Rome, succeeded in making photographic records of radiations given off by living substances, including blood and saliva.

In 1940 Dr Wilhelm Reich (d. 1957), Austrian-born American scientist, discovered *orgone*, a non-electromagnetic force which he believed was present everywhere in an uninterrupted continuum. In animals this energy existed in the form of sexual energy and the life force that sustained animate existence. Orgone in men could be increased by proper breathing exercises which changed the red blood cells into orgone energy and stimulated the sexual impulses. In his laboratory he built accumulators of orgone energy, but fell foul of the American authorities for his experiments. He was arrested and died in prison.

In 1940 a Russian electrical technician, Semyon Davidovich Kirlian, inventor of a method of high-frequency photography, observed what came to be termed *bioplasmic energy* radiating from living organisms. Subsequently his photography revealed the astonishing bioluminescence of all living things, in the shape of brilliantly coloured flares and patterns shooting forth from the body like fantastic fireworks displays. It was called bioplasmic energy because it was believed to emanate from the bioplasmic body or etheric* double. A great deal of experimental work continues to be done with Kirlian photography, both in the USSR and the USA.

In 1945 the Czech scientist, Robert Pavlita (b. 1914), advanced the hypothesis of *psychotronic energy*, the vital power from human beings that is somehow involved with psychic phenomena, and which lies behind psychic faculties such as dowsing and PK (psychokinesis*, or moving objects by thought alone). He invented a psychotronic generator which draws off, accumulates and stores human bioplasmic force. Once charged with it, the generator will be able to do what a psychic can do.

In about 1950 L. E. Eeman (d. 1958) spoke of the *X Force*, the name he gave to the biomagnetic force present in the human body. Eeman believed in the polarity of the physical system, the right and left sides being positive and negative, and the back of the head and base of the spine, positive and negative respectively. In his system of co-operative healing, which resembled Mesmer's, he made his patients hold copper wires which were connected to various parts of one another's bodies, so that by an exchange of polarities they mutually healed one another.

In 1960 Dr Francisco Racanelli of Florence suggested the existence of *bioradiant energy* in all living bodies, and thought that by means of passes, in the manner of the early magnetizers, it would be possible to heal the sick. His ideas were taken up by several experimenters but did not meet with much success.

The Soviet mathematician and neurophysiologist, Dr Genady Sergeyev of Leningrad University, studied several aspects of parapsychology, made experimental investigations in telepathy, telekinesis and radiations from the human body. In 1963 by means of a detector he was able to pick up electrical and magnetic *biological fields* several feet away from the human body. He believed it was possible for the energy from living bodies to be transferred to non-living matter.

In 1965 Dr Bernard Grad of McGill University, Montreal, suggested that some *X Factor* of unknown energy flowing from the human body could affect the growth of plants. He said that a person's mood and state of health affects this energy, and felt that it had the 'widest implications' for medical science. His experiments demonstrated that the energy emanating from a healer's hands could speed up the healing of open wounds in small animals.

At Rosary Hill College, Buffalo, Sister Justa Smith, a Franciscan nun and a biochemist, experimenting with a Hungarian-born healer, Oskar Esterbany, who had worked for a time with Dr Grad, found that healing rays from his hands could considerably increase the activity of enzymes. The Nobel Laureate Professor Szent-Györgi, as a result of his own work in the field of bioelectrics, suggested the interflow between subatomic particles and 'the cellular machinery' in biological processes.

Dr Shafica Karagulla of Beverly Hills, California, has done much work on the powers of sensitives, and notes that such persons constantly report being able to see three sets of force fields around any individual: (1) a 'vital field', which reflects the physical condition; (2) an 'emotional field', which reflects the feelings; and (3) a 'mental field', which reflects the mental activity.

In east and west the subject continues to receive intensive investigation, both in scientific and unorthodox fashion. To many students the existence of some form of subtle energy, as yet untapped, emanating from the human system would seem to be confirmed by the ever advancing discoveries in the field of biomagnetism, bioelectricity, nerve-waves and brain-waves, which are becoming increasingly amenable to laboratory research, and therefore more acceptable to the cautious.

Books

Bagnall, Oscar, *The Origin and Properties of the Human Aura*, Routledge & Kegan Paul, London, 1957.

Colville, W. J., *The Human Aura*, Fowler, London, 1917.

Karagulla, Shafica, *Breakthrough to Creativity*, De Vorss, Los Angeles, 1969.

Kilner, W. J., *The Human Atmosphere*, Kegan Paul, Trench, Trubner, London, 1920.

Lakhovsky, Georges, *The Secret of Life: Cosmic Rays and Radiations of Living Beings*, True Health Publishing, London, 1951.

Ostrander, Sheila and Schroeder, Lynn, *PSI: Psychic Discoveries Behind the Iron Curtain*, Sphere Books, London, 1973.

Ousely, S. G. J., *Science of the Aura*, Fowler, London, 1964.

Stanley, Krippner and Rubin, Daniel (eds), *Galaxies of Life: The Human Aura in Acupuncture and Kirlian Photography*, Interface, New York, 1973.

Szent-Györgi, Albert, *Bioelectrics. A Study in Cellular Regulation Defence and Cancer*, Academic Press, New York, 1968.

Walker, Benjamin, *Beyond the Body*, Routledge & Kegan Paul, London, 1974.

BIORHYTHM

The cyclic periodicities or recurrent phases of mood and behaviour that are observed in living organisms. The rhythmic flow of energy and activity is found everywhere in nature, from the circling of the heavenly bodies, the movement of the sun, the waxing and waning of the moon, the seasons and the weather, to the cyclic biological changes in animals and men. Biorhythm is the study of these cycles as they affect all species, but in particular man.

It is well known that human life is subject to certain rhythmic fluctuations that operate in all physiological activities, and are associated with the functions of the body. These rhythms may operate at intervals ranging from microseconds to several years, and the human organism has a built-in biological clock by means of which these rhythms are timed and to which they are adjusted. Their longer or shorter periodicities are to a considerable degree related to the seasons, cosmic rays, constellations, sunspot and sun movements, phases of the moon and other cosmobiological factors. They are also connected with the age and sex of the individual. Human well-being is cyclic in character, and man is subject to individual and collective low and high points. There are known to be a host of diseases that occur in cycles in epidemic form.

Many of our ordinary activities have a rhythmic character: the measured progression of walking and running, the contractions of peristalsis, the rhythm of coition, the contractions of travail. It has been established that there are rhythmic cycles in most physiological processes: the rate of cell division, the discharge of neural impulses, temperature, blood pressure, pulse rate, metabolism, energy levels, blood-cell count, haemoglobin levels, the volume and chemistry of the urine, bowel and kidney function, brain activity, the level and rate of manufacture of amino-acids, alkalines, semen, oxygen and body sugar.

In short or long waves these cycles are a universal biological phenomenon. The polarity of the brain cells shows changes which occur in fractions of a second, as revealed by electroencephalographs. The regular heartbeat and pulse rhythm is between sixty to eighty beats per minute in human beings. The cycle of respiration or in-and-out breathing is between fifteen to twenty breaths a minute. Rhythmic contractions occur every eight or ten minutes inside a woman's body throughout the whole of her child-bearing period (Tabori and Raphael, 1971, p. 173).

A very important series of rhythms is interwoven with the night-and-day cycle. Such rhythms are called circadian (Lat. *circa dies*, 'about a day') since they occur roughly once every twenty-four hours. In a very real sense it would seem that everyone is a different person at different times of the day. A cycle of magnetic change takes place in the human body about once every twenty-four hours. The best known of circadian rhythms is that of waking and sleeping, usually in the ratio of sixteen hours' wakefulness and eight hours' sleep. The body temperature, which is low in the morning and higher at night, shows brief fluctuations within this range, both during waking and during sleep. Sleep itself is cyclic, going through between four to six stages every night. Within the sleep period there are dream intervals every ninety minutes or so. The cycle of urine flow is lower at night. The 'alkaline tide' or rise in the alkalinity of urine comes about an hour after waking up in the morning. This does not seem to be connected with the acid secretions occurring with digestion, for it is found even if one has not had breakfast. Birth and death seem to be constellated around certain periods of the day or night. Most human births normally occur between midnight and 6 a.m., with the peak at about 4 a.m. On the other hand the twilight period, both dawn and dusk, when vitality is at a low ebb, is the time when most deaths occur.

Any disruption of the normal day-and-night cycle can have an unusual effect on the human organism, as recent studies indicate. It was first observed among night workers on rotating shifts, who suffered slight mental disturbances as a result of the constant alteration of their sleeping times. The matter was brought more strikingly to attention by the irregular schedules forced on people due to high-speed air travel. It has been found that when a person is suddenly transported from one part of the world to another by jet airliner he is slightly out of gear both mentally and physically because his built-in physiological timing is thrown out of rhythm. It has been suggested that diplomats and business executives suffering from such disorientation may not be fit to make important decisions until a day or two after the journey when the rhythm has had time to readjust itself. Air hostesses on jet planes have menstrual irregularities, and, if pregnant, risk miscarriage during early pregnancy, not so much because of motion sickness, plane vibration, emotional stress or sudden climatic change, but because of the abrupt changes in time-rhythms to which they are subjected.

The two- or three-day cycle appears to be connected with the progress of certain diseases. Critical periods usually stretch over two or three days, and determine the final outcome. Certain recurrent fevers return every second day (tertian), or every third day (quartan). It has been found that human beings have a fortnightly electrical rhythm, which often coincides with the lunar phases, and these determine the behaviour and moods of the individual in general.

Other observers have found a twenty-one- or twenty-five-day cycle, during which the physical constitution makes one complete change-over, affecting strength, vitality and sexual desire. Wilhelm Fliess (d. 1928), German physician and associate of Sigmund Freud, studied human biorhythms and found a bisexual character in every person, male and female. The male element in every person had a cycle of twenty-three days, during which strength, energy and aggressiveness were predominant, after which the female element took its place, lasting twenty-eight days, during which time creativity, love and sensitivity were predominant. Then, there is the twenty-eight-day biological cycle affecting women, and governing ovulation and menstruation.

The cycle of hormonal changes is said to alternate every thirty-two days, and determines the chemistry of the internal secretions which are poured into the bloodstream. The output of the thyroid gland, for instance, has a strong influence on the emotions and moves from high to low after thirty-two days. The cyclothymic rhythm is said to alternate at thirty-five-day intervals, so that one's emotions vary in a curve that rises to a peak every five weeks, resulting in alternating periods of depression and exhilaration. Every forty days there appears to be an intellectual rhythm, affecting one's grasp of practical things, alertness, concentration and memory.

Many cycles are seasonal, and cause changes as the seasons change from year to year. Children show spurts of growth in spring, and adults and children secrete a 'summer hormone', probably thyroid, which reduces the body heat during the hot months.

People even speak of a 'conscience rhythm', when there is a heightened sense of moral awareness, resulting in an increase in church-going and good works. This takes place every thirty-six months when, it has been found, many people who have evaded income tax make voluntary contributions to the government to placate their conscience. Then there is the forty-one-month 'splurge-urge', when people go on a spending spree and cannot resist the impulse to buy things.

Traditionally, every seven years the human being passes through certain life phases. He is a child till the age of seven; reaches puberty at fourteen; is an adult at twenty-one; is a householder at twenty-eight; acquires proficiency in his profession by thirty-five; is a public figure by forty-two; a senator by forty-nine; reaches eminence at fifty-six; and is ready for the end at sixty-three.

Furthermore, every nine years there is said to be a cycle of wickedness, when a man feels like breaking the shackles of convention. The 'seven-year itch' is really the nine-year itch.

Soviet scientists have discovered a curve that rises every eleven years, resulting in a growing upsurge of discontent and general unease, leading to mass movements. The Russian professor, A. L. Tchijevsky, traced a relationship between this particular cycle and the heightened activity of sunspots.

The separate cycles of each biorhythm are joined like large and small interlinked rings, and the determining pattern they form at any one time has not been worked out yet. But, according to the experts, it is these rhythms that make a man what he is, influence his character and conduct, make him happy or grumpy, accident-prone, lucky, fretful or optimistic, and so plunge him into situations leading to success, divorce, popularity, sickness, murder, disgrace or death.

Psychologists suggest a method of 'body charting' to enable one to study one's rhythms of mood and emotion, to enable one to adjust one's activities accordingly. This could be put to many practical uses. The Ohmi Railway Company of Japan has stored in a computer the biorhythms of each of its five hundred bus drivers. Drivers are informed beforehand of their 'bad days', and reminded to be extra careful. In 1969, the first year of the experiment, the drivers achieved a 50 per cent drop in accidents.

Books

Brown, F. A. *et al.*, *The Biological Clock*, Academic Press, New York, 1970.

Cloudsley-Thompson, J. L., *Rhythmic Activity in Animal Physiology and Behavior*, Academic Press, New York, 1961.

Conroy, R. and Mills, J. M., *Human Circadian Rhythms*, Williams & Wilkins, Baltimore, 1971.

Harker, J. E., *The Physiology of Diurnal Rhythms*, Cambridge University Press, London, 1964.

Huff, Darrell, *Cycles in Your Life*, Gollancz, London, 1967.

Lazarsfeld, Sophie, *The Rhythm of Life*, George Routledge & Sons, London, 1934.

Luce, Gay Gaer, *Body Time*, Temple Smith, London, 1972.

Mills, J. N. (ed.), *Biological Aspects of Circadian Rhythms*, Plenum Press, London, 1971.

Smith, E. L., *Tides in the Affairs of Men*, New York, 1939.

Sollberger, A., *Biological Rhythm Research*, Elsevier, New York, 1965.

Tabori, Paul and Raphael, Phyllis, *Beyond the Senses*, Souvenir Press, London, 1971.

Thommen, George, *Biorhythm*, Crown Publishers, New York, 1964.

Ward, R. R., *The Living Clocks*, Knopf, New York, 1971.

Wenli, J. H., *Biorhythm. A Scientific Exploration into the Life Cycles of the Individual*, Crown Publishers, New York, 1961.

Wolf, W. (ed.), *Rhythmic Functions in the Living System*, New York Academy of Sciences, 1962.

BIRTH

Birth is the physical process of coming into the world experienced by the child, as distinguished from parturition or childbirth (*see* pregnancy) which is the physical process undergone by the mother in bringing forth her young.

Why a child is born at one time and not another is a mystery, but it has been suggested that cosmobiological factors play a decisive part in it. To start with, conception itself appears to be linked with cosmic and planetary influences and these may well determine the child's exit from the womb nine months later. Other even stranger family factors perhaps also have a bearing. Johann Kepler (d. 1630) said, 'When a mother is great with child and the natural time of delivery approaches, nature selects for the birth a day and hour which correspond astrologically to the nativity of the mother's brother or father.'

Yet another contributive element is the particular disposition of certain heavenly bodies, including the stars and planets governing the child's character. Statistical research also suggests that the moon is very closely linked with human birth-times, so much so that that heavenly body has been called 'the great midwife'. More births take place during the waning than the waxing moon, with the maximum number occurring just after full moon and the minimum at the new moon.

Then, because of the human body's natural adaptation to a day-and-night rhythm, most births tend to begin towards the end of the night or early morning, although of course some do take place at other times. In hospitals today a dangerous complication is introduced by the fact that doctors and staff find it increasingly inconvenient to attend confinements at all hours of the night, and by means of drugs and injections administered to the mother adjust delivery time to a more suitable hour, which may not be physiologically or astrologically best suited to the child. Because of this induced alteration the child is born in what has been termed a 'confused period', which may cause disturbances throughout its later life.

In popular belief the time of a child's birth is of extreme importance, for it determines the course of its whole future career, and astrologers calculate a birth chart (horoscope) from it. For astrological purposes a child born in the late evening is regarded as having been born in the early hours of the following day. In popular superstition a child born at midnight has the faculty, throughout its life, of seeing spirits. In human typology children born before midday tend to be 'larks', and after midday, 'owls'.

The whole process from conception to birth is very precarious. It has been calculated that out of every hundred conceptions, between 12 to 15 will be dead within a month, and will be passed out in the form of a heavier than normal menstrual flow. In the next five or six months a further 10 to 15 will die as 'spontaneous miscarriages', most of them rejected by nature because of some definite abnormality. In Britain alone about one thousand foetuses are spontaneously aborted every day. Out of those that survive this process of elimination, roughly 2 per cent are born dead, even in developed countries. Gerald Leach says, 'Clearly, we should think ourselves lucky to have got out of the womb alive and well.'

Miscarriages serve an essential biological function in eliminating, by a perfectly natural process, all embryos that are not capable of surviving. With modern medical advances, however, many such imperfect foetuses are saved, with the result that an appreciable proportion of children survive to carry through life some disability or abnormality, physical or mental, and perhaps transmit it to their own children in the future.

Members of the early Hippocratic school in ancient Greece believed that the foetus took an active part in its entry into the world. Even today doctors suspect that changes in the hormonal secretions in the foetus trigger, through the placenta, the mother's uterine contractions. During the early centuries of the Christian era it was commonly believed that both mother and child had to co-operate in delivery, and when delivery was long delayed, sweets and knick-knacks were laid between the thighs of the woman and the unborn child was coaxed out with sweet words.

It has been said that for some weeks before birth the foetus is aware of the catastrophic nature of its forthcoming experience and looks forward to it with great trepidation. Occasionally its fear is expressed vocally. Cases have been recorded of children crying out while still in the womb, from about twelve hours to a few minutes before birth. This cry, called *vagitus uterinus*, 'uterine cry', may sound like a whimper, or like a bleat, a howl or yelp. People who have heard it describe the experience as unforgettable, and one of the most eerie imaginable. It is entirely different from the first normal cry the baby makes after birth and which marks the beginning of breathing.

If electrodes are attached to the abdomen of an eight-month pregnant woman they can register the EEG of the unborn child. These show gentle irregular pulsations with occasional convulsive discharges such as are characteristic of minor epileptic seizures. It is as though the child were aware that the resources of its little 'private pool' of amniotic fluid and the oxygen supply available would shortly become inadequate for its needs. As the days pass the insufficiency increases and with it the petty seizures until, in the words of Grey Walter, 'at the appointed phase of some maternal tide, half suffocated, the baby thrashes its way to freedom'. Dangers await the foetus throughout its existence, but they are seldom greater than when the child emerges into the outer world. 'The journey down the four-inch birth canal is probably the most dangerous we ever take,' says biologist Lyall Watson.

The newborn baby is suddenly exiled from a soft, warm, secure nest within the womb (which some psychologists suggest is the archetype of the Garden of Eden, and symbolical of the Golden Age) into an awkward and painful existence outside, and he longs to return to the lost paradise. In times of stress throughout his later life he tends to assume that once secure position in the womb, comfortably curled up.

Otto Rank (d. 1939), one of Sigmund Freud's disciples, was the first to propound the psychological concept of the birth-trauma, the profound mental shock that is part of the infant's experience in being born, and that is the root cause of fear, anxiety, dependency and insecurity in later life. Rank considered the birth-trauma to be more important than the Oedipus complex as a source of emotional disturbance.

A newborn child was commonly regarded as an unclean creature. The *Mahabharata* says, 'Man is born out of lust, engendered by blood and semen, and emerges mixed with excrement and water.' The Roman orator Pliny (d. AD 114) said, 'It is humiliating to the pride of man to consider the pitiable origin of this most arrogant of creatures.' St Augustine (d. 430) wrote, 'Inter faeces et urinam nascimur' (We are born between excrement and urine). The Cathars of the twelfth century expressed their view by saying that a child was conceived in base desires, born of brutish urges and animal postures, encased for nine months in the body of an unclean creature, and expelled from the womb in a cataract of blood, mucus and dead tissue.

Many superstitions are connected with birth, and omens are read from the manner in which a child enters the world. It is a bad sign for the baby to be born with teeth, or with grey hair, or to emerge in any way other than head first. A footling, a child born feet-first, was regarded as having healing gifts in his feet (he could cure pains by touching the sufferer with his toes), but was generally believed to be unlucky for his parents.

It is especially fortunate if the child is born with a *caul*, the part of the amniotic membrane in which it is enclosed in the womb. Cauls were greatly treasured and often sold for high prices. Fragments of it were carried like talismans and were believed to bestow eloquence in debate, give clairvoyant powers, and preserve one from danger at sea.

Books

Gauquelin, Michel, *The Cosmic Clocks*, Peter Owen, London, 1969.
Gebhard, P. H., *et al.*, *Pregnancy, Birth and Abortion*, Harper, New York, 1958.
Hodson, G., *The Miracle of Birth: A Clairvoyant Study of Prenatal Life*, Theosophical Publishing, London, 1929.
Huntingdon, E., *Season of Birth, Its Relation to Human Abilities*, John Wiley, New York, 1938.
Leach, Gerald, *The Biocrats*, Jonathan Cape, London, 1970.
Rank, Otto, *The Trauma of Birth*, Kegan Paul, Trench, Trubner, London, 1929.
Ratcliff, J., *La Naissance*, Paris, 1953.
Rechung, Rinpoche, *Tibetan Medicine*, Wellcome Institute, London, 1973.
Walter, W. Grey, *The Living Brain*, Duckworth, London, 1953.
Watson, Lyall, *Supernature*, Hodder & Stoughton, London, 1973.

BISEXUALITY

The presence in every individual of the characteristics of both sexes. It is to be distinguished both from androgyny and from transsexuality.

Androgyny (Gk. *andros*, 'man', *gynē*, 'woman') is an abnormal condition where the primary and secondary physical attributes of both male and female sexes are present in a single person. Children are androgynous to start with, both male and female principles actively co-existing within them. Old people who are past sexual competence, although asexual, are likewise regarded as androgynous. The virgin* is similarly a male–female person. The truest marriage provides an androgynous experience for both partners. There is a mysticism about androgyny, and it symbolizes wholeness, totality and unity. The belief that the androgyne or hermaphrodite represents a complete being and is a source of sacred power is prominent in many mythologies.

Also to be distinguished from bisexuality is the concept of *transsexuality*, which is the imitation by one sex of the genital attributes and functions of the other, sometimes in an attempt to reduce the distinctions between male and female in order to achieve a harmonious equilibrium. According to the Freudians there exists a degree of frustration and privation in both sexes because each lacks a sense of completeness, and finds in the other sex something that could help in its own wholeness. This is spoken of as *sex envy*, suggesting an opposition of the sexes on the basis of a mutual sense of insufficiency. Each sex therefore desires for itself the sex organs, social status and functions of the opposite sex. In occult terms this is interpreted as the nostalgic yearning of an originally androgynous being to be made whole again.

In women the basis of transsexism lies in what psychologists call *penis envy*. According to this theory the female often regards herself as destitute of an important element in her make-up. To Aristotle (d. 322 BC) a woman was a 'sterile male', or a 'crippled male', and he held that essentially the female body was that of an unfinished or mutilated man. Even Sigmund Freud regarded women as *hommes manqués*, creatures who fell short of being men.

Another facet of the same complex is found in sexophobia, as manifested in the fear of the sex organs of the other. Girls may fear the *penis aculeatus*, 'the pricking penis', the raping sword of the phallus, which hurts and invades the female.

In the male transsexing arises from *vagina envy*, which manifests in a desire for and an envy of the female reproductive organs, the female breasts, lactation, menstruation, pregnancy, child-bearing. Men are said to envy the mysteries of woman, including her physical attributes and physiological functions. The woman's fear of the sharp penis is analogous to the male's fear of the *vagina dentata*, 'toothed vulva', and rites are performed in many tribal societies which seem to symbolize the male's victory over these fears.

In contrast with androgyny and transsexuality, bisexuality is normal and universal. In the course of human ontogenesis, or development in the womb, it is seen that the genital organ starts the same in both sexes. In the male it develops into a kind of genital bud, which atrophies in the female; and in the female it leaves open the orifice, which closes in the male. Every human being bears traces of the anatomical bisexuality of the embryo. Ancient anatomists too held that in man the female sex organs exist in a state of latent development, and in women the male organs are present in rudimentary form.

Biologists affirm that every single cell in a human body is either male or female; all the cells in a man's body are male, and in a woman's body all are female. Whether this is so or not, it is also affirmed that all cells possess the characteristics of both sexes. It is known that every person secretes both male and female hormones, androgens and oestrogens respectively. Only the male produces more androgens, while the female produces more oestrogens. Neither cells nor glands are at the service exclusively of a single sex. The German physician, Wilhelm Fliess (d. 1928), maintained that he had discovered the bisexual character of all living cells, and succeeded in converting Sigmund Freud to his belief.

Furthermore, there is a bisexuality even in the mind. Carl Gustav Jung (d. 1961) speaks of the existence, in the unconscious of the human psyche, of an element that properly belongs to the sex opposite to one's own, so that each person is bisexual and androgynous. Thus in man there is an anima, or female aspect; and in the female, an animus or male side to the psyche.

No male is wholly male, no female wholly female. Human males possess breasts and frequently experience transient, small-scale changes in them during adolescence. In certain circumstances both male and female can develop the forms of sexuality opposite to their own. Such sex reversal is common among animals, and occurs less frequently among men and women as a change of sex. Sigmund Freud was convinced that all human beings are born with bisexual tendencies, and he spoke of 'the great enigma of the biological fact of the duality of the sexes'.

In medieval occultism the truly bisexual being, like the androgyne, was spoken of as *utriusque capax* (Lat. 'capable of both'), that is, complete, whole and self-sufficient.

Books

Adler, Alfred, *Study of Organ Inferiority and Its Psychical Compensation*, Daniel, London, 1938.

Baumann, Hermann, *Das Doppelte Geschlecht*, Berlin, 1955.

Benjamin, Harry, *The Transsexual Phenomenon*, Julian Press, New York, 1966.

Bettelheim, Bruno, *Symbolic Wounds: Puberty Rites and the Envious Male*, Thames & Hudson, London, 1955.

Eliade, Mircea, *The Two and the One*, Harvill Press, London, 1965.

Ferenczi, S., 'An Anal Hollow-Penis in Women', *Further Contributions to Psychoanalytic Theory*, Institute of Psychoanalysis, London, 1926.

Fontaines, Halley de, *Contributions à l'etude de l'androgynie*, Paris, 1933.

Freud, S., 'Some Psychological Consequences of the Anatomical Distinction Between the Sexes', *Collected Papers*, Hogarth Press, London, 1950.

Greenacre, Phyllis, 'Penis Awe and Its Relation to Penis Envy', in R. M. Loewenstein (ed.), *Drives, Affects and Behavior*, International Universities Press, New York, 1953.

Nunberg, H., *Problems of Bisexuality as Reflected in Circumcision*, Imago, London, 1949.

Rangell, L., 'The Interchangeability of Phallus and Female Genital', *Journal of the American Psychoanalytic Association*, I, 1953.

Wegener, E., *Man Into Woman*, Jarrolds, London, 1933.

BLOOD

The vital essence of a living thing. The Bible says, 'The life of the flesh is in the blood' (Lev. 17:11). Some occultists affirm that the vital essence is actually an invisible and intangible vapour, whose medium is blood, and that it is not the heart that causes the blood to flow, but the spirit within the blood. Life is sustained by the polarity between physical breath and the pneuma. It is sometimes said to be the vehicle of dreams, intimately linked to the invisible world, and constitutes one of the most important 'signatures' connecting the material and astral spheres.

The supraphysical potency of blood remains operative whether within the body or without. Because of the terrifying psychic potentiality and intense sacrosanctity of blood it has been universally surrounded by taboos, and put to countless ritual uses. Except as an aphrodisiac and as a 'vehicle' in certain black magical rites, the blood of menstruation is never used, as it is considered a dangerous source of psychic pollution.

Blood sacrifices are offered in all religions and religio-magical cults. The Babylonians, Greeks and other ancient peoples believed that gods and demons were attracted by the smell of shed blood, especially blood drawn from the bodies of those violently slain. The blood of men and animals released in sacrifice was thought to draw down from the spiritual world the hidden potencies that abide there. From the emanations of shed blood discarnate entities build up appearances and make themselves visible.

Blood has great magnetic power, and an inexplicable fascination for many people, both repelling and attracting in some strange manner. Havelock Ellis (d. 1939) remarked, 'There is scarcely any natural object with so profoundly emotional an effect as blood.' It can cause a person to faint, make his head reel, while irresistibly attracting him, and at the same time inspire him with disgust, nausea, or even give rise to murderous passion. Havelock Ellis thought it probable that the reason underlying sexual murders was 'nearly always to shed blood and not to cause death'.

Blood, especially that of virgin boys and girls, was regarded as a healing agent in diseases like leprosy and syphilis. The afflicted parts or organs had to be washed in the substance. The application of blood to the skin caused it to glow with supernatural beauty. Because she believed in this popular superstition, the notorious Hungarian countess, Elizabeth Bathory (d. 1616), murdered over six hundred girls so that she might bathe in their blood and preserve her complexion.

Blood was believed to be the source of two life-sustaining liquids: milk, which is blood filtered through the breasts; and semen, which is blood filtered through the testes.

Books

Ellis, Havelock, *Studies in the Psychology of Sex*, Random House, New York, 1936.

Fishman, A. P. and Richards, D. W. (eds), *Circulation of the Blood*, Oxford University Press, New York, 1964.

Hackett, Earle, *Blood: The Paramount Humour*, Jonathan Cape, London, 1973.

Macfarlane, R. G. and Robb-Smith, A. H. T. (eds), *Functions of the Blood*, Blackwell, Oxford, 1961.

Penrose, Valentine, *The Bloody Countess*, New English Library, London, 1972.

Seeman, Bernard, *The River of Life. The Story of Man's Blood from Magic to Science*, Museum Press, London, 1962.

Stibbs, A. M., *The Use of the Term 'Blood' in Scripture*, Tyndale Press, London, 1947.
Trumbull, H. C., *The Blood Covenant*, Redway, London, 1887.

BODY

The material element in man*, was known to the Greeks as *soma*, the gross, dense, carnal, animal or natural body and the arena of the senses*, as distinguished from the asoma* or non-material element. In life the body is the medium for the physiological, etheric and certain mental functions; esoterically it is the temporary vehicle of the astral body and the soul. The Orphics (c. 550 BC) called the body 'the prison-house of the soul'. Indeed, they sometimes equated *soma*, 'body', with *sema*, 'tomb'.

Physiologically many highly complex metabolic and autonomic processes such as digestion and absorption, disease-resistance and immunity, blood circulation and breath, interact in man, and help in maintaining the integrity of the organism.

In its functional aspects the body has, in past concepts, been compared to a town, with aqueducts, baths, fountains and sewers; to a house with courtyard, well, kitchen and living-rooms; to a clock with an intricate mechanism; to a heat-engine fuelled by food. The machine analogy invariably extended to man as a whole, whose bodily and mental functions at all levels were described in purely mechanical terms.

Today, another interpretation based on physics is rapidly gaining acceptance. The human body is increasingly seen as a pulsating system of energy fields, dynamically interacting with all other energy fields in the cosmos and responding to countless local and cosmic factors. The body's own bioflux radiations belong to its etheric system.

From earliest times all man's bodily activities have been invested with an esoteric and magical meaning. This fact is still especially marked in primitive societies, where eating, drinking, coition, sleeping, defecation and other natural functions, are surrounded by strict taboos. Childbirth, puberty and death are attended with special transition rites and observances.

The body as a living unit is also studied in terms of its external form. The physiotaxis* or placement of the limbs was regarded as having a particular occult significance. The symbolism of the body is therefore never ignored in any consideration of the total man. Modern psychologists speak of *kinesics* or body-language, the non-verbal mode of communication that goes on between two or more people by their gestures, postures and movements. Their glances, the movement of eyebrows, their grimaces, the way they stand, the distance they keep between themselves and others, the way they hold their arms, the tensions they betray, all speak a language that can be interpreted with great clarity.

In recent years many efforts have been made to gain a better understanding of the varying dimensions of body-experience and the means of enlarging the boundaries of such experience and so creating a deeper awareness of the body. Besides breathing, massage and similar techniques, a number of structural and movement therapies have been developed.

Many such therapies are traceable to the Australian, Frederick Matthias Alexander (d. 1955), who first emphasized the importance of holding and moving the body in a natural and relaxed manner for better health and mental fitness. The Austrian-born American psychiatrist, Wilhelm Reich (d. 1957), said that certain tensions or 'armour blocks' were built up in the head, neck, chest, waist and pelvis (*see* physiotaxis) and his therapy provided a means of release from these blocks. Something on the lines of Alexander is currently being done by the American, Ida P. Rolf, whose 'rolfing' is a method of 'structural integration' working on the deeper muscles and joints, based on the proper positioning of the limbs in work and play. A Chilean named Oscar Ichazo, who runs a development centre in Arica, Chile, teaches a system that is a mixture of physical culture and mysticism, largely influenced by the philosophy and practice of G. I. Gurdjieff.

The interrelation of the body with the wider sphere of the total material environment has been subject to a great deal of metaphysical speculation. The ancient Greeks, proceeding on the analogy of the elements, divided the human body into four zones, each associated with one of these elements, as follows: (1) the aeric, associated with the element of air, and centred in the liver, bile and gall bladder; (2) the hydric, with water, located in the bladder; (3) the telluric, with the earth, located in the intestines; and (4) the pyric, with fire, located in the heart and lungs. Astrology correlated the parts of the body with the zodiacal houses and traced their correspondences, so that each part was ruled by one of the twelve astrological signs and the seven 'planets'.

Ancient and medieval anatomists working on the microcosm principle divided the body into three main regions, thus: (1) the cranial region or head, related to the empyrean or highest heaven; (2) the thoracic region or chest, related to the caelum or sky; and (3) the abdominal region or viscera to the elementarium or elements. Further, as the ideal norm of all 'harmonious proportion*' in nature, man's body became the standard classical measure in art and architecture.

From the religious and mystical standpoint, the body serves as a training ground for the soul in a material environment, the medium through which the spirit might advance. The Bible speaks of the body as the temple of the Holy Ghost (I Cor. 6:19), adding that it should be used as an instrument for the glorification of God. Plato (d. 347 BC) believed that the new-born soul learns truths while it is in the body, and learns them with the help of the senses. It is the direct link between the world of ideas and the world of phenomena.

It is generally agreed by thinkers both eastern and western, that life in a physical body provides unique opportunities for achieving spiritual emancipation. A recurrent theme in folk myth and legend is the yearning that disembodied or elemental beings have for the sanctuary of a material body through which they too might take part in the privileged activities of man, and so achieve maturity and redemption. The Hindu philosopher, Shankara (d. 838), said that birth in a human body was one of the blessings for which a person should daily give thanks to God.

The Russian-Buriat mystic, George Gurdjieff (d. 1949), liked to tell the story of a man who wakes up from a state of apparent sleep to discover that he is actually dead, and separated from his body for ever. It is only then that he realizes the enormity of his failure to make the best use of his life. He has now lost the chief instrument of life's fulfilment, his body, and recalls with agonizing regret all the good that he might have achieved while still alive.

Books

Barlow, Wilfred, *The Alexander Principle*, Gollancz, London, 1973.
Birdwhistell, Ray L., *Introduction to Kinesics: An Annotation System for Analysis of Body Motion and Gesture*, University of Louisville, 1952.
Burnet, Macfarlane, *The Integrity of the Body*, Oxford University Press, London, 1962.
Cannon, Walter B., *The Wisdom of the Body*, 2nd edn, Kegan Paul, Trench, Trubner, London, 1939.
Crile, George W., *The Bipolar Theory of Living Processes*, Macmillan, New York, 1926.
Eckstein, Gustav, *The Body Has a Head*, Collins, London, 1971.
Edsmann, C. M., *The Body and Eternal Life*, Ventenskaps Society, Lund, 1946.
Fast, Julius, *Body Language*, Souvenir Press, London, 1970.
Fisher, S., *Body Consciousness*, Prentice-Hall, Englewood Cliffs, New Jersey, 1973.
Fisher, S. and Cleveland, S., *Body Image and Personality*, Dover, New York, 1968.
Goldstein, Kurt, *The Organism*, New York, 1939.
Hall, Manly Palmer, *Man, the Grand Symbol of the Mysteries*, Philosophical Research Society, Los Angeles, 1947.
Howe, E. G., *The Invisible Anatomy*, Faber, London, 1939.
Lenihan, John, *Human Engineering: the Body Re-examined*, Weidenfeld & Nicolson, London, 1974.
Lowen, Alexander, *The Betrayal of the Body*, Macmillan, Ottawa, 1967.
Luce, Gay, *Body Time*, Temple Smith, London, 1972.
Pressman, A. S., *Electronic Fields and Life*, Plenum Press, New York, 1972.
Schilder, Paul, *The Image and Appearance of the Human Body*, John Wiley, New York, 1964.
Tiller, William A., *Energy Fields and the Human Body*, New York, 1972.

BONES

The most enduring part of the physical organism, bones have been known to survive many hundreds of thousands of years. The bones of prehistoric man have been found in an almost perfect state of preservation in conditions that have reduced even rocks to rubble. They have survived heat, cold and water. Everywhere men have attached religious importance to bones.

Skeletons figure in magical, occult and necrophilic rites, as a *memento mori*, a reminder of death, to familiarize participants with the idea of mortality, and to make them reflect on the afterlife and on the transience of this world and of the flesh. In certain oriental and shamanistic ceremonies the candidate for initiation is told to imagine his body stripped of flesh to the bone, and to meditate on his own skeletal form. Sometimes the presiding shaman or the candidate himself wears a costume that looks like a skeleton, to suggest that the rites pertain to the realm of the dead.

Bones have been regarded not only as a symbol of death, but also of life, and it is believed in many parts of the world that a spirit can be summoned by possession of one of the bones of the departed, and even that a living being can be reanimated from its bones. The Bible relates how the prophet Ezekiel was carried to a valley full of bones, and how by God's command the bones came together and formed living men (Ezek. 37:10). Medieval Jews believed that after death the vital principle remained locked in a tiny bone fragment called *luz*, situated at the base of the spine*, from which the body would be resurrected for the final judgment.

The practice of bone-pointing is prominent in primitive witch cults. Here one of the longer bones of the human arm or leg is used. It is emptied, dried and filled with the hair, nails, blood or excrement of the chosen victim. Incantations are sung over it, reputedly causing cramps, diarrhoea and death. Bon priests of Tibet use the human thigh-bone, preferably of a criminal or someone who has died a violent death, as a trumpet to summon spirits. The finger-bones of sorcerers are converted into rosaries used in black magic. In all communities the skulls of great men are believed to have magical power and are honoured and preserved and sometimes used as oracles. The bones of saints are precious relics of the church, and miracles are sometimes attributed to them.

Bones and bone-powder have medicinal and aphrodisiac virtues. Charred and powdered corpse-bones were a basic ingredient in love unguents and love philtres.

Books

See under body *and* head

BRAIN

Brain, or encephalon, the most highly organized material substance on earth, is that part of the central nervous system lying within the cranium, the protective helmet of bone. There is a distinct structural difference between the head and the body. The body is built like a vertebrate (soft tissue covering a bony structure); the head is built like a crustacean such as a crab (bony structure covering a soft tissue).

The brain consists of (1) the forebrain or prosencephalon (Gk. *pros*, 'before'), consisting of the cerebrum*; (2) the interbrain or diencephalon (Gk. *dia*, 'through') consisting of the thalamus* and hypothalamus; (3) the midbrain or mesencephalon (Gk. *mesos*, 'middle'), consisting of the brain stem, that is, medulla and pons; and (4) the hindbrain or metencephalon (Gk. *meta*, 'after'), or cerebellum.

Lying below the covering folds of the cerebral cortex and deep inside the cerebral hemispheres, at the border of the brain stem and diencephalon, is the very old *limbic system* (Lat. *limbus*, 'border'), which is associated with the instinctive functions of eating, fighting and mating. In the evolutionary process, parts of the limbic system, along with the brain stem, are thought to have first appeared some 500 million years ago, and represent the first swelling of the spinal cord to form the head. The limbic system also contains the emotional areas linked with the senses of pleasure and displeasure. In

1954 the American physiologist, James Olds, discovered that stimulation of this area produced strong sensations of pleasure in the subject. A rat fitted with an electrode by which it could stimulate itself, did so thousands of times every hour for days at a time, to the exclusion of food, sex and sleep.

Included in the limbic system are the *amygdala* (Lat. 'walnut'), associated with the primitive emotions of fear and aggressiveness, or flight and attack, necessary for survival; and the *hippocampus* (*see* nose), also in the temporal lobe, having a role in memory formation. Without a hippocampus a patient could, for example, read the same story every day with renewed interest, since he would not recall it a few hours after having read it.

The *brain stem*, as big as one's little finger, lies at the base of the skull cavity, and is the extension of the upper end of the spinal cord. Usually regarded as forming the midbrain, the brain stem is also some 500 million years old. A switchover of nerves takes place in the brain stem; here the nerves originating in or coming from the left side of the body, switch over to the right hemisphere of the brain, and vice versa. For this reason injury to one side of the skull shows its effects, such as paralysis in hemiplegia, on the opposite side of the body.

The upper end of the spinal cord passes through the *foramen magnum* (Lat. 'great opening'), the hole in the floor of the skull, and ends in the *medulla oblongata*, which is a prolongation of the spinal cord. The medulla oblongata is one of the oldest parts of the brain. In its earliest stages of growth the human central nervous system is a long stretched tube, the so-called medullar tube, the anterior end of which grows more quickly, to form the embryonic brain-bag. The medulla oblongata is connected with the fourth ventricle, and serves as an organ of communication between the spinal cord and the rest of the brain. In it are situated centres that govern such autonomic functions as breathing, the heartbeat, the regulation of blood vessels and body temperature, and certain reflexes that accompany swallowing. Continuous with the medulla and projecting a little to the front of it, is a wide band of nervous tissue which forms a bridge (Lat. *pons*) over the two halves of the cerebellum, and is called the *pons varolii*. The medulla and the pons together form the brain stem.

In the brain stem, especially the medulla oblongata, is a nerve net known as the *reticular formation*, consisting of millions of neurons in a matrix of fibres, from which long branches are sent out to every part of the body. It thus participates in every neural function, and co-ordinates and filters information in the brain. It is the centre of arousal and wakefulness, and regulates awareness. Mechanical, electrical, surgical or chemical interference that puts the reticular formation out of action, produces coma and sometimes death. Lying longitudinally along the brain stem is the *raphe* system, which becomes active in the sleeping brain. If the raphe system is destroyed the patient suffers from chronic insomnia.

The *cerebellum*, 'little brain', or hindbrain, although not actually part of the brain stem is connected with it. It lies in the lower back part of the skull and regulates equilibrium and the co-ordination of muscular movements such as maintaining balance in walking. The cerebellum is a 'mirror-image' of the cerebrum, but the right cerebellar hemisphere controls the right of the body, and the left the left of the body. Injury to the cerebellum produces a staggering gait, palsy and slurred speech. The pons and cerebellum are believed to have first appeared in reptiles about 300 million years ago.

Originating from or near the brain stem, and attached mainly to the pons and medulla, are twelve pairs of *cranial nerves* (as distinct from the spinal nerves), which control smell, sight, taste, hearing, facial skin, swallowing and so on. For instance, the *trigeminal* nerve (the fifth cranial nerve) controls the muscles of chewing, and supplies sensations such as pain, heat, cold and touch, to the face, eyes, nose, mouth, tongue and teeth. It is the nerve of toothache and facial neuralgia. Inflammation of this nerve can cause the most excruciating pain. The tenth cranial nerve, known as the *vagus*, descends vertically and sends branches to the ear, neck, lungs, heart and abdominal viscera. Since it controls breath and digestion, the vagus is also called the *pneumogastric* nerve. Because it reaches from the head to the heart, the vagus is regarded as a nerve of particular importance by occultists, who sometimes speak of it as the tree of life.

Man's brain is larger than the combined brains of ten prehistoric reptiles, some of which were 100 feet long and had brains the size of a walnut. According to evolutionists, during the Pleistocene age one million years ago, man's brain suddenly started growing at a phenomenal rate. The roof-brain, that is, the neocortex, became almost like a 'tumorous overgrowth', leading to man's great stride forward. All hominoid apes that exist today, chimpanzees, gorillas and orang-utans, have remained the same as they were then, but one type, man alone, began a steep upward climb. His brain had grown about 350 per cent during that time. Why this sudden growth took place is an unexplained mystery. Scholars like Maerth hold that human evolution as we know it began when man's simian ancestors discovered that by eating the brains of their fellows they increased their sexuality and also their capacity for thought. In support of the theory they allude to the many folk and traditional remedies of the Chinese, Tibetans, Hindus and Arabs, that record the use of human brain as a stimulant, an aphrodisiac and a medicine.

But the precise relationship between the size of the brain, even the brain-bark, and intelligence, is not established. Several great men, including geniuses like Voltaire and Lord Byron, had smaller than average brains. The largest human brains, in fact twice the normal size, belong to idiots. Besides, Amerindians, Japanese, Eskimos and some southern Africans have brains of a larger capacity than Europeans.

So the brain remains very much of an enigma, and there are still many unanswered questions about this 'three-pound mass of repellent convolutions'. The brain has also been referred to as 'the great ravelled knot', and Sir Charles Sherrington (d. 1952), the father of modern neurology, called it 'the enchanted loom'. But what this loom is, and the nature of its specific functions, is only beginning to be dimly understood.

The geography of the brain has been roughly mapped and demarcated. The cerebrum is divided into certain sections or lobes, each seemingly responsible for some specific function. The frontal lobe, behind the forehead, is the seat of creativity; the temporal lobe, at the temples and above the ears, governs memory; the parietal lobe, from the sides to the top middle of the brain, governs motor functions, especially co-ordination; and the occipital lobe, at the back of the head, the visual areas. The location of these and other controlling areas across the cortex has been discovered by neurosurgeons on the basis of stimulation experiments. The maps of the cortex thus revealed show areas for motor activity (a strip across the top of the cerebrum), muscular response, voice control (vocalization, lips, jaw, tongue, throat), ideational speech, sight, hearing and several other faculties.

But the whole theory of the localization of cerebral functions has sometimes been thrown in doubt. The exact 'site' of memory is unidentifiable, and the controlling or willing centre unknown. Some neurosurgeons believe that there is no single region of the cortex specifically and exclusively connected with a particular function or sensation, and that when one part of the brain is damaged, another part can take over its functions quite efficiently. Operations have been performed in which large areas of the brain were removed without the crippling effects that might have been expected from brain mapping (*see* mind–body). In effect, there do not seem to be any specific areas readily and unequivocally identifiable with fixed and precise functions. The cortex is equipotential.

Hence the geography of the brain has had to be drastically revised from time to time. The larger part of the brain appears to consist of 'silent areas', since little is known about them; they yield little or nothing to experimental probing, and seem to be unused. In 1949 an eminent physiologist, R. W. Gerard, could write that 'our present understanding of mind would remain valid and useful if, for all we knew, the cranium were stuffed with cotton wadding'. Many psychologists believe that this holds true even today.

Hippocrates (d. 359 BC) regarded the brain as the seat of the intellectual faculties, but Aristotle (d. 322 BC), who noted that the brain tissue does not feel pain, concluded that it could not be connected either with thinking or feeling. He identified the heart as the intellectualizing control centre of the body, and the brain as a gland which served as a cooling system, supplying the cold humours to prevent the overheating of the body by the furnace of the heart. The Moslems adopted the same idea. The *Book of El-Habib* says, 'Man's head resembles a condensing apparatus.'

William James (d. 1910) believed that we use only one-tenth of our mental capacity. The greater part of our faculties is still untouched. According to the best modern authorities there are practically no limits to the possibilities of the human brain. The brain has properties that are chemical, electrical and magnetic. It emits waves, receives messages, interprets, intercepts. American psychologists say that there are differences in the two hemispheres of the brain (*see* cerebrum); and Soviet scientists have found that there is a difference in potential between the front and back of the brain. The back exhibits great activity during telepathic and telekinetic experiments. The brain has no parallel with anything else we know and is the nearest thing to a science-fiction organ, bridging the physical and psychical realms. The mind–body* relationship, which is virtually the brain-body relationship, is still largely unsolved.

Some people regard the brain as a defence mechanism for controlling the impressions received by our senses* and protecting us from an overwhelming surplus of information. Immanuel Kant (d. 1804) held that the brain is not the cause of our thinking, but an organ that restricts thought, and that although it is essential to our animal or sensuous consciousness, it 'may be regarded as an impeder of pure spiritual life'. And Henri Bergson (d. 1941) suggested that the function of the brain is to act as a filter to eliminate unwanted sensations. It keeps out countless impressions. The brain thus acts as a 'reducing valve', admitting to consciousness only those experiences which are relevant to survival. In xenophrenic* states this filter is bypassed or put out of action.

Books

Asimov, Isaac, *The Human Brain: Its Capacities and Functions*, Nelson, London, 1965.
Barcroft, Joseph, *The Brain and Its Environment*, Yale University Press, New Haven, 1938.
Bergson, Henri, *Creative Evolution*, Macmillan, London, 1911.
French, John D. (ed.), *Frontiers in Brain Research*, Columbia University Press, New York, 1962.
George, F. H., *The Brain as Computer*, Pergamon Press, London, 1961.
Groch, Judith, *You and Your Brain*, Cassell, London, 1964.
Lassek, A. M., *The Human Brain: From Primitive to Modern*, Blackwell Scientific Press, Oxford, 1957.
Maerth, O. K., *The Beginning Was the End*, Michael Joseph, London, 1973.
Neumann, John, *The Computer and the Brain*, Oxford University Press, 1958.
Pfeiffer, John, *The Human Brain*, Gollancz, London, 1955.
Poynter, F. N. L. (ed.), *The History and Philosophy of the Brain and Its Functions*, Blackwell, Oxford, 1958.
Rose, Steven, *The Conscious Brain*, Weidenfeld & Nicolson, London, 1973.
Sheer, Daniel E., *Electrical Stimulation of the Brain*, University of Texas Press, Austin, 1961.
Simeons, A. T., *Man's Presumptuous Brain*, Dutton, New York, 1961.
Walter, W. Grey, *The Living Brain*, Duckworth, London, 1953.
Woodridge, D. E., *The Machinery of the Brain*, McGraw-Hill, New York, 1963.

BRAIN WAVES

The popular term for the weak electrical impulses generated by the brain, especially the cortical layers of the cerebrum. The fact that the brain of man and animal is the source of varying electrical potential was first discovered by the English physiologist, Richard Caton (c. 1875), who detected tiny currents in the living brain of a dog on which he had performed an experimental operation.

A number of telemetrical devices have since been invented in order to study the functions of the living body, of which the electroencephalograph (abbreviated EEG) is used in recording 'brain waves'. The EEG machine as we know it today was developed as a result of the pioneering work in 1929 of Dr Hans Berger (d. 1941), a German psychiatrist at the University of Jena, who discovered and recorded the first brain waves, which for some time were called Berger waves, after him. In the EEG, metal disc electrodes or highly sensitive receivers are placed against various parts of the scalp, and the faint electrical impulses are picked up and amplified. These impulses are relayed into a machine where automatic pens trace the 'brain prints' on slowly revolving drums of graph paper (the electroencephalogram). The impulses are measured in so many vibrations (cycles, rhythms, frequencies, pulsations or waves) per second.

EEG recordings have been taken, from the mother's abdominal wall, of a child during the seventh foetal month. Infants and children have characteristic brain rhythms. From the age of ten the brain rhythms of childhood undergo a change of pattern and gradually conform to the range of rhythms typical of the adult. Individual differences in brain rhythms are very striking. No two persons have identical EEG rhythms, which tend to remain characteristic for each individual and are as distinctive as fingerprints. W. Grey Walter thought that they may in some degree be used to measure acquired differences of personality. Noting that international misunderstanding could be due to statesmen having different thought patterns, he further suggested that 'perhaps a diplomat should have his alpha-type endorsed on his passport' (Karlins and Andrews, 1973, p. 42).

The EEG of a sleeping person differs from that of the same person when he is awake, and this again changes when he is meditating, or angry. Furthermore, brain waves are altered by loud music, temperature, headache, excitement (an orgasm produces a convulsive EEG), illness and other changes in xenophrenic states. Aspirin causes excessively slow waves; coffee, an acceleration. It has been found that drugs having a stupefying effect on the cerebral cortex (ether, chloroform, morphine, scopolamine) result in a decreased electrical activity of the cortex; while with narcotics which have only a specific stupefying effect on the thalamus (such as veronal, somniphene, dial, luminal and other barbiturates) there is a considerable increase in the electrical activity of the cortex.

The normal EEG recording consists of many different frequencies, and each EEG pattern is named after the frequency that predominates. Various types of waves have been distinguished in this way.

Delta waves, from 1 to 3 cycles per second, have the slowest oscillation and deepest amplitude of all. Such waves occur in unconsciousness and in profound oblivious sleep, hence called 'delta sleep', where the sleeper is immobile and not dreaming, and occasionally in passive somnolent states. In the late foetal stage, at birth and for some months after birth the EEG pattern follows an irregular delta rhythm. The same pattern is sometimes recorded in epileptic seizures. During delta activity no useful work can be done.

Theta waves, from 4 to 7 cycles per second. This is regarded as an inspirational rhythm, reached during the hypnagogic stage just before sleep. It is associated both with creative hallucinations and occasional anxiety. The theta state is one of 'reverie', as distinct from daydreaming. Researchers believe it might be possible to explore higher levels of awareness and creative consciousness by developing the theta state. Zen practitioners are said to go past alpha into theta during meditation and trance.

Alpha waves, between 8 and 13 cycles per second. An idling rhythm associated with pleasant feelings. It appears best when the eyes are closed and the person is conscious but calm, passive and relaxed, during which time the rhythm is clean and synchronized. Alpha waves are disrupted by attention, concentration on a problem, or by emotion, when they become erratic, jerky and desynchronized. They also disappear during sleep, when the weaker delta waves take their place. Alpha waves are rare in children before the age of ten, and are found only in short bursts before puberty. They are common in adults and faster in women than men. Zen and yoga meditation produce an increased alpha rhythm. It is sometimes accompanied by distortions of time and space. Few or feeble alpha rhythms indicate a person with a vivid visual imagination. Persistent or strong alpha rhythms indicate non-visualizers who prefer auditory, kinaesthetic and tactile modes of perception. If alpha rhythms persist when the eyes are open it is a sign of mental illness of the kind that ends in withdrawal from reality.

Beta waves, between 14 and 26 cycles a second, are the waves with the highest frequency, and are found in practically all normal waking states. Beta are the brain waves of the normally active mind. They seem to increase during concentration, tension, and anxiety, and diminish or disappear if the functioning of the cerebral cortex is interrupted. The presence of beta waves means that the brain is being used for normal everyday work, with attention focused on the outside world, on calculating, shopping and so on. Beyond beta some researchers have recorded *gamma* waves, with frequencies higher than 26 cycles per second. Not much is known about them so far, and if any waves beyond 26 cycles per second are recorded they are treated as an extension of beta waves.

Following the discovery of the seemingly close association between brain waves and mental states, a method of controlling these rhythms has been evolved, in order to create desirable states of consciousness at will. In cybernetics (the theory governing the control-mechanism of self-regulating systems), the term feedback is used for the return information on the effects of any controlling action. In physiology and psychology, *biofeedback* is applied to the adjustment of one's body to reactions 'fed back' to the mind as a result of earlier experience. Biofeedback is a constant and natural bodily process, which takes place all the time, helps in maintaining physical homeostasis and mental equilibrium, and is involved both in the conscious control and the unconscious regulation of all physical activity. It is estimated that there are over 2,000 feedback systems built into the human body.

More specifically, biofeedback denotes the control of normally involuntary reactions by conscious and systematic effort. It is a training procedure, usually with the aid of telemetric devices (such as variations of the EEG) for regulating the physiological functions and mechanisms that are regarded as being outside one's control, such as heartbeats, blood pressure, sweating and other involuntary reflexes and functions. It applies some of the principles of autogenic training (*see* nervous system).

It is known that in certain eastern meditative systems such as Zen and Yoga, these autonomic processes can be brought under conscious control.

But while techniques of meditation require years of effort to become effective, biofeedback training claims to do it in a matter of weeks, even days. Much research has been conducted since 1958 on biofeedback control, especially of alpha waves, by Dr Joe Kamiya of the University of Chicago, and other researchers have elaborated on his findings. Some feel that with biofeedback training one might be able to achieve the 'alpha experience' by mastering the EEG rhythm changes and thus produce 'instant enlightenment' on demand.

Several types of versatile biofeedback machines are manufactured commercially. When connected to the subject, the machine amplifies his brain waves, heartbeat, the vibrations of his vocal cords, the tension of his muscles, and a flashing light, a moving needle, a clicking noise, a high whine, a low buzz or a steady tone, will tell him whether he is doing well or not. This monitor provides him with all the information he needs to begin to control his responses. Thus, he learns to keep his heartbeat down to a safe pace, and achieve the serene alpha state at will, and even sustain it.

A great deal of criticism has been directed at EEGs in general and alpha rhythms in particular, especially when used for these purposes. It has been pointed out that the physiological basis of the different waves is not yet understood to any satisfactory degree. The borderline between the various brain rhythms and the corresponding mental states said to be associated with them is neither clear nor consistent. The two hemispheres of the cerebrum sometimes have different rhythms; thus the right hemisphere may be generating alpha, while the left is in beta. A minute later the frequency may be reversed.

It has also been observed that the function of the alpha rhythms is still obscure. Alpha waves do not necessarily coincide with feelings of relaxation and well-being. They are sometimes registered without the subject feeling relaxed, and when he is actually anxious and apprehensive. Some people produce almost continuous alpha rhythms and some exhibit none at all. No correlation has been found between alpha waves, and intelligence or personality.

Some experts believe that alpha rhythms are not a record of the brain at all, but may be activated by a tremor of the optic muscles or optic nerves. They can allegedly be produced by such methods as rolling the eyes up and back; by closing the eyes; by blinking; by opening the eyes in the dark and straining to look at something; by twitching or tensing the muscles of the forehead; by frowning or gritting the teeth; by holding the breath; or simply by expecting alpha waves.

Books

Barber, T. *et al.*, *Biofeedback and Self Control*, Aldine-Atherton, Chicago, 1972.

Barnes, Thomas C. *Synopsis of Electroencephalography*, Hafner, Philadelphia, 1968.

Brazier, Mary, *A History of the Electrical Activity of the Brain*, Pitman Medical, London, 1961.

Erlanger, J. and Gasser, H., *Electrical Signs of Nervous Activity*, Pennsylvania University Press, 1937.

Glaser, Gilbert H., *EEG and Behaviour*, Basic Books, 1963.

Hill, Denis, *Electroencephalography*, Macdonald, London, 1963.
Jacobson, E., *Progressive Relaxation*, University of Chicagó Press, 1938.
Karlins, Marvin and Andrews, Lewis, *Biofeedback: Turning on the Power of Your Mind*, Garnstone Press, London, 1973.
London, P., *Behavior Control*, Harper & Row, New York, 1969.
Stevens, Leonard A., *Explorers of the Brain*, Angus & Robertson, London, 1973.

BREASTS

Breasts, or mammary glands (mammae), crowned by the areolae, from which sprout the nipples, are a characteristically feminine equipment, and one of the chief outward signs of womanhood. From the shape, position, condition and comparison of the two breasts it was believed to be possible to judge the age of the girl, the race, the sexual type, character, whether virgin or not, whether mother or not, the kind of dress usually worn and the type of occupation. The intelligence of a girl can also presumably be gauged from the size of her breasts. A survey of childless women conducted in Texas concluded that the bigger the breasts the smaller the IQ.

Not uncommon in medical annals are cases of women having more than two breasts (polymastia), more than two nipples (polythelia), or false nipples situated outside the area of the bosom (hyperthelia or pseudothelia). The anthropologist Hermann Klaatsch says, 'There is still frequently at least one additional breast, above the real breast, even in European women. It has no teat and very rarely gives milk.' And he states that it can sometimes be seen on the breast of well-formed women, and classical statues like the Venus of Milo show it. Anne Boleyn (d. 1536), second wife of Henry VIII, was multi-breasted.

In medieval Europe such extra breasts and nipples were regarded as the certain sign of a witch, as witches were believed to suckle their familiars from these teats. Since the extra nipple, called a *bigg*, was frequently concealed in some intimate part of the body, usually in the sexual parts, witchfinders conducted a thorough examination of the body in their search for it. Any mole, corn, wart or other protuberance, or excessive development of the clitoris, could be pronounced a bigg, and the woman burnt on this evidence alone.

For various reasons the breasts were sometimes excised. In some cases it was a form of disgrace, torture or punishment. Ancient Greek chronicles record that the Amazons (Gk. *a-mastos*, 'without a breast'), a tribe of warrior women of the Caucasus, used to cut off the right breast so that they could draw the bow more effectively. The Skoptsi, a Russian sect which survived till the beginning of the present century, practised male castration and mutilation of female breasts, because these were regarded as conducive to sin.

Beautiful breasts were commonly regarded as the highest mark of feminine beauty, and it was the fashion in many places for women to be clothed from neck to ankles, but to have the breasts exposed. In classical Greece the cult of the female bosom is found richly reflected in literature and art. A favourite Homeric epithet of admiration for a woman was *bathykolpos*, 'deep-bosomed'. In Christian Europe exposure of the breasts followed the vagaries of fashion, although it was always opposed by the Church. Tudor women wore bodices which displayed the nipples, a fashion which returned in the eighteenth century. Revealed breasts were also a sign of virginity, and Queen Elizabeth I (d. 1603) often wore gowns that exposed her breasts for reasons of state, to show her virgin status.

Breasts have a prolific symbolism. The association patterns built up in the infant's mind with the maternal bosom are regarded by psychologists as the origin of a wide range of cultural and social activities. Fascination for the breast is very deep-rooted, stemming from ancestral experience. As a phylogenetic inheritance, it is found in every person, even those who have never been nursed directly at the breast.

The comfort that comes to the child from being held against the bosom makes a woman the shelter and refuge, and a source of security against the cruel world outside. This was one aspect of the mother goddess. The oral satisfaction found in sucking, and all its associated pleasures, is thought to have led to the cultivation of the culinary arts. The milk that comes from the breast and nourishes the infant makes the mother the symbol of abundance and generosity. Sigmund Freud pointed out that a child's first erotic object is its mother's breast, and around the breast centre not only mother love, but sexual love, starting with the pleasure of kissing.

Because of their shape and smoothness, breasts symbolized the curve, the circle, the rotunda, the globe. Man's appreciation of beauty, based on a remembrance of the mother's bosom, accounts for the development of sculpture and the plastic arts. The earliest pottery is believed to be fashioned in direct imitation of the female breasts, and the making of pots in many places had a religious bearing, connected with the worship of the Great Mother.

Books

Binder, Pearl, *Muffs and Morals*, Harrap, London, 1953.
Klaatsch, H., *The Evolution and Progress of Mankind*, Unwin, London, 1923.
Neumann, Erich, *The Great Mother*, Pantheon, New York, 1955.
Ploss, H. H. and Bartels, M. and P., *Woman*, 3 vols, ed. F. J. Dingwall, Heinemann, London, 1935.
Sierksma, F., *The Gods as We Shape Them*, Routledge & Kegan Paul, London, 1960.
Smith, Anthony, *The Body*, Allen & Unwin, London, 1968.

BREATH-MAGIC

Breath-magic involves a knowledge of the different kinds of pneuma* or vital breath-energy generated within the system, an understanding of the principles of breath-retention*, the ability to direct the pneuma to various organs of the body for the purpose of invigorating them, and the utilization of pneumic energy for various purposes, largely sexual.

It is to be understood that like sweat and other bodily substances manufac tured within the system, breath differs in people both in health and sickness in moments of peace and in times of passion. The pneumic power of a mother's breath cooing to her infant has a different quality from that of an angry and jealous woman. The one is soft, soothing and full of tenderness, poured out from the mother's loving spirit; the other is harsh, searing and vengeful, springing from the soul envenomed with hatred.

In certain kinds of breath-magic the pneuma is directed to areas of the body which are the centres of the bodily fluxes, such as the brain, which is the centre of the cerebral fluids; the heart, the centre of the haematic fluids; the solar plexus, the centre of the astral fluids; and the testicles, the centre of the seminal fluids. The fluids from these various centres become etherealized, and the released energy converted into a vaporous substance that is used for the purpose chosen by the practitioner.

In the Tibetan esoteric practice of tummo the pneumic current is directed towards the transformation of the seminal fluids. Both inspiration and expiration techniques are brought into play to convey the energy to and from the male vessels to the heart. During inspiration, in the language of occultism, the lower door of energy is opened and seminal power conveyed to the brain; during expiration the upper door of energy is opened and the seminal power is carried back again down the front of the body towards the perineum. The principal organs involved are the lungs, testicles, heart and brain. In the process the semen becomes heated and vaporized, then united with the breath and transformed into energy. The energy is then diffused throughout the body, which becomes heated to an extraordinary degree and thus rendered immune to the intensest cold.

Breath control plays an important part in tantrik sex magic, both in controlling the coital process and in absorbing female energy. It is believed that breath-retention* in a special manner 'arrests the semen', and prevents ejaculation. The Sanskrit text *Goraksha Samhita* says, 'So long as the breath is in motion, the semen moves about. When the breath ceases to flow the semen is arrested.'

Again, the pneumic essence exhaled by the female partner during intercourse can also be utilized by the male. But one must be careful to select the right partner and to ensure that she is stimulated in the right manner. The coital breath of a woman who is indifferent to the act is of neutral value for the male; if she actively dislikes her partner and is filled with revulsion or hatred for him, her breath can do him harm. According to the Chinese, the female's breath during satisfactory intercourse is charged with yin essence, and the sipping of this vitalizing breath is one of the oldest occult methods of rejuvenation, if the woman can be brought to the proper pitch of desire. Hindu manuals also recommend the savouring of this breath. After duly preparing the woman for intercourse by preliminary love-making, the man should effect penetration and immediately apply his mouth to hers and draw in her breath as she breathes. According to the manuals this will prolong his erection and increase his retention capacity.

Finally, the breath that is exhaled by a woman at the moment of orgasm, especially after satisfactory intercourse, is full of very potent energy. But this orgasmic breath requires special methods of intake by the male if he is to benefit from it, for in most cases the power is short-lived and is very rapidly dissipated.

Books

Cakravarti, Candra, *Sex Life in Ancient India*, Mukhopadhyay, Calcutta, 1963.
Campbell, Joseph (ed.), *Spiritual Disciplines*, Routledge & Kegan Paul, London, 1960.
Garrison, Omar, *Tantra: The Yoga of Sex*, Academy Editions, London, 1972.
Gulik, R. H. van, *Sexual Life in Ancient China*, Brill, Leiden, 1961.
Rechung, Lama, *Tibetan Medicine*, Wellcome Institute, London, 1973.

BREATH-RETENTION

The act whereby the breath drawn into the lungs is held there for some time, forms an integral part of certain mystical and magical practices. Such retention is believed to put in great reserves of vitalic energy. This appears to be supported by the common experience that a heavy object becomes easier to lift if one takes a full deep breath and holds it while one lifts (*see* respiration).

Most major mystical systems have evolved their own methods of breath control. Indian and African wonderworkers who practise suspended animation are able to stop their breathing for long periods, and can allegedly be buried without danger for several hours, and, according to their claims, even days. They retain in their lungs a small reserve of air which would be used in case an accident should bring them out of their trance; they would then take a few shallow inhalations and return to their trance state.

In the sufi practice of *zikr* (repetition of God's name), the devotees are trained in certain respiratory exercises. Several sufi leaders were credited with the ability to suspend their respiration for two or three hours while in trance. Like the sufis, the eleventh-century Christian monks of the middle east, known as the hesychasts, combined breathing and breath-retention techniques with their religious devotions. Among western mystics, Emanuel Swedenborg (d. 1772) declared that when communing with spirits he hardly breathed for half an hour at a time. In the United States, the 'archnatural respiration' of Thomas Lake Harris (d. 1906) also involved an element of breath-retention.

It is said that breath can best be retained in a watery element, which has a larger proportion of the etheric and pneumic substances conducive to breath-retention. Among mammals the aquatic animals can hold their breath longest. For example the seal (forty minutes), and the sperm whale (two hours). The ideal aim of many occult breathing techniques is embryonic respiration, that is, breathing 'internally', like the embryo in the amniotic fluid within the womb; in other words, to still the breath (*see* eupnea).

Probably the most intensive method of all was evolved by the taoists of China. The taoist method of respiration calls for (1) inhaling; (2) retaining the breath; (3) purifying the in-breathed air; and (4) circulating the purified air to various parts and organs of the body, especially the brain, heart and sexual zone. The potency of this air is absorbed for the nourishment of the body, the increase of mental powers, the expansion of the spirit and the attainment of immortality.

In breath purification, the breathed-in air is subjected to the influence of the internal fires and cleared of all impurities so that only an extremely rarefied and refined essence of air remains in the body. This energy-essence of the breath (*ch'i*) is purer even than the purest mountain air. The process of refining causes the air to expand. As it expands it tries to escape, seeking outlets through the mouth (or nose) and the rectum (*see* flatus). To prevent any such loss the operator, before beginning the exercise, inserts a wooden plug into his anus and puts a clamp, like a clothes peg, on his nostrils. Later, when he acquires proficiency he can dispense with these aids.

At the same time the saliva is also purified. Taoists believe that this distillation of the head can provide the practitioner with all the nourishment he needs for life, if he learns to absorb it. The secret lies in the technique of collecting the 'brain-dew' (*see* ros) as it seeps into the mouth, of harmonizing it with the purified air, and of swallowing and absorbing its precious essence. According to certain accounts one need go no further than this stage to be on the road to immortality.

Having acquired proficiency in the preliminary techniques the adept lies down, turns his tongue up and back against the roof of his mouth, contracts the anus, presses the middle of each palm with the middle finger of the opposite hand, and taking a series of slow deep breaths holds his breath for the length of thirty units of time (today counted in seconds). He then proceeds on the 'little tour', sending the *ch'i*, or breath energy, through the chest and heart. He then progressively increases breath-retention by five units of time every lunar month until he can hold his breath for 150 units, at which stage he sends the *ch'i* on the 'big tour', directing his breath through the heart, neck, chest, abdomen, liver, kidneys and sex organs, and passes the residual impure air out of the anus. At each stage he stimulates the organs concerned and controls their functions.

Further progress involves even longer periods of retention, and each period brings its own reward. When he reaches 300 units he learns to send the breath up the spine and into the head. There is danger here that the air might seep out of the cranial sutures and it must therefore be directed in the proper manner. At this stage he no longer sees or hears with his external organs, but has an inner perception of things. At 500 units he ceases to think in the clouded confusion that characterizes the thoughts of ordinary men. Now he learns to keep a column of vitalic air within the spine. At 1000 units he is on the threshold of immortality, and is able to feed the various gods who dwell in the body, and make them subservient to his will.

Ultimately, the purpose of breath-retention in taoism is to unite the breath-energy (*ch'i*) and the semen-energy (*ching*), and by meditative visualization and self-conjugation, to create within the body the mysterious seed known variously as 'the golden pill', 'the embryonic pearl' or 'the immortal foetus', that will ensure his physical immortality. An ancient Chinese text says: 'One holds the breath and it is collected; when collected it expands; when expanded it moves downward. Proceeding down it becomes quiet; when quiet it solidifies and then begins to germinate. When germinated it reaches the upper regions to the crown of the head. Then one lives for ever.'

It is to be noted that holding one's breath for long periods of time can be very dangerous, and many incautious neophytes have done themselves serious injury as a result of breathing practices carried out in ignorance.

Books

Gulik, R. H. van, *Sexual Life in Ancient China*, Brill, Leiden, 1961.
King, Francis, *Sexuality, Magic and Perversion*, Neville Spearman, London, 1971.
Luk, Charles, *Taoist Yoga: Alchemy and Immortality*, Rider, London, 1970.
Needham, Joseph, *Science and Civilisation in China*, vol. 2, Cambridge University Press, 1956.
Regardie, Israel, *Art of True Healing*, Helios Books, Toddington, 1964.
Walker, Benjamin, *Sex and the Supernatural*, Macdonald, London, 1970.
Welch, Holmes, *The Parting of the Way*, Methuen, London, 1957.

BUTTOCKS

Formed by the expansion of the gluteal muscles, buttocks enable a man to stand perfectly erect, and exist in no other animal. They are the hallmark of the human being and are regarded as a special gift of God. It was commonly believed in Europe that the devil had no buttocks and that though he could assume any shape, even human, he could not simulate the buttocks. When he appeared before his followers at the sabbat gatherings he wore a head where his buttocks should have been. The same disability appears in the devil's minions: the Germanic Frau Holle and the Norse Huldren are described as beautiful to behold from the front, but with a rear hollow as a rotten tree-trunk and full of putrefaction.

Exposure of the buttocks was hateful to the devil as it reminded him of his deficiency, and such exposure was used to exorcize or banish the malice associated with the evil eye and witchcraft. Martin Luther (d. 1546), tormented by visions of the devil and by nightly suggestions inspired by him, knew no more effective means of self-defence than exposure of his own hind quarters to the prince of darkness.

Among men themselves, baring the buttocks was the sign of the passive homosexual and of servitude, and it was regarded as a disgrace for one man to bare his backside to another. The Bible tells of the humiliation of Egyptian and Ethiopian war prisoners who, 'with their buttocks uncovered' (Isa. 20:4), were led away to captivity by the king of Assyria.

In women the size and shape of the buttocks and hips vary according to race, and this again is due to diet, climate, habit and custom. Different shapes develop as a result of carrying children on the back or across one hip, or working at floor level as when grinding corn, and in the postures assumed in kneeling, sweeping, sowing and so on.

Because of the prospect of greater sexual pleasure and the promise of abundant progeny from a woman with generous pygeal endowments, man has generally tended to select such a woman as his mate. Male preference for shapely feminine gluteals is believed to be a heritage from the practice of early man, who copulated from behind like the animals. Sexual accent on this region is further emphasized by tattooing and painting them, thus adding aesthetic appeal to the charms provided by nature.

The Greeks held *kallipygia* (or eupygia), 'beautiful buttocks', to be more aesthetically gratifying and alluring than any other part of the female body. The only temple named after a part of the human body was raised by the Greeks to Venus Kallipygos, 'Venus of the Beautiful Buttocks', built, it is said, following a dispute between two sisters as to which had the more graceful posterior.

A characteristic feature of the women of certain African tribes like the Bushman and Hottentot, is the condition known as steatopygy, an abnormal accumulation of fat on the buttocks, a shape highly esteemed among their men. Many statuettes of the Mother Goddess discovered in various sites in Asia and Europe show enormous gluteal development, and this has been taken as evidence of a prehistoric population in these areas with a pronounced tendency to steatopygy. There is a marked incidence of this feature in certain parts of Italy and Spain today, and to a lesser extent in France. Perhaps some old instinct favouring steatopygy brings the bustle-like fashion periodically back into circulation in western countries from time to time, even in modern days.

Books

Cooper, W. M., *A History of the Rod: Flagellation and Flagellants*, John Hotten, London, 1870.

Licht, Hans, *Sexual Life in Ancient Greece*, George Routledge, London, 1932.

Neumann, Erich, *The Great Mother: An Analysis of the Archetype*, Pantheon Books, New York, 1955.

Passemard, L., *Les Statuettes féminines dites Vênus stéatopyges*, Nimes, 1938.

Ploss, H. H. and Bartels, M. and P., *Woman*, ed. E. J. Dingwall, vol. I, Heinemann, London, 1935.

CELL

The unit of life, consists of a cell-substance called protoplasm, in the centre of which is its brain, the nucleus, which is the central directorate of the cell. The name cell was first given to these biological structural units by the natural philosopher, Robert Hooke (d. 1703), of the Royal Society. The nucleus contains chromosomes, rod-shaped bodies usually occurring in pairs. Cells increase by dividing, and when a cell divides the chromosomes double so that each daughter cell has the original number of chromosomes.

Each biological species has a fixed number of chromosome pairs. Men and women have 23 pairs, or 46 chromosomes in each cell of their bodies, except in the sex cells which have only 23 chromosomes each. When sperm and ovum fuse at conception the new organism contains 23 pairs, or 46 chromosomes. In the ovum or female sex cells, all the 23 chromosomes are the same, and are called X-chromosomes. But in the case of male sperm, some sperms have 23 X-chromosomes, like the ova, while others have 22 X-chromosomes plus one Y-chromosome. If at conception a sperm with all X-chromosomes joins an ovum, the child will be a girl. If a sperm with a Y-chromosome joins an ovum the result will be a boy.

Every chromosome contains a long thread-like DNA (abbreviation of deoxyribonucleic acid) molecule, each molecule in turn consisting of four nucleic acids arranged in the form of a twisted ladder like a parallel double spiral. The nucleic acids are linked in pairs along the ladder. DNA, or a minor variant known as RNA (ribonucleic acid), is found in all living matter.

A specialized configuration of the nucleic acids at a particular position in the coiled DNA strand is a gene, the biochemical unit which transmits hereditary characteristics, probably by influencing the chemical activity of the cells. The DNA molecule is made up of a number of such genes, which are responsible for registering, storing and transferring the genetic information that is passed on from parent to offspring. This information transmitted in the biochemical code-patterns is recorded in the DNA strands. We are conceived and born with a perfectly programmed set of hereditary factors. All cells, somatic and sex, have the same coded information housed in their DNA strands or genes and this information is repeated endlessly throughout the body.

Thus every cell in the body, and not the sex cells alone, contains the entire genetic code, carrying the instructions and the potential to produce a complete man, yet a cell which is required to produce only a hair at a particular part of the body, does this and no other work. Each cell or collection of cells is specialized for its function, whether in liver, heart, or eye, and knows exactly what it has to do. No one knows why or how the DNA in the brain cell, for instance, ignores the countless coded instructions for doing all the other work in the body, and confines itself to its own job of keeping the brain functioning. Apparently the other instructions it contains are muffled. Wherever found, the DNA, although capable of building any other kind of cell, builds only the kind of cell that can be used for the organ it occupies. In most creatures only the sex cells now have the power to reproduce the whole body, but science, by means of 'genetic engineering', still hopes to untangle the potential of the other cells, so as to create a total being from any cell in the body.

In an experiment carried out in 1967, a somatic or body cell (not a sex cell) was used for the reproduction of a toad. The cell was taken from the toad's gut (it could have been taken from any part of the toad's body) and the mechanism for the division of the cell was supplied from the protoplasmic substance of a rabbit. Another complete toad was reproduced as a result.

Each cell is therefore a viable ent, a self-contained and self-sufficient organism. It is a vital unit: it lives, breathes, consumes nourishment, excretes waste, reproduces itself. It possesses its own 'brain' in the nucleus, and has an intelligence. Some biologists maintain that each cell (and not the sex cell alone) has its own sex. Every cell in a man's body is male, and every cell in a woman's body is female (*see* bisexuality).

Each cell absorbs energy, receives the impulses that make up behaviour, records what has been done. Biologists think that it is possible that the chemical and molecular 'memory' of a personal experience might be transmitted from the brain cells to the reproductive cells and thus to another generation. These experiences may be 'coded into the molecules', as it were, so that certain ancestral experiences and instincts may already pre-exist in the organism. The cosmic consciousness* of the mystic, the collective consciousness of C. G. Jung, the reincarnationist's experiences of *déjà vu*, could all be plausibly explained in terms of such an inherited memory.

It has further been established that every cell of a living body is a microscopic dipolar battery, which generates tiny electrical charges of low voltage, producing a biochemical current and creating organic electricity by chemical reactions inside the cell.

Another miracle of the cellular world is that there is a constant process of death and regeneration going on in the body. Every day billions of our body cells perish, and billions of new cells replace them, so that in a few months we have none of the cells we had before. Yet there is no break or discontinuity in the takeover, and the coding of the new cells, their molecular memory, the 'messages' they carry, their specialization, power and adaptability, are all identical with the ones they have replaced. The nature of the permanent essence underlying this flux remains to be explained.

All cell activity including cell division is influenced by the sun and moon and other cosmobiological factors, and the operations of these factors probably result in mutations. The cell, like the atom, is a miniature universe. Its immense potentiality is only just beginning to be appreciated. The cells of the nervous system* alone are a prodigious masterpiece whose wonders have still not been brought to light.

Books

Alexander, Rolf, *The Power of the Mind*, Werner Laurie, London, 1956.
Anonymous, *Some Unrecognized Factors in Medicine*, Theosophical Publishing House, London, 1939.
Bleibtreu, John, *The Parable of the Beast*, Gollancz, London, 1968.
Cameron, G. Roy, *Pathology of the Cell*, Oliver & Boyd, London, 1952.
Eccles, John C., *The Physiology of the Nerve Cells*, Oxford University Press, 1960.
Pauling, L. C., *The Structure of Molecules and Crystals*, Cornell University Press, 1960.
Sager, Ruth and Ryan, F. J., *Cell Heredity*, John Wiley, New York, 1961.
Schroedinger, E., *What is Life? The Physical Aspect of the Living Cell*, Cambridge University Press, 1958.
Watson, James D., *The Double Helix*, Weidenfeld & Nicolson, London, 1968.

CEREBRUM

A mass of nervous tissue which fills most of the upper portion of the skull. It is the largest part of the brain*, comprising about 80 per cent of brain matter, and is popularly regarded as the brain proper. It has an outer layer known as the cerebral *cortex*, also called the brain-bark or roof-brain, about one-eighth of an inch thick, which covers the brain as a rind covers an orange, and is highly folded and fissured, giving the brain its characteristic crumpled look. Because of the colour of its nerve cells it is often referred to as 'grey matter'. The cortex is the seat of the higher intellectual processes, thinking, reason, memory; its function seems to be to abstract, integrate, compare and store experience. The cerebral cortex is not homogeneous in its activity, since different areas seem to control different functions. It operates at full awareness when one is all attention, and is less aware when performing routine or habitual operations. At night, as sleep comes, the cortex falters and remains in abeyance.

At birth the infant's cortex is virtually non-functional. It is the last portion of the brain to develop in the growing child and is the first to suffer the ravages of old age. In evolutionary terms it was the last to develop, and is not more than one million years old.

The rest of the cerebrum is made up of two *hemispheres*, consisting of nervous tissue thrown into many folds found reflected in the cortex. This extensive folding increases its surface area. In appearance it consists of a number of grooves called sulci (sing., sulcus), and ridges called gyri (sing., gyrus), forming the convolutions. The arrangement of the folds is never quite alike in two brains, and even the right and left hemispheres of any single brain show marked differences. The hemispheres are divided into a number of separate regions or lobes, which seem to be associated with particular sensory functions (*see* brain).

Hippocrates (d. 359 BC) described the human brain as being double, separated by a delicate membrane in the middle, each half performing a different function. A hollow canal from the liver passed up the right side of the body to the brain, and another from the spleen passed up the left side of the body to the brain. Both these hollow canals were filled with pneuma* and were connected by many fine subsidiary vessels to all the other parts of the body. The two halves of the brain made different contributions to the bodily system.

The existence of two hemispheres has suggested to some authorities a double consciousness in man. The two hemispheres have different 'brain waves'*; they also provide a positive and negative electrical polarity, and a positive and negative magnetic polarity. One eye, one ear, one side of the body is different from the other and forms an occult opposite* to the other. Each hemisphere largely controls the opposite side of the body; the right lobe directs the left side, and the left lobe the right side, but only one hemisphere is dominant in any individual. Unlike the cerebrum, the right hemisphere of the cerebellum controls the right side of the body, and the left hemisphere the left of the body.

In both right- and left-handed persons, the left cerebral hemisphere is usually the dominant one, and more immediately at the service of the waking brain, being responsible for speech and certain other waking activities. The functions of the non-dominant right hemisphere are so far poorly understood. Certain animals tend to use the hemispheres in rotation. Dolphins, for instance, appear to sleep first with one eye open and then the other, changing every few hours, using each hemisphere alternately.

As a result of recent experiments on the functions of the brain, conducted by Robert Ornstein and other scientists in California, psychologists have tentatively classified human types, and indeed human institutions and races, on the basis of the left and right cerebral hemispheres.

The *left hemisphere* people, or those who have the left side of the brain developed, are better adapted for rational, logical, objective, analytical and sequential processes of thought. They are articulate, think and speak rapidly and can do difficult calculations. They have a high verbal faculty and an excellent memory for words. They tend to look to the right when thinking. They make good lawyers, and most of the 'lower' categories of the major professions of the practical world are left-hemisphere dominant. As a whole, the western materialistic civilization is left-hemisphere dominant too. Broadly speaking, the left hemisphere is the waking or conscious hemisphere.

The *right hemisphere* people, with the right side of the brain dominant, have strong instinctive, non-rational, intuitive, subjective, artistic and emotional tendencies. They are spatial rather than verbal. They possess a strong imagination and 'simultaneous' processes of thought. Possessed of good visual memories they are slower in expressing their thoughts in words, but have a better gift for language. They tend to look to the left when thinking. They are the artists, musicians, poets. Eastern and primitive peoples are right-hemisphere dominated. They are non-verbalizers and tend to use simple arithmetic. The right is the dreaming and imaginative hemisphere.

It should be added that while such correlations have been said to exist, some researchers find no evidence to support them.

It would appear that the *corpus callosum*, 'hard body', with its millions of fibres connects the two hemispheres and enables them to function as a unit. In what are called 'split-brain' experiments the nerves in the corpus callosum connecting the two hemispheres are severed, and the result, according to Roger Sperry, a biologist of California, is the division of the mind into two independent spheres of consciousness. Sometimes there is a conflict of wills in the individual, as though there were two separate minds inside one head.

One patient, for instance, would wash only the right side of his body and put on only the right sock and shoe, and forget the other. Another patient would try to put on his pants with one hand and pull them off with the other. Usually this conflict wears off as there appears to be a reconciling force that harmonizes the anomaly after a time. When one hemisphere is removed by surgery the other seems to have the capacity to reorganize and compensate, and take over the functions lost with the destroyed tissue, much as one surviving kidney does the work of two.

Books

Bonin, Gerhardt von, *Essay on the Cerebral Cortex*, Springfield, Illinois, 1959.
Calder, Nigel, *The Mind of Man*, BBC, London, 1970.
Campbell, Anthony, *Seven States of Consciousness*, Gollancz, London, 1973.
Ornstein, Robert, *The Psychology of Consciousness*, Jonathan Cape, London, 1975.
Penfield, W. and Rasmussen, T., *The Cerebral Cortex of Man*, Macmillan, New York, 1950.
Woodridge, D. E., *The Machinery of the Brain*, McGraw-Hill, New York, 1963.

CHILDHOOD

Childhood is conveniently divided into certain distinct stages, starting with the neonate or newborn infant and ending just across the threshold of puberty.

Each stage has its own characteristic features, its own problems and its own psychology.

The understanding of the child's mind is a matter of profound interest to the psychologist. Some conceive of the newborn's mind as being in a state of 'buzzing confusion', the term used by William James (d. 1910) to suggest the unorganized chaos of unrelated and unidentifiable impressions that make up the 'psychology' of the infant. Others, notably John Locke (d. 1704), taking a concept from ancient Greece, stated that the mind of a child is a *tabula rasa*, a clean slate, upon which life's experiences are imprinted as they occur.

This is disputed by many authorities ancient and modern who contend that the mental equipment of every individual, including the infant, far transcends what his own experience can teach. Plato (d. 347 BC), for instance, spoke of archetypal ideas belonging to a Real World which the child has known before birth and possesses at birth, although the vision of this past glory progressively fades as the child grows up and loses touch with that world. Others say that the child also shares in the evolutionary past and the 'collective unconscious'* of mankind. Just as important are the prenatal engrams or imprints left on the brain of the fœtus* as a result of its experiences within the womb. It is clear that the mind of the newborn child is not blank at birth, but already bears the stamp of its evolutionary past, with all the programming of its ancestral, racial and parental inheritance, in addition to the scars of its treatment in the womb.

After birth the infant very slowly learns to establish its relationship with the world. It knows that it can get attention by crying, by moving about, by stretching out its hands. This is thought to establish its belief in the magical power of supplications, spells and occult gestures. The grown man's will to dominate nature is an extension and projection of that early experience by which the child was able to control his infant environment.

Children, it seems, strangely share in more than a single range of experience and live very close to another dimension. They share with animals in an intuitive perception of the overtones of nature. Their thought processes also resemble those of primitive peoples of simple societies. Like them they have an instinctive belief in the reality of dreams and fantasies. Occultists say that the astral and physical bodies of infants are not in complete alignment, a fact which accounts for their lack of co-ordination and their inability to adjust to the practical realities of everyday life. A rather precarious balance, with transient phases of discoincidence during the waking state, is attained between the ages of five and ten, but the coincidence of the two bodies is stabilized more securely some time during puberty. Thereafter, discoincidence takes place, as with all normal adults, only during sleep, trance or other xenophrenic states.

The factors that go to form a person's character are largely fixed in childhood. The state of health in the early years determines the vulnerability and immunity to disease in the life of the adult. Toilet training, the weaning trauma, sleeping habits, the development of the libido through its normal oral, anal and sexual phases, the behaviour of parents, the attitude of siblings, all play a great part in the future of the adult. When a child is old enough to enter into closer association with other children, the mystique of what sociologists call the 'peer group' influences his manners, speech, pronunciation, attitude to religion, morality, society and his whole outlook on life and the world.

Children at this time lead a life parallel with that of adults, separate from them and outside the family circle. They have their own folklore, their own language, their own games, sometimes differing with each locality, each school and each age group. These are acquired not from their elders but from other children and are handed down from generation to generation for centuries. It has been pointed out that the games played by the street boys of London till the beginning of the present century survived from the time of Nero (d. AD 68). Many of the gestures, formulae, jokes, puns, riddles, responses, tongue-twisters, jingles, preserve a great deal of very old magical and occult symbolism. Many are concerned with morbid subjects revolving around murder, suicide, battles, epidemics like the Black Death, skeletons, graveyards, funerals and ghosts. Scatology is prominent but sexual subjects are conspicuous by their absence.

Childhood ends with adolescence, the period in life when the youthful person grows up to become a man or woman. This great milestone in the development of the individual is marked by the onset of puberty when another area of energy and experience is opened up and liberated. At puberty the gonads begin to ripen and release potent hormones into the bloodstream, causing important changes in mind and body and resulting in a great reorganization of the whole personality.

The immediate pre-sexual and post-sexual period of adolescence is a magical time. But a desire for activity and adventure may lead to unsocial, callous and even violent behaviour. In many communities, tribal and modern, it has been felt that if the gushing waters of youth were not channelled to irrigate and fertilize they would flood and destroy, and that it is necessary to harness and if need be to choke the turbulent springs. Various puberty rites of adjustment and indoctrination, some of extreme harshness, were therefore common in primitive communities. In the west compulsory military training used to provide both an outlet for the aggressive instincts and the discipline and training for life in society.

Besides the physical and mental concomitants of adolescence, sensitives point out that there is often a definite aura about young people that suggests a highly charged field of biomagnetic energy. Many psychic and spiritualist manifestations are associated with adolescence. Girls and boys of pubertal age were universally employed as scryers as if they were easily able to cross the boundary between two worlds. Often the force generated by young people can cause actual disturbance in the physical surroundings. Poltergeist phenomena, which almost invariably occur in a house where an adolescent is present, may be due to this pubescent energy.

Books

Cohen, Yehudi, *The Transition from Childhood to Adolescence*, Aldine Books, Chicago, 1964.

Erikson, E., *Childhood and Society*, 2nd edn, Norton, New York, 1963.
Fleming, C. M., *Adolescence: Its Social Psychology*, Routledge & Kegan Paul, London, 1963.
Opie, Iona and Peter, *The Lore and Language of Schoolchildren*, Oxford University Press, 1969.
Opie, Iona and Peter, *Children's Games in Street and Playground*, Oxford University Press, 1969.
Pfister, Oskar, *Love in Children and Its Aberration*, Allen & Unwin, London, 1924.
Piaget, Jean, *The Child's Conception of the World*, Kegan Paul, London, 1929.
Symonds, Percival, *Adolescent Fantasy*, Columbia University Press, 1949.
Tanner, J. M., *Growth at Adolescence*, Blackwell, Oxford, 1962.
Wickes, Frances, *The Inner World of Childhood*, Appleton, New York, 1940.

COITUS

Coitus between man and woman brings into operation all the sensory faculties of the partners, and is the source of the greatest physical pleasure known to man.

The coital postures assumed by the mating couple are of great variety. Known as the *figurae veneris*, 'shapes of love', they may involve not only the sex organs but also the mouth, as in oralism, thighs, armpits, breasts, anus and other parts of the body. All coital postures are variations of three basic groupings: (1) the man and woman face each other; (2) the woman has her back turned to the man; and (3) the partners are in reversed positions, that is, they have their heads at opposite ends of each other. Variations are introduced by the partners standing, sitting, leaning or lying down; by one partner being positioned above the other, or the two lying side by side; by the legs of the couple being spread apart, bent, or placed together. The placement of the hands provides further changes. The art of sexual postures reached a high degree of sophistication in certain eastern countries, notably China, Japan, India and the middle east. The *Kamasutra* of the Indian exponent, Vatsyayana (fl. AD 450), had a number of imitators, one of whom lists no less than 729 variations, most of them valueless and ludicrous.

The postures assumed during intercourse played a part both in therapeutics and occultism, and members of even the most primitive societies were guided in their sexual conduct by certain prohibitions. How people copulated was as important as whom they copulated with. In many early matriarchal societies the woman assumed the top position and squatted over the man who was supine beneath her. But in medieval Europe it was believed that for a woman to assume the superior position was a heinous offence that would have evil consequences for the family, and if practised on a wider scale would bring disaster to the whole community. It was thought that the Flood was caused by the vile custom of women mounting upon men in the sexual act. It was prohibited in Islam, and according to tradition Muhammad is reported to have declared, 'Cursed be he that maketh himself earth and woman heaven.'

Another posture that was regarded as inviting divine anger was that in which the man's penis entered the vagina from the rear. Known as coitus *a tergo* (from behind), or rear-entry, this was classed as a reprehensible animal posture, since most animals face the same direction while mating. Medieval theologians believed that this position afforded most pleasure because of the additional impact of the woman's buttocks, and they therefore put a ban on its use. Couples engaging in this kind of intercourse, *more canino*, 'in the manner of a dog', or *more ferarum*, 'in the manner of a beast', were liable to seven years' penance. Coitus a tergo also provided opportunities for anal intercourse, which was another reason why the church prohibited the act of *venus aversa*, 'coitus from the rear', or *venus praepostera*, 'coitus in reverse order'. The only posture permitted for husband and wife united together in Christian wedlock was face to face, or *venus observa*, when the couple could see each other, with the woman on her back and the man kneeling or lying above her.

In ancient societies coitus was often performed in conjunction with rites for fertilizing the soil. This was done by *coitus interruptus*, in which the male withdraws his member immediately prior to orgasm so that the sperm is emitted outside the vagina. Fertility rites in many early cultures included the union of men with domestic animals in order to promote fertility among the herds; promiscuous union of men and women of the tribe in order to render the women more fertile; and finally the ritual sex act, either with women, or by masturbation, when the life-bearing semen was ejaculated on the freshly ploughed soil in order to fecundate the womb of Mother Earth.

That coitus interruptus was practised in ancient Canaan is suggested by the story recorded in the Bible about Onan, the son of Judah and Shuah. The latter was a woman of Canaan, a country notorious for its practice of heathenish rites which the Jews held in abomination, and it seems that Shuah instructed her son Onan in these practices. When he was commanded by his father Judah to have union with his brother's wife in order to raise children, Onan lay with her but at the moment of emission he 'spilled it on the ground' (Gen. 38:9). For this sinful act God slew Onan. The term onanism is now commonly applied to male masturbation.

What is known as *coitus prolongatus*, is the postponement, inhibition or prevention of ejaculation during the sexual act, by special retentive techniques. The human average for retention ranges from ten seconds to ten minutes, but protracted coition can last from half an hour to three or four hours. Hasty ejaculation, where the semen is precipitated as soon as the penis becomes erect (*ejaculatio praecipitata*), or prematurely within a few seconds after entry (*ejaculatio praecox*), is always a cause of humiliation to men. Women generally need more stimulation than men in order to achieve sexual climax, and this cannot be done without retentive power on the part of the male. Men who are able to retain their ejaculation and produce one or more orgasms in a woman have a feeling of great satisfaction and achievement, because the woman's ecstasy and loss of control gives them a sense of dominance and power, and fulfilled masculinity.

Sexologists point out, however, that a quick male sexual response is quite normal among mammals, and in the case of a man is not to be taken as a sign of inferior performance, no matter how inconvenient and unfortunate this may be for his partner. The continuance of the species does not depend on the female orgasm. Alfred Kinsey says that it would be difficult to find another situation when an individual with a speedy and intense response was regarded as anything but superior, and in most instances that is exactly what the man who has a rapid ejaculation is.

Be that as it may, any man would prefer to have greater control over his ejaculatory timing, and for this reason many methods have been evolved in an attempt to postpone the reflexes that start the ejaculatory process. The ability to control emission is particularly important in sex-magical rites, since it is necessary to utilize the orgasmic energy of as many women as possible, one after the other, and this cannot be done if one's semen is easily expended. Chinese, Central Asian (Crimean and Tartar), Indian and Arab masters advise that one should have intercourse with a woman and bring her to orgasm as often as possible, each time absorbing her expended energy, by sipping the released power through his penis. If he is capable of continuing he should then proceed to have intercourse with a fresh partner.

Among the Arabs deliberate prolongation of coitus is known as *imsak* (Arabic *amsāk*, 'retention'), the essence of the art being to avoid over-tension, to preoccupy the mind with other matters (mental calculations are useful), to breathe in a special rhythm, to press on the perineum and certain other points in the body, to compress the anal sphincter. The application of ointment to the male organ to render it insensitive, and special meditative techniques are also helpful. Arab occultists believe that it is impossible to work any form of sex magic unless the art of prolonged erection and coition is mastered first.

Kabbalist sects who advocated retention based their teaching on the Biblical text which puts under condemnation the man 'whose seed goeth from him' (Lev. 15:32). In further support Christian kabbalists practising acclivity* also invoked the New Testament verse which refers to the sinlessness of the man whose 'seed (Gk. *sperma*) remaineth in him' (1 John 3:9), for it is through the seed that he is regenerated.

A further advanced technique of sex restraint is *coitus reservatus*, in which coition is carried on without the male partner (in rare cases either partner) coming to a climax. It is a form of stimulation without consummation, advocated in a number of sex cults as a way to mystical illumination and a heightening of the spiritual and psychic faculties.

One form is known as Udhrism, named after the Arab bedouin cult of the Beni Udhri (or Udhra), the 'sons of virginity' who used this method to attain states of spiritual exaltation. The cult of Udhri love, very select and limited, spread from Baghdad to Spain between the tenth to thirteenth centuries, and thence to the rest of Europe. The eleutherian sects such as the Brethren of the Free Spirit who flourished till the sixteenth century practised a secret *ars amandi*, 'love art', quite distinct from the animal act of copulation, which they called a *modus specialis*, 'special method' of sexual union, not contrary to nature, but used, it was said, by Adam in Paradise. This is now known to have been coitus reservatus. The same technique was adopted by a sect of the Familists and some Perfectionists.

Among the latter, John Humphrey Noyes (d. 1886), founder of the Oneida community in New York State, advocated what he called 'male continence', in which the male partner in sexual congress refrained from emission, and only the woman could reach orgasm, once or several times. Intercourse was to last up to at least an hour. Noyes believed that the separation of the amative (sexual) from the propagative (procreative) functions placed coition in the same category as ordinary social intercourse, like conversation, shaking hands and kissing. Intercourse without intent to procreate, and accompanied by male orgasm, was properly to be classed with masturbation.

Noyes declared that if treated as a purely social accomplishment, coitus reservatus can, with training, become one of the fine arts, ranking above music, painting and sculpture, differing from them by its superior intensity and beauty. When each is married to all, the refining effects of sexual intercourse are increased a thousand-fold. A man and woman in intimate physical union, said Noyes, have one of the noblest and sweetest encounters possible, amounting to a spiritual experience.

An elaboration of male continence is *karezza*, the term given to a more prolonged coitus reservatus, in a book of that name written by an American physician, Dr Alice Bunker Stockham (d. 1912) of Chicago. In karezza climax is not permitted for either man or woman, unless of course they wish to have children. Desire is allowed to reach a high point of tension by preparation, and when at length penetration is effected, there should be alternate periods of 'slow, controlled motions', and absolute quiescence, during which the partners exchange spiritual fluids. After about an hour physical tension will subside although the male will still be in a condition of tumescence, but this time there will be a greatly heightened intensity of emotion, psychic exaltation and sublime spiritual joy, that will be infinitely superior to a normal climax. Hence it is also called *coitus sublimatus*.

Strange feelings will follow this stage, feelings of hovering in the air, a sense of ecstatic bliss, an awareness of new power, a consciousness of transcendent life. Karezza may be repeated after two or three weeks, but some find it preferable to wait three or four months. The subtle interaction of anticipation and continence, recollection of past experience and desire for the next, are supposed to heighten the faculties and cause the workaday world to become suffused with a wonderful delight. Karezza was believed to reduce the incidence of nervous disease, increase vitality, bestow youthfulness and prolong life. Modern sexologists repudiate these claims and warn that such practices can be very damaging.

In general occultists tend to class all forms of coitus as a force-generating activity, creating psychic power and opening up the interior faculties of both the partners, individually and unitedly. It leads to trance-like states, however transient, and provides a brief experience of the borderline area between two dimensions. Besides the body, other factors are drawn into the ambit of operation during sexual intercourse. Sex energy is the most volatile form of biological energy. There are differences in bioelectrical potential between man and woman and an exchange of these two types of electricity takes place during sexual union. Some occultists describe sexual intercourse as the union between the male-electrical and female-magnetic energy-fields, with the couple providing a channel for the induction of forces from the cosmic to the earth planes. This biodynamic energy charges the surrounding atmosphere. In the case of a highly charged couple, their love-making can activate their environment, and give rise to various psycho-kinetic manifestations, causing objects to move, sounds to be heard, lights to appear, and even small explosions to occur.

There is a definite connection between sexual energy and the higher psychic and ecstatic states. Tantrik adepts speak of an inner light that illumines the psyche during *maithuna* or sexual union, as the couple achieve nirvanic consciousness. The luminescence descends from the top of the head and suffuses the sex organs with a jet of five-fold light. Occultists say that sometimes when sexual stimulation is kept up for a prolonged period between two persons without actual union and climax, the bodies of the partners become surrounded by a kind of halo of bluish-green light.

Coitus therefore provides a tremendous source of powerful impulses from the occult point of view, and a great deal of sex magic* and sex mysticism* centre around it. Though each partner provides his or her own kind of sex energy, the man's contribution is minimal compared to the female's. It is her contribution that is important, and her gynergy that is utilized for ritual and magical purposes.

Sometimes the sexual act is elevated to a transcendental activity and a cosmic mystery. The sex organs are a minicosm within the microcosm that is man. Several religions regard sex within wedlock as a sacrament. Muslims and Zoroastrians are enjoined to utter a silent prayer before sexual union, for it is believed to be consummated in the presence of God who has provided the pleasures that accompany it, and furnished the blessings that follow its fulfilment. 'Sex is not just a buzz in the genitals, or a form of biophysical electricity streaming through the flesh, but an occult power attuned by invisible strings to the resounding harmonies of the cosmos' (Walker, 1973, p. 43).

Books

Cakravarti, C., *Sex Life in Ancient India*, Mukhopadhyay, Calcutta, 1963.
Eliade, Mircea, *The Two and the One*, Harvill Press, London, 1961.
Gillette, Paul J., *Psychodynamics of Unconventional Sexual Behavior and Unusual Practices*, Holloway House, Los Angeles, 1966.
Gulik, R. R. van, *Sexual Life in Ancient China*, Brill, Leiden, 1961.
Kinsey, Alfred C. *et al.*, *Sexual Behavior in the Human Male*, Saunders, Philadelphia, 1948.
Noyes, J. H., *Male Continence*, Oneida, New York, 1872.
Stockham, Alice B., *Karezza, Ethics of Marriage*, Chicago, 1896.
Urban, Rudolph von, *Sex Perfection and Marital Happiness*, Dial Press, New York, 1965
Walker, Benjamin, *Sex and the Supernatural*, Harper, New York, 1973.

COLLECTIVE UNCONSCIOUS

Collective Unconscious, in the theory put forward by Carl Gustav Jung (d. 1961), is the inherited unconscious, the sum total of all the knowledge acquired by mankind, representing the residual thinking-substance containing the imprints of countless generations of man's ancestral experiences. It is to be distinguished from what mystics call Cosmic Consciousness*, which is not a residue from man's past, but a World Mind, the all-pervasive mental element inherent in all things animate and inanimate.

The collective unconscious is the common psychic factor that lies behind the whole panorama of our individual and collective experiences as human beings. Since it is a collective, transpersonal, universal, archaic nucleus of memories, shared by all members of the race, it is also called the racial consciousness or group soul. A similar idea is illustrated in Plato's *Theaetetus*, where every soul is said to contain a wax tablet upon which certain concepts common to mankind are imprinted by a seal (*sphragis*), so that men everywhere have the same archetypal images, and the same instinctive urges.

Man's mind is not as exclusive as he would like to believe, for one stratum of it is composed of these common primeval images, or archetypes, which constitute its structure, and is a heritage from which he cannot escape. Some part of the minds of all individuals are the common property of all. Just as ontogeny, the development of the individual embryo, summarizes phylogeny or the evolution of the race of mankind, so does the individual mind summarize all human experience; and just as rudiments of our earlier evolutionary states are present in our bodies, so are our earlier mental states present in the mind. Jung says, 'The body has an anatomical prehistory of millions of years, so also does the psychic system.'

The collective unconscious containing as it does elements common to the entire human race tends to produce identical responses in all peoples, primitive or sophisticated, savage or civilized. It embraces memories and primeval fantasies made up of a complex tapestry from family, clan, race and animal legacies. As a residue of archaic psychic life it constitutes, as it were, a store of 'psychic fossils' buried in the unconscious.

The minds of all men are thus interconnected. Dr Gardner Murphy, president of the American Society for Psychical Research, spoke of individuals as volcanic islands projecting above the sea. Underneath they slope to a common interconnected ground. Something of the same kind is conceived by Pierre Teilhard de Chardin (d. 1955) who speaks of the 'myriads of thought-grains of men, which form a single vast collectivity of consciousness on a sidereal scale'. The common ground of humanity forms the collective unconscious.

Every major situation with which a person is confronted tends to stir in him the submerged vestiges of ancient memories, and his personal attitudes are simulations of ancestral reactions to earlier situations of a like nature. His instinct for self-preservation, his search for food and a mate, his seemingly irrational fears, his strange premonitions, his inexplicable intimations, his unaccountable fascination with the numinous in life, all spring from the collective unconscious. By virtue of this uniform inheritance all men share a common imagery in dreams, have similar motifs in their mythology, a common symbolism in artistic expression and common religious instincts, for which no personal and individual experiences can account.

Books
Jaffé, Aniela (ed.), *Memories, Dreams, Reflections of C. G. Jung*, Pantheon, New York, 1962.
Jung, C. G., *The Structure and Dynamics of the Psyche*, Routledge & Kegan Paul, London, 1960.
McDougall, William, *The Group Mind*, Cambridge University Press, 1927.
Teilhard de Chardin, Pierre, *The Phenomenon of Man*, Collins, London, 1959.

CONGRESSUS SUBTILIS

Sexual congress in which one of the partners is not in bodily form. The non-physical consort, according to occult lore, may be the devil, or one of his minions, the spirit of a dead person, the astral double of a living person, or any etheric *eidolon* created by magical means. The human partner is usually unconscious and it is his subtle body that actually participates in the act of intercourse, which takes place on the astral planes. Night pollution is sometimes said to result from such activities. The curious tradition of such intercourse is very old and is found in all parts of the world.

According to the Franciscan friar and student of medieval European belief on the subject, Ludovico Maria Sinistrari (d. 1701), demoniacal spirits are able to create for themselves a magical body with a tangible form made from the aerial and other elements by means of which they have intercourse with human beings. Sinistrari also adds that a demon can enter and animate the corpse of a recently dead human being and have intercourse with a man or woman in this manner.

He further states that phantom beings dedicated to the service of Satan also exist, who seek sexual intercourse with men and women for the purpose of corrupting them. Such beings are known as incubi (male) and succubi (female). In the kabbalistic tradition the seductive Lilith, daughter of Satan, was a succubus; she visited Adam in his dreams and had several offspring by him.

In Hindu and Buddhist belief certain primeval hags of preternatural power, known as dakinis, periodically select mortals for intercourse, assuming a voluptuous shape in order to lure them. Union with these beings is one of indescribable pleasure, but the experience can end disastrously for the unwary, for they are said to 'suck a man's testicles dry'. Tantrik and taoist adepts seek union with these beings in order to learn the hidden mysteries of the astral planes.

In medieval European tradition certain semi-material nature-spirits known as elementals, born of the etheric elements in nature, such as fairies, nymphs, naiads, melusines, lorelei, sylphs and sirens, who are anxious to acquire a soul by intercourse with humans, sometimes seduce mortals and sleep with them. The legends of many renowned families in Europe speak of such elementals among their ancestors.

Medieval witch lore tells how by applying the flying ointment to her body a witch would attend the sabbat in her subtle form and have intercourse with demons, while her physical body was actually lying insensible at home. The

Malleus Maleficarum (1486), a handbook on medieval witchcraft written by two Dominican monks, describes witches who are seen lying on their backs in fields and woods, the lower part of their bodies exposed up to the navel, their thighs and hips moving in a manner suggestive of carnal copulation with an unseen entity, climaxed by the agitations of venereal orgasm. Sometimes, although rarely, at the end of the act a very black vapour, about the size and height of a man, is seen to rise into the air from the body of the witch.

Occasionally demon entities assault individuals and have congress with them against their will. In the reports of medieval inquisitors this most secret and abominable experience sometimes occurred in public, in a few cases even in the midst of an exorcism carried out to banish the demon. It was done in order to tempt onlookers who would be filled with libidinous ideas at the sight of the exhibition. Sister Madelaine, a young novitiate of an Ursuline convent at Marseilles who accused the French priest Louis Gaufridi (d. 1611) of debauching her, went through such a performance during a public rite of exorcism.

Followers of the left-hand path often seek for opportunities of intercourse with non-physical beings. In his work on Hindu tantrik practices Sir John Woodroffe refers to a ritual of sex magic known as *prayoga* practised by tantrik adepts. They work in the lower astral plane using ancient sexual techniques in order to acquire or augment occult power by drawing on *nayika siddhi*, 'female energy', from female creatures on that plane. By methods of concentration and magical evocation they bring into visual form and give a kind of materiality to succubus-like entities whom they use for sexual purposes. J. Marquès-Rivière, speaking of the same ritual, says: 'I was able to know personally the absolutely depraved and abnormal sexual appetite of these false yogis.'

Modern black magicians of western countries practise congressus subtilis in various ways. Occultists maintain that it is possible for a magician in his astral form to visit a sleeping woman and have congress with her physical body. It is also possible for him to occupy the body of a woman's husband and have intercourse with her through him. This would involve what is known as expersonation*, or the temporary dispossession of another person's physical body and its occupation by the magician. This cannot happen in normal circumstances but is rendered easy in the case of drug addiction on the part of the husband.

The passion engendered by such types of intercourse can be very intense, and occultists describe it as infinitely more satisfying than normal physical intercourse when both partners are in their physical bodies. In the throes of sexual passion the astral body may even assume a degree of materiality during the embrace. Aleister Crowley (d. 1947) says, 'There are many cases on record of children having been born as a result of such unions.'

Some magicians believe that it is possible for those who are in possession of the requisite knowledge and skill to conjure up the spirit of a dead person and have sexual relations with it. This is referred to as spectrophilia, 'sex intercourse with a spirit'. In J. K. Huysmans's novel *La-Bas* (1891), based on a close study of the operations of contemporary sorcerers, Madame Chantelouve who conducted the hero to a black mass ceremony claimed that she was able to enjoy the embraces of deceased personalities such as Gérard de Nerval, Charles Baudelaire and others.

Finally, it is also said to be possible to attract the astral bodies of living men while they are asleep and use them for sexual congress. The Abbé Joseph Antoine Boullan (d. 1893), the Abbé Louis van Haecke (d. 1912) and other more recent magicians claimed to be able to use for such subtle intercourse the astral bodies of persons both living and dead.

Books

Crowley, Aleister, *Magick in Theory and Practice*, Castle Books, New York, n.d.
Grant, Kenneth, *The Magical Revival*, Frederick Muller, London, 1972.
Laurent, E. and Nagour, P., *Magica Sexualis*, Falstaff Press, New York, 1934.
Marquès-Rivière, J., *Tantrik Yoga: Hindu and Buddhist*,, Weiser, New York, 1970.
Sinistrari, L. M., *Demonality, or Incubi and Succubi*, ed. by Montague Summers, Fortune Press, London, 1927.
Summers, Montague (trs. and ed.), *Malleus Malleficarum*, Pushkin Press, London, 1951.
Woodroffe, Sir John, *The Serpent Power*, Ganesh, Madras, 1931.

CONSCIOUSNESS

(Lat. *con*, 'with', *scio*, 'to know') is the subjective factor that characterizes awareness. It commonly designates the normal waking consciousness, the private experience that one is aware, 'present' and on the surface. It is a psychological, even physiological concept, as distinguished from mind, which is largely a philosophical one.

This waking consciousness is the mental glow that results from impressions created by the shifting and changing panorama of the world impinging on the senses. It is the psychic condition experienced by the ego or personality during all its self-aware activities. Through consciousness the ego exercises the faculties of (1) perception, that is, the apprehension of things, through the sense organs; (2) cognition, the understanding of what is presented to the senses; (3) memory, the recall and recognition of past experience; (4) thinking, the process of reasoning, sifting, analysing and making judgments; (5) feeling, or experiencing emotion and pathemic states; and (6) willing or activity.

The waking consciousness is a series of disconnected awareness phases integrated and given continuity by memory, which itself is intermittent and disjointed. According to G. I. Gurdjieff (d. 1949) even the person who imagines that he is wide awake is in a state of light hypnosis. Much of this limited consciousness is a mechanical reflex, an automatic activity carried on by the neuronal, ganglionic or cerebral systems, and almost exclusively a matter of the brain and sense organs. As such it is properly the sphere of the neurophysiologist and behaviourist. It has no primacy over the rest of the mind except that it is best fitted for dealing with the practical needs of everyday life. Friedrich Nietzsche (d. 1900) deplored the 'absurd over-valuation of consciousness', and went so far as to state that, 'The waking and rationalizing consciousness is a danger, and whoever has lived among conscious Europeans knows in fact that it is an illness.'

Man possesses both practical information and intuitive insight, but only a small fraction of this knowledge can be present in his consciousness at any given time. All the rest of it, the part not at the moment lit up by his conscious awareness, represents the subconscious, preconscious or subliminal consciousness, which can be tapped by memory. Beyond this again is the huge mass of data stored in the unconscious*, most of which cannot normally be recalled and seldom rises to the surface or forms part of conscious awareness.

The conscious mind is adapted to interpret symbolically and through the extremely limited range of the sense organs, the material it receives. It is an obfuscating medium which interferes with most ranges of higher perception. Only rarely is it capable of affording some manifestation to the higher self. Only in brief spurts and obliquely can the average conscious mind obtain a glimpse of the higher reality. Awareness as communicated through the brain has been described as awareness received through a filter, a veil, a net, a scrambling device, a distorting mirror. It hinders true perception and can be an obstacle to truth, blinding a man to the vision of the greater reality. We cannot through our normal consciousness know what it is like 'out there'. Consciousness has therefore been termed the Slayer of the Real. Some degree of xenophrenia* is a prerequisite to the higher ranges of perception, and anything that arrests the process of 'thinking' and 'reasoning' puts one nearer to this knowledge.

As understood in mysticism and the occult and in various parapsychological contexts, consciousness includes not only the awake and aware states, but also all states of so-called unconsciousness, since it is now fairly well established that psychic activity continues without interruption, even if what is experienced during xenophrenic states cannot be recalled to memory.

In its most extended sense, consciousness covers the full range of the individual's awareness, including all the ranges of his subconscious and unconscious. Conscious awareness as commonly understood is thus only a transient wave in an infinite ocean. It might be described as the subjective aspect of universal mind, localized in the individual and constituting his individuality, enabling him to know a kind of reality from within. In the final analysis consciousness becomes a mode of energy.

Books

Abramowski, E., *Le Subconscient normal*, Paris, 1914.
Abramson, H. (ed.), *Problems of Consciousness*, J. Macy Foundation, New York, 1950.
Adrian, E. *et al.*, *Brain Mechanisms and Consciousness*, Blackwell, Oxford, 1954.
Campbell, Anthony, *Seven States of Consciousness*, Gollancz, London, 1973.
Eccles, J. C. (ed.), *The Brain and Conscious Experience*, Springer, Heidelberg, 1966.
Eriksen, R., *Consciousness, Life and the Fourth Dimension*, Knopf, New York, 1923.
Jastrow, J., *The Subconscious*, Houghton Mifflin, Boston, 1905.
King, C. Daly, *States of Human Consciousness*, University Books, New York, 1936.
Magoun, H. W., *The Waking Brain*, Thomas, Springfield, Illinois, 1958.
Metzner, Ralph, *Maps of Consciousness*, Macmillan, New York, 1971.
Münsterberg, H. *et al.*, *Subconscious Phenomena: A Symposium*, Rebman, London, 1910.
Neumann, E., *The Origins and History of Consciousness*, Routledge & Kegan Paul, London, 1954.

Rose, Steven, *The Conscious Brain*, Weidenfeld & Nicolson, London, 1973.
Tart, Charles T. (ed.), *Altered States of Consciousness*, Wiley, New York, 1969.
White, John (ed.), *The Highest State of Consciousness*, Doubleday, New York, 1972.

CONSPIRATION

(Latin 'co-breathing'), a technique in which the breathing rhythm between two or more persons is reciprocally harmonized, to establish mental resonance and 'sympathy'. It is used in healing and magic for mental rapport. Thus, an adept may synchronize his breathing rhythm with that of his pupil in order to learn what is passing through the latter's mind or to understand his weakness, so that he might provide him with the help he needs.

In conspiration therapy the physician alters the patient's breathing tone, by harmonizing his healthy and power-charged breath with that of the patient, to enable the sufferer to participate in his own healthy rhythm. This healing rhythm can then be 'locked' so that the easy breathing continues even when the physician departs.

The breathing rate is believed to be connected not only with the heartbeat, the pulsing of the brain and the metabolic rate, but also the sexual centres, and considerable use is made of conspiration in sexual magic. For instance, the magician concentrates on the breathing rhythm of his intended female victim, who should not be more than about six feet away from him. He gauges her rhythm by the rise and fall of her breast. He begins to breathe in unison with her, and when the breaths have been harmonized thus for about three minutes, he suddenly contracts his anus for a few seconds. This serves to 'lock' their breaths. He now relaxes and slowly increases the rate of breathing, concentrating on her sexual zone. Sorcerers have been known to induce uncontrollable orgasms in women by this means.

The American mystic, T. L. Harris (d. 1906), evolved a breathing technique which he called 'archnatural respiration', which may have employed a kind of conspiration. His disciple, Laurence Oliphant (d. 1888), had his own method known as sympneumata, which involved the use of sexual power. Both Aleister Crowley (d. 1947) and George Ivanovitch Gurdjieff (d. 1949) were expert at 'co-breathing', but no record of their teaching on this point seems to be extant.

Some people have been able to seduce women by merely approaching them after arousing their desire in this manner. One woman described how Gurdjieff once looked at her and then began to inhale and exhale in a peculiar way, and, as she put it, 'struck her through her sexual centre', causing her nearly to faint.

Books

Ahmed, Rollo, *The Black Art*, John Long, London, 1936.
Oliphant, Laurence, *Sympneumata*, Edinburgh, 1885.
Pauwels, Louis, *Gurdjieff*, Douglas, Isle of Man, 1964.
Stephensen, P. R., *The Legend of Aleister Crowley*, Mandrake Press, London, 1930.

CORPSE

The dead body was believed to be surrounded by a sacred and dangerous contagion, and in the past those who had been psychologically or spiritually close to it (relations, friends, mourners), and had physically approached or touched it (physicians, corpse-bearers), or those who performed the obsequies (priests), were shunned until they had ceremonially purified themselves. In many ancient societies, especially in hot, tropical climates, notably in India and Egypt, attendants and corpse disposers were a class apart, generally despised as untouchable and polluted. Even the sight of a corpse could bring pollution. Among the Ibo people of Nigeria the sight of a corpse was held to be spiritually contaminating, and a priest had to shield his eyes if he should chance to meet or pass one on its way to burial.

The dead were believed to emanate a highly potent psychic aura which resided in the body itself. Corpses therefore had to be properly and ritually consigned to the elements (earth, fire, water) or given to animals or birds to pick clean.

In other countries the belief that a corpse or parts of a corpse had special occult and curative virtues was also widely prevalent. All manner of diseases were thought to be cured by the touch of a hanged man. After public executions of highwaymen and other felons in Europe, the hangman used to sell the bones, flesh and blood. The 'hand of glory', the pickled hand of an executed criminal the fingers of which were used as candles, was believed to confer invisibility. Toothache was charmed away if the face was touched with the fingers of a dead child. Birthmarks, carbuncles, herpes and similar skin complaints, disappeared if similarly treated. The human brain, liver, gall, were highly prized for various medicinal purposes, being used as cures for epilepsy, paralysis and apoplexy. The brain dissolved in spirits of wine was especially recommended as a nerve tonic and an aphrodisiac. Pliny (d. AD 79) said that if a circle were traced around an ulcer with a human bone it would prevent the ulcer from spreading. Dried human fingers tied on a string were worn as a magical necklace in Africa, Melanesia and among the North American Indians. Every bone in the human skeleton was put to some magical purpose.

Witches, sorcerers and magicians in all parts of the world, without exception, resorted to human cadavers for the success of their operations at the sabbats, at the black mass and in necromantic rites. The fat of dead men and the charred bones of corpses were among the chief ingredients in witches' salves and love philtres. The brain, flesh, heart, liver and private parts were offered to the spirits in magical ceremonies. In fact, the sale of the flesh of corpses for magical rites was well enough established in Scotland by the sixteenth century for James VI (d. 1625) to legislate against such desecration in his Act of 1602, but the trade continued in England and Scotland till well into the seventeenth century.

Many aspects of the occult centre around the corpse. Zombies are soulless bodies reanimated by magical means. The use of ancient mummies was once common in the pharmacopoeia of the middle east and Europe. Human fat was used in anointing during the black mass and was an important ingredient in the flying ointment used by witches. Head-hunting, skulls and skull cults, skeletons and skeleton lore, the occult significance of the skin, teeth and hair, are all aspects of the same mystique attached to the dead body. The climax of this morbid fascination is reached in necrophilia, where the sorcerer has sexual intercourse with a dead body.

Books

Brendann, E., *Death Customs: An Analytical Study of Burial Rites*, Kegan Paul, Trench, Trubner, London, 1930.
Frazer, J. G., *The Golden Bough*, abr. edn., Macmillan, London, 1922.
Garnier, J., *The Worship of the Dead*, Chapman & Hall, London, 1901.
Rhodes, H. T. F., *The Satanic Mass*, Rider, London, 1945.
Summers, Montague, *The Vampire, His Kith and Kin*, Kegan Paul, Trench, Trubner, London, 1928.
Wernert, P., 'Culte des Crânes. Représentations des esprits des défunts et des ancêtres', pp. 51–102 of M. Gorce's *L'Histoire générale des religions*, 5 vols, Paris, 1944–51.

COSMIC CONSCIOUSNESS

Also called cosmic mind, world mind, cosmic psyche, cosmic consciousness is the psychic element in the cosmic ether, and shares many of its characteristics. All-pervasive, coexistent and merged with matter, it is the field of mental vibrations, the source of all mental energy and understanding, and the factor that constitutes the awareness of things. The world is pervaded by the cosmic consciousness and all objects and elements forming the universe share in a kind of common mind. Sir James Jeans (d. 1946), the famous astrophysicist, observed: 'Today there is a wide measure of agreement regarding the non-mechanical nature of reality. The universe begins to look more like a great thought than like a great machine.'

The human mind is fed from the limitless reservoir of the cosmic mind of which it is a part and to which it is channelled. The area of its operation in the human being is a kind of supra-consciousness that lies dormant in man. At a profounder level therefore there is in every man a region where all can be known. Many thinkers through the ages have been aware of this transcendent fact.

The Islamic philosopher, Averroes (d. 1198), taught that while we have separate bodies we do not have separate minds. He said that every individual shares in the universal mind or soul, and derives from this common source similar, if not identical, ideas 'like an aquatic plant with many heads showing above water, but all meeting in one great root beneath the water'. The profoundly mystical experience of this universal mind is one of indescribable illumination and understanding. St Thomas Aquinas (d. 1274), having gone through such an experience, declared that in comparison with it, all his learning was 'as straw'. Another mystic, Jacob Boehme (d. 1624), recalling his own moment of revelation, wrote: 'The gate was opened to me so that in one quarter of an hour I saw and knew more than if I had been many years at a university.'

Modern philosophers and psychologists have sometimes probed the same depths. 'In our innermost being,' wrote Arthur Schopenhauer (d. 1860), 'we are secretly aware of sharing in the inexhaustible springs of eternity.' The great pioneer in psychical research, Frederick Myers (d. 1901), believed in the existence of a universal telepathic link connecting all mankind. William James (d. 1910), eminent psychologist, held a similar view. 'We live immersed in a continuum of cosmic consciousness', he wrote, a little of which filters into the individual human mind. James did not deny the possibility of an interaction between the slumbering faculties of the individual mind and a 'cosmic environment' with consciousness of some sort. Henri Bergson (d. 1941) also held that the universal mind was aware of everything, everywhere, but that for us this knowledge was modified by the limitations of the human brain. Carl Gustav Jung (d. 1961) had similar intimations of a universal overmind. This is to be distinguished from his concept of the 'collective unconscious'*, which represents the experiences of mankind inherited by each individual.

The whole subject of cosmic consciousness was examined by Dr Richard Maurice Bucke (d. 1902), a Canadian surgeon and president of the American Medico-Psychological Association. At the age of thirty-five he had an overwhelming experience that coloured all his subsequent thinking, so that he was in the unique position of having both experienced and deeply studied the phenomenon, which he described in his authoritative book on the subject. He states that a person who experiences cosmic consciousness will acquire more enlightenment in a few moments of his rapture than in months or years of study, and a great deal that cannot be learned by any amount of study. He himself saw and knew that the cosmos is a living, thinking and feeling presence.

Adepts, sages, prophets, seers, poets and mystics, and men of extraordinary power and vision like Zoroaster, Lao Tzu, Buddha, St Paul, Plotinus, Muhammad, Blake and Swedenborg, have been able to tap the well-springs of the cosmic mind. Through a kind of transpersonal consciousness they lose awareness of the self and receive illumination and understanding of the ultimate significance of human destiny and the living principles of the universe.

Lesser men, in varying moods or at certain critical moments in their daily lives, may also have fleeting glimpses of smaller radiances from the lucent cosmic ocean and feel the touch of the infinite, often becoming vividly aware of life's profounder mysteries. This may happen in moments of ecstasy*, when in love, in the presence of death, in various xenophrenic* states. Manifestations of psychic power and paraperception, 'hunches' and premonitions, the operations of the sixth sense and second sight, visions of the fourth dimension, may all be explained as a leakage into individual consciousness of some of the material from the cosmic mind, that the ordinary brain would normally exclude.

Cosmic mind is Objective, Total, Pure or Transcendent Consciousness. Fed from this unseen source the human mind has a potentiality without limits, and greatly exceeds the capacity of the nervous system to contain it. The immense surge of power would be too much for man, and it is therefore channelled and filtered through the brain and senses, and a great deal is shut out in the process.

A French physicist, Olivier Costa de Beauregard, has suggested, from recent developments in cybernetics, that the physical universe must possess a psychic 'underside', which is the source of information embracing all possible knowledge, of which consciousness in animals and men are little crystallizations.

Books

Bucke, R. M., *Cosmic Consciousness: A Study in the Evolution of the Human Mind*, Innes, Philadelphia, 1905.
Cassirer, Ernst, *The Individual and the Cosmos in Renaissance Philosophy*, Barnes & Noble, New York, 1963.
Jeans, James, *The Mysterious Universe*, Cambridge University Press, 1930.
Nomad, Ali, *Cosmic Consciousness*, Advanced Thought Publishing, Chicago, 1913.
Reinhardt, Karl, *Kosmos und Sympathie*, Munich, 1926.
Roy, M. C., *Cosmic Consciousness*, Madras, 1910.
Stromberg, G., *The Soul of the Universe*, Philadelphia, 1948.
Walker, Benjamin, *Beyond the Body*, Routledge & Kegan Paul, London, 1974.

CROWD

It is a commonplace observation of psychology that the behaviour of an individual can differ remarkably from that of the same person when he finds himself part of a crowd, contributing to and influenced by the 'group thought'* of a large multitude of people. Instances of group behaviour are frequently found in the animal kingdom, even among insects. No one knows how or why a communal unit is formed in a colony of ants, termites or bees, but there appears to be a definite identity in this mind, which is centrally co-ordinated, and operates unitedly, each individual or sub-group performing specific functions related to the group as a whole.

The instinct to act in unison, though usually to the individual's detriment, is perhaps best seen in the behaviour of human crowds, whether at a lynching or a football match. On such occasions the mind of the individual seems to surrender itself to another, larger mind, and can easily take on a strange and at times frightening new aspect. Gustave Le Bon (d. 1931) expressed the view that by merely becoming part of an organized crowd, 'a man descends several rungs in the ladder of civilization; in a crowd he is a barbarian'. Each man feels that he is not responsible for what is happening and therefore can let himself go. He is swallowed up. The emotional contagion in some crowds is so strong that few can resist it, and otherwise rational individuals may find themselves shouting with others in tones they would scarcely recognize as their own.

The 'psychology' of the mob belongs to a lower level than that which usually governs the individual of reason and judgment. The level of the crowd, the 'beast with many heads', is often base, instinctive and primitive. Its reactions are more cruel, more irrational, and distinctively regressive, like those of the *sans culottes* of revolutionary France. The *polloi* or multitude are obtuse and easily aroused to hysteria. As C. G. Jung (d. 1961) said, 'A hundred intelligent heads massed together make one big fathead.'

The psychic upheaval in a large concourse of people who succumb to the spell of a powerful preacher or are subjected to a high degree of emotional excitement, as at a revival meeting or political rally, seems to set up disturbances in the atmosphere around them. In ecstatic religious meetings these have been reported as creating effects that are actually palpable and visible. The air becomes charged with strange electrical impulses and there is a sensation of radiant waves all about, and spontaneous phenomena may occur resembling those seen in a seance room. Such were the levitations and aerial music during the manifestations of the French convulsionaries (c. 1730), and the earth tremors that rocked the house when John Wesley (d. 1791), the founder of Methodism, preached.

Occultists speak of a psychic energy that overflows from multitudes who come together to participate in a common emotional experience. Their released feelings flood the atmosphere, liberating what is called an *aura magnetica* (lit. 'magnetic breeze') which impregnates the surroundings and affects all those who come within the range of its influence.

Books

Canetti, Elias, *Crowds and Power*, Gollancz, London, 1962.
Félice, Philippe de, *Foules en délire: Extases collectives*, Paris, 1947.
Freud, Sigmund, *Group Psychology and the Analysis of the Ego*, Hogarth Press, London, 1959.
Hoffer, Eric, *The True Believer: Thoughts on the Nature of Mass Movements*, Secker & Warburg, London, 1952.
Jung, C. G., *The Practice of Psychotherapy*, Routledge & Kegan Paul, London, 1954.
Le Bon, Gustave, *The Crowd: A Study of the Popular Mind*, Benn, London, 1929 edn.
McDougall, William, *The Group Mind*, Cambridge University Press, 1927.
Reinwald, Paul, *Vom Geist der Massen*, Pan-Verlag, Zurich, 1946.
Riesman, David, *The Lonely Crowd*, Yale University Press, New Haven, 1950.
Sighele, Scipio, *La Foule criminelle. Essai de psychologie collective*, Alcan, Paris, 1892.
Thrasher, F. M., *The Gang: A Study of Gangs in Chicago*, University of Chicago Press, 1936.
Tiger, Lionel, *Men in Groups*, Nelson, London, 1968.
Trotter, W., *Instincts of the Herd in Peace and War*, Unwin, London, 1916.
Whyte, W. F., *Street Corner Society*, University of Chicago Press, 1955.

DREAMS

The visual imagery experienced during sleep*, dreams represent one of the most extraordinary mysteries of life. Everyone dreams, but no one knows the cause of dreams. Modern research indicates a close connection between dreams and the REM (rapid eye movement) phase of sleep, when the eyes under the closed lids move about rapidly as though the sleeper were watching something. Dreams seem to take place on the borderline of two worlds. There is a fantastic distortion of time, place and possibility, which we accept without question in the dream plane.

Many modern students believe that dreams can be telepathic, warning or precognitive. In his book, *An Experiment With Time*, John William Dunne (d. 1949) says that part of our dreams often anticipate future events and cut right across the time segment. Dreams have also inspired countless creative works and provided solutions to problems that have baffled the waking state, a fact vouched for by men in all walks of life.

Bernard Palissy (d. 1589) made one of his most beautiful ceramic pieces on dream inspiration. Jean de La Fontaine (d. 1695) composed one of his major works, *The Fable of Pleasure*, after prompting from a dream source. The poet, John Dryden (d. 1700), used to eat raw meat to procure dreams of splendour. Isaac Newton (d. 1727) said that the solution to many of his mathematical problems came to him in sleep.

Giuseppe Tartini (d. 1770), struggling to complete a sonata, dreamed that Satan appeared to him and played it on the violin for him. Tartini awoke and immediately noted it down, and named the composition *The Devil's Trill*. Voltaire (d. 1778) conceived a whole canto of his *Henriade* during sleep. His somewhat less distinguished contemporary, the philosopher Etienne de Condillac (d. 1780), said that he often continued and concluded in his dreams the metaphysical discussions he began while awake. Wolfgang Mozart (d. 1791) confessed that much of his music came to him in dreams. The Marquis de Condorcet (d. 1795), French mathematician and philosopher, resolved many mathematical problems in his sleep. He once dreamed the final steps of a difficult equation that had puzzled him through the day.

The German poet, Friedrich Klopstock (d. 1803), was convinced that many of his poems were dream-inspired. Like Dryden, Ann Radcliffe (d. 1823), author of *The Mysteries of Udolpho*, gave inspiration a helping hand, and deliberately ate indigestible foods to procure the nightmares she used in her Gothic tales. Johann Wolfgang Goethe (d. 1832) admitted that he solved scientific problems and conceived poems in his dreams. The beginning of S. T. Coleridge's (d. 1834) extraordinary poem, *Kubla Khan*, was received in the same way, and so were many of the best stories of Edgar Allen Poe (d. 1849). Even the idea of Mary Shelley's (d. 1851) supernatural classic, *Frankenstein*, came to her in a dream.

In a succession of three vivid dreams Professor Jean Agassiz (d. 1873), the Swiss naturalist, was guided to the correct decipherment of an indistinct impression of a fossil fish on a stone slab, with all its missing features perfectly restored. Dr Hermann Hilprecht, the Babylonian scholar, dreamed in 1893 that he was visited by a 'tall thin priest of Nippur', ancient Mesopotamia, who explained to him the precise arrangement of certain inscriptions on some fragments of agate that had been puzzling him for some time.

In 1865 the chemist, Friedrich Kekulé (d. 1896), puzzling for weeks over the arrangement of atoms within a molecule of benzene, dreamed one night that the atoms were dancing before him in long chains in a snake-like manner; one of the snakes suddenly got hold of its own tail, and when Kekulé awoke this ring structure suggested to him the arrangement he sought. The Russian chemist, Dmitri Mendeleev (d. 1907), saw his entire periodic table of elements laid out clearly in a dream.

R. L. Stevenson (d. 1894) dreamed the story of *Dr Jekyll and Mr Hyde* as well as plots for numerous other stories. Henrik Ibsen (d. 1906), during three feverish weeks, used to scramble out of bed in a semi-somnolent condition to write down the lines of his *Brand*, which arose tumultuously in his mind as he drowsed. Through a dream Otto Loewi (d. 1961), Nobel prizewinner, established the theory that nerve impulses are transmitted by means of chemical substances. He awoke from sleep one night, jotted down something on a piece of paper and in the morning was unable to decipher the scrawl, but later realized that it was the design of an experiment to demonstrate his hypothesis. Albert Einstein (d. 1955) always kept a notebook by his bed to jot down any helpful dreams that might contribute to his mathematical work. Niels Bohr (d. 1962) dreamt about a curious model of the solar system, the model of the atom on which the whole of modern atomic physics is based.

The time factor is a puzzling problem in the study of dreams. The opium dreams of Thomas De Quincey (d. 1859) stretched to seventy or more years on some nights. The French dream researcher, Alfred Maury (d. 1922), relates that he once had an elaborate dream which ended with his being caught and guillotined. He awoke in terror to find that the bed-tester had fallen on his neck. His conclusion was that while dreaming of the Revolution, the dramatic denouement was flashed through his mind in a fraction of a second to bring it into accord with his sudden experience of the bed-pole falling on his neck. In the same way any local noise that awakens a sleeper may be transmitted instantaneously to fit into his dream sequence as if it were actually part of the dream he is having at the time.

No one knows what causes dreams. They were once regarded as messages from the gods, guardian angels or ancestral spirits, counselling and forewarning the dreamer. Others believed that demons and elemental spirits emerged from their haunts when a man was asleep, and enacted their fantasies in his mind. Some held that a man's own spirit wandered off and its adventures were communicated to the sleeper as dreams.

Dreams may be a shadowy continuation of our waking state, a muddled recapitulation of our recent daytime experiences. Many medical researchers tend to account for dreams entirely in terms of the physiological or emotional state of the sleeper. Glare on the eyelids, spots before the eyes, ocular spectra, indigestion, painful menstruation, a full bladder, sexual tension, fever, cold, noise, anxiety, fear, anger, can all give rise to dream sequences to suit the situation. But it must be said that although such stimuli may find their way into dreams they are by no means the sole cause of dreams.

In the occult view each of the four components of the total man (physical, etheric, astral and spiritual) contributes data to the dream content from its own plane. All four become superimposed, as it were, in varying degrees of intensity, and make up the composite imagery of the dream.

Dreams frequently release the lower element in man. Plato (d. 347 BC) in his *Republic* said, 'In all of us there is a lawless side like a wild beast, that peers out during sleep.' St Augustine (d. 430) thanked God that he was not responsible for his dreams. Friedrich Nietzsche (d. 1900) said, 'In dreams some primordial relic of humanity is at work which we are unable to reach by a direct path. The dream provides a hint of man's archaic inheritance, of what is psychically innate in him.' Dreams therefore are something primordial, visceral, epigastric, intuitive.

Alfred Adler (d. 1937) held that a person's disabilities would lead to an attempt to make up for them not only in real life, but in dreams. The dreamer would create dream situations where he is successful, charming, attractive, rich and happy. In other words dreams compensate for his feelings of inferiority. Sigmund Freud regarded most dreams as secret wish fulfilments. 'Every dream is a repressed desire,' he said. He emphasized the sexual nature of dreams and said that most dreams treat of sexual material and give expression to erotic wishes. C. G. Jung (d. 1961) regarded dreams as an integral and personal expression of the individual consciousness but often concealing a deeper archetypal or universal symbolism.

A fairly common belief among primitive and tribal peoples is that dreams are real and represent an actual world, and they often hardly distinguish between dream life and everyday existence. For example, a man might take snake-bite treatment on awaking from a dream of being bitten by a snake. Many children, even in advanced communities, are similarly unable to separate dreams from reality. Thinking men too have had their doubts. It is pointed out that just as it is impossible for a sleeper to judge that he is asleep (for then he would have to be simultaneously awake), so it is impossible for the ordinary person to be sure that he is actually awake, for what we call waking might well be a form of sleep from which we have to be aroused to see the real world.

Eminent thinkers have expressed the same view. The Chinese philosopher, Chuang Tzu (d. 286 BC), once dreamed that he was a butterfly and on awaking could not be sure whether he was Chuang Tzu who had dreamed that he was a butterfly, or actually a butterfly now imagining that it was Chuang Tzu. According to Blaise Pascal (d. 1662), 'Apart from faith there is no telling whether a man is awake or asleep.' René Descartes (d. 1650) wrote, 'I am not aware of any signs by which waking can be distinguished from sleeping.'

In dream laboratories in various centres around the world dream phenomena are being studied on scientifically established principles in an attempt to unravel some of the secrets hidden in dreams. One recurring problem is that the medium of recollection does not seem to be the memory of normal consciousness. A dream swirls away and begins to fade as soon as we wake up. And as for the dreams one has had earlier in the night, they are usually lost altogether and leave no trace in the memory.

Most dream experiences are unreal, remote, irrational. St Thomas Aquinas (d. 1274) said that logical syllogisms go wrong in dreams, and Sigmund Freud (d. 1939) observed that the dreamer cannot do arithmetic. Wilhelm Wundt (d. 1920), German psychologist, called dreaming a state of 'normal temporary insanity'. To which a modern psychologist adds that dreams allow each of us to go quietly and safely insane every night of our lives.

Books

Diamond, E., *The Science of Dreams*, Eyre & Spottiswoode, London, 1962.
Dunne, J. W., *An Experiment With Time*, Faber, London, 1934.
Fisher, C., *Dreaming and Sexuality*, New York, 1966.
Freud, Sigmund, *The Interpretation of Dreams*, Allen & Unwin, London, 1961 edn.

Grunebaum, G. E. von and Caillois, R., *The Dream and Human Societies*, University of California Press, Berkeley, 1966.
Kramer, Milton (ed.), *Dream Psychology and the New Biology of Dreaming*, Springfield, Illinois, 1969.
Lincoln, J. S., *The Dream in Primitive Culture*, Cresset, London, 1935.
Mackenzie, N., *Dreams and Dreaming*, Aldus, London, 1965.
Ratcliff, A. J. J., *The Nature of Dreams*, Nelson, London, 1939.
Ullman, Montague *et al.*, *Dream Telepathy*, Macmillan, New York, 1973.

DRINKING

Drinking in primitive communities is often hedged in by taboos. The preparation of ceremonial drinks, especially intoxicants, is usually attended by ritual, and the people set apart for preparing them are restricted in their activities, prohibited from larger social contact and from sexual intercourse for some time before, so that they might devote their energies to their duties.

Many kinds of drinks are used for ritual purposes: alcoholic beverages like spirits, beers and wines; drinks spiced with vinegar, salt and seasonings; infusions like tea, the preparation of which is still occasionally attended by semi-religious ceremonial in the far east; blood; the juice and sap of fruits and plants, regarded as the 'blood of the tree'; milk, which is 'blood filtered through a gland'; semen, or 'blood filtered through the testes'; urine, taken either ritually or therapeutically; drugged drinks for the attainment of xenophrenic states; aphrodisiac drinks to increase sexual desire and capacity.

Originally drinking was confined to religious occasions. One drank in honour of the gods and of the dead. In certain cult rites at which the deity was invoked to participate, the bread and wine were served as part of a 'sacramental meal' and were believed to be infused with the essence of the blood and flesh of the god. Among the warlike communities of the ancient world, such as the Scythians, Gauls and Norsemen, it was common practice to convert the skull of enemies into drinking vessels. Drinking from a skull gave one health and vitality, and the word *skoll* (i.e. skull) meant to drink one's health. Often a piece of toasted bread accompanied the wine served to guests, and those who drank raised their drinking cups and called down good wishes for the health of the others and then ate the toast and drank the wine, whence comes the custom of 'toasting', or drinking a toast of good will.

Huge quantities of mead and wine were consumed in early European societies. It is said that in England St Dunstan (d. 988), disturbed at the excess of drinking among the villagers of Devon, ordered wooden pins or pegs to be fitted into drinking tankards at intervals, and each person (as many as eight persons drank from one tankard) had to drink only as far as the next peg. Hence the 'peg' became the measure of an alcoholic drink.

Most transit periods of life called for the goodwill of the gods, and this was accompanied by a drinking rite. Births, marriages, deaths, victory celebrations, fervent wishes and blessings for the successful outcome of a venture, welcoming loved ones, guests, friends, and parting from them ('one for the road'), were made auspicious occasions by drinking. Even today, many people who do not normally drink at all, celebrate with a drink on such special occasions.

But drinking, like eating, is an activity not devoid of its perils. In a number of tribal societies, those who wish to drink, first retire to some place where they cannot be watched, or else drink unobtrusively after turning their backs on those present. Whenever the king of Dahomey wanted to drink, a curtain had to be held up to conceal him. In the last century the son of a Congo chieftain of Loango was put to death because he had inadvertently seen his father drinking. In other Congo states a bell used to be rung at each draught as the chief drank, and at the same time a boy standing before him would brandish a spear to keep off any spirits who might try to enter his body along with the liquid imbibed.

In medieval Europe similar precautions were taken, though for different reasons; one guarded against attack, but by living enemies. At drinking parties a large bowl was passed around and each person as he received it had to take it in both hands and stand up to quaff the drink. With his hands occupied and his breast exposed he was in a vulnerable position, so before taking a drink he would request his neighbour or other member of the party to be his 'pledge', that is, to protect him. When the fierce Danes held sway in England, the English never dared to drink in their presence, and even when permission was given they would not do so unless the Danes had pledged their safety. Many instances are recorded in history of men slain while in this defenceless position, notably Edward the Martyr (d. 978), king of the English, who at the instigation of his stepmother, was murdered as he raised his cup. Till the middle of the eighteenth century the custom prevailed at Queen's College, Oxford, for scholars to put their thumbs on the table while waiting on their fellows. In many parts of Germany the inferior placed his two thumbs on the table when a superior drank. This precaution was necessary to 'disarm' the serving man.

Similarly, 'tasting' used to be the common preliminary rite in ancient times. Generally the first drink was taken by the chief of a tribe because he had to be served first as the representative of the god. It also symbolically lifted the taboo that prohibited drinking on ordinary occasions, and neutralized the mana that inheres in sacramental drinks. It was also an assurance to guests that the drink was not poisoned.

Even today in western society the man ordering a bottle of wine for his companions, or offering wine to guests, often has the first sip from his glass and then has the other glasses filled. This is a survival of the old 'tasting' custom, by which the host 'approved' the drink, and ensured that it was free from poison. In Moslem countries the ruler had an official taster, and only after he had tried the sultan's food and drink in his presence without ill effects, did the latter partake of them himself.

Books

Chambers, R. (ed.), *The Book of Days: A Miscellany of Popular Antiquities*, vol. II, Edinburgh, 1878.

Crawley, E., *Dress, Drinks and Drums*, Methuen, London, 1932.

Fielding, W. J., *Strange Superstitions and Magical Practices*, Blakiston, Philadelphia, 1945.

DYING

Dying, the process during which life ebbs away and death supervenes, is perhaps the most awesome of all human transition states. To help the dying a number of religions have evolved an *ars moriendi*, 'art of dying', a technique for dealing with the whole process attending the final moments.

Descriptions of the actual dying process are many and varied. In the case of those who die a normal death in bed, it would seem that the vital energy begins to shrink and retreat, starting from the feet and working upwards. The sensation is one of growing coldness, numbness and paralysis, often accompanied by strange sounds of buzzing, snapping, singing and humming, inside the head and outside. The strength drains away, the muscles relax and there is a slow sinking of vitality.

Often the mind remains active, and reviews its past life. Like a rushing panorama of vivid pictures, memories of forgotten places, dimly-remembered people, scenes and incidents from the past, some important, some apparently trifling, come floating before the mind's eye of the dying person as in a vision. There is some truth in the popular idea about the thoughts of drowning men as they go down for the third time.

Scenes of the past give way to another phantasmagoria, seemingly of another dimension, when it appears as if two worlds have merged, this world and that, like one picture superimposed upon another, for the soul's connection with the body is loosened. A man *in articulo mortis*, 'at the point of death', flickering on the borderland between two planes, is said to be *fey* (lit. 'doomed'), a word which describes the power of prescience that he possesses at this time; he becomes clairvoyant and can see into the future.

During the moments immediately preceding death all physical energy is withdrawn, there is a growing stupor, sensibility evaporates, awareness of surroundings is lost, and there is a swooning drift into nothingness. Students of astral projection believe that during the last phases of dying the physical body is unconscious, that is, brain consciousness is in abeyance, and all sensations and thoughts pass into the astral body, so that the whole process of dying is gradual, easy and natural, and seldom involves physical pain or fear.

Although it would seem that man leaves the world as he entered it, in a state of oblivion, occultists believe that the consciousness that vanishes at death is not extinguished but merely withdrawn, for use in some other form, or if it is extinguished it is only a blackout of the brain consciousness, after which another awareness emerges which we carry with us into the next sphere. We depart from here with another, *theta*, consciousness (*see* xenophrenia), into other dimensions, and other fields of experience.

Books

Barrett, William, *Death-Bed Visions*, Methuen, London, 1926.

Comper, F. M. M., *The Book of the Craft of Dying*, Longmans, London, 1917.

Eissler, Kurt, *The Psychiatrist and the Dying Patient*, International Universities Press, New York, 1955.

Feifel, H. (ed.), *The Meaning of Death*, McGraw-Hill, New York, 1959.

Flammarion, Camille, *Death and Its Mystery*, Unwin, London, 1922.

Glaser, B. G. and Strauss, A. L., *Awareness of Dying*, Aldine, Chicago, 1965.
Hinton, John, *Dying*, Penguin Books, Harmondsworth, 1974.
Kübler-Ross, Elizabeth, *On Death and Dying*, Macmillan, New York, 1969.
Osis, Karlis, *Deathbed Observations*, Parapsychology Foundation, New York, 1961.
Welby, H., *Signs Before Death*, London, 1825.

EAR

The ear receives sound waves and transforms their vibrations into mechanical impulses that stimulate certain nerve-endings, which in turn transmit them to the brain, where by some mysterious process they are given a meaningful interpretation. The fluid in the labyrinth of the middle ear acts like a spirit level, governing our sense of equilibrium, and disorders of the semicircular canals within the ear lead to giddiness and difficulty in maintaining balance.

The shape and size of the ear, the absence or presence, and the configuration of the lobe and helix, the convolutions of the outer surface, all reveal the characteristic, and, where present, degenerative, traits of the individual. Dr Amédée Joux said, 'Show me your ear and I will tell you who you are, where you come from and where you are going' (Bloch, 1968, p. 32).

From earliest times long ear-lobes have been regarded as a sign of spiritual development and superior status. Among the distinguishing marks of Buddha (d. 483 BC), and a sign of his greatness, were his large ear-lobes. Homer (d. c. 800 BC) and Aristotle (d. 322 BC) reputedly also had the same characteristic.

There is a close connection between the ears and the sexual reflexes. Our fleshy ear-lobes, absent in all other primates, are not, as they appear to be, useless appendages, but erogenous zones which in sexual excitement become swollen and hypersensitive. In ancient times severed ears were offered to the Mother Goddess as a substitute for the male organs. In Egypt devotees offered their ears to the goddess Isis, and till the early decades of the Christian era, sculptured ears were offered at the shrine of the Great Mother in other parts of the middle east.

Like the penis, the ear-lobe has no bone, and pulling the lobe was believed to elongate the male organ. The tutors of royal children in the east, while not permitted to beat their pupils, were allowed to pull their ears, for this involved no loss of honour and assisted in making the young boys sexually more vigorous.

The boring of the ear-lobes has been widely practised in all parts of the world from early times. The purpose of this operation is not only to facilitate the wearing of earrings for beauty, but to protect the wearer from evil influences, the adornments serving as talismans. This practice was also thought to have some therapeutic value. In certain places in Germany, Scotland and Ireland, ear-piercing was believed to be good for the eyes; it also sharpened the mind and drew off 'bad humours'. Till recently there was a custom current in Carmarthenshire, Wales, in which, from the waxing of the moon, children from miles around were brought to certain village wise-women, to whom the art had been handed down hereditarily. They would make an incision in the cartilage of the child's ear as a cure for 'backwardness' of various kinds. In India there exist certain orders of 'ear-split' yogis whose ears are mutilated by the cartilage being bored, cut, or torn on initiation, to render them more receptive to the etheric nuances of 'unstruck sound' that no one else can hear.

The ear provides its own unique method of communication and understanding; what is heard is totally and entirely different from what is seen, belonging to a completely different order of experience. In esoteric theory the ear consists of a network of superfine ganglia directly connected with the interior organs of perception, so that the whispering of an occult doctrine by the master to the disciple activates the network and communicates instantaneous enlightenment and transpowerment*.

There is a natural limit to one's tolerance to sound that is both physiological and psychological. The worst kind of sound is what is broadly called noise. Today there are more sources of noise than ever before: aircraft, pneumatic drills, traffic, high-powered machinery. The constant repetition of strident, harsh, metallic and penetrating noises is injurious to body and mind. Many patients in mental hospitals are the victims of noise.

Even more insidious in their damaging effects than the cacophony of these harsh sounds are the vibrations produced by certain kinds of music. The very real ravages wrought by such music are only now beginning to be appreciated. Electronic amplifiers which raise the volume of sound to the limits of tolerance, destroy the delicate hair cells attached to the membranes of the inner ear and can cause deafness after even brief exposure.

There are psychic effects as well. It is well known that many jazz musicians of the twenties and thirties drove themselves to dementia. Psychologists declare that those exposed for several hours to the noisy cacophony of today's pop rhythms, and this includes both the musicians and their listeners, remain in a dazed and trance-like state for some time thereafter. Medical research has shown that pop music with its loud insistent beat causes the amount of blood pumped into the heart to double, resulting in a marked deterioration of the breathing rate and impairing brain activity.

In the long run this continuous assault on the senses raises the reflex level of the nervous system and leads to progressive impotence. Contrary to general belief, many pop stars are sexually subnormal. Furthermore, following the need for the strong sensory stimulus to which they are accustomed, many pop addicts inevitably drift into drug addiction.

The sense of sight is said to be the most important of the senses. While this is true in practical life, it is occultly true that auditory impressions have a more powerful impact on the psyche than visual impressions, for sound vibrations affect not only the physical organism, but the asomatic elements as well. Plato (d. 347 BC) in his *Timaeus* describes sound as a stroke impressed on the air, which passes through the ear, and profoundly stimulates the head, brain, liver and the blood, penetrating even through to the soul.

The philosophers of the Renaissance repeatedly emphasized that it was of vital importance for the well-being of the soul that the ear be provided with a 'proper diet', and just as it is harmful for the lungs and the digestive organs to take in poisonous air and food, so it is injurious to the spirit for the ear to hear the wrong sounds. Silence was infinitely to be preferred to the demoralizing tones of vulgar music.

Books

Bloch, Iwan, *Strange Sexual Practices*, K & G Publications, Hemel Hempstead, 1968.
Burns, William, *Noise and Man*, John Murray, 2nd edn, London, 1973.
Davis, H. and Silverman, S. R., *Hearing and Deafness*, Holt, Rinehart & Winston, New York, 1966.
Eyle, P., *Ueber Bildungsanomalien der Ohrmuschel*, Zurich, 1891.
Kryter, K. D., *The Effects of Noise on Man*, Academic Press, London, 1970.
Stevens, S. S. and Davis, H., *Hearing: Its Psychology and Physiology*, John Wiley, New York, 1938.
Weaver, E. G., *Theory of Hearing*, John Wiley, New York, 1949.

EATING

As an intimate personal function, eating is attended with psychic hazards and hedged in by stringent taboos. Anthropologists have found that one can learn a great deal about the structure of a society by studying the eating rules prevalent in it. There is often a strange protocol about commensal relations, and whom you eat with is often more important than whom you sleep with. A Hindu of high caste would have no objection to sleeping with a low-caste woman, but would never eat with her.

In ancient communities every stage connected with the eating of food was marked by ceremonies: the diet or the kind of food sanctioned by the religious code; the mode of acquiring it, whether by hunting, fishing or harvesting; the preparation of the raw foodstuffs; and the final act of eating it.

Prayers such as grace before a meal are an expression of thanks to God for the blessing of food. But they are also said in order to avert any danger that might come through eating it. Impure food can make a man ill or kill him, but equally the wrong kind of food (beef for the Hindu, pork for the Muhammadan) can contaminate the psyche. It has been said that the avoidance of eating, as in fasting, arises partly from fear of being polluted.

In many places custom dictates that food be eaten in silence and solitude, and to eat and talk at the same time is a serious breach of propriety amounting to sin. Eating in solitude is obligatory especially on those of high rank. In many parts of Africa no one was allowed to see the chieftain having a meal, and in Dahomey it was punishable by death. In ancient Mexico a wooden screen used to be placed in front of the Aztec king during meals so that no one might see him eat.

When a man eats he breathes into his food some of his own psychic emanations, which impregnate it. Any fragments of food that fall to the ground belong to the chthonic deities who absorb with great relish the human vital breath contained in it. The remains of one person's food are also prohibited for everyone else. Many primitive sorcerers make juju with the food left by others, so people are very careful to dispose of any food left over so that no one can get at it for evil purposes.

Eating, like defecation and the sexual act, is regarded as a rite which once begun must be completed. In some parts of the world a man once he has started eating will not be called away to do anything until he has finished, and if compelled to leave will not resume the repast but throw the food away.

A certain quantity of air is carried into the stomach along with the food one eats, and this is audibly expelled in eructation or belching. Such a sound would be considered offensive in the west today, but till the seventeenth century in the best European society belching was the correct expression of approval for a good meal served by a good host. Even today, peoples of the near east feel complimented when a guest belches during or after a meal, regarding it as a token both of appreciation of the food and of a replete stomach. The prophet Muhammad (d. AD 632) said, 'If any man belch and say *al-Hamduli'llah* (Praise be to God), he averts seventy diseases, of which the least is leprosy.'

But belching is an offence during worship, and a priest who belches during service renders the rite void. Hierophants therefore never performed their ceremonies after a meal. It is strange but true that some people have chemically hyperactive gases in the stomach which are dangerously inflammatory, and have been known to cause small spontaneous explosions (Smith, 1968, p. 466).

The food eaten undergoes the process of digestion, part being assimilated by the body, the rest passing out as faeces. The repugnance associated with faeces has led to the belief that in the case of supernatural beings and supreme adepts digestion results in a magical transformation. They ingest food, but they do not digest it and eject the superfluous. They have another power by which food is instantly dissolved and miraculously diffused in the body.

Books

Auddy, C., *The Diet of the Ancient Hindus*, Calcutta, 1916.
Bleibtreu, John N., *The Parable of the Beast*, Gollancz, London, 1968.
Crawley, E., *The Mystic Rose: A Study of Primitive Magic*, 4th edn, Watts, London, 1932.
Frazer, J. G., *The Golden Bough*, abr. edn, Macmillan, London, 1922.
Smith, Anthony, *The Body*, Allen & Unwin, London, 1968.

ECSTASY

A state of mental and spiritual exaltation when the mind is suddenly raised to a rare level of experience far more profound than that of daily consciousness. As originally used the term implied a rapturous bewilderment when the person in the ecstatic state was for a time out of his senses and suffered a brief mental derangement.

Often it is of short duration. But in that brief moment the soul is dissolved in the infinite and life becomes an 'eternal now'. The experience is profound and incommunicable. 'I knew a man in Christ,' said St Paul, 'whether in the body or out of the body I cannot tell, who was caught up to the third heaven and heard unspeakable words, which it is not lawful for a man to utter' (2 Cor. 12:2).

Ecstasy may be theistic or atheistic, Christian or pagan, deistic or pantheistic, materialistic or idealistic, and can result in feelings of elation or melancholy, joy or sadness, fearlessness or fright, serenity or eroticism. It can cover the full scale of human experience, and may range from the deep joy of a purely physical sensation, intensely felt, to the *rapture* which abruptly, uncontrollably and violently seizes the saint or prophet, and displays before his vision a glimpse of another dimension. Reality lies beyond the ken of human consciousness in its normal state, and some form of exaltation is necessary to apprehend or experience the other dimension.

Ecstasy is a condition when the centre of perception shifts from the physical to the spiritual world, when the consciousness is withdrawn from the circumference to the centre, during which there is an exaltation of the faculties, and a blissful trance-like state supervenes, accompanied by visions. In the supreme moment of ecstatic beatitude it is even possible for the body to die, for it can no longer contain the soul. The experience is known as the *mors osculi**.

The sense of ecstasy is 'immediately' and not rationally felt, but at the same time certain distinctly physical symptoms accompany the event, and often the physical and psychical sensations seem to meet and merge. Thus, a person in ecstasy may feel tides of warmth which often reach a pitch where they are described as 'hot' or 'burning'. He has a sensation of light that can be of dazzling brilliance. Thrills (lit. 'piercings') or sensations of tingling pass in waves over his body. His breathing is impeded, or it may be accelerated, he feels suffocated, his heart overflows with emotion, tears come to his eyes and he may cry out as if in agony.

The subjective experience is almost beyond description. He is filled with a profound and mystical sense of boundless release, newness, peace and fulfilment. He is radiant and aglow, as if lit up from within, and he has the feeling that he is walking on air or lying on a cloud. His soul seems to dissolve and he loses all awareness of his physical surroundings, deeply absorbed in his experience.

Like the symptoms, the circumstances that evoke ecstasy are varied. The saint, mystic or prophet may become enraptured as a result of deep meditation or contemplation of divine things. In a lower range the philosopher or scientist might have an experience of inspired elation while solving, or at having solved, a metaphysical or mathematical problem. The feeling bordering on ecstasy has come to people while worshipping in a cathedral, or listening to a symphony, reciting or hearing poetry, or seeing a play. The vast wastes of the desert, the solitudes of the mountain or deep forest, the roar of waterfalls, the fury of thunderstorms, have all at some time or other brought on a state of rapture. Overwhelming emotions like great love, deep sorrow, joy, or even raging anger, can make one lose one's reason and plunge one into a state closely akin to ecstasy (*see* xenophrenia).

A still lower range of ecstatic experience may be precipitated by bodily sensations and related emotions, such as those that accompany childbirth, love-making and orgasm.

Books

Beck, P., *Die Ekstase, ein Beitrag zur Psychologie und Völkerkunde*, Haake, Bad Sachsa im Harz, 1906.

Laski, Marghanita, *Ecstasy: A Study in Some Secular and Religious Experiences*, Cresset Press, London, 1961.

Leuba, J. H., *The Psychology of Religious Mysticism*, Kegan Paul, London, 1929.

Lewin, B. D., *The Psychoanalysis of Elation*, Hogarth Press, London, 1950.

Lewis, I. M., *Ecstatic Religion*, Penguin Books, Harmondsworth, 1971.

Tart, Charles (ed.), *Altered States of Consciousness*, John Wiley, New York, 1969.

Walker, Benjamin, *Beyond the Body*, Routledge & Kegan Paul, London, 1974.

ECTOPLASM

A strange substance extruded from the etheric body* of a spiritualist medium during trance, out of which the form of a spirit entity may materialize. It is also referred to as *ideoplasm* or *psychoplasm*, since the subconscious thoughts of the medium or the sitters are believed to have something to do with its creation. The alternative term *teleplasm* is used for it when materialization takes place at a distance from the medium's body.

Certain facts have been noted about the nature of ectoplasm and its formation. It seems to be a semi-material substance, with both material and non-material characteristics. It exudes in vaporous form from the pores of the medium's body, or in slightly more solid form from the top of the head, breast, solar plexus, finger-tips; or from the bodily orifices, the mouth, ears, nose, eyes, sex organs or anus. Its consistency to begin with is misty. Emanuel Swedenborg (d. 1772) spoke of it as a kind of small visible cloud which steamed from the pores of the body and fell downwards on the carpet. Other observers have compared it to the condensation of a nebula or to a mass of swirling steam.

When the hand is put through it, the feeling experienced has been described as of touching a spider's web, fine threads, a veil-like material or elastic cords. After a few minutes outside the body ectoplasm assumes greater substantiality, and is then said to be moist, cold, sticky, semi-liquid, pasty, rubbery, and yielding to the touch and sometimes, though rarely, dry and hard. During the materialization of a spirit form it may be attached to the body by a cord which may be clearly visible. This cord is reminiscent of the human umbilical cord, and has been compared to the astral cord.

Ectoplasm has a smell reminiscent of ozone. It varies in colour, being mostly white, sometimes grey, and more rarely black. It is mobile and undulating in action. If suddenly grasped without warning or permission, or exposed to bright light, it rapidly dissolves and disappears, or snaps back like elastic into the medium's body with lightning speed, often causing the medium considerable pain. With the medium's permission small specimens have been cut off for chemical and microscopical analysis and have been found to bear a remote resemblance to animal tissue. It burns to an ash, leaving a smell as of horn, and chemical analysis shows the presence of salt and phosphate of calcium. Hundreds of photographs have been taken of the phenomenon, both by normal and by infra-red light.

At a seance, ectoplasm may be drawn partly from the medium and partly from the sitters.

Books

Barbanell, Maurice, *Spiritualism Today*, Herbert Jenkins, London, 1969.
Bisson, J., *Les Phénomènes dits matérialisation*, Paris, 1914.
Brackett, E. A., *Materialized Apparitions*, Rider, London, 1912.
Fodor, Nandor, *Encyclopedia of Psychic Science*, Arthurs Press, London, 1934.
Geley, Gustave, *Clairvoyance and Materialization*, London, 1927.
Pearsall, Ronald, *The Table-Tappers*, Michael Joseph, London, 1972.
Richet, Charles, *Thirty Years of Psychical Research*, Collins, London, 1923.
Schrenck-Notzing, A. von, *Phenomena of Materialization*, Kegan Paul, London, 1920.

ENCRATISM

(Gk. *en*, 'in', *kratos*, 'strength'), a discipline of sexual restraint practised in religious and occult groups with the object of developing spiritual and psychic power. It gained prominence among the gnostics especially under Saturninus (c. AD 110), the Syrian founder of an encratite sect who advocated abstinence from flesh and wine, and in particular, from sexual activity, so that *gnosis* or mystical enlightenment might be received. It was also encouraged by certain agapetae Christians. Encratism covers all forms of sex abstinence and sex restraint, particularly for males. It is highly extolled in the Chinese, Buddhist and Hindu esoteric systems as a means of increasing physical stamina, mental energy and spiritual power. All great spiritual leaders at the critical period of their careers were celibates. They were thus overflowing with vital energy which they were able to utilize.

Yogic schools regard ejaculation and the loss of semen* as detrimental to body, mind and spirit, and teach that sexual energy should be transmuted into psychic force. It is believed that by retaining his semen the yogi becomes physically more alive, mentally more alert and spiritually more receptive. He acquires supraphysical powers which enable him to influence the processes of nature and the cosmos. He can overcome death and achieve immortality. Seminal energy when conserved spreads over the whole body, makes the skin glow, tones up the muscles, brightens the eyes and sharpens the senses. It makes the mind alert, activates the psychic faculties and opens the channels of extra-sensory power, such as telepathy, clairvoyance, mind-reading, mind-projection, the ability to create and control thought-forms*.

Encratism may take many forms, depending on the person practising it. There are people who are natural celibates, and do not feel the sexual urge strongly enough to trouble to seek satisfaction for it. There are the natural bachelors, such as Julian the Apostate (d. AD 363), Isaac Newton (d. 1727) and William Pitt (d. 1806), who were said to have refrained from sexual intercourse altogether. Again, the celibacy that results from castration is not encratism, because the seminal energy is no longer available for utilization. Nor is the enforced celibacy of monastic institutions where female companionship is denied, since that leads to frustration and repression, which causes mental disorders and muddies the psyche.

Chastity and sexual purity through unyielding self-control is the basis of true encratism. It exists in a situation where a man, equipped with the full sexual apparatus, possessed of a normal sexual appetite, moves about freely in the company of the opposite sex, but does not indulge in sexual intercourse, or if he does refrains from ejaculation. It is said that one of the thirty-two signs of Buddhahood is that 'the organs of sex are hidden by nature', signifying not the absence of the organs but the complete control of the sex instinct. Jain texts prescribe several aids to suppressing sexual desire and so conserving energy: cold baths, physical exercise, the use of anaphrodisiacs, meditation, devotion, prayers, the reading of pious books, associating with holy persons, religious observances, breath control, and as far as possible, minimum contact with the opposite sex.

Conversely, encratism as a power-discipline recommends the use of sex. Here one excites and stimulates the latent energy and then refrains from expending it. In one form the woman is sought but not touched. Certain aspects of the philosophy of Courtly Love and the troubadours were based on this ideal. Here it was believed that physical possession puts out the flame of desire, that fulfilment bears no fruit, that love dies with orgasm, that passion flowers under adversity, that true love is based on desire for physical fulfilment yet is divorced from it, that love only endures while desire remains inflamed. The aim of love is not to arrive but to travel hopefully. 'Delightful the pain, pleasant the toil, sweet the longing, and joyous the suffering of love unfulfilled.' In the words of one troubadour, 'He knows little or nothing of the service of women who wishes to possess his lady entirely, for when he receives the final gift he ceases to yield his heart.' A gnomic saying attributed to another troubadour, Marcabrun (c. 1150), goes: 'It is not the beloved that ennobles the lover, but the love of her.'

A still more difficult form of encratism advocated physical contact, sometimes including intercourse, but without orgasm. One variety is found in shunamism in which a man sleeps naked beside a nude woman but refrains from physical contact. Still another is udhrism, reputedly practised by the bedouin tribe of the Beni Udhra, where the man makes love to a nude woman but does not penetrate her. In Europe and America certain bundling and kissing sects of the eighteenth and nineteenth centuries were also encratite in their excursions around the realm of orgasm without actually achieving it. The final and most exacting forms of abstinence sanctioned every variety of sexual pleasure, including penetration by the male, but without ejaculation on his part. At its most advanced this type is found in karezza and other varieties of coitus reservatus and acclivity*.

By suppressing sexual energy encratism in all its forms becomes a prelude to xenophrenic states in varying degrees. It is well known that sexual abstinence is conducive to ecstatic conditions and euphoric hallucinations. These start by taking the form of erotic fancies, but later develop into symbolical visions. The process can be accelerated by taking aphrodisiacs and so heightening the tortures of sexual abstinence.

Celibacy and continence are widely practised for occult purposes. It consists in raising tension without the relief of orgasm, and by special methods spreading this tension and raising the basic impulse to torturous ecstasy in order to dynamize the psyche and heighten the mental and spiritual faculties and thus achieve mystical illumination and enlightenment.

Among magicians encratism is commonly used as a means of generating energy and exercising fascination. This is done by refraining from sexual intercourse for a period of three months at the same time concentrating on the woman one wishes to attract. The surplus semen passes out in nocturnal emissions, but the residue is said to be reabsorbed into the system and permeates the body. This diffuses a magnetism so powerful that it acts at a distance on the ova of the female on whom attention has been concentrated and irresistibly attracts her.

Books

Davenport, John, *Sexagyma*, p.p. London, 1888.
Denomy, A., *The Heresy of Courtly Love*, D. X. McMullen, New York, 1947.
Dixon, William Hepworth, *Spiritual Wives*, 2 vols, Hurst & Blackett, London, 1868.
Hardmann, O., *The Ideals of Asceticism*, SPCK, London, 1924.
Laurent, E. and Nagour, P., *Magica Sexualis*, Falstaff Press, New York, 1934.
Schroeder, T. A., *The Erotogenesis of Religion*, p.p. New York, 1934.
Walker, Benjamin, *Sex and the Supernatural*, Macdonald, London, 1970.

ENDOCRINE GLANDS

Those glands whose secretions do not pass through any ducts but pour directly into the bloodstream as it circulates through the glands. Hence also known as ductless or internal secretion glands. The chemical substances manufactured by them are called hormones (Gk. *hormaein*, 'to excite') which are of vital importance for the physical and mental balance and well-being of the individual. The endocrine glands have an almost magical potency, and are responsible for the basic physiological functions. They affect behaviour, and control the mental states. When an endocrine gland produces too much or too little of its particular hormone, it affects growth, metabolism, emotional and sexual development and the total personality, in many strange ways. The endocrines are associated with specific human types, and in occultism with the plexuses.

The endocrine glands include: (1) the pineal*, which lies in the midbrain; (2) the pituitary* at the base of the brain; (3) the thyroid and parathyroids in the neck; (4) the thymus in the chest; (5) the adrenals, above the kidneys; (6) the pancreas, behind the lower part of the stomach; and (7) the gonads (ovaries and testes) which produce the reproductive cells.

The *thyroid* is situated on either side of the Adam's apple, and is larger in women and children than in men. Underactivity of the thyroid results in lack of initiative, obstinacy and mental degeneration. The changes in the personality of Henry VIII towards the end of his life, when he became a suspicious and jealous despot, have been attributed to thyroid failure. The thyroid type is lean, clean cut, with thick hair, bright eyes, even teeth, impulsive, restless, sanguine, mercurial. Example: Percy Bysshe Shelley.

The *parathyroids*, buried in the thyroid tissue, control the metabolism of calcium and phosphorus in the body. The parathyroid type is passive, vegetative, sensitive, warm, feminine, emotional, artistic, nervous, physically unstable. Example: John Keats.

The *thymus* gland consists of two large masses situated in the upper part of the chest, at the root of the windpipe. It is the gland of youth, and regulates early physical and mental development, and shrinks after puberty. Its failure to regress at the proper time inhibits the ageing of the body and delays sexual maturity. Thymus types are delicate and frail, artistic and sensitive.

The *adrenals* (Lat. *renes*, 'kidneys') or suprarenals are twin glands lying above the kidneys. The medulla or inner core manufactures a powerful secretion called adrenalin, 'the emergency hormone', which is poured into the bloodstream to meet any situation of fight or flight, for adrenalin excites both courage and fear. Jealousy, hate, ambition, fear, rage, lust, the struggle for wealth, power and success, all stimulate the adrenals. Adrenalin is thus the source of 'instant karma', for retribution always follows indulgence in passion and the emotions, and people suffer because of its action. Some physiologists believe that it might be possible to alter consciousness by some natural bodily secretion, like a certain by-product resulting from the decomposition of adrenalin. When administered artificially the effects of this substance resemble those of mescalin and certain other drugs. But it can be produced spontaneously in the human body, and it is conceivable that it might be possible to manufacture it by an act of will. The adrenal type is hairy in face and body, vigorous, passionate, fierce, full of mental energy, assertive, aggressive, easily moved to anger.

The *pancreas* secretes digestive juices, but there are certain islet cells (the islets of Langerhans) embedded in it which secrete insulin. This hormone controls the absorption of sugar by the body. When the islets fail to produce enough insulin, diabetes results. Insulin promotes the deposition of sugar by the blood, and is thus an opposite* of adrenalin, which impedes deposits. The pancreatic type is full and rounded, 'moon-faced', passive, moody, introspective.

The *gonads* or sex glands (ovaries and testes) produce gametes or sex cells (ova and sperm). People of the gonad type, both male and female, are masterful and have strong sexual instincts.

Books

Allen, Edgar (ed.), *Sex and Internal Secretions*, Baillière, Tindall & Cox, London, 1939.
Beach, F. A., *Hormones and Behavior*, Hoeber, New York, 1948.
Berman, Louis, *The Glands Regulating Personality*, Macmillan, New York, 1921.
Cobb, I. Geikie, *The Glands of Destiny*, Heinemann, London, 1927.
Green, R., *Human Hormones*, Weidenfeld & Nicolson, London, 1970.
Leak, D., *The Thyroid and the Autonomic Nervous System*, Heinemann, London, 1970.
Pickford, Mary, *The Central Role of Hormones*, Oliver & Boyd, Edinburgh, 1969.
Whalen, R. E. (ed.), *Hormones and Behavior*, Van Nostrand, New York, 1967.
Young, W. C. (ed.), *Sex and Internal Secretions*, Williams & Wilkins, Baltimore, 1961.

EPIGASTRIUM

(Gk. 'upon the stomach'), the region in the middle of the upper abdomen in front of the stomach, and roughly extending from the sternum or breastbone downwards to just above the navel. This is the site of one of the most important of all plexuses*, known by such names as: the epigastric plexus, or the coeliac (Gk. *koilia*, 'belly') plexus, because of its location; and the solar plexus because of the cluster of nerves that radiates from it. It is closely associated with the stomach, spleen, gall-bladder, the adrenals, and with the six lower bones of the twelve thoracic vertebrae of the spine.

The solar plexus is a network of nerves spreading out like a great octopus, which acts as the control centre for the nervous system of the abdominal viscera. The gastric nerves, branching off the vagus nerve, are connected to the sympathetic nervous system via this plexus. The solar plexus is therefore regarded as the ruler of the sympathetic system, regulating the digestive and other vegetative functions, and is spoken of as the 'abdominal brain'. Furthermore, all the emotional reactions are reflected in the epigastrium, which lies in front of the aorta, the main artery from the heart. In colloquial Arabic the epigastrium is picturesquely called 'the mouth of the heart'.

Being a very sensitive area, it is at this spot 'just above the belt' that the boxer aims his blow to make his opponent groggy. Even normally, when the muscles are held loose, a light tap in this region can be distressing. In certain nervous diseases like epilepsy and migraine, and during all times of emotional stress, there is a feeling of knotting in the epigastrium as if the tensions were being concentrated there.

In occultism the epigastrium, as a major centre, frequently figures as a focus of psychic illumination, and a point of contact between the physical and astral planes. Many cases are on record where the transposition of the senses involves the epigastrium, so that blindfold subjects can identify things presented to the stomach area as if it were equipped with its own visual sense.

Many people too, who have experienced astral projection, have stated that the point of exit seems to be in the epigastric region. A few believe that the astral cord lies curled up in the same area when the two bodies are in coincidence, and that when the astral moves away from the physical body they are joined together by the cord which emerges from this point. Some indeed have averred that during projection a ray of light is emitted from the epigastrium sufficient to illuminate the objects in the room.

In esoteric exercises this plexus is stimulated by concentration on it, combined with breathing techniques.

Books

See under plexus

ERECTION

The distention, lengthening and stiffening of the penis*, is caused by the flooding of blood into its spongy tissue, and not by the presence of a bone, as in some animals. The *os penis*, or penile bone, is found in dogs, cats, seals, bears, rodents, bats, and all primates, but not in man. Erections occur at all ages, even in baby boys. They can be provoked by fear, by the need to urinate, by aphrodisiacs, by the desire for intercourse, and by strangulation, or by severe injury to the spinal cord. Fatal injury to the neck, as happens in hanging, has the same effect. A slight degree of erection also occurs regularly in sleep during REMs. Inability to have an erection is a basic form of impotence.

There is supposed to be an erection point in a man's back, above the sacrum, between two to five inches from the base of the spine, where the spinal nerves are connected with the cerebral area governing the sexual system. The point apparently differs in different men, and even in the same man at different times.

In many primitive societies the phallus was thought to have a separate life, mind and movement. It was man's other self, his alter ego, which was believed to harbour a spirit who controlled it. It was an appendage directed by another being who had to be placated by incantation and magic; by witchcraft too, it could be rendered immobile and useless. Plato (d. 347 BC) in his *Timaeus* said, 'In men the nature of the genital organs is disobedient and self-willed, like a creature that is deaf to reason, and it attempts to dominate all because of its frenzied lusts.' Even St Paul wrote, 'I see another law in my members, warring against the law of my mind, and bringing me into captivity to the law of sin which is in my members' (Rom. 7:23). St Augustine (d. 430) declared that the pudenda (from the Latin *pudere*, 'to be ashamed') were so named, 'because they reveal the shame of men who can control all parts of the body to obedience but not these parts'. To some extent the monk Severius (d. 432) voiced the view of the early church when he said, 'Man is the work of God down to the waist, the work of the devil below.' It was the devil and his minions who controlled the penis.

Erection is uncontrollable by man, and normally when sex desire is aroused the penis swells automatically. On the other hand, it sometimes remains flaccid in spite of every enticement. Leonardo da Vinci (d. 1519) wrote in one of his notebooks about the unruly member:

> It sometimes has intelligence of its own, and although the will of man desires to stimulate it, it remains obstinate and unresponsive. Sometimes it starts to move without permission of the man, whether he is sleeping or waking. Often the man is asleep and it is awake; and many times the man is awake and it is asleep. Frequently the man wishes it to act and it does not desire to do so; many times it wishes to act and the man is compelled to forbid. It seems therefore that this creature has a life and intelligence separate from man. Man is therefore wrong in being ashamed to give it a name or to exhibit it, seeking constantly to conceal what he ought to adorn and display with ceremony as a ministrant.

In sexual mysticism the penis in its flaccid state signified death; and when *in forma arrecta*, 'in upright form', it symbolized the resurrection.

Books
See under penis

ETHERIC BODY

The densest of the asomatic* or non-physical elements of the body, is so called because it was once believed to be composed of etheric substance. In the beginning of the present century psychical researchers in Europe and America were led to believe that the etheric body was lodged between the atoms of the physical body and defined it as the 'intra-atomic quantity'. They claimed to have demonstrated that human beings at the moment of death lose about two or three ounces in weight, presumably due to the departure of the etheric double. French researchers took photographs which apparently showed a misty ball of light over the body at the moment of death. Subsequent experiments failed to confirm these findings and this line of investigation was discontinued. Sensitives, however, have never ceased to report luminous mists and vaporous forms separating from the bodies of dying persons and animals, and rising out of sight.

In esoteric tradition the etheric body is subject to natural law, survives the death of the physical body, usually for a few weeks or so, and then disintegrates and disperses. The precise distinction between the etheric and astral bodies is not always clear, and the terms are often used synonymously, but according to occultists the etheric body has certain qualities that clearly distinguish it from the astral.

Though normally invisible, it is none the less regarded as having a very refined type of materiality, and is therefore known by such designations as the fine body, the subtle body, the between (or tween) body, the unifying body (since it integrates the astral with the physical), the counterpart body or the double. As the phantom body it may appear as a ghost, although there are other reasons for such apparitions. It is also the beta body, a step beyond the physical, which is the alpha body.

The etheric system underlies the sensory reactions of the five senses, including pleasure and pain; it brings about the awareness of brain consciousness, and governs all the needs and functions of the physical body, such as hunger, the sexual urges and procreation. The term *p'o* in Chinese, meaning the physical soul, has the alternative meaning of 'semen'. The etheric body is the vehicle of life-energy, and of the instinctive and mechanical responses of the individual, and is therefore called the vitalic body, energy body, instinctive or reflex body. Most psychic healing is directed at the etheric body. Because its emanations are part of the human aura it is called the auric body. Some think it is the factor responsible for nervous energy, so it is known as *nervengeist* (German, 'nerve-spirit'). Sometimes called the pre-physical body or the body veil, it is identified with the ectoplasm of mediumistic materialization phenomena.

Since it was said to have the properties of what was known in earlier physics as the 'electric fluid', or 'animal magnetism', it was called the electric, magnetic or fluidic body. The etheric double is the body of the subtle arteries and the plexuses (therefore also called the plexal body). Like the astral body it has a pearly luminosity and is called the luminous, radiant or shining body, or the body of light.

Soviet scientists after decades of intensive study with highly sophisticated instruments have established the existence of an energy-system they call the bioplasmic body, which functions along with the physical, and whose brilliant emanations can now be photographed. Many of its characteristics bear a remarkable similarity to those of the etheric body of tradition.

Books

See under astral body

EUPNEA

(Gk. *eu*, 'well', *pneō*, 'to breathe'), the condition of breathing at the ideal rate. The normal breathing rate of the human adult is roughly fifteen breaths a minute, representing the number of times a complete respiration is taken. This rate differs, depending on the bodily activity and emotional state of the individual at the time. Emanuel Swedenborg (d. 1772) declared that the movement of the brain synchronizes with that of the lungs and not with that of the heart, and this has since been established. The heart and lungs also operate together in close rhythm, but have different rates. At rest respiration is four times slower than the pulse.

Besides physical exertion, any violent emotion or intense sensation raises the breathing rate. Rage, hatred, terror, anxiety, sexual arousal, music (especially loud music with a strong beat), all cause an acceleration of breathing. Fast breathing can produce anaesthesia and reduce susceptibility to pain. Most xenophrenic states are associated with a change in the rate of breathing.

During the astral operations of shamans and mediums in trance, the rate varies but is not consistent; in a few cases it is slightly slower than normal, but as a rule more rapid. Mediums have been known to breathe so heavily and so fast, sometimes reaching 300 breaths a minute without tiring, that it was found impossible to simulate it artificially. Harry Price (d. 1948) made an attempt to simulate the phenomenal breathing rate of Rudi Schneider (d. 1957), which was often likened to a steam engine or a tyre being pumped up, but could not continue for even seven minutes, whereas Schneider used to breathe at an incredible speed without stopping for as long as seventy-five minutes.

Very rapid breathing, known as hyperpnea or polypnea, can exhaust the carbon dioxide content of the blood and so bring about a cataleptic trance. Prolonged shouting, singing, chanting, as practised in ecstatic cults, produce a like result. A neurotic disorder known as hyperventilation is characterized by deep and rapid breathing, which the patient is aware of but cannot control. This provokes dizziness, anxiety, fainting, greyouts, blackouts and eventually tetanic spasms. The state is related to dyspnea or shortness of breath, usually the result of an insufficiency of oxygen in the blood, and follows certain diseases of the lungs, heart and blood.

The establishment of a eupnic rate is a matter of great importance in occultism. Since the respiration is synchronous with the slight expansion and contraction of the brain, and is also linked with the pulse, breathing affects both the mind and the metabolic rate. Experts in respiration are not unanimous about the ideal rate, but they are clear that it should be slow. While rapid breathing might be necessitated by certain exigencies, such as running, any undue increase in the rate should be avoided as far as possible. Breathing should not normally be noticeable.

Just as exertion and excitement cause an acceleration in the speed of breathing, so tranquillity results in a more leisurely rhythm. Slow breathing indicates a calm and unruffled mind, unperturbed by passion.

Occultists say that ten breaths per minute are normally sufficient, but if one can manage with five that is excellent. In certain types of meditation when the emotions are still, the rate falls to four a minute. In very profound meditation there may be no perceptible breathing at all.

The reduction of the breathing rate to any considerable degree only comes with long practice and forms the objective of certain breath-retention* techniques. Taoists have specialized in this area, their aim being to reach the eupnic ideal in two stages: (1) to imitate the exceedingly slow breathing of animals during hibernation; and having mastered that, (2) to return to the breathing manner of the embryo as it floats in the amniotic fluid in the womb. The embryo does not breathe, but keeps its breath closed and internal. Mastery of this 'embryonic respiration' ensures immortality.

Books

Cannon, Alexander, *The Power Within*, Rider, London, 1950.
Carrington, Hereward, *The Invisible World*, Rider, London, 1947.
Price, Harry, *Rudi Schneider*, Methuen, London, 1930.

EXHALATION

Exhalation, or expiration of the breath in respiratory techniques, is not as a rule dealt with in any great detail as compared with inhalation. Most texts on breathing are either silent on the subject or speak of it as of no great consequence. But advanced adepts lay great emphasis on exhalation, on its duration, and on the arrest of the lungs after exhalation, regarding the process as being even more important than inhalation.

It is known that inhalation reduces the quantity of blood in the brain, causing the brain to shrink in size. Expiration has the opposite effect, for then the brain refills slightly and re-expands. Expiration is classed as positive and masculine, while inspiration is negative and feminine. By making use of the expiratory phase it becomes possible to utilize breathing as an aid to increasing the potentiality of the brain.

Expulsion is practised by blowing out the air in one long slow stream, or in a series of short breaths as in puffing, coughing, whistling, roaring or other animal sounds, the time taken being of great importance. A related technique called insufflation*, or breathing upon a person, is used in various healing and cult rites.

In Chinese magical practices exhalation is a slow process, for it is meant to restore the equilibrium between the lower and upper plexuses and re-settle the generative energy that is agitated by each inhalation. The Japanese texts on *hara* (*see* plexus) say that for inhaling a moment is enough, but one should exhale in a long slow out-breathing, pressing down on the tanden (just below the umbilical plexus) and keeping back enough breath to say a few words.

In Hindu esotericism the 'locking' of the lungs after the breath is expelled is called *hinaka*, 'lacking', in the sense of deficiency. But Buddhists regard this condition, as they do all privative states, as a manifestation of *shunyata*, 'voidness', an important philosophical category. The empty state of the lungs therefore symbolizes the Universal Essence.

If not properly done under the supervision of an expert, emptying the lungs and holding the breath while retaining the deflated posture can lead to the maladjustment of the 'gearing', as it were, and disorganize the normal breathing rhythm, causing considerable distress to the student.

Books

See under respiration

EXPERSONATION

The dissociation of the individual consciousness or astral double from one body, and its transference to another. It is human possession as distinct from demon possession. A large part of the tradition concerning expersonation belongs to folklore but a small residue is still preserved as a living practice in secret cults. It is an arcane operation of extreme antiquity whose techniques were known in earliest times in Egypt, Greece, China, Tibet and India.

There are several kinds of expersonation. Thus, an adept may expel the vitalizing spirit of an animal and possess its body for various reasons. This may be done in order to enjoy the thrill of sexual activity in animal shape, or to acquire the knowledge accessible only to members of the animal species. Aleister Crowley (d. 1947) notes that the Egyptian *Book of the Dead* contains many chapters detailing how the astral entity of a dead man can assume the form of certain animals such as the hawk and crocodile, and in this guise go about the earth, 'taking his pleasure among the living'. Hindu legend tells of rishis assuming animal form and having intercourse with the beasts of the forest. In African animal-cults and in Voodoo, weird rites are said to be performed in which persons temporarily occupy the body of an animal.

Most forms of expersonation involve two human beings. Thus, allegedly, an aged adept may discard his own worn-out body and forcibly dispossess a youthful person and occupy his body, without any break in the continuity of his consciousness. Or a man may temporarily occupy the body of another man and thus have congress with his wife. This is said to be a common yogic miracle, and Hindu rishis have employed it in order to experience sensual pleasure without polluting their own bodies.

Two adepts can mutually agree to exchange consciousness temporarily. In Tibetan mysticism, a rite known as *trong-jug*, meaning 'transference' or 'inspiration', involves an exchange between the minds of two persons, so that they might benefit from each other's experience and knowledge. It belongs to the *tam-gyud* or 'whispered' tradition, and is held to be a very secret teaching, never communicated except by the master to a single pupil, and then only when the master is at the point of death.

In the process known as 'overshadowing', a master projects his soul into the disciple's body, the disciple being willing and receptive so that he might understand the esoteric teachings. Ancient adepts were said to enter the body of a youthful, inexperienced or unjust king and rule on his behalf for the good of the people.

Another kind of expersonation is seen in the Tibetan rite of *pho-wa*, in which a priestly expert sits by the side of a dying man and assists him in transferring his consciousness from his own dying physical body to his astral double, so that he might remain aware of his own condition in the dying and after-death state, and also plan his next incarnation. In some cases the lama will accompany the man through his dying and early after-death states.

Black magicians in the east practise expersonation in necromantic rites in which a corpse is reanimated, either by the sorcerer himself or by a spirit forced out of another body. Bon priests of Tibet are notorious for the horrible rituals in which they lengthen their own earthly days by appropriating the life-force of a pupil who dies a miserable death by slow attenuation or starvation. These victims must in all cases be voluntary.

It is generally admitted that it is not easy to dispossess another consciousness from its bodily habitation. If a yogi leaves his own body and cannot immediately possess the body he covets, the astral connection between his consciousness and his body, very tenuous when separated for the purpose of permanent possession, may easily break, and he will find himself in a kind of living hell, fully conscious as a human being, but without a bodily vehicle to fulfil the requirements of its earthly sojourn.

The *Zohar*, a famous kabbalistic compilation, refers to the possibility of a disembodied soul overshadowing, and seemingly possessing another personality, presumably in order to assist that person in his bodily incarnation. Furthermore, since there is always an 'averse' side to good, there are also believed to be evil beings who may overshadow and possess men to mislead them.

States vaguely resembling expersonation and the feeling that one has entered into another person's mind, or that someone else has entered one's own mind, are encountered in xenophrenic experiences under the influence of hypnosis, and psychedelic drugs. In earlier times hypnotism was explained as 'entering another's body'.

Books

Bloomfield, Maurice, 'On the Art of Entering Another's Body: A Hindu Fiction Motif', *Proceedings of the American Philosophical Society*, Philadelphia, 1917, 56, 1–43.

Crowley, Aleister, *Magick in Theory and Practice*, Castle Books, New York, n.d.

David-Neel, Alexandra, *With Mystics and Magicians in Tibet*, Penguin Books, Harmondsworth, 1936.

Eliade, Mircea, *Yoga, Immortality and Freedom*, Routledge & Kegan Paul, London, 1958.

Hoffmann, Helmut, *The Religions of Tibet*, Allen & Unwin, London, 1961.

Oesterreich, T. K., *Possession, Demoniacal and Other, among Primitive Races in Antiquity, Middle Ages and Modern Times*, Kegan Paul, London, 1930.

Sinistrari, L. M., *Demonality, or Incubi and Succubi*, Montague Summers (ed.), Fortune Press, London, 1927.

Stafford, P. G. and Golightly, B. H., *LSD, The Problem-Solving Drug*, Award Books, New York, 1967.

Waite, A. E., *The Secret Doctrine in Israel*, Weiser, New York, 1914.

Walker, Benjamin, *Beyond the Body: The Human Double and the Astral Planes*, Routledge and Kegan Paul, London, 1974.

EYE

Perhaps the most intricate and wonderful of all the bodily organs. Modern experiments in perception show that there are over seven million varying shades of colour between which the eye can differentiate, although we classify them into a dozen broad groups.

According to the physiologist, Sir Charles Sherrington (d. 1952), the eye has something like 137 million 'seeing elements' or light-sensitive cells among its other marvels, and he adds, 'To picture its complexity beggars any imagery I have.' A century earlier Charles Darwin (d. 1882) wrote, 'I remember well the time when the thought of the eye made me cold all over.' A century earlier still the philosopher, David Hume (d. 1776), said: 'Anatomize the eye and survey its structure and contrivance; and tell me, from your own feeling, if the idea of a contriver does not immediately and forcefully flow in upon you.'

Embryologically and anatomically the eye is an extension of the brain, and is in effect an exposed part of the brain. Richard Gregory has suggested that the evolution of the brain followed that of the eye, and that the development of the visual system demanded the complex brain structure for analysing and interpreting it.

Seeing is regarded as a form of contact. The ancients, including the Platonists and Stoics, and subsequently medieval scholars and kabbalists, believed that a stream of energy, 'a lucid spirit, an unburning vivific fire, similar to the fire of the sun, from which it originally proceeds', went forth from the eye, regardless of distance, to contact its objective, and so caused it to be seen. Galen (d. AD 201) held that vision is produced by rays of light emitted from the eyes. Leonardo da Vinci (d. 1519) thought that a beam of light streamed out of the eyes, which thus came into contact with the object seen.

Today neurophysiologists have cause to believe that movements of the eye give out very tiny electrical discharges, and that the eyes 'act like small batteries in the head since the retina is positively charged with respect to the cornea' (Stevens, 1973, p. 216). Soviet scientists have found by experiment that the human gaze has immense energy, and they are said to have substantial proof that the eyes in fact send out rays (Ostrander and Schroeder, 1970, p. 150) which are picked up by the pineal gland.

Ordinarily the eye is a comparatively neutral and receptive organ, but when intent is added to the look it can charge the glance with irresistible power. Every feeling of the heart is transmitted through the eye. An imperious look sends forth a magnetism that seems to command homage; the stern eye of authority withers every contradiction and impels obedience; and such looks can be as compelling as if they held their subjects in a grip of steel. The eye can communicate feelings of reverence and sympathy, love and lust. A woman looked at with lust has in a psychic sense already been violated. Note Christ's saying that a man who looks upon a woman with lust has 'committed adultery with her already in his heart' (Matt. 5:28).

What is known as the *evil eye* is the power to cause ill luck by a glance accompanied by feelings of envy, jealousy, hatred, malice, contempt, hostility, astonishment or exaggerated admiration. The power of the evil eye is believed to reside in every person to a greater or lesser degree, and it operates in a flash, so that the first glance even of an ordinary man, if tinged with envy, can send forth the malign influence.

Sight, involving as it does 'contact' with the object seen, can contaminate. The Hindu caste system includes certain 'unseeable' categories, the sight of whom, according to the orthodox, causes pollution. Children are said to be especially susceptible to such contagion and should never be allowed to look at corpses or other unclean things, or be permitted to watch intimate acts like coition, or attend sacred rites like religious ceremonies, since all holy things have a dangerously potent aura.

Philosophers, psychologists and physiologists tell us that seeing, which we take for granted, is actually a very complicated matter. Bishop Berkeley (d. 1753), the idealist philosopher, in his *Theory of Vision*, written at the age of twenty-four, held that seeing was really an act of interpretation, and that a congenitally blind person whose vision was restored would find it impossible to recognize an object by sight, which he had previously known by sound and touch alone, and that he would have no idea of its relative distance.

Such was the case with the blind man healed by Jesus who when his sight was restored said, 'I see men as trees, walking' (Mark 8:24), and it was only when Jesus touched his eyes again that he saw clearly. Evidence culled from the experience of people blind from birth, whose sight was restored, either spontaneously or through surgery, shows that they are confused for several weeks, in some cases months and even years, by their newly acquired sight.

Health and disease are supposed to be easily discerned from the eyes, especially the *iris*, the coloured part of the eye, whose black centre, the *pupil*, helps the adjustment of the eye to changes in the intensity of light. There is a direct relation between pupil size and mental and emotional reactions. Pupils expand when looking at something interesting, pleasant and appealing, and contract when exposed to something distasteful and unappealing. In emotional situations pupil reactions are connected with an increase in the heart rate and blood pressure, more rapid respiration and greater sweating.

In popular superstition a cross-eyed person, that is, a person with a squint, was thought to bring bad luck to those who saw him before noon. On the other hand, in some places, such as among the Mayas of ancient Central America, cross-eyes were believed to be highly auspicious, bringing good fortune to the person possessing them and to all who saw him. A major Maya deity, Itzamma, was cross-eyed, and so were several other of their gods. In the east the deliberate crossing of the eyes is an accepted aid to meditation, and to this end yogis fix their eyes on the tip of the nose, or else with closed eyes focus them on the forehead.

This latter form of concentration allegedly helps in the opening of the *third eye*, an invisible organ of spiritual perception and second sight, traditionally said to be situated in the middle of the forehead at a point a little above the place where the eyebrows meet. It is regarded as the channel of supreme wisdom and sublime intuition, and confers almost divine knowledge. Normally the third eye is closed, but it can be opened by certain occult exercises. The pineal gland is said to have a part in the opening of the third eye; some occultists indeed believe it to be the seat of the third eye.

The visual sense is the only one of the senses that can be cut off immediately and automatically from sensation. The gentle lowering of the eyelids, which effects this isolation, is more than the mere closing of a shutter. As the lids fall the eyeballs roll upwards and certain mechanisms in the brain are suspended for an instant. In a cryptic way the same conditions accompany *blinking*: there is a fractional movement of the eyeballs upward and an infinitesimal mental blackout. Psychologists believe that in certain exceptional individuals a succession of such short periods of blinking may constitute a microsleep, and provide a plausible explanation for the strange phenomenon of insomnolence. Curiously, it is not possible to keep the eyes open while sneezing.

In xenophrenic states the rate of blinking tends to drop, and if the eyes are not shut the condition of *staring* is gradually approached. Staring causes eye-strain due to fatigue of the optic muscles, and nervous exhaustion. Just as a drug acts on the nerves so does staring seem to act on the eyes. The unfocusing of the eyes while staring creates double vision, the normal consciousness is relaxed and subconscious powers seem to rise to the surface. Often a kind of euphoric meditation supervenes, such as the brown study produced by gazing into a fire or at a burning candle, followed in some cases by a state of genuine trance.

Books

Alder, Vera Stanley, *The Finding of the Third Eye*, Weiser, New York, 1949.

Davson, H. (ed.), *The Eye*, Academic Press, New York, 1962.

Elworthy, F. T., *The Evil Eye: An Account of an Ancient and Widespread Superstition*, Murray, London, 1895.

Gregory, R. L., *The Intelligent Eye*, Weidenfeld & Nicolson, London, 1970.

Ostrander, Sheila and Schroeder, Lynn, *PSI: Psychic Discoveries Behind the Iron Curtain*, Sphere Books, London, 1970.

Pirenne, M. H., *Vision and the Eye*, Chapman & Hall, London, 1948.
Révész, G., *The Psychology and Art of the Blind*, Longmans Green, London, 1950.
Sherrington, Charles, *Man on His Nature*, Cambridge University Press, London, 1953.
Stevens, Leonard A., *Explorers of the Brain*, Angus & Robertson, London, 1973.
Walls, G. L., *The Vertebrate Eye and Its Adaptive Radiation*, Bloomfield Hill, Michigan, 1942.

FACE

Of the five organs of sense, three, the eyes, nose and ears, are prominently on the face. Important physiognomical features such as the beard, moustache, wrinkles and dimples also form part of the facial composition.

The human face is not symmetrical; there may be, and usually are, striking differences between the right and left sides. By sticking together two right halves and two left halves of the same full-face photograph, two completely symmetrical full-face photographs will be obtained, each made up of two halves of the same side. These two portraits will show up the two different personalities of an individual. The right-face picture is said to reflect the inner life, the personification in depth of the real, spiritual self. The left-face picture is the external or public side, the social personality, the man as he wishes to appear to the world. Most persons recognize the portrait of the left profile as their own, but rarely of the right.

The ancient study of *physiognomy* is the method of judging a person's character, aptitudes, capabilities, temperament, from his outward physical appearance, especially from the face. The study of physiotaxis* and 'harmonic proportions'* are included in this art. Evidence of the application of phrenological principles is found in Egypt, Babylonia, China and India. The Greeks had their experts too. It is recorded that one exponent of the art named Zopyrus (d. 400 BC) examined the features of Socrates and read there several vices. The company present mocked the physiognomist but Socrates defended him saying that he was right; he had indeed once strongly tended to those vices and lusts, but had conquered them by reason. Among the Jewish kabbalists, secret teachings were never imparted to those who did not possess the requisite facial features.

A general rule for judging intelligence is to view the face in profile and mark a point above the top of the ear and see how much of the head lies in front and how much to the back of this point. The more the head lies in front the more intelligence is shown; if the point lies in the middle the intelligence is average; if more of the head lies to the rear it shows a more material, plodding, obtuse and even dull character.

In physiognomy, a broad chin shows fidelity and permanence of attachment to family and friends. A narrow, short and round chin shows an easy-going, warm, but not passionate nature. A very pointed chin is a sign of some unseen bodily defect. A long chin extending downwards reveals power and ability to command; a short chin, a yielding nature; a receding chin, weakness of will but stubbornness; a cleft chin, a compassionate, trusting and even gullible person.

Looked at full face the jaw should be narrower than the forehead. A wide jaw shows a tyrannical, obdurate nature. The square jaw line, great will, and quickness of decision. The size of the jaw is an important indication of strength and energy.

Wrinkles on the face are read from the lines on the forehead (horizontal lines, benevolence; perpendicular, thought), around the eyes (crow's feet show sympathy and a sense of humour), around the mouth (upturned, cheerful; downturned, complaining). Dimples on the chin reveal the flirt.

Books

Bell, Charles, *The Anatomy and Philosophy of Expression*, Longmans, London, 1806.
Lavater, J. K., *Essays on Physiognomy*, Simmonds, London, 1804.
Rees, Grace, *Character Reading from the Face*, A. G. Elliott, London, 1950.

FAITH

The confident belief in a positive outcome. While faith itself is a passive state, it is at the same time one of assured hope and fervent expectation. It gives strength to the imagination* and permits beneficent forces to operate upon the mind. Faith dynamizes the psyche and creates the conditions necessary for hopeful affirmations to be made and fulfilled. It not only affects the person himself, but also others who come within its influence. In the view of Paracelsus (d. 1541) anything can be accomplished by faith, for powerful forces act miraculously through a human mind which is in trustful harmony with a larger dimension.

Faith is the bedrock of religion and forms the basis of belief in a divine power and hope in a future life. Just as the snags that lie in the way of true knowledge spring not from superstition but scepticism, so the chief obstacle between God and man is not ignorance but unbelief. Lack of faith is a form of death, both in a moral and spiritual sense. Once the greater faith is lost, many favourable influences cease to be effective in the lesser sphere. In the words of Tertullian (d. AD 230), 'It is not difficult for Satan to seal the eyes of the body, once he has sealed the eyes of the soul.'

In healing, faith acts as a powerful suggestion and has great therapeutic and restorative value. The most powerful weapon in the physician's armoury of cures is faith, for cures work best when there is confidence. But if faith warms the heart, disbelief shrivels the psyche and disperses power. Disbelief brings an almost universal blight for it dismisses from the sphere of human experience all life's inexplicable wonders. As faith declines miracles become fewer, for man's doubt affects the things around him, even inanimate things. Bishop Garsias (c. 1489) declared, 'In modern times many stones lack the virtues once attributed to them.' Jerome Cardan (d. 1576) accepted magic when it was mentioned in the Bible, and he accepted it from Homer and Virgil, but he said the growing scepticism of his day had reduced its power and it was now largely a thing of bygone times. Today students say that with the revival of interest and a renewal of belief in these matters, the powers of the occult world are once more beginning to be manifest.

Experiments in ESP and thought transference indicate that the attitude of the experimenters unconsciously affects the subject's faculty and has a marked influence on the final result. A subject needs to believe in a system if that system is to work. If the scientist is a sceptic his disbelief will upset the delicate operation of the subject's psychic abilities. Sensitives, including those who work with instruments, such as dowsers and radiesthetists, know that disbelief and negativism can cause palpable interference with their operations. The presence of a sceptic, lay or academic, in a seance can cause a distinct 'jamming' that inhibits phenomena.

Faith, according to the mystics, sustains the universe. Using his own striking symbolism William Blake (d. 1827) said, 'If the sun and moon should doubt, They'd immediately go out.'

Books

Freud, Sigmund and Pfister, O., *Psychoanalysis and Faith*, Hogarth Press, London, 1963.
Haldane, J. B. S., *Fact and Faith*, Watts, London, 1934.
Sherrington, Charles, *Man On His Nature*, Cambridge University Press, London, 1953.
Ward, J., *Naturalism and Agnosticism*, Black, London, 1899.

FAT

The greasy substance consisting mainly of adipose tissue found in various parts of the animal body, and in certain vegetable substances, fat figures in many forms of occult rites and magical practices.

Animal and human fat is sometimes used in its crude form, but more often in specially prepared salves and ointments. It is massaged into the body as a protective coating against the cold. Fats and oils of various kinds are used in ritual anointing. They are added to beauty preparations to soften the skin. Many healing medicaments contain fat. The ancient Egyptians applied serpent's fat to tumours, and recommended rat's fat for rheumatism, and crocodile fat for sex stamina. In sympathetic magic animal fat is widely used as a medium for the transmission of the animal's qualities. Folklore and legend tell countless stories of sorcerers being transformed into animals or transforming their victims into animals by magical ointments, usually made with the fat of the animal in question.

The most potent of all fats was that of a human victim. We find human fat being used in magical and sorcerous operations throughout the world, for the superlative virtues of human fat as a curative and magical ingredient were universally prized. It was put into magic ointments, love charms, medicinal preparations. The Australian aborigines would kill an enemy to obtain his kidney fat to make their weapons strong, to strengthen themselves and to cure the sick. Medieval witches melted the fat of infants for their flying ointment which they would rub on their bodies to be transvected to the sabbat. Grease from the fat of a corpse was regarded as an invigorating salve if applied to the sexual parts, accompanied by the recitation of suitable spells. Not a few magical recipes in the old grimoires begin with: 'Take the fat of a young child . . .', an unbaptized infant being preferred.

Buddhist, especially tantrik, sorcerers make use of lamps fed with human fat during their necromantic rites. In Europe till the seventeenth century a special magical unguent used to be made from the flesh and fat of a hanged man, and applied to the bolts and doors of a house to keep out evils, plagues and sickness. Killing ointments were of course always made with the fat of a corpse and then surreptitiously rubbed on the clothing of the intended victim. During the Middle Ages in Italy many such *unctori*, 'greasers', were allegedly caught at their nefarious occupation and suffered torture and death for their crimes.

Physiologically, fat serves a useful purpose. Besides keeping the body warm, the layers and pads of fat distributed around the body act as a protective cushioning and covering. They also act as food reserves, so that in lean times the body falls back on the fat stored.

Fatness in women is greatly favoured in many countries. Fat women are regarded as giving more sensual pleasure to the male during sexual intercourse. They make cheerful companions, are good mothers, affectionate wives and rear healthy children. The Great Goddess of prehistoric times was always depicted as a very fat female figure with steatopygous buttocks* and huge pendulous breasts. In some places, even today, wives and concubines are so excessively fattened that they lose the use of their limbs. Some are regarded almost as family heirlooms. In Nubia, Nigeria, Hawaii and Tahiti, voluptuously fat women were once in high demand.

Fat was frequently associated with prosperity and plenty, and the expression to eat or live off 'the fat of the land' (Gen. 45:18) meant living in wealth and luxury and enjoying the best that life has to offer. In the Bible a generous and diligent person who puts his trust in the Lord will 'grow fat and prosper'. At the same time the Bible speaks of proud and wicked persons as being 'inclosed in their own fat', and stupid persons as having hearts that are fat. Such a derogatory association is found in current expressions like 'fat-head' or 'fat-brained', for a dull-witted individual.

The only Biblical story about an obese personality is the one about Eglon, whose name means 'circle', and who is described as 'a very fat man' (Judg. 3:17). He was a king of the Moabites and for long oppressed the Israelites until slain by Ehud the Benjamite.

In human* typology the fat person is classed as a pyknic, endomorphic, viscerotonic, apoplectic and extraverted. Fat people are commonly regarded as less neurasthenic and more outgoing than any other type.

Books

Hughes, Pennethorne, *Witchcraft*, Longmans Green, London, 1952.
Mitchell, S. W., *Fat and Blood, or How to Make Them*, Lippincott, Philadelphia, 1877.
Najjar, V. A. (ed.), *Fat Metabolism*, Johns Hopkins Press, Baltimore, 1954.
Neumann, Erich, *The Great Mother*, Routledge & Kegan Paul, London; Pantheon Books, New York, 1955.
Ploss, H. H. and Bartels, M. and P., *Woman*, vol. I, ed. F. J. Dingwall, Heinemann, London, 1935.

FLATUS

The gas accumulated in the stomach and intestines which is expelled as a 'rude noise'. The misdemeanour of breaking wind was deemed a sacrilege during priestly rites, so that a priest guilty of flatus during service rendered it void. For this reason, states Plutarch (d. AD 120), tubers, onions, garlic, cabbage, beans and pulses were forbidden to hierophants because they created intestinal wind. The Egyptians held that the easing of flatulence during service mortally offended the gods, and Zoroastrians likewise believed that a belch or crepitus during a prayer rendered it invalid. Some Persian tribes regarded the voiding of wind as so indecent that the culprit who made the sound in the hearing of any of the elders was banished from the tribe.

On the other hand, there were scatological cults in which the worshippers dedicated their crepitus, along with their faeces, to fertility deities, and there may be a reference to this type of offering in the Bible: 'Wherefore my bowels shall sound like an harp for Moab, and my inward parts for Kir-haresh' (Isa. 16:11). The Moabites, like other tribes of ancient Canaan, were notorious for the undisguised naturism of their religious practices.

The inhabitants of ancient Pelusium in Lower Egypt venerated the flatus, which they worshipped in the symbol of a swollen belly, or in the image of an infant deity 'with its arse upward' as though in the act of crepitation. Samuel Purchas (d. 1626) in his *Pilgrimage* refers to the Egyptian beetle-gods that crawl 'out of their privies, their dreadful deitie, the Onion, and their stinking farts which had their unsavorie canonization and which they worshipped at Pelusium'.

The Romans of the imperial period, despite their lapse into luxury and sexual indulgence, were very conscious of the indignity of breaking wind in public. Suetonius (d. AD 160) relates that the emperor Claudius (d. AD 54), having heard of a person who out of shame held in his flatulence while eating and nearly died as a result, wanted to publish an edict sanctioning this breach of table etiquette among the Romans.

Certain sects among Hindus and Arabs regarded crepitation as an act of purification, for by this means evil spirits were expelled from the body, and those in the vicinity were driven off. Loud discharges were therefore permitted even in the presence of others. Hindu yogis believe that they rid the body of impurities and prepare it for union with the divine if, after certain rites, they alternately break wind and belch a number of times, at the same time repeating the formula, 'Glory to those keen ebullitions which escape above and below' (Edwardes, 1965, p. 273). So highly were some Arabs esteemed for their ability in this direction that one of them was given the title Abu-es-Zirteh, 'father of farts'. He was a courtier at the Egyptian court in the eighteenth century and could break wind in time to music after he had had a meal of beans.

The connection between gastric wind and penile erection is well known, and there are certain esoteric techniques of erecting the phallus during intercourse and keeping it erect by controlling the anal wind. In yoga the rectal wind is called *apana*, which controls not only excretion but also erection and ejaculation. In Chinese taoist magic two kinds of breath were distinguished: one was the 'embryonic air', responsible for penile arousal, which had to be retained in the body, and the other was the noxious gas generated as a result of the digestive process, which had to be expelled through the rectum at a seemly moment. If, as sometimes happened, the embryonic air also sought to escape by the same exit, the magician prevented this by inserting a wooden plug into the anus (*see* breath-retention).

The curious lore of flatus is not unknown in Europe and figures both in literature and social customs. In medieval England a person who held lands in fief by serjeantry in the region of Heminston, Suffolk, was obliged to come to court each year on Christmas Day and in the presence of the king of England perform 'one saltus, one sufflatus and one pettus', that is, jump, whistle and fart.

The uninhibited freedom with which Englishmen broke wind and spoke of it in company was frequently mentioned in the journals and letters of foreign visitors to their shores. John Brand (d. 1806) in his *Popular Antiquities* says that the early grossness of manners in the matter of breaking wind would exceed belief. In the stage directions of the old Morality Plays it was not unusual to find some such direction as: 'Here Satan letteth a fart.' Although Martin Luther expressed the belief that Satan fled in dismay from human flatulence, the medieval stage manager found the popular association between crepitation and Old Bendy hard to resist. In any event, Satan was supposed to arrive and depart in a smell of sulphur. Crepitation is commonly believed to 'summon the devil', and when one is guilty of the act in a loud manner it is advisable to invoke a good spirit by 'touching wood', a practice observed to the present day among schoolboys in certain old schools.

St Paul spoke of Satan as 'the prince of the power of the air' (Eph. 2:2), and a control over the 'pneumatic elements' was claimed by those who paid him homage, although this control was confined to the basest thaumaturgy. Ben Jonson (d. 1637) said that one of the tricks of the rosicrucians and other wonder workers was that they 'could draw farts out of dead bodies'.

A number of treatises have been written on this subject. One is entitled *The Benefit of Farting Explained* (1761). Another, published in Paris, is entitled *An Essay on Wind, With Curious Anecdotes on Eminent Peteurs, Written for the Edification of Windbound Ladies and Gentlemen* (1877). The famous orator, Charles James Fox (d. 1806), is credited with the authorship of *An Essay Upon Wind* published anonymously in London. Benjamin Franklin (d. 1790) was also said to have written *The Technique of Farting*.

Books

Bloch, Ivan, *Sexual Life in England*, Corgi, London, 1965.
Bourke, J. G., *Scatologic Rites of All Nations*, Lowdermilk, Washington, D.C., 1891.
Brand, John, *Popular Antiquities*, London, 1777.
Dubois, J. A., *Hindu Manners, Customs & Ceremonies*, 3rd edn, Clarendon Press, Oxford, 1906.
Dulaure, J. A., *The Gods of Generation*, Panurge Press, New York, 1933.
Edwardes, Allen, *The Jewel in the Lotus*, Lancer, New York, 1965.
Perry, Charles, *A View of the Levant*, London, 1743.

Purchas, Samuel, *Purchas his Pilgrimage*, London, 1626.
Taylor, G. Rattray, *Sex in History*, Thames & Hudson, London, 1959.

FOETUS (or fetus)

A distinction is made in medical literature between foetus and embryo. After fertilization has occurred, the ovum grows rapidly within the womb, and in the early stages of its development is known as the embryo. By about the end of the third month of pregnancy, when the eyes, nose and limbs begin to form and the sex characteristics become recognizable, it is known as a foetus.

The gestatory period generally tends to be dismissed as an introductory phase of no great consequence to the individual, the foetus being thought of as just something to be kept alive until it emerges as a child. But it is now increasingly realized that this phase is one of profound importance and may be a decisive factor in determining the character and conduct of the individual in later life. Samuel Taylor Coleridge (d. 1834) said, 'The history of man for the nine months preceding his birth would, probably, be far more interesting, and contain events of greater moment, than all the threescore and ten years that follow it.'

In many ways the foetus in the womb leads an independent existence. The ancients erroneously believed that the blood of the mother flowed into the foetus, nourished it and contributed to its growth, but in fact no blood actually flows from mother to child, and the blood-cell characteristics of the child are not necessarily those of its parents. The nervous system of the mother and foetus are also quite separate, although the emotional state of the mother can have lasting effects on the behavioural development of the uterine organism. The placenta and foetus originate from the same cell, and the mother's internal secretions also pass through the placenta and into the circulation of the foetus and have a bearing on the physical and mental development of the child.

The child* thinks its own thoughts, has its own volition, and to some extent even determines its own affairs. The mind of the child at birth was once held to be a *tabula rasa*, 'clean slate', upon which life's experiences begin to be recorded only after its emergence from the womb. But it is now known that the new-born child is as well equipped mentally as it is physically. It is evident that an infant's mental life begins long before its first cry at birth.

While the mother has no control over the child's ancestral inheritance, she does have considerable control over its welfare while she carries it within her. All peoples in times past had their pregnancy* taboos, prescribing what should be done and what avoided, so as to protect the foetus from evil or harmful influences.

It was thought that a woman's intense desires and emotions can mark a child's body. Popular superstition still attributes birthmarks to a violent reaction to some experience on the part of the mother, like fright at the sight of a mouse. Hermann Boerhaave (d. 1738), celebrated Dutch physician, said that a pregnant woman who was shocked at the sight of an epileptic fit might cause her infant to become epileptic.

In Victorian times expectant mothers were warned to be careful not to expose themselves to any unpleasant situations. It was suggested that they visit art galleries and look at beautiful paintings, listen to soft and uplifting music, think beautiful thoughts, so that the child might be cultured, healthy and happy. Some such regimen of calm activity and a pleasant environment was insisted on in many cultures of the past.

It has long been known too that the mother's physical illness, diet, psychological and emotional stress, can adversely affect the foetus, and may result in physical malformation, and permanent mental and emotional disturbances. The embryo is a very plastic entity, easily moulded and shaped by the mother's thoughts, feelings and actions. For her part, a pregnant woman is in a highly impressionable condition both physically and mentally and is susceptible to many trifling emotional tensions which she inevitably transmits to her child.

Experiments in age-regression suggest that the experiences of the growing organism in the womb are registered at an incredibly early age. Many fateful tendencies and predispositions are apparently established at the foetal stage in a person's development. The feeling of euphoria, ease and security we feel in rocking movements stems from the soothing motion of the mother's body, the rhythm of her heartbeats, the rise and fall of her lungs. Heavy sedation, smoking, drugs, drink, adversely affect the foetus, and later the child and the man, and thus further contribute to the total birth experience. Already, even before birth, a child can become addicted to the drugs taken by the mother.

The womb can be a very disturbing place, for all the mother's movements are picked up by the embryo. A loud noise can startle the unborn child, and mothers have known it to hammer on the walls of the womb in protest. It is also a very noisy place, for all the internal sounds of the body at work are also picked up. So is the sexual act between mother and father. Some doctors are inclined to advise against sexual intercourse after the middle period of pregnancy, and some psychologists add their warning, if for different reasons. Nandor Fodor for example held that the foetal consciousness may remember the violence of pre-natal intercourse. Normally, if a pregnant woman has sexual intercourse in the early months of pregnancy it does not do the foetus any harm, but if she submits under duress or with feelings of guilt, resentment or anxiety, it can seriously affect the physical and psychological well-being of the child.

Recent evidence further suggests that the foetus is intellectually receptive while in the womb, and that the unborn child is capable of learning. After the fifth month of prenatal age the human foetus can distinguish between certain tastes, will respond to pitch, vibration and tone, and is influenced by a wide range of chemical and psychological stimuli. The psychiatrist, Denys Kelsey, believes that by the fifth month the unborn baby is aware of itself as an individual, of its sex, of its position, of the length of time it has been in the womb, and of the interrelationship of its various limbs (Grant and Kelsey, 1972, p. 44). Some of this information may be picked up telepathically from its mother. Then, the infant knows it must be born, just as we know we must die. Some psychologists say that the foetus plays an active part in its own birth*, and co-operates with its mother in delivery.

It is known too that many outside influences operate on the foetus. These include cosmobiological factors like cosmic rays and night-and-day radiations. Dr Eugen Jonas of Czechoslovakia has shown how conception is influenced by the major heavenly bodies. After almost two decades of research he has come to the conclusion that the viability of the embryo is influenced to a great extent by the disposition of planetary bodies, and that cosmic influences also determine the time of parturition.

Books

Blondel, J., *The Power of the Imagination on Pregnant Women, and Its Effect on the Foetus*, Strasburg, 1756.

Cole, F. J., *Early Theories of Sexual Generation*, Clarendon Press, Oxford, 1930.

De Beer, G., *Embryos and Ancestors*, Clarendon Press, Oxford, 1958.

Flanagan, Geraldine, *The First Nine Months of Life*, Heinemann, London, 1963.

Gebhard, P. H. *et al., Pregnancy, Birth and Abortion*, Harper, New York, 1958.

Grant, Joan and Kelsey, Denys, *Many Lifetimes*, Gollancz, London, 1972.

Harrell, R. F. *et al., The Effect of Mothers' Diets on the Intelligence of Offspring*, New York, 1955.

Hodson, G., *The Miracle of Birth: A Clairvoyant Study of Prenatal Life*, Theosophical Publishing House, London, 1929.

Liggins, G. C. *et al., Foetal Autonomy*, Ciba Foundation, London, 1969.

Montague, A., *Prenatal Influences*, C. C. Thomas, Springfield, Illinois, 1962.

Rogers, M. E. *et al., Prenatal and Paranatal Factors in the Development of Childhood Behavior Disorders*, Baltimore, 1957.

Spelt, D. K., 'The Conditioning of the Human Foetus *in utero*', *Journal of Experimental Psychology*, 1948, 38, 338–46.

FORESKIN

The foreskin or prepuce is the natural covering of the glans, or head of the penis, and as such was once thought to be the protective element of the phallic system. In many places the foreskin is regarded as a source of defilement, and it is said that the devil hides under it, perhaps an allusion to the smegma, the evil-smelling secretion that quickly forms under it, or to the fact that it is the crown of the penis-head, which is the domain of evil powers.

Mostly, the prepuce is symbolic of virility, and its excision was a sacrificial offering to the deities in many communities. This procedure, known as circumcision, in which the foreskin is cut off, often forms part of the puberty rites of young males. In many western countries till the early decades of the present century, the prepuce used to be removed in the belief that it checked masturbation, and today in America and certain places in Europe, most male children are routinely circumcised at birth in hospital. The prepuce is sometimes regarded as a pathological structure, and circumcision is believed to remove the defect and to prevent such diseases as penile carcinoma (cancer), and also impotence.

Jews, Arabs and other Semitic peoples always cut off the foreskin of male children, because it is regarded as a sign of uncleanliness. Some men are born without the foreskin, a condition known as aposthia; it has no ill effects. The prophet Muhammad, according to popular tradition, was born circumcised, that is, he lacked a foreskin.

In some places the prepuce was thought to be intimately connected with the person to whom it belonged, and it had to be carefully preserved, hidden or destroyed, for fear that someone should obtain it and by magical means disfigure the penis or cause the testicles to swell. In some places the prepuce is placed in a small box and carried around the neck as a charm.

Books

Bryk, Felix, *Circumcision in Man and Woman*, New York, 1934.

Cabanes, Augustine, *The Eroticon: Scientific Marvels of Human Sexuality*, Falstaff Press, New York, 1933.

Gennep, A. van, *The Rites of Passage*, University of Chicago Press, 1960.

Nunberg, H., *Problems of Bisexuality as Reflected in Circumcision*, Imago, London, 1949.

Remondino, A., *A History of Circumcision*, F. Q. Davis, Philadelphia, 1891.

GAIT

Denotes the manner in which the body is carried while walking, running, dancing, stepping, marching. The way a man walks, his deportment, is often an indication of the kind of person he is, or his mood at the time. The person who strides out boldly with firm step is obviously a man with a purpose, determined, forceful, forthright. A slouching, shuffling walk, with dragging feet, characterizes one who is indolent, defeated or dejected. The swaggering gait of the blusterer and bully, the stagger of the drunkard are matters of common observation.

Divination or character reading by the gait is known as *pateomancy* (Gk. *pateō*, 'to walk or tread'). According to this study short, quick steps denote a brisk and active, but rather contracted mind, even tending to bigotry; long, quick steps are an indication that the person will accomplish much; long, slow steps point to the thinker; a shambling walk marks the individual who has received a great buffeting from life and has succumbed; a person with an easy determined step will accomplish what he sets out to do with little outlay of energy; the tendency to roll from side to side while walking reveals a man who lacks direction; the mincing and affected walk betrays a shallow and pretentious individual; a tendency to bounce up and down suggests corresponding ups and downs in the person's moods; a limp is a sign of cruelty.

The gait of a patient can give physicians an indication of the state of his health, and may point to the ailment from which he is suffering. Thus, heels stamped on the ground and eyes fixed downwards might suggest locomotor ataxia; a stiff-kneed walk, arthritis; short, agitated movements, Parkinson's disease; turned-out toes, flat feet; a dragging leg, a stroke; high-raised knees, neuritis.

A particular tread is appropriate to a particular occasion. The dance is full of stylized steps, each of which is relevant to a special mood, musical rhythm or beat. Marching is a disciplined group activity that serves to promote uniformity and obedience to commands. Jumping, leaping and acrobatic movements serve their own designs. They may be light and tripping, or heavy and determined, steady and purposeful, or stealthy and furtive. For certain types of magical circumambulation Aleister Crowley recommends 'the pace of the tiger who stalks the deer'.

Stepping, when ritually performed, is a dynamic occult operation involving determined and willed movement in a set direction. Most secret societies have ritual stances and steps, laid down by tradition, which are part of the ceremonial, or serve as a means of transit from one grade to the next. Some steps in freemasonic rites symbolize stepping over a grave; some, climbing a spiral staircase, performed in an inward or outward spiral, and either deasil or withershins. The 'regular step' in freemasonry, forming a tau cross with the two feet, is derived from the Templars, and was once thought to mean trampling on the Cross.

Stepping over a prostrate body is considered very harmful, and degrading to the one lying down, and the natives of many tribal societies have a great fear of it happening to them. In some places stepping over a sleeping man is as insulting as spitting in his face.

Books

Allport, G. W., *Studies in Expressive Movements*, Macmillan, New York, 1933.
Crowley, Aleister, *Magick in Theory and Practice*, Castle Books, New York, 1929.
Fellows, John, *The Mysteries of Freemasonry*, London, 1866.
Le Roux, H. *et al.*, *Acrobats & Mountebanks*, London, 1890.
Murphy, J. P., *Mannerisms and Their Relation to Psychic Life*, New York, 1915.
Shallow, J., *The Templars' Trials*, Stevens, London, 1888.

GESTURE

Gesture is a movement of the body expressing an emotion or mood, revealing an inclination, intention, sentiment or idea. It is to be distinguished from posture*, which is more or less static. A gesture is the result of a natural discharge of nervous tension, a conscious or unconscious kinaesthetic reaction to an inner stimulus, and ultimately an instinctive response.

Involuntary gestures and mannerisms are an accurate clue to inner tensions and conflicts, but so are voluntary ones. A man may try to conceal his feelings by deliberate and calculated gestures designed to mislead, but a careful reading even of such gestures will reveal the man within, for no one has full control of all the responsive movements of his body, and certain unrehearsed signs will betray him. All gestures are visible expressions of a person's mind.

Gestures preceded but did not create speech. When speech evolved, gestures supplemented it, and have therefore been called the elder brother, and not the father, of speech. They spontaneously accompany emotion and are the backbone of rhetoric and oratory. The word itself is derived from the Latin *gestus*, meaning the dramatic movements of the orator or actor.

Individuals and nations differ widely in their habits of gesture, depending on their temperament, character, upbringing, mental and emotional development and race. Gestures, it appears, are absolutely essential in communication for some people; the Bubis of west Africa cannot talk in the dark because their language depends so much on gesture. Mediterranean peoples gesticulate a great deal; the Neapolitans and Sicilians use more gestures than other Europeans, the Nordics perhaps the least.

Though gestures may involve one or more parts of the body, those made with the hands are the most revealing of all. Such are the ancient manusigns, forming the subject of cheironomy, the ritualized mudras of the hierophant, the stylized gestures of the dance, the gestures found in sign-language, the handshake, and in the universal movements that accompany threat, benediction, prayer, welcome and so on. Handwriting, forming the subject of graphology, is a series of acquired symbols executed by the hand, and reveals in its own way the character of the person writing. It has been called 'a chain of crystallized gestures'.

The face too is very revealing, as seen in movements of the eyes and eyelids, the dilation of the nostrils in anger or moments of passion; of the lips in pouting, smiling, snarling. Movements involving the head may indicate agreement or disapproval, and many other shades of favour and disfavour. The nod was regarded as a peculiarly binding and sacred form of promise, and an expression of the will, because the head, the holy seat of the life-soul, was involved in the gesture. Sucking motions, including kissing and smoking, suggest a desire for nourishment, whether physical, mental or spiritual. Sucking the thumb and biting the nails express anxiety and insecurity, and a desire to revert to an earlier, more comforting period of life.

Rocking and to-and-fro movements are relaxing and provide soothing gratification for the nervous system. Children seek for rhythmic pleasure since it is reminiscent of the gentle sway within the womb, and, after birth, the mother's arms. Adults who rock want peace, and a reversion to infantile security. Movements involving the legs and feet, including the gait*, no less than the hands express the whole physical and emotional condition of the person, for the way a person carries himself and the manner in which he walks are relevant to the kind of person he is. Gestures of prostration are based on national and traditional custom, but also have a symbolical significance.

Hitting movements, either with the open palm or the closed fist, or a desire to kick out, with the intention of frightening, threatening or hurting, are signs of intense, aggressive emotions. In extreme cases they become autistic (self-directed) or auto-aggressive, so that a person who cannot vent his rage on others, hurts himself, bangs his head against the wall, bites his hands, or otherwise injures himself. It betrays frustration, unappeased urges, and, ultimately, suicidal tendencies.

The gestures of a well-adjusted person are easy, flowing, co-ordinated, spontaneous and rhythmic. Tension is revealed in erratic, sudden, cryptic and halting movements. The extravert has expansive and outward gestures. The introvert has inward-directed or enclosed gestures. Many gestures are psychosomatic and represent a physical reaction to mental states. This was found to be the case in word-association tests, when random words provided a stimulus for unconscious gestures and so revealed their true emotional association.

One of Freud's followers, Sandor Ferenczi, pointed out that during the first years of a child's life, the infant learns that its gestures, like the movements of its arms and legs, stretching out to reach for something, as well as grimacing and crying, actually achieve their object, bring it the attention it seeks and the thing it craves. From this the child, and later the man, learns to invest gestures with a magical significance. Reciprocally, the very young child reacts to a number of simple gestures and movements made by the mother, even before it learns to associate them with sounds.

Cornelius Agrippa (d. 1535), the famous German occultist, held that ritual gestures used by magicians in ceremonial magic were devised to express the abstract and occult power of numbers, by bodily notation, as it were. There are in fact hundreds of such age-old symbolical and esoteric signs, formalized by tradition and custom as found in various religious and hermetic rites. In religious and ritual gestures the body assumes a certain position and takes on a certain configuration in order to become a focus of psychic energy. The formulary of signs and gestures often reaches great complexity when incorporated within the workings of occult and secret societies and each movement is directed towards a particular magical end.

Books

Adams, Florence, *Gesture and Pantomimic Action*, Werner, New York, 1891.
Akiyama, A., *Buddhist Hand Symbols*, Yokohama, 1939.
Alport, G. W., *Studies in Expressive Movements*, New York, 1933.
Bell, C., *The Anatomy and Philosophy of Expression*, Longmans, London, 1806.
Coomaraswamy, A. K., *The Mirror of Gesture*, 2nd edn, New York, 1936.
Critchley, M., *The Language of Gesture*, Edward Arnold, London, 1939.
Efron, D., *Gesture and Environment*, King's Crown Press, New York, 1941.
Krout, M., *Autistic Gestures*, Albany, New York, 1935.
Lamb, Warren, *Posture and Gesture*, Duckworth, London, 1965.
Murphy, J. P., *Mannerisms and Their Relation to the Psychic Life*, New York, 1915.
Onians, R. B., *The Origins of European Thought*, Cambridge University Press, 1951.
Saunders, E. D., *Mudra: A Study of Symbolic Gesture*, Princeton University Press, 1960.
Wolff, Charlotte, *A Psychology of Gesture*, Methuen, London, 1945.

GROUP THOUGHT

The psychic power unitedly engendered by a number of people mentally and emotionally bound in a common purpose. Avicenna (d. 1037) stated that when several persons meet together in a sacred place they powerfully move to sympathy the forces of the supernatural spheres by their common devotion. Men and women bound in such communion are said to form a psychic group-field and create forces that work on the physical situation and bring about spiritual and material changes in the environment.

It is further believed that the thoughts of families, tribes, nations, all generate their own collective group energy, forming a gestalt, an organized configuration, sustained by their beliefs and traditions and coloured by their sentiments. In the case of national units with their own type of culture and religion, this thought-form finds expression in the typically national trends as revealed in their religion, philosophy, literature, art, music and architecture.

Religious sentiments are strongly individualistic, and the thoughts engendered by different religious groups have their own characteristic forms. In this view, the Hindu temple and the Moslem mosque represent inevitable patterns created by the impulses arising from the beliefs and practices rooted in their respective faiths. Occultists say that during a church service performed with ritualistic solemnity, a gigantic thought-form is gradually built up, swelling up from below like an iridescent phantom cathedral that can be seen by sensitives.

An understanding of the genesis of group thought and a knowledge of how to utilize the power created by collective concentration has been claimed by many occult groups. In western witchcraft the members of a coven assemble in a circle, each concentrating on a matter of mutual interest, and by the magnetism of their collective thought-force build up a 'cone of power', a cone-shaped charged field which rises above the circle, and which is then directed towards a specific purpose. English witches like to claim that by such a massive concentration of will, in combination with other rituals, their ancestors destroyed the Spanish Armada in 1588. When news of the approaching Spanish ships reached England the covens met and conjured up the devastating northwesterly gale that crippled the enemy fleet. By a similar group effort they again prevented the country's invasion after Napoleon had made vast preparations for an attack on England in 1803.

In May 1940 over four hundred Hampshire witches, having prepared themselves by fasting, congregated in the New Forest to prevent yet another invasion, this time by Adolf Hitler. To create the necessary whirlpool of power they divested themselves of their clothes and performed their rites while some of their number scourged themselves, with the result, we are told, that a dense fog arose that obscured the English channel. At the same time a powerful negative idea was projected into Hitler's mind, and the German invasion (Operation Sea Lion) was called off. It is said that the rite also called for a human victim; an aged member who volunteered deliberately neglected to apply the usual protective coating of grease to his body on that freezing night, and was dead within a fortnight.

American witches perform similar rites. On Lammas Day (1 August) 1971, several covens in California joined in an attempt to bring the Vietnam war to an end, in order that certain members among them might not be drafted. The subsequent withdrawal of the US forces from Vietnam was cited as proof of their success.

A somewhat different attempt was made in 1938 by Heinrich Himmler, the Gestapo chief, who faked charges against General von Fritsch whom the

Nazis wanted out of the way. During the trial Himmler, a believer in the power of magical and group concentration, assembled twelve (the number of a coven) SS officers in a room near the courthouse, made them sit in a circle and concentrate on the proceedings so as to achieve the outcome desired. As it happened von Fritsch was cleared in spite of their efforts (Cavendish, 1967, p. 272).

The alleged visible and invisible manifestations of group thought are explained by occultists as a mass projection of forces from the combined unconscious of those participating, the success depending on their powers of concentration, their unity of purpose and their faith.

Books

Burland, C. A., *The Magical Arts*, Barker, London, 1966.
Cavendish, Richard, *The Black Arts*, Routledge & Kegan Paul, London, 1967.
Freud, Sigmund, *Group Psychology and the Analysis of the Ego*, Hogarth Press, London, 1959.
Gardner, G. B., *Witchcraft Today*, Rider, London, 1954.
King, Francis, *Ritual Magic in England*, Neville Spearman, London, 1970.
McDougall, William, *The Group Mind*, Cambridge University Press, 1927.

HAIR

Hair is regarded in occultism as one of the most extraordinary parts of the body. It belongs to the element of earth as it is solid and tangible; to the element of water since it is free and flowing; to the element of fire since it is fed from the furnace of the brain; and to the element of air since it is light and can be blown by the wind. It is animal since other animals also have hair; it is characteristically human since no animal has hair quite like a man's; it is vegetable since it is parasitic like a plant. Hair is both living, since it grows, and dead since it is without sensibility. As such it constitutes a link between this world and the next. It has its own life, grows more rapidly than anything else, and continues to grow after the death of the body.

Hair is a source of vital strength and magic power, for the life principle resides in it. It forms a crown encircling the head, the most sacred part of the body and is full of personal mana. It plays a role in all forms of the head-taboo. It was a substitute for the whole body, and its sacrifice to the deities was an acceptable surrogate for a human victim. In Byblos in Phoenicia women had the alternative of sacrificing their virginity to strangers in honour of the goddess Ashtart, or shaving the head and offering her their hair.

Youths dedicated to the service of the deities also cut off their hair, thus giving rise to the custom of tonsure, or shaving a priest's head, which was believed to have originated in Egypt. The hairless or tonsured head was said to represent emasculation (which was demanded in many shrines dedicated to the Great Goddess); or was a symbol of the circumcised phallus; or of the solar disc; or of innocence and purity. The Mosaic law enacted against tonsure (Lev. 21:5), but the Church allowed the practice for certain monastic communities. Often associated with the tonsure was the scalp-lock, a strand of hair left uncut, like a pigtail. Some think it was left to mark the bregma, the occult aperture at the top of the cranium.

In certain communities a razor is never allowed to touch a man's head. Young men of the Jewish sect of the Nazarites were dedicated by their parents to God for a certain number of years, and during this period their hair was never cut. The child Samuel was probably a Nazarite, and so was Samson. Many sects in India, notably the Sikhs, prohibit men from ever cutting their hair.

Among warrior nations of the Mediterranean world, long hair was regarded as a disadvantage as it provided a handle for an opponent in battle. So short hair eventually became a symbol of manliness. St Paul said, 'If a man have long hair it is a shame unto him' (1 Cor. 11:14). In most places in Europe long hair came to be regarded as a sign of degeneracy and immorality. Oliver Cromwell (d. 1658) made the close-cropped skull of the Roundheads a feature of puritanism, in contrast to the Cavaliers of the king's party, in whose shoulder-length ringlets every vice was believed to be lurking.

Because of the power inherent in hair, great precautions were taken in primitive societies in the selection of a barber, in appointing an auspicious time for cutting, and in the disposal of the remains. Special days were set apart for the purpose and spells and incantations recited. Because hair could be used for many magical operations directed against the owner, care had to be taken that it should not fall into the hands of sorcerers. The cut hair was therefore buried in a secret place. Tribal peoples would sometimes release their prisoners of war only after shaving off their hair, which was kept as a 'hostage', so that if they gave trouble, punishment could be inflicted on the hair and the owner thus made to suffer.

The hair of women differs from that of men and was supposed to have great attractive power over men and nature. It was a temptation to the male and women were enjoined to attend church with their hair covered so as not to distract the men of the congregation. Witches knew the power that lay in their hair, and tossed their loosened tresses in ritual dances as a love charm, or bent down and shook their hair while uttering a curse. In many places in Europe the bride used to go to her wedding with her hair hanging freely down, but after the ceremony it was either cut a little, to signify the curtailment of her power and independence, or was bound up to symbolize her new responsibility. Letting one's hair down still implies behaving in a free and unrestrained manner.

The reason why hair grows on one part of the body and not another, and why growth in one region does not encroach on adjacent areas, is a mystery. The quality of hair in different parts of a person's body varies considerably. The hair of the eyebrows differs from that of the lashes; of the head from that of the pubes. There is a connection between the eyebrows and the pubic hair, the thickness, colour, and texture of the eyebrows giving a good indication of the hair on the pubes. A sonnet to a lady's 'eyebrow' was a euphemism for a verse dedicated to a woman's sexual charms. Chivalric knights of the Middle Ages dedicated to Courtly Love wore the pubic hair of their mistress in their hats as a token of service to them.

Character reading from the hair is known as trichosomancy, with special significance attached to the areas where baldness spreads in men. The natural waves and whorls, the direction of the growth, the cow's licks, are read for signs. Horripilation, commonly called goose-flesh, is believed to be the body's instinctive reaction in situations of ague, itching, sexual desire, fright and various mystic states. If a person suddenly gets goose-pimples without apparent cause it means that he is passing over a spot where something very grave will happen to him or to a loved one, at some time in the future.

Books

Berg, Charles, *The Unconscious Significance of Hair*, Allen & Unwin, London, 1951.

Mackay, Charles, 'Influence of Politics and Religion on the Hair and Beard', in *Extraordinary Popular Delusions*, London, 1856.

Myres, J. L., *Anthropology and the Classics*, Oxford University Press, London, 1908.

HAND

Hand, called by Aristotle 'the organ of organs', is the active agent of the human system. With the sensitive antennae of the fingers, the hand is responsible for man's evolution from the near-animal to the civilized state.

The medieval philosophers liked to point out that the hand and the 'unruly member' (the phallus) were the only two parts of the body that acted independently. But only the hand, 'man's other self', acted intelligently. No other part of the human body is so intimately associated with human behaviour. With his hands man works, defends himself, reveals his feelings, creates his works of art and builds his civilization.

The hand is virtually the principal instrument of man's cerebral system, what Immanuel Kant (d. 1804) called 'the visible part of the brain'. It seems that the brain cannot think without the hand becoming involved. All strong emotions are reflected in imperceptible ideodynamic movements of the hand. More nerves run from the brain to the hand, especially the fingertips, than to any other part of the body. One of the first places in which sweat appears in stress and anxiety states is on the palms of the hands. This psychogalvanic response, as it is called, is used extensively in lie-detector tests, which measure the electrical resistance of the skin.

The fingertips are equipped with an incredibly delicate sensory apparatus, each tip containing several million nerve cells. On its surface are ridges called rugae, dotted with tiny pores. The rugae develop in the foetus by about the eighteenth week of pregnancy and remain without undergoing any change until the skin disintegrates after death, unlike the larger crease lines of the palm, which are constantly changing. Accidents may obliterate them or they may be removed by some deliberate process like sandpapering, but if the skin recovers, the original pattern returns exactly as before.

The tracery of these papillary ridges seems to have intrigued mankind from earliest times, and some students have suggested that the curious labyrinthine carvings, found in certain ancient burial passages of neolithic tombs, may have been copied from the fingerprint patterns of the personage buried there, to be preserved as a kind of magical identification. Others think that the vortices of concentric lines may bear some relationship to the convolutions of the brain.

When the fingertips of the two hands are placed together, a circuit is set up with the brain that is believed to assist thought. People in deep thought will often talk with their fingertips pressed together, as if unconsciously aware of the need to establish such a current to assist their concentration. If a man wishes to recall something he has forgotten, his hand will instinctively touch his forehead to contact with his fingers the source of his thinking.

The hands of certain people are believed to send out powerful radiant and healing waves. This is found in the laying on of hands to transmit blessing or grace, and the therapeutic practice of touch-healing. In ancient Greece those who healed with their hands were known as *cheirourgos*, 'hand-workers', from which comes the English word surgeon. The Jews said that the hands of holy men at prayer gave out a radiance, and the early Christians believed that saints could send forth a flame from their fingertips. Modern high-frequency photography seems to confirm that the hands do send out strong bio-luminescent rays, and the fingertips of those who are natural healers emit them with greater force (*see* bioflux).

The *thumb* is the king of the palmar kingdom. According to anthropologists, the development of the thumb marked an important step forward in the anatomical and cultural evolution of the human race. In Chinese palmistry the thumb is considered so important, that often the whole character, state of health and future are read from the thumb alone. In the classical world the thumb was regarded as sacred to Venus and in hand-gestures it still has a phallic significance.

A large thumb denotes strength of character, practicality; a small thumb weakness and lack of force. The first phalange (top segment) shows will, decision, ability to command; the second (middle) phalange shows logic, judgment, reason. The third phalange, the 'ball of the thumb', called the Mount of Venus, shows love, sympathy and passion. Hiding the thumb in the closed fist is a defensive, introverted, disturbed gesture, of one seeking protection or feeling persecuted.

The other *fingers* of the hand also come in for detailed interpretation in palmistry and symptomatology. Long, slender fingers show a slow-moving, painstaking, detail-loving person. When very long, a cowardly, cold-blooded and servile individual. Where there is an exceptionally long bone-growth and extraordinary flexibility we have the condition known as arachnodactyly, 'spider-fingers', also known as the Marfan syndrome after the French paediatrician, Antonin Marfan (d. 1896), which is a sign of heart disease, paralysis or tuberculosis. Short fingers show the quick and alert person, impatient, forthright, blunt. Smooth fingers indicate the artist, and knotty joints the philosopher.

Clubbed fingertips indicate aggression, jealousy and violence, with a tendency to heart-disease. Spatulate tips show the practical and realistic person. Square tips: love of routine, system, regularity. Conic (tapering): impulsiveness, intuition, idealism, love of art.

The *index finger* or forefinger was regarded as the venomous finger and, in contrast to the ring finger, was never used in healing. A wound touched with the index finger would take long to get well. The index is the finger of Jupiter and is believed to relate to the conscious ego, and the manner in which a person presents himself and adapts himself to the world.

The *middle finger*, also called the medius, the digitus impudicus, digitus obscenus, or digitus infamis (immodest, obscene, disreputable), or the fool's finger. It is dedicated to Saturn and is usually the only finger that is kept unringed. The extended middle finger, like the thumb, represents the phallus. In palmistry the finger of Saturn indicates the degree of balance between the conscious and unconscious aspects of a person's life.

The *ring finger*, also called the leech (doctor's) finger, the digitus medicus, or physician's finger. It is the healing finger, and when stroked over a wound is believed to heal it. Medieval apothecaries used to mix their medicaments and potions with this finger. All ointments should be rubbed on with the ring finger, never the forefinger. In the Samothracian mysteries, which were celebrated in ancient times in scattered centres in the Aegean Sea, the ring finger was enclosed in a finger-stall of magnetic iron, and this 'idaeic' finger (named after Mount Ida in Crete) was used in healing ceremonies. Even today rings are mostly worn on this finger, especially of the left hand, and it is called the annular, or ring-bearing finger. In palmistry it is the finger of Apollo and is related to the emotions and the arts.

The *little finger*, also called the auricular or ear finger, not because one can conveniently clean one's ears with it, but because it indicates one's capacity for 'hearing' or inspiration. The British Druids used to stop their ears with it as an aid to prophecy. Contact of the tip of the little finger with the ear-hole was believed to assist psychic vision. At seances the sitters in the circle touch with their little fingers, the little fingers of those beside them, thus forming a psychic link. The little finger is directly related to parental relationships and sex. It indicates the unconscious ego. It is the finger of Mercury and is related to oratory, law and business.

In popular superstition the possession of extra fingers, known as *polydactylism*, was a sign of great good or great evil. Persons with a sixth finger in the right hand are born to be lucky. Those with a sixth finger in the left hand will have misfortune, like Anne Boleyn (d. 1536), second wife of Henry VIII, who was executed. Those with six fingers on both hands, like the Philistine giant Gath mentioned in the Bible (1 Chr. 20:6), will make their name for good or ill in some spectacular way.

The study of hand gestures is known as *cheironomy* (Gk. *cheir*, 'hand', *nomos*, 'rule'), which covers both ritual and spontaneous movements. The graceful flowing movements of the hands show a person at ease, and possessing taste and refinement. When this trait is exaggerated and the gestures become stylized and artificial, we have the effeminate and 'arty' type. In the same way one can distinguish the unruffled hands of the poised and dignified individual; the masterful hands of the strong personality; the aggressive hands which are known by their abrupt and violent movements; and the materialistic hands which hang down, heavy and stolid.

The man with a fidgety mind does not know where to put his hands; he toys with a handkerchief, button, cigarette, or drums on the table, revealing the nervous temperament of one who lacks assurance. The person who constantly rubs his hands together betrays an ingratiating, hypocritical, unctuous character. Limp hands show lack of fixity of purpose. Hidden palms with fingers closed or almost closed over them betray the secretive, miserly and cautious person. Where a man constantly tries to hide his hands by putting them in his pockets, he shows that his deeds and thoughts do not bear close inspection. The man who hides his hands behind his back is cautious, or endeavouring to restrain himself from saying what he would like to, out of a sense of politeness.

More specifically, cheironomy relates to the gestures of occult symbolism and religious ritual, when the hands are arranged in certain stylized *manusigns* (Lat. *manus*, 'hand') or hand-signs. Here each gesture, by virtue of its symbolic significance, is believed to contain a particular potency. The ancient Egyptians attached great importance to ritual gestures, especially those of the pharaoh who was a god incarnate. For this reason when he was depicted in sculpture or painting without a clearly defined gesture, he was usually shown in a pose of immobility so as not to draw down harmful forces that might result from a manusign incorrectly rendered.

The Greek cheironome, 'hand-position', was known in Hindu and Buddhist ritual as a *mudra* (Sanskrit, 'seal'), and played a major part in religion, ritualism, mime-drama and the dance. There was a highly elaborate code of stylized gestures, several hundred in number, but all variations on four basic hand positions, namely: the open palm, the hollowed palm, the hand with the finger-tips together and the closed fist. One or both hands were brought into play in their symbolism.

The western world too has its heritage of symbolical cheironomes. One of the earliest was the horn sign, made by doubling the thumb, folding the ring and middle fingers over it, and raising the first and little fingers to make horns. In the V-sign the index and middle fingers are raised, which again originally symbolized, horns, sometimes said to be the horns of Satan. What is called the phallic thumb is a priapic sign, made by thrusting the thumb between the first and second fingers of the closed hand. The upraised thumb, signifying the upraised phallus, was a symbol of life, success, prosperity. The down-pointing thumb was a sign of defeat, the veto sign that condemned gladiators to death.

In certain countries, a closed hand with the first finger alone outstretched, is regarded as a sure protection against the evil eye. Crossing the middle finger over the forefinger was a symbol of coition. According to an old superstition the act of coition is lucky, and brings good fortune, hence the use of phallic and coital amulets for good luck. Keeping the fingers crossed is therefore keeping at coition during the performance of an enterprise whose outcome is uncertain. A circle formed by thumb and forefinger, with the other fingers raised and slightly bent, is a symbol of the vulva, and means that all is going well.

The phallic medius is the upraised middle finger, with thumb and the other fingers doubled up, representing the erect virile member, the bent fingers on either side being the testicles. Reproductions of this cheironome made in metal, bone or other substance were very popular amulets in the ancient world and were widely used in Greece and Rome. An extended middle finger denotes unnatural vice or homosexuality, and making this sign at someone signifies, 'Go fornicate with yourself', or 'Stick it up your arse'. It is vulgarly referred to as the 'up yours' gesture.

Books

Bell, Sir Charles, *The Hand, its Mechanism and Vital Endowments*, Wm Pickering, London, 1833.
Berry, T. J., *The Hand as a Mirror of Systemic Disease*, Davis, Philadelphia, 1964.
Cummins, H. and Midlo, C., *Finger-prints, Palms and Soles*, Philadelphia, 1943.
Hutchinson, Beryl, *A Handbook on Hands*, Rider, London, 1953.
Nurnburg, Walter, *Hands at Mass*, Chapman & Hall, London, 1951.
Révész, G., *The Human Hand: A Psychological Study*, Routledge & Kegan Paul, London, 1958.
Saunders, E. D., *Mudra: A Study of Symbolic Gesture*, Princeton University Press, 1960.
Sorell, Walter, *The Story of the Human Hand*, Weidenfeld & Nicolson, London, 1968.
Wolff, Charlotte, *The Human Hand*, Methuen, London, 1942.

HARMONIC PROPORTIONS

Harmonic proportions, divinely designed, are said to be enshrined in the human figure, and their exposition has been of great interest to artists and thinkers from very early times. Basically all canons of proportion in art and architecture are established on elaborations of the golden section, the relationship of the part to the whole. The rule of the golden section is applied to the unequal division of a line so that the lesser part is to the larger part, in the same proportion as the larger part is to the whole line. More intricate proportions emerge from triangles, squares, rectangles, circles and other geometrical figures.

In the occult view all relationships are best exemplified in the human being, who as a microcosm represents the greater cosmos around him. Male and female embody two subtly different but mutually related proportions that form the basis of all configurations in heaven and earth.

In the course of centuries, from the time the canons were first sought and established, there have been numerous schools of thought on the subject. Although there is an underlying unity in the harmonic proportions as set out by various civilizations, there are also slight deviations in each norm which are determined by race and the period of history at which the norms were fixed.

The ancient Egyptians took the length of the middle finger as the measure. The body was nineteen times as long as this finger. Certain Egyptian monuments and buildings are believed to be based on human proportions set out by the priests from a study of occult physiogeometry. The temple of Luxor for instance, built by Amenhotep III (c. 1500 BC), is to the scale of an idealized man.

The Greeks worked out their own canon, which they regarded as absolute. Both Phidias (d. 432 BC) and his contemporary Polyclitus believed that there was only one perfect and correct proportion of the parts of the human body. But later Greek sculptors had their own norms, notably Praxitiles (fl. 365 BC) whose wonderful Aphrodite was measured again and again for centuries to yield the secrets that underlay the perfect harmony of the female form.

The Roman architect, Vitruvius (c. 15 BC), in his book on architecture, set out a wider system relating the proportions of man to the universe, and observed that the best design for temples was that based on the symmetry of the human form. He stated that a man's body with arms and legs fully extended fits both into a square and a circle, an axiom that was repeatedly quoted by later writers.

Renaissance artists, notably Leonardo da Vinci (d. 1519), revived the classical norms and illustrated these ancient ideas in their drawings. Leonardo wrote:

> If a man has his hands and feet extended and a pair of compasses centred at his navel, the fingers and toes of his two hands and feet will touch the circumference described therefrom. And just as the human body yields a circular outline, so too a square figure may be formed from it. For if we measure the distance from the soles of the feet to the top of the head, and then apply the measure to the outstretched arms, the breadth will be found to be the same as the height.

Ideally, the span of a man's outstretched arms is equal to his height. Ten times the length of his face, eight times the length of his head, or six times the length of his foot, also equals his height. The distance from the wrist to the tip of the middle finger equals the distance from the edge of the hairline on the forehead to the point of the chin. In other words the length of the palm equals that of the face. From the chin to the nose-tip is a third part of the face, and the same from the nostrils to the eyebrows, and again from the eyebrows to the hairline.

The distance between a woman's breasts is half that between the breasts and navel (this was a Gothic norm). The two breasts and navel form an equilateral triangle. The distance between the breast line and navel is the same as the distance between navel and crotch.

In Hindu iconography the face-length proportions were regarded as characteristic for different beings, and these were followed in their sculpture. The body of the gods was eleven times the length of the face; that of goddesses nine times; men eight times; women seven times; goblins four times; rats twice; ogres had bodies exactly as long as their huge faces (Walker, 1968, p. 199).

In the study of human proportions as laid down in esoteric anatomy, the relationship of the various parts of the body determines the character and destiny of children, youths, men and women. Proportions are studied in intricate detail, with reference to the distances between the crown of the head and the forehead, the ears, eyes, nose, chin, the hollow of the neck, the line of the nipples, the navel, sexual organs, buttocks, hips, anus, the line behind the knees, the ankles and toes.

Books

Birkhoff, G. D., *Aesthetic Measure*, Harvard University Press, 1933.
Borissavlievitch, M., *The Golden Number*, Alec Tiranti, London, 1958.
Ghyka, M., *The Geometry of Art and Life*, Sheed & Ward, New York, 1946.
Hambidge, Jay, *The Elements of Dynamic Symmetry*, Dover, New York, 1967.
Harré, Rom, *The Anticipation of Nature*, Harrison, London, 1965.
Scholfield, P. H., *Theory of Proportion in Architecture*, London, 1958.
Schwaller de Lubicz, R. A., *Le Temple de l'Homme*, 3 vols, Caractères, Paris, 1958.
Stirling, William, *The Canon: An Exposition of the Pagan Mystery Perpetuated in the Cabala as the Rule of All the Arts*, London, 1897.
Vitruvius, *The Ten Books of Architecture*, Cambridge, Mass., 1914.
Walker, Benjamin, *Hindu World: An Encyclopedic Outline of Hinduism*, vol. I, Allen & Unwin, London, 1968.
Wittkower, Rudolf, *Architectural Principles in the Age of Humanism*, Warburg Institute, London, 1949.
Zeising, Adolphe, *Der goldene Schnitt*, Leipzig, 1884.

HEAD

The capital of the kingdom that constitutes the physical organism, the king in the capital, the crown of the king. The head is the seat of the chief sensory organs, the centre of intelligence, the source of thought, the habitation of the spirit. It holds the brain, bregma, ventricles and the occult ros. In art it is sometimes shown surrounded by a halo. The sacrosanctity of the head accounts for the importance attached to the head-dress, the skull, head-hunting, the scalp-lock and the hair.

In primitive societies the head is believed to contain the protective spirit of man and is very sensitive to injury or disrespect. After the death of important personages the head was treated with special care because of the mana believed to reside in it, and it was often regarded as a talismanic object and revered as a relic. Sometimes the head was dried and preserved, but sometimes the skull alone was given homage. In many tribal communities the skulls of chieftains and revered ancestors were inlaid with mosaic of coloured stones, or beautifully painted, and set up in the temple or household shrine and worshipped. Even in western countries skulls were preserved in private houses because supernatural powers were attributed to them.

Situated in the skull is the bregma or fontanel, the meeting point of three major bones at the top of the head. In the foetus and young infants the bregma is open, since the bones are not quite joined, and the area is soft to the touch. The sutures usually unite before the end of the second year. The bregma is regarded as the point of entry and exit of the soul. What the Hindus call the aperture of Brahma corresponds to the bregma, which is the site of the most important of the occult plexuses, the sahasrara. Tibetans reputedly practise a form of yoga in the course of which the bregma opens spontaneously and this provides a means of spiritual enlightenment.

A great many occult phenomena are connected with the bregma. It is an area of consciousness, a centre of meditation, a focal point for the divine light to enter the soul, a place through which the invisible world may be made visible.

The occult practice of the headstand directs the flow of vital fluids towards the bregma and helps the absorption of the ros*, or heavenly dew, which is received through it. There are several ways of doing the headstand, but all of them involve nothing more than just reversing the natural order of the normal erect stance, and standing on the head. The headstand changes the direction of certain secret rivers and tributaries of the subtle body so that they move towards the hidden caverns and reservoirs of the head. In esoteric parlance, the conjoined fluids flow towards the nuptial chambers of the brain, and here a union is enacted between the lower and upper potencies, when the fluidic energies are 'set on fire', and a state of bliss and illumination supervenes.

The study of phrenology is based on the alleged location of the mental faculties in definite areas of the human brain, and purports to find a relation between these areas and the intellectual, emotional and moral aptitudes and capabilities. When the section of the brain governing a certain faculty is well developed it is thought to press upon the skull and cause a bump on the surface that can be felt by pressure.

In phrenology the brain is divided into five broad zones, which are further demarcated into thirty or forty 'organs' or bumps, each governing a particular faculty. These are distributed as follows. (1) The domestic or social zone, located at the back of the head, starting from the part just above the neck and going upward to just below the crown. The organs in this region govern amativeness or sex desire; philoprogenitiveness or love of offspring; habitativeness or love of home; friendship and sociability. (2) The selfish or animal zone, located on both sides of the head. Starting from behind the ears and working around the ears to the temples we have the organs governing alimentiveness, leading to greed and drunkenness when well developed; combativeness; destructiveness. (3) The prudential or aspiring zone, forming a band from ear to ear (but excluding the selfish zone), over the crown of the head, and containing the organs of acquisitiveness, secretiveness, circumspection, self-esteem, approbativeness, conscientiousness. (4) The moral zone at the top of the head, from the crown forward to the hair line. It governs hope, spirituality, veneration, benevolence, idealism, sublimity. (5) The intellectual zone, in the front, including the forehead, the temples and the area around the eyes.

Books

Blofeld, John, *The Way of Power*, Allen & Unwin, London, 1970.
Coates, J., *Phrenology: How to Read Heads*, Foulsham, London, 1920.
Ferrier, David, *Cerebral Localisation*, London, 1886.
Hedderly, Frances, *Phrenology: A Study of Mind*, L. N. Fowler, London, 1970.
Onians, R. B., *The Origins of European Thought*, Cambridge University Press, 1951.

Rele, V. C., *Asanas for Health and Vigour,* Bombay, n.d.
Walker, Benjamin, *Beyond the Body,* Routledge & Kegan Paul, London, 1974.

HEART

The central muscle of the physiological system, the heart holds the supreme place among the organs of the body as the symbol of our being, and the seat of our thoughts and emotions, of love, courage and the conscience. Physically, its ceaseless operation is the nearest thing we have to perpetual motion. For no accountable reason it beats, a tiny node of specialized tissue within it acting as a pacemaker, regulating its throb and causing it to alternate between dilation (diastole) and contraction (systole) sixty to eighty times a minute. This beat is closely connected with breathing and is responsible for the pulse beat. During the lifetime of the average man of sixty-five, it beats 2,600 million times.

Great importance was given to the *ab* or heart in ancient Egypt. It was regarded as prompting, guiding and planning. It was the abode of the soul, enabling man to distinguish good from evil. During the process of embalming, the heart was not always extracted from the body, but if it were, it was placed in a jar under the protection of the god Tuamutef. In the *Book of the Dead* six chapters are devoted to formulae for protecting the heart and restoring it to the deceased in the after-life. It was his heart that was weighed in the balance in the judgment hall of Osiris to decide his ultimate destiny.

According to the Greeks the physical principle or 'life' of the body resided in the blood, which was stored in the liver, and distributed through the veins; while the psychic principle resided in the pneuma or breath which was stored in the brain and distributed through the arteries. Both these systems met in the heart. Aristotle regarded the heart and not the brain as the thinking or control centre of the body. He also spoke of certain very fine thread-like tendons that went from the heart to all the larger tendons of the body as in a marionette. Hence the notion of one's 'heart-strings' being tugged.

The heart was popularly held to be the abode of the divine principle. The Hindu philosopher, Shankara (d. AD 838), in his commentary on one of the Upanishads says that the god should be meditated on 'in the form of a light of the size of the thumb situated in the cavity of the heart'. Paracelsus (d. 1541) also describes the Dweller in the heart, as a 'bluish flamelike body' the size of the last joint of the thumb. This was the central heating principle of the body.

William Harvey (d. 1657) was the first to discover and establish the circulatory system and to demonstrate that the heart acted like a pump. His contemporary, René Descartes (d. 1650), entered into personal disagreement with Harvey on the subject maintaining that the heart was a heater or furnace and not a pump. Sir Kenelm Digby (d. 1665), member of the Royal Society, also subscribed to the latter theory of the heart as a furnace or cauldron in which the blood was heated and spiritualized.

But apart from its physiological functions, whether as heater or pump, a great deal more has been ascribed to the heart. Some authorities feel that it is our heartbeat that has contributed to the development of our consciousness of rhythmic intervals and our appreciation of repetitive sounds, like handclapping and drumming, and of measure of time and space. The appeal of rhythm is universal, perhaps arising from the steady heartbeat of the mother which calms the infant in the womb.

Furthermore, the location of the heart on one side of the body may have fostered a natural tendency to move more towards one side when walking. Apes lurch vaguely to one side more than the other as they walk. When a person is lost in the desert he tends to walk not in a straight line but in a wide circle, which may be either clockwise or anticlockwise. Most people tend to turn to the right, perhaps in order to counteract the weight of the heart on the left side. This lop-sidedness, it is suggested, may have guided the evolution of movement in a circular direction, for example, ring dances. Children love to whirl and rotate.

Some experts attribute laterality or one-sidedness in men to this fact that the heart is on one side of the body and not in the middle. Still others suggest that because the heart gives one a sense of the pulsating life within, and a sense of 'interiorness', it may have been the origin of introspection and philosophical speculation.

Books

Budge, E. A. Wallis, *The Mummy*, 2nd edn, Cambridge University Press, 1925.
Hackett, Earle, *Blood: The Paramount Humour*, Jonathan Cape, London, 1973.
Hartshorne, M., *Enshrined Hearts of Warriors and Illustrious People*, London, 1875.
Pianhoff, A., *Le 'Coeur' dans les textes égyptiennes*, Paris, 1930.
Willius, F. A. and Dry, T. J., *A History of the Heart and Circulation*, Saunders, Philadelphia and London, 1948.

HETEROSEXUALITY

The state of sexual attraction towards a person of the opposite sex is socially approved as the right kind of relationship, other states being regarded as abnormal or perverse. Psychologists today believe that during puberty and adolescence an inclination towards heterosexuality is not necessarily the predominant feeling. Sometimes homosexuality or other 'abnormalities' persist beyond adolescence, and this too is not considered unusual. The tendency is therefore to speak not of homosexuals but of individuals who have a preference for such satisfaction. All men and women latently possess both instincts, homosexual and heterosexual, and the functioning of certain glands, or social circumstances, brings one or other to the fore.

But heterosexuality is bound up with the human organism in a way that homosexuality is not. Men and women represent different variations of energy, and when they come together sexually can attain a high degree of spiritual illumination not possible with an 'equal' partner. Occultists believe that the positive male force can be the stimulator and the negative female force the dormant potential, in a partnership of polarity for setting up a circuit and starting the flow of forces generated by their encounter.

In heterosexual sex magic the vital current has a characteristic type of power. But continued heterosexuality becomes devitalizing, and the currents interflowing through the partners become weaker and are soon neutralized of their electrical and magnetic potentials. That is why conjugality, or husband and wife relationship, while necessary for the continuance of the race, is self-defeating in terms of recharging one's vitality.

Aleister Crowley (d. 1947), who practised all forms of sexuality, said that the use of a woman in sex magic 'is more dangerous to the career of the magician', and for those engaged in such rites women are a deep and dangerous pit. They have a powerful sexergy and a vampire-like faculty of drawing up strength from men, which is physically manifested during invagination.

Oriental systems of sex magic are also aware of the slow equalization and consequent attenuation of power that results from continued intercourse with a single partner. They therefore advocated the use of a succession of women, so that from each partner the magician could draw a high quantum of energy, before their mutual potentials had a chance of being rendered impotent.

Books

Charles, Edward, *An Introduction to the Study of the Psychology, Physiology and Biochemistry of the Sexual Impulse,* Boriswood, London, 1935.
Gulik, R. H. van, *Sexual Life in Ancient China,* Brill, Leiden, 1961.
Stoller, Robert, *Sex and Gender,* Hogarth, London, 1968.
Symonds, John, *The Great Beast: The Life of Aleister Crowley,* Macdonald, London, 1971.
Walker, Benjamin, *Hindu World,* Allen & Unwin, London, 1968.

HUMAN TYPES

Human types are based on the variations in physical appearance, mental faculties, temperament, character and personality in general, as found in both men and women. Tabulations based on sex and age are excluded from such a scheme. Thus, it is commonly believed that body build is related to a certain kind of behaviour; that the fat man is jovial, the thin man a recluse, and each has his characteristic pattern of conduct. In spite of the many objections that might be raised to this kind of classification, it has a long tradition in history, and the idea of *somatotypes,* 'body types', continues to be propounded by psychologists today.

Ethologists who study animal and human behaviour point out that human nature is not infinitely adaptable, since each person inherits a number of genetically determined tendencies. These together with his own adjustment to his environment make up his personality. There are therefore obvious limitations to the number of possible types into which human beings may be categorized.

In the past a rough and ready scheme of classification was by *race,* colour of skin, hair, eyes and so on, on the basis of which certain broad characteristics were attributed to the various ethnic groups. Some degree of scientific justification can be found for such a scheme, arising from the undoubted influences of climate, topography, diet and cosmobiological factors. Earlier classification by *caste* or class was perhaps originally based on race, and came in the wake of conquest, and later on occupation, further confirmed by hereditary privilege. The main castes of antiquity were arranged somewhat in this order: (1) rulers, chieftains, kings; (2) philosophers, mystics, sages; (3) warriors, generals, soldiers; (4) merchants, including tradesmen and farmers; and (5) serfs, who worked in all occupations in a servile capacity.

Another typology is based on the *mental* faculties, so that men are divided into: (1) thinkers, or those with the intellectual qualities predominating, such as philosophers, priests, mathematicians; they are usually tall and slender and have triangular faces; (2) willers, or doers, men of action, with the motor or active qualities predominating, such as warriors, athletes, merchants; they are heavily built and have square faces; (3) feelers, or those in whom the pathemic* or emotional qualities are highly developed, such as artists, poets, musicians and prophets; they are small and slender and have long faces.

A popular classification is based on the *astrological* correspondences between the twelve signs of the zodiac and the people born under these signs. Each sign governs those born roughly between the 21st of one month and the 20th of the next month. Thus: (1) Aries (March-April) are assertive and enterprising; (2) Taurus (April-May) plodding and conservative; (3) Gemini (May-June) inconsistent and restless; (4) Cancer (June-July) reserved and loyal; (5) Leo (July-August) self-assured and courageous; (6) Virgo (August-September) conventional and pedantic; (7) Libra (September-October) romantic and easy going; (8) Scorpio (October-November) secretive and intense; (9) Sagittarius (November-December) freedom-loving and tactless; (10) Capricorn (December-January), disciplined and cautious; (11) Aquarius (January-February) intuitive and idealistic; (12) Pisces (February-March) indecisive and gullible.

Palmistry distinguishes seven types, named after the seven 'planets', and determined by the shape and development of the finger* related to the particular planet, or the corresponding mount (the small pad of flesh) beneath the finger or elsewhere on the palm. Broadly speaking: (1) Apollo or Sun (ring finger) types are versatile and lucky; (2) Moon (lower outside edge of palm) imaginative and inconstant; (3) Mars (across middle of palm) reckless and outspoken; (4) Mercury (little finger) practical and articulate; (5) Jupiter (forefinger) ambitious and dignified; (6) Venus (ball of thumb) amoral and frivolous; and (7) Saturn (middle finger) taciturn and avaricious.

Religious motivation and the approach to religious dogma, and an individual's inclination to a particular way of finding spiritual satisfaction or expressing the religious instinct, lead to a further grouping under three headings, namely, those who seek the way of (1) knowledge, a theoretical and intellectual approach, which is that of the scribes, rabbis and pandits; (2) works, such as acts of charity, the observance of religious and social duties, active help to one's neighbour; this is illustrated in the Bible by Martha, who was busy about the house (Luke 10:40); and (3) faith and devotion, illustrated in the Bible by Mary, who sat at the feet of Jesus and heard his words (Luke 10:39).

Another very common classification of individuals is based on their general attitude to life, and to their fellows: (1) the optimist takes a cheerful view of things; and (2) the pessimist takes a dismal view. This is expressed in the couplet, 'Two men looked through the prison bars, One saw the mud the other the stars.'

Many divinatory procedures and methods of 'fortune telling' are also devoted to the classification of human types, depending on an individual's gestures and movements, manner of speaking, outward behaviour. For instance physiognomy studies the face, and phrenology the cranium. In earlier times the nature and quantity of the internal humours* formed the basis for a system of medical diagnosis. Something on similar lines has been evolved in our own time by certain healers who determine the endocrine* class to which a person belongs, on the presumed connection between the glandular secretions and the temperament.

Types are further distinguished by the natural predisposition of persons to certain diseases. Four main classes are named: (1) the colitic, who tends to suffer from ulcerative colitis, gastric and bilious troubles; he is nervous, emotionally immature, anxious, fearful, dependent on others, narcissistic; (2) the coronary, suffering from heart disease; he has a respect for authority, is a hard worker and a meticulous observer of rules and rituals; (3) the consumptive, emotionally tense, strongly sexed, artistic; (4) the arthritic, extraverted and optimistic, but critical and cantankerous.

A number of typological theories are also associated with individual exponents, who have sought to tabulate human temperaments under some manageable scheme. The school of the Greek physician, *Hippocrates* (d. 359 BC), spoke of two 'habits' that distinguished men, namely, (1) phthisic (Gk. *phthisis*, 'wasting') characteristic of tall thin individuals, with a tendency to phthisis or tuberculosis; and (2) apoplectic (Gk. 'struck'), characteristic of full built and heavy individuals, disposed to stroke and heart conditions.

The Roman physician, *Celsus* (fl. AD 50), who wrote on medicine and military affairs, observed that a person is normally restricted and secretive about himself, but relaxes when he is under the influence of alcohol. On the principle of *in vino veritas*, 'in wine the truth', he said that everyone when in his cups could be listed in one of three categories: (1) the aggressive type who wants to fight when he is drunk; (2) the sociable type who likes to dance and sing; and (3) the sentimental type, who usually weeps and becomes maudlin.

Hindu authorities, like the physician *Charaka* (d. AD 180), classified men into three groups according to the predominating *guna* or 'quality' they possessed, namely: (1) satvik, having the quality of satva, 'goodness'; they were of medium height and build, pure-minded and wise, like the sage; (2) rajasik, having rajas, 'passion'; they were tall, muscular, passionate, energetic, like the warrior; (3) tamasik, possessing tamas, 'darkness'; short in stature, corpulent or thick-set, dull, slow-witted, such as the tradesman or serf.

The scholastic and medieval authorities of Europe usually followed the

Hippocratic or humoral scheme of typology, and made little or no original contribution to the subject. Robert *Burton* (d. 1640), in his massive collation of ancient theories, *The Anatomy of Melancholy,* speaks of three types of melancholy, springing from (1) the head, (2) the heart and (3) the liver. The natural temperament of the individual predisposed him to his particular type of gloom. The nature, seat, causes and symptoms of each variety of melancholy in all their ramifications were learnedly traced to their sources. Burton himself had the 'hepatic melancholy', and it was long believed that he ended his life by suicide.

John *Brown* (d. 1788), physician, and founder of the Brunonian system of medicine, divided all diseases into two main classes and regarded men as fitting into these categories according to their temperament and disposition. These were (1) sthenic (Gk. *sthenos,* 'strength'), 'strong' or 'exciting' diseases, to which athletic or motoric (active) types were susceptible, and which could be cured by debilitating drugs like opium, or by bleeding; and (2) asthenic, submissive or depressive diseases, to which ascetic, usually tall, cerebral, feeling and sensitive persons were susceptible, and which could be cured by stimulants like wine and brandy. Diagnosing asthenia in himself, Dr Brown followed his own system, treated his complaint in the prescribed manner, and died from alcoholic cirrhosis.

The poet, Samuel Taylor *Coleridge* (d. 1834), made a more metaphysical dichotomy of human beings in characteristic fashion. He declared, 'There are two classes of man, beside which it is next to impossible to conceive a third. Every man is a born Aristotelian or a Platonist. The one considers reason a quality or attribute; the other considers it a power.'

The German physiologist, physician and artist, Karl Gustav *Carus* (d. 1869) of Leipzig, spoke of three types of men, namely: (1) the athletic, muscular and well-built; (2) the asthenic, slender and weak; and (3) the cerebral or intellectual. Each had a distinctive personality and could be successful and happy only if his work were in accord with his temperament.

In his *Origins of Tragedy* the German philosopher, Friedrich *Nietzsche* (d. 1900), differentiated between Apollonian and Dionysian art, a dichotomy that has been applied to the two main human types: (1) the Apollonian who is sober, moderate, orderly, conservative, mechanistic, classical; he is referable to 'space', and proficient in or appreciative of the plastic arts, and partial to opium; such were Spinoza, Locke and Hume; (2) the Dionysian who is ecstatic, exuberant, lacking in order and regularity, rebellious, romantic, vital; he is referable to 'time', and proficient in or appreciative of music, and partial to alcohol; such were Boehme and Nietzsche himself.

Francis *Galton* (d. 1911) divided people into (1) verbalizers, who think by name or sound, and (2) visualizers, who think by form, image or outline. Modern researchers have a simple experiment for determining the two categories: swing a pendulum before someone's eyes for a minute, then ask him to shut his eyes and think of the swinging pendulum; the visualizer's eyeballs will move, the verbalizer's will not.

Sir William *Osler* (d. 1919), the eminent Canadian physician, also placed men in two categories but with a different approach, namely, (1) the lark, who wakes up early, spontaneously, chipper and alert; his brain warms up fast, he does his best work in the early part of the day, and goes to bed early at night; a rebel, he resists convention, although he tends to be introverted; and (2) the owl, who often uses an alarm clock to wake up, is slow to rise, and is unpleasant and sour-faced in the early morning; he warms up gradually, and reaches his maximum alertness in the late afternoon or early evening; he loves late nights and goes to bed late; he is a routine man, a plodder, and generally extraverted.

In his essay on 'The Powers and Limitations of Science', William *James* (d. 1910), the great American psychologist, spoke of two kinds of mind, each creating different models of the universe, namely, (1) the scientific or academic, predominantly masculine and outgoing, like Benjamin Franklin; and (2) the mystical and intuitive, predominantly feminine, like William Blake.

Alfred *Binet* (d. 1911), French psychologist, in 1903 brought forward his theory of two principal psychological types: (1) the introspective, who were subjective, abstract in thought and speech, favoured ancient thought, were imaginative, spontaneous, had a good idea of time, could describe inner states and were inclined towards art, poetry and mysticism; (2) the externospective or extraspective, who were objective, concrete in thought and speech, favoured contemporary thought, were practical, lacked spontaneity, had good ideas of space, and could describe the external world, and excelled in law and the sciences.

Ivan *Pavlov* (d. 1936), Russian 'reflexological' psychologist, who after experiments with dogs concluded that behaviour is built up of 'conditioned reflexes', found that animals conditioned to react to two distinct stimuli become confused at a stimulus that is not clearly identifiable as one or the other. Dogs respond in one of two ways to such borderline stimuli, and Pavlov accordingly concluded that there were two basic types of dogs. Later behaviourists extended this distinction to men: (1) excitable people, who become anxiety-ridden and worried at indecisive border-line stimuli and situations; these people want clear-cut living and clear demarcation of their lives and laws; and (2) inhibited people who are able to resist dubious stimuli, which resistance often 'festers' in the mind.

Emil *Kraepelin* (d. 1926), German psychologist, also spoke of two types, variously named by his followers: (1) cyclothymic, cycloid or manic depressives, who were theatrical and erratic, made broad gestures and movements, and were said to be syntonic, or 'in tune' with their environment; they were often pyknic (thick-set) in appearance; and (2) the schizothymic, schizophrenic or schizoid, who were inhibited, cautious, tense, made bodily movements that were indrawn and restrained, and were said to be dystonic or out of tune with their environment, and were often asthenic (thin) in appearance.

Dr E. *Spranger* (c. 1928) categorized man in six classes: (1) theoretical, interested in the discovery of truth and in abstract principles; (2) economic, concerned with the practical and utilitarian; (3) aesthetic, concerned with form and harmony; (4) social, inspired by love of people; (5) political, motivated by power and authority; and (6) religious, moved by mysticism.

The Hungarian psychologist, Franz *Voelgyesi* (c. 1930), grouped men into two classes, as (1) psychoactive, extraverted, commanding, performing, worshipped, intellectual, masculine; and (2) psychopassive, introverted, obedient, witnessing (spectators), worshipping, emotional, feminine.

Dr William *Sheldon* (c. 1940) and his collaborators produced a threefold system of somatotyping based on the early human embryo, which is formed like a tube of three layers, each giving rise to different organs and structures: the endoderm or inner layer, developing into the viscera, the mesoderm or middle layer developing into muscle, and the ectoderm or outer layer developing into nervous tissue. The relative development of these layers differs in different embryos and results in the three types of men and women. Sheldon's system is based on three physical 'morphs' and three temperamental 'tonias'. (1) The endomorph is soft, fat and gut-dominated, and has the viscerotonic temperament, loves good food and comfort, and tends to gall-bladder complaints. He is amiable, emotional, tolerant, extraverted, family-loving. When upset he seeks sympathy. He fears solitude and death. (2) The mesomorph is big-boned, square, and muscle dominated: he has the somatotonic temperament, and goes in for sports and physical activity. He is assertive, aggressive, and loves power. He demands physical activity when upset. He tends to arterial and heart disease, fears old age and infirmity. (3) The ectomorph is slender, small boned, weak muscled, and nerve dominated, in keeping with his cerebrotonic temperament. He has fast reactions, is alert, sensitive, introverted, delicate, highly sexed, but socially inhibited. Capable of prolonged mental concentration. Under stressful conditions he seeks solitude. As a rule he does not take to drink. Tends to colds and chest complaints.

Karen *Horney* (d. 1952) of Berlin developed her own variant of a trichotomous division of human types, based on the manner in which men and women react to others in personal and social encounters. There are (1) those who move towards others, and are friendly, sociable and compliant; (2) those who move against others, are misanthropic, anarchistic and aggressive; and (3) those who move away from others, who are the withdrawing, aloof, reclusive and contemplative type.

Ernest *Jones* (d. 1958), psychologist and biographer of Sigmund Freud, made a clear twofold division on the lines of idealism on the one hand and materialism on the other. In his own biography he said that in his view the distinction between those who believed in the possibility of mental processes and beings existing independently of the physical world, and those who did not, was 'the most significant of all human classifications', and he felt that further human progress could be measured by the passage of men from the one class to the other.

Carl Gustav *Jung* (d. 1961), Swiss physician and psychologist, used two broad categories very much on the lines of Binet. He spoke of (1) introverts, who are speculative, idealistic, secretive, dreamers, preferring solitude, having few intimate friends, easily disturbed and made anxious by excitement and change, for example, Hamlet; and (2) extraverts (or extroverts), the men of action, who are outgoing and need strong stimulus, and are not concerned with the opinions of others, like Napoleon.

Ernst *Kretschmer* (d. 1964), Professor of psychiatry and neurology at the University of Marburg, classified men under three main types: (1) asthenic, tall and thin, with a lean and hungry look, tending to introversion and schizophrenia; (2) pyknic, short and round, thick-necked, tending to extraversion and cyclothymia, i.e. manic depression; and (3) athletic, strong and muscular, tending to epilepsy. To these three a fourth class is sometimes added, namely, leptosomic (Gk. *leptos*, 'slender'), of slim, medium build, and 'medium' temperament.

Dr Daly *King* (d. 1962), American physician and psychologist influenced by the teachings of G. I. Gurdjieff, spoke of three basic types of man: (1) intellectual man, dominated by the cerebral system; (2) emotional man, dominated by the autonomic (basal-gangliar) system; and (3) practical man, dominated by the spinal-cord system.

The English psychologist, Hans Jurgen *Eysenck* (b. 1916), and a number of others correlated the four humours* of classical physiology with modern studies in personality analysis. We then have four types as follows: (1) choleric (extraverted, unstable), the warrior; (2) melancholic (introverted, unstable), the recluse; (3) sanguine (extraverted, stable), the ruler; and (4) phlegmatic (introverted, stable), the philosopher.

The most recent classification follows on researches undertaken since 1973 in California, based on the two cerebral* hemispheres. Left-hemisphere oriented persons are described as practical verbalizers, and right-hemisphere oriented persons as intuitive visualizers.

The tabulation of the various human types into two, three and four main categories is given below.

Division into two categories (*see also* opposites)

fat	thin
pyknic	asthenic (Kraepelin)
sthenic	asthenic (Brown)
apoplectic	phthisic (Hippocrates)
liable to stroke	liable to tuberculosis
liable to heart trouble	liable to nervous trouble
alcohol oriented	opium oriented
jovial	saturnine
sanguine	melancholic (*see* humoralism)
cycloid (manic-depressive)	schizoid (schizophrenic)
cyclothymic	schizothymic (Kraepelin)
hysteric	schizophrenic
Apollonian	Dionysian (Nietzsche)
reserved, restrained	excitable, exuberant (Pavlov)
Attic	Rhodian
Classical	Asiatic
active	thoughtful
commanding	obeying (Voelgyesi)
performing	witnessing (Voelgyesi)
worshipped	worshipping
psychoactive	psychopassive
extraspective	introspective (Binet)

extravert	introvert (Jung)
optimist	pessimist
conscious dominated	unconscious dominated
left-hemisphere dominated	right-hemisphere dominated (*see* cerebrum)
syntonic, or in tune with environment	dystonic, or out of tune (Kraepelin)
sociable	reclusive
permissive	restrictive
expansive gestures	restrained gestures
banking, science, law, business	poetry, art, religion, mysticism
owl	lark (Osler)
reasoning (intelligence)	instinctive (intuition)
willed	spontaneous
practical	imaginative
objective	subjective
thinking	feeling
good idea of space	good idea of time
plastic arts	musical and poetic arts
interest in contemporary thought	interest in ancient thought
concrete thought and speech	abstract thought and speech
can express outer states	can express inner states
verbalizer	visualizer (Galton)
Aristotelian	Platonist (Coleridge)
materialist	idealist (Jones)
influenced by egos (personalities)	influenced by issues (principles)

Division into three categories

fat or medium	thin	muscular
pyknic	asthenic	athletic (Kretschmer)
cerebral	asthenic	athletic (Carus)
endomorph	ectomorph	mesomorph (Sheldon)
cerebral	ganglionic (autonomic)	spinal (King)
gall-bladder complaints	neurasthenia	heart disease
head-dominated	heart-dominated	liver-dominated (Burton)
thinker (cognitive)	feeler (affective)	willer (conative)
intellectual	emotional	active (practical)
satvik (good and wise)	rajasik (passionate)	tamasik (dull and brutish) (Charaka)
seeks the way of knowledge	seeks the way of faith	seeks the way of works
truth	beauty	goodness
viscerotonic	cerebrotonic	somatotonic (Sheldon)
fears solitude and death	fears crowds	fears old age and infirmity
likes comfort	likes mental activity	likes physical activity such as sport
tends towards others	moves away from others	acts against others (Horney)
sings, when drunk	weeps, when drunk	fights, when drunk
in stress seeks family and sympathy	in stress seeks solitude	in stress seeks activity

Division into four categories

athletic	asthenic	pyknic	leptosomic
warrior	poet, artist	ruler	mystic
physical	astral	etheric	spiritual

HUMORALISM

choleric	melancholic	sanguine	phlegmatic
coronary	consumptive	arthritic	colitic
epileptic	neurasthenic	cyclothymic	schizophrenic
unstable-extravert	unstable-introvert	stable-extravert	stable-introvert
active	emotional	thoughtful	intuitive
passionate	depressive	cheerful	lethargic

Books

Jones, Ernest, *Free Associations*, Hogarth, London, 1959.

Jung, C. G., *Psychological Types*, Kegan Paul, Trench, Trubner, London, 1923.

Kahn, Fritz, *Psychological Types*, London, 1949.

King, C. Daly, *States of Human Consciousness*, University Books, New York, 1963.

Kretschmer, Ernst, *Physique and Character*, 2nd edn, Kegan Paul, Trench, Trubner, London, 1936.

Lowen, A., *The Physical Dynamics of Character Structure*, Grune & Stratton, New York, 1958.

Macauliffe, L., *Les Tempéraments*, Paris, 1924.

Mead, M., *Sex and Temperament*, George Routledge, London, 1935.

Mottram, V. H., *The Physical Basis of Personality*, Penguin Books, Harmondsworth, 1949.

Semeonoff, Boris (ed.), *Personality Assessment*, Penguin Books, Harmondsworth, 2nd edn, 1970.

Sheldon, William H. *et al.*, *The Varieties of Human Physique*, Harper, New York, 1940.

Spranger, E., *Types of Men: The Psychology and Ethics of Personality*, Halle, 1928.

HUMORALISM

(Lat. *humor*, 'moisture'), an ancient medical doctrine based on the notion that a person's nature and disposition, and the diseases likely to afflict him, were determined by the proportions (Gk. *krasis*, 'mixing') of the four cardinal humours or fluids in his body.

The physical basis of the theory was the 'opposite' nature of heat and humidity, set forth by the Pythagorean philosopher, Alcmaeon of Crotona (c. 450 BC), from which the four categories of hotness, dryness, wetness and coldness were derived. The philosopher, Empedocles (d. 425 BC), first laid down the four 'roots' or elements, namely, fire, earth, air, water, which provided the framework on which the humoral system was established. The Greek physician, Hippocrates (d. 359 BC), associated these elements with the four cardinal fluids in the body: gall, black bile, blood and phlegm. Aristotle (d. 322 BC) attributed to these fluids the qualities of hot-dry, cold-dry, hot-wet, and cold-wet. But it was Galen (d. AD 210), another Greek physician, practising in Rome, who first systematically expounded the humoral theory as it came to be applied in healing practice in Europe and the Middle East for over a thousand years.

The principal features of the system are summarized below:

(1) The human body contains four primary fluids called humours, which regulate its functions.

(2) These humours are mixed in certain combinations, and the temperament (Lat. *temperare*, 'to blend') and character (Gk. 'stamp') of each person is determined by the proportion of these humours in his body. We still speak of a person being even-tempered or good-tempered.

(3) Physical and mental health and well-being depend on the eucrasis (right mixture), symmetry (right measure) and isonomy (right action) of these four vital fluxes.
(4) In humoral pathology the disproportionate combination of humours produces distempers, vapours, megrims, murrains and disease in general. To be 'out of humour' originally meant to be ill or indisposed; 'good humour' and 'ill humour' still retain traces of their ancient associations. The bitterness of gall contracts the mouth, and we still speak of a wine being 'dry' (bitter or sour, as opposed to sweet) and of dry humour, which originally meant the 'bitterness' of a person's wit.
(5) Morbid fluids generate morbid airs, and both these often take refuge in the channels of the body and clog them, and these 'peccant humours' must be periodically eliminated by egesis (excretion), diuresis (urination), emesis (vomiting), sudoresis (sweating), haemesis (bleeding), eructation (belching), flatulation (breaking wind), esemination (ejaculation), lachrymation (shedding tears).
(6) In the case of actual disease, the effects of excessive humours had to be counteracted by applying treatment, or following a regime, of the 'opposite' nature. For example, cancer, a cold-dry disease, due to an excess of black bile, had to be treated by hot-wet medicines, by eating hot-wet foods like onions and honey, and by living in a place with a hot-wet climate and soil.

A great deal was added to the doctrine of humours during the middle ages, and it was further linked with colours (red, green, yellow, blue), tastes (bitter, sour, salt, sweet), the planets (Mars, Saturn, Venus, Jupiter), the seasons (summer, winter, spring, autumn), and so on. The humoral table given here tabulates the basic feature of the early humoral system, without the later correspondences, about which there is much confusion.

Source	sun	earth	sky	sea
Element	fire	earth	air	water
Nature	hotness	dryness	wetness	coldness
Quality	hot-dry	cold-dry	hot-wet	cold-wet
Bodily organ	gall-bladder	spleen	liver	lungs (or brain)
Humour	gall, i.e. yellow or red bile, also called choler (Gk. *cholē*) (Lat. *bilis*)	black bile (Gk. *melan cholē*) (Lat. *atra bilis*)	blood (Gk. *haima*) (Lat. *sanguis*)	phlegm (Gk. *phlegma*) (Lat. *pituita*)
Temperament	bilious or choleric	melancholic, splenetic or atrabilious	haemic or sanguine	phlegmatic or lymphatic (Lat. *lympha*, water)
Character	excitable quick-tempered violent	pessimistic brooding suspicious irritable	optimistic lively impulsive hopeful	unemotional cold tranquil sluggish

	energetic	obstinate	communicative	callous
	impatient	avaricious		
	assertive	timid	warm-hearted	dull
	bold			
Disease	jaundice	cancer	apoplexy	rheumatism
	cholera	paralysis	neurasthenia	colds
		epilepsy		worms

Books

Heidel, W. A., *Hippocratic Medicine,* Columbia University Press, New York, 1941.
Moon, R. O., *The Relation of Medicine to Philosophy,* Longmans, London, 1909.
Robin, P. A., *The Old Physiology in English Literature,* Dent, London, 1911.
Thorndike, Lynn, *History of Magic and Experimental Science,* vol. I, Columbia University Press, New York, 1923.
Walkington, Thomas, *The Optik Glass of Humors,* London, 1607.

IDEODYNAMICS

The involuntary, almost imperceptible movements made by a person under the influence of a prevailing idea. These movements, quite unconsciously carried out, are prompted by the tendency of thought to cause reflexes in the nervous system and so find expression in movement. Though not normally perceptible to any but a trained observer or a sensitive person, these ideomotor movements have been recorded by various biotelemetric devices and have conclusively established that a man's thoughts, feelings and interests cause minute physical reflexes in his body.

Thus, if a person is made to watch a pendulum, his hand soon begins to move very slightly to and fro. If he hears footsteps outside a door his whole body tends to move very slightly towards the direction of the approaching sound. A similar curious synchronization has been noted between the desire to perform an action, or simply the thought of the action, and the minute movements of the muscles necessary to perform it. Experiments have shown that the mere thought of doing something even while lying quite still tends to produce incipient muscular activity or changes in muscular tension in the appropriate part of the body. When to the process of thinking an element of emotion is added, then a whole range of dermal, cardiac, glandular and metabolic activities are immediately set in motion. Emotive thinking, or thought coloured by passion, can induce sweating, an increase in the respiratory rate, palpitations and a host of other physiological symptoms. The study of psychosomatics proves the dynamic influence that the mind has on the body.

It has also been noted that physical mediums in trance carry out barely perceptible mimetic actions while some telekinetic phenomena are taking place in the seance room. Thus, if an object placed on the table is being lifted, there is a very slight corresponding micromuscular movement of the medium's hand as if she were carrying out the operation by an extension of her own hand.

Perhaps the most interesting of all ideomotor movements are those connected with what is known as endophasia, 'inner speech', or silent articulation. Almost all thought and visualization cause an innervation (excitation) of the vocal apparatus, including the lips, tongue and larynx (voice-box), which in turn result in unconscious whispering or subvocal speech. Even when the lips are closed and there is no sound at all, a sensitive instrument will pick up the vibrations of the speech organs. Delicate recording instruments have shown that when we write we actually make the same movements of the laryngeal muscles that we would normally make in speaking. Similar unconscious movements of the vocal muscles occur when we are reading silently.

Besides these very subtle movements, thought causes easily discernible changes in the muscles of the speaker's face and neck, affects his gestures and alters the rhythm and rate of his breathing. Flushing, blushing, tremors, facial expressions, bodily tension, all supplement the visual sign language by which we unwittingly communicate our thoughts and feelings.

A large proportion of telepathic and thought-reading phenomena can be explained by the accurate picking up by an experienced practitioner of these involuntary clues. In what is known as cumberlandism, lip-reading or muscle-reading, the trained expert notes and interprets these tell-tale signs together with all the more obvious clues. So, when a person consults a palmist, clairvoyant, sensitive or diviner, he gives away a great deal of information without being aware of it. By the faintest facial or muscular reactions of surprise, doubt, hesitation, disappointment, acquiescence, he provides the sensitive with a score of helpful cues as to the correctness of her statements, and thus guides her in her reading.

Books

Beard, George M., *The Study of Trance, Muscle-Reading and Allied Phenomena*, Putnam, New York, 1882.

Carington, Whately, *Matter, Mind and Meaning*, Yale University Press, 1949.

Dessoir, Max, 'Experiments in Muscle Reading and Thought Transference', *Proceedings of the Society for Psychical Research*, 1887, vol. 4, part X.

Jastrow, J., *Fact and Fable in Psychology*, Macmillan, London and New York, 1901.

Osty, E., *Supernormal Faculties in Man*, Methuen, London, 1923.

Rawcliffe, D. H., *The Psychology of the Occult*, Rockliff, London, 1952.

Sugden, E. H., 'Note on Muscle Reading', *Proceedings of the Society for Psychical Research*, 1883, vol. I, part IV.

Thomas, J. F., *Beyond Normal Cognition*, Boston, 1937.

IMAGINATION

The power of visualizing, or forming images in the mind, is one of the most important mental activities. The Greek word for thought, *eidos*, also signifies a creative picture. Aristotle (d. 322 BC) said, 'To think is to speculate with images.'

Imagination is not to be confused with eidetic imagery, which is the ability, possessed by many children and preliterate peoples, to reproduce with vivid clarity a visual image of what one has previously seen. Sometimes the image may be so vivid as almost to create a hallucination of its reality.

Imagination implies the operation of the will, as opposed to fantasy (or phantasy), which is an uncontrolled indulgence in wishing and day-dreaming. Everyone gives in to occasional fantasy, since it is not possible to be ever vigilant over one's thoughts, and sometimes it is pleasant to take refuge from the tensions and frustrations of reality. But healthy adults limit their indulgence in it. On the other hand, children, the immature, the neurotic, the mentally disturbed, retreat constantly into the world of fantasy, and live in a pretence of courage, noble birth, success, wealth, glamour. Fantasy does not include volition; it is a form of dreaming. According to Henri Bergson (d. 1941), 'Willing and waking are one and the same thing.'

The visual imagination is the key to a great many magical operations, since it can reinforce the power of thought. In magic and occultism the imagination is used as a compelling and concentrated thought-force to conjure up and hold in the mind's eye a clear idea of the desired objective in order to make it happen. The medieval physician and philosopher of Padua, Peter Abano (d. 1318), in speaking of the power of imagination, cites the case of a man who cast down a camel by merely imagining its fall.

Imagination draws the blueprint upon which the will acts. The Nuer people of the Upper Nile believe that God created the world and everything in it out of nothing, by imagining it. In every work of significance an imaginative pattern must be set first; this stimulates the will, and both thereafter operate together to create what is sought. In this partnership the will is always subordinate to the imagination and can be rendered immobilized by it. A man can run without trepidation along a plank of wood if laid on the ground, but when it is placed like a bridge across a chasm he will be unable to do so, and if forced to try will crawl over it like a terrified child, because the idea of falling is so vividly presented to him by the imagination.

Through the ages men have expressed their belief in the immense power of the imagination. The Arab philosopher, Abu Muhammad al-Ghazali (d. 1111), said: 'The earnest imagination hath power to work effects on things, for if a man intensively imagine that it rains, then, though the weather be fair, it may soon be cloudy, and indeed rain.' Paracelsus (d. 1541), German physician and alchemist, expressed it thus: 'Imagination is creative power. He who can think imaginatively discovers the latent forces in nature. Imagination takes priority over all. Resolute imagination can accomplish anything.' Napoleon (d. 1821): 'Imagination rules the world. It operates on all spheres of activity and existence.' William Blake (d. 1827), poet and mystic: 'What is now proved was once only imagined.' Émile Coué (d. 1926), French psychologist: 'When the will and imagination are in conflict, the imagination invariably gains the day.' Karl Pearson (d. 1936), scientist and mathematician, said that even the laws of science were 'products of the creative imagination'. W. B. Yeats (d.

1939), poet and occultist, held that if strongly enough formulated, imagination 'realizes itself in the circumstances of life acting either through our own souls, or through the spirit of nature'. Sir James Frazer (d. 1941), folklorist: 'Imagination works upon a man as really as does gravitation, and may kill him as certainly as a dose of prussic acid.'

Books

Atkinson, J. W. (ed.), *Motives in Fantasy, Action and Society*, Van Nostrand, New York, 1958.

Bundy, M. W., *The Theory of Imagination in Classical and Medieval Thought*, University of Illinois Press, 1927.

Freud, Sigmund, *Creative Writing and Day-Dreaming*, Hogarth Press, London, 1959.

Johnson, Raynor, *Nurslings of Immortality*, Hodder & Stoughton, London, 1957.

McKellar, Peter, *Imagination and Thinking*, Basic Books, New York, 1957.

Osborn, A. F., *Applied Imagination*, Scribner, New York, 1953.

Rugg, H., *Imagination*, Harper & Row, New York, 1963.

Rycroft, Charles, *Imagination and Reality*, Hogarth Press, London, 1968.

Weaver, Warren, *Science and Imagination*, Basic Books, New York, 1967.

Yates, Frances, *The Art of Memory*, Routledge & Kegan Paul, London, 1966.

INHALATION

Inhalation or inspiration, the indrawing of breath, is the first stage in the process of respiration, by which air is exchanged: inhalation enables the lungs to use the oxygen drawn in; exhalation* gets rid of the carbon dioxide.

Breathing techniques take into account a number of factors involved in the process of inspiration, all of which have an important bearing in breath-magic. These are as follows: (a) the nature and quality of the air inhaled; (b) the rate of inhalation, whether slow or fast (*see* eupnea); (c) whether the breath is inhaled through the nose (warm) or the mouth (cold); (d) whether it is drawn in one long breath, or in a series of short jerks; (e) whether air is inhaled through a constricted or an open throat; and (f) the depth of the inhalation.

In occult physiology the act of inspiration introduces vitalizing pneumic energy into the body, the bio-plasmic energy of modern science, which plays a paramount role in the well-being of the individual. It disperses the energy to the minutest parts of the physical system and revivifies them, providing a negative and feminine charge of power, in contrast to the positive and masculine charge of exhalation.

Highly intricate methods have been devised to receive, store, circulate and utilize this pneumic energy, and the manner in which the indrawn breath is received becomes of considerable importance in healing and strengthening the various organs of the body, and the physical and etheric systems as a whole.

For this purpose it is necessary for the pupil to learn how to direct the air. Initially he has to concentrate on the point at which the air enters the body, which can be easily localized at the opening of the nostrils, which the air seems to strike gently as it enters. By stages he will learn to shift this point of entry or initial impact further and further inside, so that the air is felt entering not at the nostrils but at a point in the interior of the nose; then deeper down, in the palate; then the throat. After several months of practice he should be able to feel the air strike any part of the interior of the body he desires: the top of the head, the forehead, the back of the neck, the navel, the perineum, and, it is said, even the toes.

It then becomes possible to direct the pneumic energy to any part that needs re-energizing or healing.

Books

See under respiration

INSPIRATION

The strange influence that stimulates the creative or imaginative impulse, commonly believed to be prompted by divine or supernatural agency, and sometimes equated with possession. The word 'inspiration' is derived from the inhalation of trance-inducing fumes from somniferous incense that the ancient oracles used to burn to help them attain a prophetic state.

Inspiration is a condition of sublime xenophrenia which descends in a sudden flash without warning, sometimes in a vision, sometimes during work, and sometimes during some commonplace activity. At the moment of inspiration, as in ecstasy, an individual finds himself seemingly in contact with another force beyond the self. The mind is overwhelmed, feeling and understanding become intensified to an extraordinary degree, and one is able to grasp instantly and as a whole something that had so far been perceived only vaguely and in fragments.

Divine inspiration was usually associated with prophets, sages and men of exalted wisdom, but inspiration of another order is the common experience of poets, artists, authors, musicians and even scientists, some of whom have accomplished their best work under the stimulus of an external impulse that cannot be accounted for. This experience is vouched for by the inspired men themselves, as the following brief catalogue indicates. It is to be noted that in most cases some previous work or knowledge is necessary for inspiration to be useful, and any attempt to write a good poem or paint a beautiful picture is unlikely to be very successful, however grand the inspiration, if one is not basically competent to deal with the material. 'Fortune', said Louis Pasteur (d. 1895), 'favours the prepared mind.'

Socrates (d. 399 BC) ascribed all that was best in his life, to the guidance received from his 'daemon' or inner voice; and Plato in his *Ion* makes Socrates describe the sudden access of power that imbues the poet when the Muses inspire him:

> The authors of those great poems which we admire, do not attain to excellence through the rules of any art, or while reason remains with them. They utter their beautiful verses in a state of inspiration, possessed, as it were, by a spirit not their own, and in a state of divine insanity. For whilst a man retains any portion of the thing called reason he is utterly incompetent to produce poetry or to vaticinate, and every rhapsodist or poet is excellent in proportion to the extent of his partici-

pation in the divine influence, and the degree in which the Muse itself has descended on him.

Philo Judaeus (d. AD 50), a Jewish mystic and philosopher of Alexandria, said: 'Sometimes I have come to my work empty, and have suddenly become full. Ideas were showered upon me through some invisible power and through its influence I have become inspired and have known neither where I was, nor who was present, nor what I did or wrote.' St Teresa (d. 1583), speaking of her great mystical works, said that though they were uncontrolled and inspired, and written at immense speed without stopping to correct, they were imitative, like the speech of a parrot that repeats yet cannot understand the things he says. Jacob Boehme (d. 1624) produced many of his writings not as acts of deliberate and rational composition, but in a state of illumination, 'a motion from on high' that seized him and forced him to write. 'Before God', he wrote, 'I do not know how the thing arises in me without the participation of my will. I do not even know that which I must write, and how it comes to be written.' Madame Guyon (d. 1717) says, 'I was myself surprised at the letters which Thou didst cause me to write, and in which I had no part save the actual movement of the hand.'

The Italian poet, Torquato Tasso (d. 1595), author of *Jerusalem Delivered,* never ceased to believe that he was accompanied by a familiar spirit who prompted him in all he did, and he often had visions of angels and devils from whom he received snatches of verse which he embodied in his work. John Milton in 1643 wrote of one of his odes that it was written 'without any previous deliberation, but with a certain impelling faculty for which I know not how to account'. Johann Friedrich von Schiller (d. 1805) said of his own inspired moods, 'I have frequently wondered where my thoughts come from. They flood through me independent of the action of my mind.' William Blake (d. 1827) said that he wrote certain poems 'from immediate dictation, without premeditation and even against my will'. He insisted that he was under the direction of messengers from heaven daily and nightly, and stated on his death bed that the credit for all his works belonged not to himself, but to his 'celestial friends' who dictated to him. John Keats (d. 1821) was often astonished at some of his own work which struck him as 'the production of another person rather than my own'. In the opinion of Johann Wolfgang Goethe (d. 1832), all great human achievements, including works of art and literature, are beyond anyone's control and 'are to be regarded as unexpected gifts from above'. According to Alfred de Musset (d. 1857), 'It is not work, it is listening; it is as if some unknown person were speaking in your ear.' The Indian sage and poet, Rabindranath Tagore (d. 1941), writing of one of his works explained: 'I am not the author of the book. I merely held the pen while a disembodied being wrote what he wished, using my pen and mind. There is an unseen hand that drives the spirit on, like a submerged propeller.'

Many musicians have confirmed the same inexplicable power that overtakes them. The life of Wolfgang Amadeus Mozart (d. 1791) is filled with instances of a sudden access of inspiration that seized him, often at the most unlikely times. The idea for the whole of the *Magic Flute* quintet came to him while playing billiards. Ludwig van Beethoven (d. 1827) said, 'Inspiration is for me that mysterious state when all the forces of nature become instruments, and the entire world seems to form one vast harmony.' Hector Berlioz (d. 1869) for long tried to complete a musical passage in vain, until one day as he rose from a dive while swimming in the Tiber the whole passage occurred to him ready formed. Richard Wagner (d. 1883), sick with dysentery and almost in a trance, suddenly felt he was sinking in a mighty flood of water, and from the surge and roar emerged the musical shape which became the orchestral prelude to *Rheingold*. Johannes Brahms (d. 1897) when gripped by the power of inspiration was in a veritable fit of trembling. He wrote, 'Vibrations thrill my whole being; ideas flow instantaneously upon me with such power and speed that I can grasp only a few. They quickly fade unless I get them on paper.' Piotr Ilyich Tchaikovsky (d. 1893) said, 'The germ of a composition comes suddenly and unexpectedly. It would be futile to try and put into words the immeasurable sense of bliss I feel. Everything in me quivers and pulsates. If that condition of soul and mind we call inspiration lasted long without intermission, no artist would survive the ordeal.' Sergei Rachmaninoff (d. 1943), another famous Russian composer, told a friend that during inspiration it would seem as if the music swirled around him, not bit by bit, but the total composition. Everything all at once. 'Whence it comes, how it begins, how can I say? It comes up within me and I write it down.'

Emily Brontë (d. 1848) expressed the view, 'The writer who possesses the creative gift owns something of which he is not always the master, something that at times strangely wills and works for itself.' William Makepeace Thackeray (d. 1863) once admitted that he had been surprised at the observations made by some of his characters. 'It seems as if an occult power were working my pen. The personage does or says something and I ask, How did he come to think of that?' Charles Dickens (d. 1870) declared that the words uttered by his characters were distinctly heard by him, and that when he sat down to write, 'some beneficent power showed it all to me'. George Eliot (d. 1880) felt that in her best works there was a 'not myself' which took hold of her and used her personality as an instrument through which the work was done.

Fyodor Dostoevsky (d. 1881), speaking of the rapture of inspired moments, wrote: 'If this state were to last more than five seconds, the soul could not endure it and would have to disappear. During these five seconds I live a whole human existence, and for that I would give my whole life and not think I was paying too dearly.' Benjamin Disraeli (d. 1881) wrote his novels sometimes as if in trance and often felt keenly the overwhelming power of inspiration. 'I often feel', he said, 'that there is only a step from intense mental concentration to madness.' Harriet Beecher Stowe's *Uncle Tom's Cabin* (1851) was, in part, 'written as though blown through the mind as with the rushing of a mighty wind'.

Great painters, working under the surge of inspiration, have often been unaware of how their work came to be done. 'My whole work', said Raphael (d. 1520), 'has been accomplished as it were, in a dream.' The pictures of Vincent van Gogh (d. 1890) came to him 'with a terrible dream-like lucidity' when he was hardly conscious of himself.

Scientists, although living in a more precise and intellectual world, have not been immune to this baffling influence. Speaking of his own subject, astronomy, Johann Kepler (d. 1630) declared: 'The roads by which men arrive at their insights into celestial matters seem to be almost as worthy of wonder as those matters themselves.' Sir Isaac Newton (d. 1727) received by direct intuitive grasp many notions that he found he could not prove. Indeed, one of his discoveries, on the roots of equations, was only proved two centuries after his death. James Watt (d. 1819) saw how the waste of heat in a steam engine could be avoided by condensing steam, in a flash in inspiration during a walk to the golf house. Sir William Hamilton (d. 1865), mathematical physicist, thought of quaternions (a new mathematical method) while strolling with his wife in the streets of Dublin. The German mathematician, Karl Friedrich Gauss (d. 1855), said that he received the solution to one of his mathematical discoveries, 'not by painstaking research but as it were by the grace of God, and as a sudden flash of truth. The riddle solved itself, as lightning strikes.' He confessed that he would not have been able to show the steps by which he arrived at it. Hermann von Helmholtz (d. 1894), German physicist and philosopher, declared that his best ideas had come to him while climbing hills on a sunny day. Henri Poincaré (d. 1912), French mathematician and physicist, told how the solution of a problem struck him suddenly as he stepped into a bus, when he was not even conscious of thinking about it at all.

The philosopher, G. W. F. Hegel (d. 1831), was convinced that he was possessed by a divine spirit that inspired his works and sometimes even dictated what he wrote. Arthur Schopenhauer (d. 1860) believed all his life that he was impelled by some spirit, so much so that he would often stop on the road and argue with it, gesticulating wildly.

Modern psychologists account for all types in inspiration as a welling-up of images and ideas from the individual's own unconscious.

Books

Anderson, H. H. (ed.), *Creativity and Its Cultivation*, Harper, New York, 1959.
Chadwick, Norah, *Poetry and Prophecy*, Cambridge University Press, 1942.
Clissold, Augustus, *The Prophetic Spirit in Genius and Madness*, Longmans, London, 1870
Hadamard, Jacques, *The Psychology of Invention in the Mathematical Field*, Princeton University Press, 1949.
Harding, Rosamond, *An Anatomy of Inspiration*, Heffer, Cambridge, 3rd edn, 1948.
Karagulla, Shafica, *Breakthrough to Creativity*, De Voss, Los Angeles, 1967.
Prescott, F. C., *The Poetic Mind*, Macmillan, New York, 1922.
Storr, Anthony, *The Dynamics of Creation*, Secker & Warburg, London, 1972.
Vernon, P. E. (ed.), *Creativity*, Penguin Books, Harmondsworth, 1967.

INSUFFLATION

(Lat. *sufflare,* 'to blow upon'), a form of exhalation* which involves breathing or blowing upon a person, specifically with the intention of influencing him in some way. Though anyone can blow hot and cold in a single breath by voluntary effort, the breath of different people varies in power, each kind of breath having its own virtue and energy, and each being charged with magnetic and electrical properties. Generally, warm breath is regarded as positive and beneficial; cold breath as negative and injurious. Animals fear cold breath breathed upon them and are repelled by it.

Just as there are natural sensitives and psychics, so it seems that there are individuals constitutionally endowed with a potent breath. There are authentic records of people with an incredibly hot breath. A young Negro, A. W. Underwood (c. 1910) of Michigan, who had the power of producing intensely hot breath, was medically examined by a panel of doctors, and in their presence, under test conditions excluding all possibility of fraud, he was able to set alight handkerchiefs and other small articles by merely breathing upon them. Later, in 1927, Charles Dawes, Vice-President of the USA under Calvin Coolidge, personally investigated the case of one William Watson, also a Negro, who could cause combustible objects to burst into flame by breathing upon them. Dawes with his team of experts absolutely ruled out trickery but could not explain how it was done.

Insufflation is used in healing, so that a sick person who is breathed upon is helped by the living breath thus poured upon him. Either warm or cold air may be insufflated, depending on the disease, but in most cases warm air produces better results. More specifically, warm breathing is good for circulatory diseases, cures gout and rheumatism, and may be used successfully against local inflammation, muscular spasms, burns, open sores and wounds. Cold insufflation soothes congestive pains, nervous disorders and heart attacks. Insufflation, for therapeutic purposes, may also be performed on oneself.

In the usual method the healer concentrates on the affected part for a short time, breathes a slow, regular rhythm for a few moments, then inhales deeply, 'energizing' his breath, and then pours the now power-charged interior breath over the affected part, disrupting and dispersing the dark vapours and thus banishing the ailment. This treatment is repeated, with firm concentration and conviction for a few minutes. Chinese taoist practitioners use a similar method after first 'harmonizing' their breath.

Insufflation also figures in rites of initiation and exorcism. In certain religious and magical cults, both ancient and modern, the priest breathes upon a child in order to imbue him with new spiritual life, or upon a novice to confirm him in the discipline to which he is committing himself. In certain initiation ceremonies the master breathes three times on a candidate, thus consecrating him, and making him a new man. Mystical insight may be communicated by this means (*see* transpowering).

There is an old belief that if with sufficient mental concentration a person breathes into the mouth of another, that person can be brought under the power of the insufflater. During the time of the witchcraft trials in Europe, many cases were reported of men and women falling under the spell of mysterious individuals who breathed into their mouths. In 1335 a woman of Toulouse named Anne Marie de Georgel confessed that once when she was outside the town a dark-skinned man of huge stature, with fiery eyes, and dressed in animal skins, came towards her across the water. He blew into her mouth and she gave herself to him, and on the following week accompanied him to the sabbat. Edmund Hartley (hanged 1596), a warlock of Lancashire, was charged with kissing his victims over the mouth and thereby 'breathing the devil into their bodies', for they suffered thereafter with fits, and behaved as if possessed.

Insufflation was often practised on the opposite sex as a means of arousing sexual passion. St Augustine (d. 430), St Jerome (d. 420) and other eminent Christian authorities denounced it as sorcery. Notorious cases of the seduction of girls by insufflation are associated with the names of three priests, Father Louis Gaufridi (burned at the stake 1611), Father Urbain Grandier (burned at the stake 1634), and Father Jean-Baptiste Girard (d. 1733), who were accused of breathing upon their victims while kissing them, thus depriving the girls of their senses, and then debauching them.

Books

Ahmed, Rolla, *The Black Art*, John Long, London, 1936.
Cavendish, Richard, *The Black Arts*, Routledge & Kegan Paul, London, 1967.
Edwards, Frank, *Strange People*, Pan Books, London.
Goldston, Robert, *Satan's Disciples*, New English Library, London, 1969.
Wheatley, Dennis, *The Devil and All His Works*, Hutchinson, London, 1971.

JOINTS

Joints of the body, where the bones meet or fit together, are regarded, like other areas of contact in occultism, as having a special significance. Such areas change the character of the two meeting forces and by serving as a transit point can produce a new force. In Hindu esoteric physiology the *marma*, 'joint', is a vital and vulnerable part of the organism.

All joints, corners, junctures and points of articulation in the human body are symbolic of power. In occultism, the immovable joints such as those between the bones of the skull, like the bregma; the slightly movable joints like the vertebrae of the spine; and the freely movable ones like the elbow, shoulder, wrist, finger (knuckles), hip, knee, ankle and toe joints, have each their own symbolism.

The elbow, joining as it does the forearm and upper-arm, is the source of the arm's mobility and strength, which is preserved in such expressions as: 'elbow-grease', for hard work; 'elbow-room', for working space; 'up to the elbows', to be completely engrossed; 'more power to your elbow', more strength for your undertaking. The elbow marks one end of a measure of which the other end is the tip of the finger, making one cubit, a very important measure of length in the ancient world. Two cubits make an ell, a word having the same origin as elbow.

The knuckles, as the articulations of the energy-charged fingers, represent a sacred part of the hand, a symbol of work and personal will. To 'knuckle down' to something is to settle down to it determinedly. A 'rap over the knuckles' is a humiliating reproof since it involves a prestigious part of the hand. Knuckles are instrumental in all knocking operations in magical ceremonies, for the sound of knocking on wood with the knuckles is believed to penetrate to the spirit world. Similarly, touching wood to avert bad luck, should be a rap made with the knuckles or finger joints. 'Knuckled' bread, or bread which has been kneaded with the knuckles, is supposed to be especially strengthening. The original salute was a raising of the hand to the head and touching the forehead with the knuckles. The knucklebones of dead men are greatly prized in primitive divinatory and magical operations. They are used as dice, or rattled in a box to summon spirits.

The shoulder is both the location of a joint and a focus of strength. Physically and spiritually a man 'puts his shoulder to the wheel' when he wishes to get things moving. In occultism an important plexus is believed to lie between the scapulae (shoulder-blades). Alice Bailey, the theosophist, says, 'The main centre for the reception of prana (vital breath) is a centre between the shoulder-blades.'

The knees are the most important of the bodily joints, and the word knee has a wide connotation in many languages, and is associated with a number of important activities, such as birth, copulation, work, locomotion, support, prayer, supplication. In several languages the word for knee and the word for phallus or begetting is the same. In the normal posture a man is usually on his knees and elbows during the act of intercourse. One of the natural postures assumed by a mother in childbirth was kneeling. In occultism the posture of standing with knees bent outwards intensifies the potency of a rite or a curse.

Books

Bailey, Alice, *A Treatise on Cosmic Fire*, 3rd edn, Lucis, New York, 1944.
Hall, M. P., *Man, the Grand Symbol of the Mysteries*, Philosophical Research Society, Los Angeles, 1947.
Onians, R. B., *The Origins of European Thought*, Cambridge University Press, 1951.

KISSING

Includes all forms of greeting and caress in which the face, and especially the lips, are brought into contact. Many senses commingle in the kiss, although it is itself an ethereal thing. In the animal world kissing equivalents include antennal play among certain insects, the billing of birds, the cataglottism of pigeons, the interlinking of trunks by elephants.

With few exceptions there are no references to the kiss in early writings. Homer and the early Greek poets do not mention it, nor is it to be found among the Celts who did not even have a word for it in their language. The Chinese and Japanese regarded the sensual kiss as immodest and the latter have no word for it either. Kissing in Japan is confined to the mother kissing her infant, or the father kissing his child till he can walk. The ancient Jews prohibited kissing between persons of the opposite sex as leading to lewdness.

The earliest recorded mention of the kiss occurs in the Egyptian pyramid texts where the word for greeting is accompanied by the nose as a determinative, so that it signified a smelling, sniffing or inhaling, for welcome, respect, joy or love. The Vedic Indians greeted one another in the same fashion, but sniffed up in shorter jerks. Melanesians believe that the air they breathe in and out contains the mana or personal aura, and to greet someone by sniffing implies a transfer or mingling of souls. Some primitive tribes simply inhaled the others' smell and 'exchanged breaths'.

The next stage after smelling led to the actual touching of noses, and eventually to the rubbing of noses. The pressure of noses in rubbing brings the lips into contact and this is believed to be the origin of the kiss. Nose-rubbing prevailed among the Maoris of New Zealand, who called it *hongi*, 'nose-pressing'. It was also customary among the Hawaiians, Tongans, Eskimos and Malays; nose-rubbing is still called 'the Malay kiss'. The giver of the kiss places his nose at right angles to the nose of the other, and sniffs and then rubs it, often to the accompaniment of soft exclamations and grunts. It lasts no longer than a handshake among Europeans.

In face-rubbing, found among certain Australian tribes, there is a more general contact of the whole face. In cheek-inhaling, as practised by some Chinese, the Yakuts and certain other Siberian tribes, the mouth and nose of the one are applied to the cheek of the other, and a long inspiration follows. Aboriginal tribes often resort to licking, so that a mother will lick her child in affection just as a cat licks its kittens. Eskimos lick each other's hands, then draw them over their own faces and bodies first, and then over the face and body of the other.

Kissing with lips, either on the lips of the other, or any other part of the body, one's own or the other's, is the kiss as commonly understood in the west. In Morocco equals greet by momentarily clasping one another's hands, after which each kisses his own hand. The Turk kisses his own finger-tips and carries the hand to his heart and head as a token of respect.

Kissing further involves a sipping or a gentle sucking, which is the usual kiss of non-sexual affection where the suction creates the characteristic sound of the kiss. In addition, there is also the factor of taste. The anthropologist, Sir E. B. Tylor (d. 1917), calls a kiss 'a salute by taste'. In fact, the English word 'kiss', and the German 'kuss', may be ultimately connected with the Gothic *kustus*, 'taste'.

The kiss of lovers involves a mutual 'exchange of lips' and 'exchange of saliva', and also biting, thus making the kiss of love a combined expression of hunger and love. The French kiss, known as the deep kiss or tongue kiss, is one in which the lovers mutually explore and caress the inside of each other's mouths with their tongues as profoundly as possible. The sexual kiss involves the application of the lips to the sexual zone of the partner as in oralism.

But the true kiss of love is given another significance. Count Baldassare Castiglione (d. 1529), Italian renaissance writer, says in his manual for courtiers:

> A man delights in joining his mouth to that of his beloved not in order to bring himself to any unseemly desire, but because he feels it gives mutual access each to the other's soul, which pour themselves each into the other's body and mingle so together that each of them has two souls and a single soul. Hence a kiss may be called a joining of souls rather than of bodies.

In a social context the kiss has a varying significance. The Romans distinguished between the *osculum* or kiss of friendship on the face or cheeks; the *basium* or kiss of affection on the lips as given to a child; and the *suavium*, the erotic kiss of lovers. The first was a sign of family and social affection, and as such was exchanged between members of the family and between friends. The habit of welcoming guests with a kiss was once common in Europe. It is sometimes said that the practice of kissing originated as a precaution to ensure that wives had not been drinking. Cato the Elder (d. 149 BC) stated that the reason why women are kissed by their relations is to discover the smell of drink. Englishwomen up to at least the seventeenth century were supposed to have had far more liberty than continental women in kissing male friends, a fact that was observed by Desiderius Erasmus (d. 1536). Kissing the hand of a lady was a form of chivalric etiquette, probably a survival from renaissance courtly practice. Kisses on one's own fingers may be blown from a distance towards the object of affection.

Kissing was also a token of spiritual communion and fellowship, and as such was permitted by the early Christians, based on St Paul's recommendation to 'Salute one another with an holy kiss' (Rom. 16:16), and St Peter's 'Greet ye one another with a kiss of charity' (1 Pet. 5:14), which gave rise to a wave of kissing sects that saw its climax in the middle of the nineteenth century in New York state.

Kissing is also a sign of reverence and homage. Because a kiss conveys the 'contagion' of sacred things, relics, statues and holy objects, such as a robe or ring, are kissed, to receive some of their holy emanation. Muslims kiss the Kaaba; Jews the *tallith* or prayer shawl, before wearing it; when entering or leaving the house they also kiss the *mezuzah,* a little container nailed to the front door holding a piece of parchment inscribed with certain verses from the Bible. Kissing the Book after taking an oath on the Bible or other holy scripture still survives in civilized countries. Ratifying or strengthening an oath by taking it on what used to be called a halidom, or holy object, serves to identify oath and object. By extension, kissing becomes the symbol of the sanctity of a pact, and promises and oaths are often 'sealed with a kiss'.

Kisses may be delivered on the head, usually by a superior in the form of a benediction; or imprinted on the ground or feet as an act of homage or reverence. In eastern countries inferiors kiss the feet of their superiors or masters. The present-day practice of kissing the foot of the pope on ceremonial occasions derives from early Roman emperor-worship. There are other occasions when the phallus and even anus of superior persons are kissed by devotees.

Kissing brings healing, so when a child falls and is bruised the mother 'kisses the place to make it well'. Kisses help to dispel enchantment, so the Sleeping Beauty is awakened with a kiss, and the toad is changed into a handsome prince by a kiss. Kissing is a sign of peace (Lat. *pax*) and concord: 'a sign that our souls are united and that we banish all remembrance of injury'. Kisses bring luck, so gamblers kiss their cards for good fortune.

Conversely, kisses can also cause harm if used with evil intent. The kiss of Judas betrayed his master. Witches were believed to have the power of communicating malice and mischief through their kisses.

Books

Beadnell, C. M., *The Origin of the Kiss,* Watts, London, 1942.
Bloch, Ivan, *Odoratus Sexualis,* Panurge Press, New York, 1934.
Dawson, W. R., 'Nose Rubbing and Salutations', in *The Bridle of Pegasus*, Methuen, London, 1930.
D'Enjoy, P., 'Le baiser en Europe et en Chine', *Bulletins de la Société d'Anthropologie de Paris,* 4th series, Paris, 1897, vol. VIII.
Hazo, Robert, *The Idea of Love,* Praeger, New York, 1967.
Nyrop, C., *The Kiss and Its History,* Sands, London, 1901.
Roth, H. Ling, 'On Salutations', *Journal of the Anthropological Institute,* 1890, 19, p. 169 *et seq.*

KUNDALINI

(Sanskrit 'coiled'), the name of a secret energy believed to reside in the perineum*, and symbolized as a tiny serpent lying in three and a half coils, fast asleep. As it sleeps it breathes and sends pulsations up the axis joining the other occult plexuses* and gently stimulates them. That, for the ordinary man, is its main function, but specialists in tantrik yoga have evolved means of activating and awakening the kundalini and sending it on a journey through the chakras till it reaches the *sahasrara,* the chakra situated at the top of the head.

The correct arousal of the kundalini involves long breathing techniques, anal exercises, the control of the semen, the chanting of mantras and super-concentration. It takes many years of training to perfect the art. When aroused the serpent starts to tremble and then becomes erect and upright, ready for its ascent. Strange sensations of sight and sound are experienced – bright fountains and cascades of coloured lights, and sounds of humming, buzzing and whistling.

The kundalini is taken through one chakra at a time, and each chakra that is activated gives the aspirant a new and enhanced degree of perception and a special kind of power. After reaching the first or lowest chakra the kundalini returns to its base and curls up in slumber. Normally several months, even years, must intervene before a higher ascent is attempted. Few adepts are able to take the kundalini to the topmost chakra, the sahasrara, the plexus crowning the head.

The kundalini is essentially a sex and fire force and its arousal can cause very unpleasant sensations in the body, sending jets of burning heat coursing through the system. Because it is connected with the sex force it can cause uncontrollable eroticism that will seek to be appeased at all costs and in any available manner.

Awakening the kundalini without proper guidance and control can be extremely dangerous. The hazards and indeed the futility of arousing the kundalini have been pointed out by more than one expert. G. I. Gurdjieff regards the power of kundalini as illusive, and warns, 'Above all, kundalini is not anything desirable or useful for man's development.'

Ralph Metzner writes of a person known to him who succeeded in raising the kundalini to the brain, 'and was quite the opposite of pleased with the outcome'. He points out that persons with prematurely opened chakras can be found in mental hospitals.

Books

Arundale, G. S., *Kundalini: An Occult Experience,* Adyar, Madras, 1947.
Krishna, G., *Kundalini,* Shambala, Berkeley, California, 1970.
Metzner, Ralph, *Maps of Consciousness,* Macmillan, New York, 1971.
Narayananda, Swami, *The Primal Power of Man, or Kundalini Shakti,* Rishikesh, 1950.
Ouspensky, P. D., *In Search of the Miraculous,* Routledge & Kegan Paul, London, 1950.
Pandit, M. P., *Kundalini Yoga,* Madras, 1959.
Rai, A. K., *Kundalini the Goddess,* Calcutta, 1908.
Rele, V. G., *The Mysterious Kundalini,* Bombay, 1927.
Walker, Benjamin, *Hindu World,* 2 vols, Allen & Unwin, London, 1968.
Woodroffe, J., *The Serpent Power,* 5th edn, Ganesh, Madras, 1953.

LATERALITY

The disposition of the body in relation to a right-and-left symmetry. The letters A and T, for example, possess right and left laterality. The term also includes up and down symmetry as is found in the letter H. At the same time it is to be noted that lateral symmetry coexists with a definite asymmetry in the human body. The heart is slightly more to the left side; the viscera and vital organs are asymmetrical; we breathe more freely through different nostrils at different times; the left testicle of the male is lower than the right; the female breasts are not symmetrically placed.

Laterality is one of the most interesting aspects of human physiotaxis. It is manifested in certain predispositions relating to sidedness, or the right and left sides; to handedness or the right and left hands; to eyedness or the right and left eyes; to footedness or the right and left feet. There is a universal belief that occult significances are concealed in the right and left sides of things. In many languages the word for right has a laudatory meaning, while the word for left has a pejorative meaning.

The right is invariably synonymous with virtue, honour, good, lawfulness, skilfulness, correctness (hence the name). It is also the side of conscious reason. In Babylonia the right hand was the hand of good omen, the left hand of bad. In Hebrew *yamin* meant the right hand, so the tribe of Benjamin (Ben Yamin) were the sons of the right hand, or right testicle, although one of their tribe, Ehud the Benjamite who slew Eglon king of Moab, was left-handed.

The left constitutes the wrong, weak, clumsy, unpropitious side; the evil, malignant, dishonourable side. It is also the side of the heart rather than the head, the emotions rather than reason, the unconscious rather than the conscious. The English word *left* itself comes from the Anglo-Saxon *lyft*, meaning weak or worthless. In Italian *mancino*, besides left-handed, also means treacherous and dishonest.

In Hebrew tradition Samael, the chief of the Satanic host, was a demon of the left. The Norse god, Tiw, who presided over war and discord, was left-handed, and the day named after him, Tuesday, was regarded as a day of quarrels, litigations and bloodshed. In many places it is still considered unlucky to meet a left-handed person, as this betokens coming quarrels and bad luck.

In the east the left hand is always used for washing the private parts, and after defecation. This usage survives in the English term 'cack-handed', from the vulgar 'cack' (Lat. *cacare*, 'to void excrement'). Meals are eaten with one hand, the right, the left seldom being used for the purpose. The Latin epigrammatic poet Martial (d. AD 105) spoke of the left hand as *manus fututrix* 'fucking hand', since it was the hand used in masturbation.

Some psychologists hold that left-handedness is often a characteristic of people who are sexually abnormal, homosexual, incestuous or impotent. There is said to be a higher incidence of left-handedness among epileptics, the blind, deaf and dumb, stammerers, the degenerate, the mentally defective, neurotics and those who are emotionally unbalanced. The emperor Tiberius (d. AD 37), a notorious pervert, was left-handed. But many men of genius have been left-handed, including Leonardo da Vinci (d. 1519), Hans Holbein (d. 1543), Michelangelo (d. 1564), Ludwig van Beethoven (d. 1827), Goethe (d. 1832), and Friedrich Nietzsche (d. 1900).

Most normally left-handed persons hold the pencil and paper on which they write in an awkward way. This is found in the writing of all scripts. Belief in sinistrality is probably due in part to the clumsiness of the left hand. So strong is the instinct that left-handedness is somehow freakish, that even ambidextrousness, or the ability to use both hands equally well, arouses a certain feeling of strangeness in the onlooker.

LATERALITY

Laterality applies not only to handedness but to footedness, where the left foot is considered unlucky. In Scotland it is considered inauspicious to enter a house with the *skir* or left foot. This unpropitious meaning of leftness attaches to many irregular situations. The morganatic marriage between two partners of unequal social status was known as a left-handed marriage, and one that was not officially recognized; the children of the left hand, that is, of a non-marital or irregular alliance, did not inherit. The bend sinister in heraldry, a diagonal stripe running from the top right-hand corner to the left lower corner, signified bastardy when emblazoned on the escutcheon. A left-handed toast is drunk to a person's downfall or ill. A left-handed compliment is one of dubious worth. People speak of getting up on the 'wrong side' of the bed, which brings bad luck through the day, which usually means the left side.

In omens and divination generally, the right side is auspicious and the left evil. In Greek augury birds flying to the right were a good sign; to the left a bad one. A common superstition has it that if a person's right ear tingles someone is speaking well of him; if the left ear, they are maligning him. Moles on the right side of the body are good, on the left unlucky. Palmistry distinguishes between the reading of the right hand (what we become) and the left (what we are). The two sides of a persons's face* show entirely different physiognomies. There are said to be opposite* forces in the right and left sides of the body.

In Latin *dexter* means right, and *laevus* (or *sinister*) means left. From the latter connotation anything sinister implies the ominous or evil side of things. In all religious cults, the right-hand path is the correct, traditional, orthodox one; and the left-hand path, the *via sinistra,* is antinomian, or associated with black magic. In politics the right wing is conservative and traditional, the left unorthodox and revolutionary.

Chinese and Japanese jackets were always closed in front by placing the right-hand lapel over the left. Hence in oriental eyes the western method of buttoning the coat left over right was regarded as a sign of western inferiority. Western clothes for women button up as the Chinese do. In Mexico it is believed that medicine taken with the right hand will benefit the liver, and with the left hand will benefit the kidneys.

Similarly, ritual circumambulation and orientation are based on considerations of the right and left sides. In all circumambulatory rites, that which is correct is served or moved through in the right way, that is, clockwise, according to the course of the sun. Moving leftward in such rites is associated with evil and death.

It is noted that dextrals or right-handers draw profiles facing their (the artist's) left; sinistrals or left-handers, facing their right. In certain xenophrenic states such as mediumistic trance, the phenomenon of *allochiry,* 'other handedness', sometimes takes place, where there is a reversal of feeling in the two sides of the body, so that if a finger of the right hand is pricked, the left-hand finger feels the pain.

During sleep, skin temperature is usually higher on the left side; during the day it is usually higher on the right. Some authorities find significance even in the way we clasp our hands together, as in prayer. If the right thumb closes over the left thumb, it is said to indicate the predominance of reason and action; if the left thumb is on top, then emotions and instincts, imagination and passivity are dominant.

How and why a child's handedness is determined is still a mystery. Psychologists believe it to be partly the result of habit, upbringing, nursing, education and environment. In the demands of primitive warfare, the shield to protect the heart was held by the left hand, leaving the right free to wield the weapon. The Hebrew word *semol*, 'left', is said to mean 'that which is covered', and the Cymric word for 'left', *asw*, is said to come from *aswy*, meaning 'shield'.

Some think handedness is inherited to some extent. Others attribute a biological reason for the overwhelming predominance of right-handedness among people. For instance, the distribution of the viscera and the asymmetrical displacement of the centre of gravity in the human body. The greater weight of the lungs and liver on the right enables a man to balance better on the left foot, leaving the right side free for action. The inequality of the blood supply to the brain in the foetal stage of development produces the unequal growth of the cerebral hemispheres. Another factor is the superiority of one cerebral hemisphere. It is known that the right cerebral hemisphere controls the left side of the body, and the left hemisphere the right side of the body, but one hemisphere is the dominant one. The superiority of one eye is still another fact to be taken into account. As a result of this ocular dominance the body is thrown slightly out of balance, leading to the use of one hand more than the other.

The placement of the heart slightly to the left of the body, and the consequent disposition of the blood vessels and arteries, may also play a part in laterality. It is a curious fact that when a person is lost in the desert he tends to walk not in a straight line, but in a wide circle, which may be either clockwise or anticlockwise, and may come right back to the point of departure. Most people naturally tend to turn towards the right. Some say this is because the earth moves to the right, and others that it is because the physiological motor impulses go more easily to the right side.

The question whether there is an absolute right or left is problematic, since it is only and always relative to the observer. When we turn around what was on the right is now on the left. Right and left therefore have no existence beyond our senses, like colour or sound. Ernst Mach (d. 1916), Austrian philosopher, believed that our distinction between right and left might be based on chemical differences.

Immanuel Kant (d. 1804) said that left and right were appearances only and existed in relation to something else that was handed. If we were completely symmetrical in all ways, we would be unable to appreciate rightness and leftness. Scientists say that to convey the notion of right and left to an inhabitant of a distant galaxy whose matter may not be the same as ours and whose physics operates on different laws, would be an impossible problem.

Books

Barsley, M., *The Left-Handed Book,* Souvenir Press, London, 1966.
Barsley, M., *Left-Handed Man in a Right-Handed World,* Pitman, London, 1970.
Blau, Abram, *The Master Hand,* New York, 1946.
Clark, Margaret, *Left-Handedness,* University of London Press, 1957.
Fritsch, Vilma, *Left and Right in Science and Life,* Barrie & Rockliff, London, 1968.
Gould, G. M., *Righthandedness and Lefthandedness,* Philadelphia, 1908.
Hertz, Robert, *Death and the Right Hand,* Cohen & West, London 1960.
Jackson, John, *Ambidexterity,* Kegan Paul, Trench, Trubner, London, 1905.
Jones, H. M., *Ambidexterity and Mental Culture,* Heinemann, London, 1914.
Lombroso, Cesare, *Left Sidedness,* New York, 1903.
Naidoo, S., *Laterality,* London, 1961.
Parson, B. S., *Lefthandedness: A New Interpretation,* New York, 1924.
Wile, Ira, *Handedness: Right and Left,* Lothrop Lee & Shepard, Boston, 1934.
Wilson, Daniel, *Lefthandedness,* London, 1891.

LEGS

Legs are associated with a host of beliefs concerning the feet, footprints, knees and sacred lameness. Legs represent the dignity, strength and nobility of man, who alone of all creatures, walks upright upon his legs. The Bible describes man's beauty in terms of his legs, as when the bride speaking of her husband says, 'His legs are as pillars of marble, set upon sockets of fine gold' (S. of S. 5:15). And in the verses telling of what pleases the Lord the psalmist says, 'He delighteth not in the strength of the horse, nor in the legs of a man' (Ps. 147:10).

Man's thighs are the sign of his physical stamina and virility. In the Bible they are sometimes used as a euphemism for the testicles. The thigh bone is the longest bone in the body, and the Latin name for it, *femur,* signifies 'that which engenders'. Dionysus was born out of the thigh of Zeus. In Hindu legend Aurva is born of the thigh of his mother, and Nishada of the thigh of his father.

The mysterious personage who wrestled with Jacob, at the place called thereafter Peniel ('face of God'), put Jacob's thigh out of joint, and renamed the patriarch Israel ('strife of God'). The precise significance of this episode in the life of Jacob has been the subject of some secret commentary.

The legs symbolize stability and power. Wrestlers smite their thighs while manoeuvring for a catch, and heroes break the thighs of their enemies. Standing on one leg alters the centre of stability and concentrates psychic power, hence formal curses are uttered while in such a stance. In one form of yogic meditation the man stands on one leg with the foot of the other leg propped up against the knee of the upright one.

The foot is the pedestal of man, in direct contact with Mother Earth, absorbing vigour from her powerful emanations. In ancient times religious and cult rites were invariably performed by priests who were unshod, to maintain this contact with the earth. According to esoteric physiology, five subtle arteries are situated in the foot: the heel (regulating occult power), the big toe (sexual rhythms), the ball of the foot (digestive processes), the arch (breathing), instep (the heart). Regular massage of these arteries was believed to be highly beneficial.

The heel has a profound significance. In Hindu occultism the heel forms the centre of one of the plexuses in esoteric lore, and bears a relation to the balance and tensions of the body. When in contact with the ground the heel emphasizes the body's association with gross and practical things. Conversely a posture with the heels raised from the ground signifies aspiration godwards, ambition, hubris and imbalance.

Injury to the foot or leg results in lameness, and ritual limping and hobbling formed part of certain ancient cults and were deliberately cultivated. A person standing on one leg assumes a form of lameness by renouncing the use of one foot. This is thought to concentrate power and give it direction. In tribal magic the sorcerer often assumed this one-legged stance when he directed a spell.

A curious physiological factor associated with lameness is that it is believed to increase sexual ability through strengthening the tendons of the groin. Footbinding in China, resulting in the deformity of the feet of girls, was said to have been practised to increase the strength of the vaginal reflexes and make women more proficient in the sexual act. It is recorded that certain Amazon princesses used to break the leg of handsome male prisoners of war whom they intended to use as sexual partners, because they found that 'the lame best perform the act of love'.

There is a worldwide superstition that the marks left by feet bear the 'contagion' of the owner and form a link with him, and that by injuring a person's footprint, such as by driving a nail into it, you can injure his feet. Because of the same belief in pathemic contagion, the footprints of saints and holy men are preserved and revered in many parts of the world, usually in commemoration of a visit. The Bible makes a reference (Ezek. 43:7) to the veneration of the place upon which the soles of feet have been set.

Books

Hall, M. P., *Man the Grand Symbol of the Mysteries*, Philosophical Research Society, Los Angeles, 1947.

Onians, R. B., *The Origins of European Thought*, Cambridge University Press, 1951.

LIBIDO

(Lat. 'desire'), the vital energy, particularly as it manifests in the dynamic sexual instincts. In common parlance libido is a lustful desire, which is conveyed to the sex organs and sensitizes them to discharge the built-up inner tensions in the pleasurable and satisfying act of sexual intercourse, which affords it relief.

In psychoanalytic theory libido is diffused through all parts of the body, which therefore constitutes an overall erotogenic zone, and is the source of all erotic (sensual) sensations. In the older theory the human infant was spoken of as being polymorphously perverse, because his sexual instincts were not yet directed to any specific areas but diffused all over the body.

Three stages mark the development of the libido, and with it the individual's ego and character, and this development determines the areas around which the component instincts become grouped. The first is the *oral* stage, which lasts for one or two years, and is found in breast-feeding and thumb-sucking in infants, survives in nail-biting in children, and biting and kissing in adults. The second is the *anal* stage which manifests in coprophilia or dirt love in children and an interest in faeces and dirt generally in later life. In adulthood it finds additional expression in collecting and hoarding things and in the love of money. The last is the *genital* stage, when the instincts are concentrated in the sex organs, although traces of the two earlier phases remain throughout life in all individuals.

Genital libido manifests in feelings of sexual excitement. It is found in animals in the form of oestrus, heat, rut or must, recurring in periodical cycles. Voltaire (d. 1778) remarked that the human being is the only animal that drinks when it is not thirsty and makes love at all times. Both men and women, he said, can have and enjoy sexual intercourse at any 'season'. But the fact is that there is a cycle of sexual hyperaesthesia, or greater intensity of desire, amounting at times to erotomania, in both men and women, which is still seen among some primitive peoples, but which has to some extent become submerged in civilized societies. Ordinarily, most women feel a greater sexual urge before and after menstruation.

Sex desire is a strong generator of bio-energy, which can be utilized in sex-magic, sex-mysticism and occultism in general. In occult terms a considerable amount of animal energy is released during the manifestations of lust. That is why occult groups of the left hand end their gatherings in orgies, permitting indiscriminate and perverse intercourse, as a result of which the atmosphere becomes charged with power which the master then utilizes for his magical operations.

Sexual stimulation of the male causes the seminal essence held in the seminal vesicles to melt and flow and give off a subtle emanation, which is accompanied by a great charge of power. But the female sex energy, called gynergy, is regarded as more important for magical purposes and is infinitely more potent. The very presence of a woman creates a special aura in the atmosphere, since she evokes sex-consciousness in man. This is augmented during her sexual desire, sexual activity and orgasm.

Chinese taoists believed that the female gave off very powerful *yin* virtues, especially during the fourth to sixth days after menstruation, and particularly during her orgasm (*khuai*). A woman when inclined for sex was saturated with yin essence of which she had an inexhaustible supply, and when so inclined she could be used in any manner, in normal sexual intercourse, sodomy or cunnilingus, and the man by special methods, including acclivity*, could absorb this energy.

Among tantriks the equivalent of yin is *shakti.* They also say that powerful pulsations of a subtle and potent energy called *kala* are given off by the female in the form of vaginal vibrations when she is on heat, when sexually aroused, and especially at the moment of orgasm.

The Jews too were aware of the gynergetic phenomenon. According to the Kabbalah, the Shekinah, or presence of the power of God in His feminine aspect, envelops all women, and abides for a short time in man only while he is in union with woman. During sexual intercourse with one's lawful spouse this Shekinah emanation is very strong indeed. But it diminishes in power and bestows only a blemished advantage to a man in illicit sexual activity with a woman. The nineteenth letter of the Hebrew alphabet, *qoph,* represents the moon, the cerebellum, the eye of the needle, the vulva, and denotes the secret energy of woman.

Women give off numerous secretions from the genital canal, as Havelock Ellis (d. 1939) has pointed out. Tantriks speak of three basic secretions: urine, the least important and the weakest; menstrual blood which has a greater quantity of the female energy but is mixed with poisonous ingredients; and the female 'seed', which is also mentioned in Chinese, Japanese, Korean and Tibetan manuals. This latter is extraordinarily rejuvenative for the man who knows how to utilize it. In all, fifteen kinds of secretions are named in eastern texts, but there is a sixteenth which is kept secret. All come from the cerebro-spinal fluid and the female endocrine glands. There is yet a seventeenth which is entirely non-physical. Many forms of sex-magic make use of gynergy and of these secretions.

Books

Charles, Edward, *An Introduction to the Study of the Psychology, Physiology and Biochemistry of the Sexual Impulse*, Boriswood, London, 1935.

De Ropp, Robert S., *Sex Energy,* Jonathan Cape, London, 1970.

Ellis, Havelock, *Studies in the Psychology of Sex,* Random House, New York, 1936.

Fleiss, Robert, *Erotogeneity and Libido,* International Universities Press, New York, 1956.

Freud, Sigmund, *An Outline of Psychoanalysis,* Hogarth Press, London, 1964.

Reik, Theodor, *Of Love and Lust,* Farrar, Straus, New York, 1957.

Walker, Benjamin, *Sex and the Supernatural*, Macdonald, London, 1970.

LOVE

The state of harmonious existence arising from personal attachment, devotion and benevolence. In its most generic sense it is a feeling of universal affection (Gk. *philia*), an inclination of the soul to kinship with all beings, such as is found in persons of high spiritual attainment.

Any classification of the many ranges of love must first consider the two great divisions of non-sexual and sexual love. Included in the former we have such manifestations as a broad humanitarianism, a love of all mankind (Gk. *philanthropia*). Not far removed is the love of one's neighbours, associates, comrades, or what is called brotherly love (Gk. *philadelphia*). It also includes Platonic love (*eros*) as defined by Plato. Popularly, though not quite accurately, Platonic love signifies the bond between the opposite sexes, but divested of all sensual passion. In the *Symposium* this love is said to work sometimes through the flesh, but in its sublimest form is an aspiration towards Truth, Beauty and Goodness. In the Christian view it is expressed as benevolence (Gk. *agape*), or spiritual love (Lat. *caritas*), rendered 'charity' in the Bible (1 Cor. 13). The love of parents for children, of children for parents, family affection, friendship, the love of one's own people, one's own tribe or community, completes the classification of non-sexual love.

Sexual love is invested with desire (Lat. *libido*), pleasure (Lat. *amor*) and lust (Gk. *epithymia*). One range of sexual love seeks deviant ways of self-expression such as homosexuality, necrophilia, bestiality. Another finds fulfilment in variations of male-female sexuality, which includes love in wedlock, romantic love, the love of the counterpart, promiscuity, free love and sex communism, troubadour love and adultery.

Students of the subject also classify the opposites found in love, namely: spiritual and carnal love; sacred and profane love; conjugal and romantic love; mature and adolescent love (calf-love); heterosexual and homosexual love; therapeutic (healing) and pathological (diseased) love.

It is important to distinguish between love that seeks fulfilment in the opposite sex, and two closely related concepts, namely, procreation and sex. Reproduction is not necessarily connected with love. The force that draws two organisms together is often independent of fertilization and procreation. Love in the sense of such mutual attraction is found in all nature, from molecule to man. Protozoa like the paramecium, which do not have to unite to produce, still seek each other and exemplify the kind of primary groping towards love, which is fulfilled in man. Again, the phenomenon of sexuality, with its overtones of lust and physical satisfaction, can be and often is independent of love.

The Talmud says that since God could not be everywhere he created mothers; thus love becomes in its earliest states of existence a form of contact with the divine, as necessary as breath. A child inadequately loved will develop into an inadequate social being. It is during the period of infant dependency that a child learns to love and respond to others. Every adult's full maturity, physical (including sexual), psychological and spiritual, depends upon the love he received as a child.

In later life, as in infancy, disappointment in love, unrequited affection, rejection in love, can lead to illness, heartbreak and even death. Literally millions of people are physically and mentally ill for want of someone to love and someone to love them. This lack of love can warp the character and undermine the personality. A great deal of neurotic, delinquent, criminal and psychopathic behaviour in adolescent and adult life can be traced to lack of love in childhood. It has been suggested that even hardened prisoners often die, not from ill treatment, but because of 'deprivation of human support and affection', as a result of which they just surrender the wish to live.

Every individual is born with an innate need to love and be loved, for love gives assurance, provides security, releases therapeutic energy, and creates conditions for healthy biological development, emotional maturity and social responsiveness. There are few aspects of love that do not possess the qualities that make it a spiritual force and an occult power.

Romantic love is the theme of poetry, song and legend. It ranges from the frenzied madness of a transient infatuation, to the permanence of a passionate attraction that defies death itself. True love grows and at the same time enlarges the personality. A man and woman emerge from their experience with renewed vigour that comes from an expansion of awareness. The aim of love is union with the other in delight, tenderness and passion. It creates new dimensions of experience. In true love everything is permitted, everything is possible, everything is sacred.

Such love, even when unfulfilled, does not diminish. Some indeed feel that love fades with fulfilment and that love's greatest intensity is reached, and indeed multiplied, in the anguish of unfulfilled desire. Such was the idea underlying much of the courtly love which was advocated and practised in certain circles in Europe during the middle ages. This was the breathless yearning of unassuageable passion that made everything around one take on a new dimension of vitality.

Love follows without fear the urges of the heart, and braves sorrow, disappointment, danger. It overrides the dictates of society and the moral code, taking little account of discretion, judgment, reason or common sense. Lovers do not feel they have sinned or done wrong; they do not ask or care to be forgiven; they feel they are above the rules of ethics and propriety, beyond good and evil, outside everyday experience. Even adultery is purified by love.

Love is the most important thing in life. It possesses absolute power and claims the complete person. No one in love can give reasons for being in love. The full intensity of love can be so consuming that everything else loses its proper proportion and nothing else matters except to be with the loved one. Gratification of the sexual instinct plays a subsidiary part in this rage of passion, and one desires above all else to merge one's inner being with the other and in the mutual surrender of sentiment, intellect, imagination and the senses, to find the whole self. Such love if unrequited makes every ambition and activity, every pleasure, all wealth and fame, seem like Dead Sea fruit which turns to ashes in the mouth Breathing becomes a conscious struggle against suffocation and the aching heart, and life becomes so unbearable that it were finding a sublime peace to end it.

Love does not necessarily produce happiness, but rather a kind of ecstasy. Often it transcends happiness. It is a thing apart, like nothing else, utterly beyond classification. In love, a man or woman is singled out for a noble and spiritual experience, and life becomes infinitely meaningful for them. But it is often a sad experience. It has been said that men and women have a secret preference for what is unhappy, and if so, love provides them with the opportunity, for it brings suffering and torment along with bliss. Both Greeks and Romans looked upon love as a sickness. Plato (d. 347) called it a 'frenzy'. In Arabic tradition too love is a sickness, and in love no person is normal or sane. Ultimately, romantic love is death-seeking. It is a type of threshold experience bordering on death, and this is found even in the sensations accompanying orgasm*.

The great lovers whose names have become legendary are not to be envied, since they are accursed, like the victims of a Greek tragedy, risking all for their fateful passion, and doomed to die in the end or to bring tragedy in their wake. Yusuf and Zuleikha (the names of Joseph and Potiphar's wife in Arabic legend), Paris and Helen, Aeneas and Dido, Antony and Cleopatra, Aucassin and Nicolette, Lancelot and Guinevere, Tristan and Iseult, Abelard and Heloise, Romeo and Juliet, Dante and Beatrice, Paolo and Francesca, were all associated with disappointment or death.

On the other hand there are those who feel that the rewards more than compensate for the drawbacks. In love the world is suddenly widened, made more profound, deepened, beautified, intensified, enriched. No other passion known to man ennobles him as love does. True love consecrates and transforms, so that the loved one appears better to behold and has excellences never seen before. Every love has a fresh virginal quality about it, for as Sören Kierkegaard (d. 1855) puts it, 'In love every man starts from the beginning.'

Finally, love has an archetypal and mystical status. It is an attempt to restore a lost identity, a return to reintegration and unity through a counterpart. Love has been called 'an affinity of being with being', 'a nostalgia for a lost continuity', 'the gravitational force of the soul'. In Plato's *Symposium* the poet, Aristophanes, describes love as the urge of an originally androgynous being to find his split-off half. Love is thus the desire and pursuit of the Whole.

Male and female have a reciprocal destiny and they find themselves in each other. Love is a hunger for unity, a cessation, even temporary, of being other and separate. It is a cosmic principle, rising over all levels of existence. It is the nearest thing to the hunger and thirst after divine experience that the saints and mystics speak about, giving one a beatific foretaste of heavenly joys.

Books

D'Arcy, M. C., *The Mind and Heart of Love,* New York, 1956.
Hazo, Robert G., *The Idea of Love*, Praeger, New York, 1967.
Morgan, D., *Love: Plato, the Bible & Freud,* Prentice-Hall, New York, 1964.
Nygren, Anders, *Agape and Eros,* Philadelphia, 1953.
Rougemont, Denis de, *The Myths of Love,* Faber, London, 1964.
Rutter, M., *Maternal Deprivation Reassessed,* Penguin Books, Harmondsworth, 1972.
Sorokin, Pitrim, *The Ways and Power of Love,* Beacon Press, Boston, 1954.

LUNGS

Lungs have been compared to bellows that draw in and expel the air. Physiologically the process of respiration*, which begins at birth and continues till death, is the means by which oxygen is absorbed by the body and carbon dioxide given out. But it has long been believed that what is actually taken in by the lungs is not merely the atmosphere around the individual, but a very special element which is the vitalizing substance of the universe still unknown to science (*see* pneuma). In occult belief the action of the lungs is to cool the furnace of the heart, and in this sense the pulmonary functions are the opposite of the cardiac functions. These two organs form a triangular system with the brain, so that all their actions are reciprocally related.

In the Chinese physiological system the lungs (*fei*) are the executives of the heart, which is the king. They are the seat of righteousness and the repository of inward thoughts. Like the stomach, the lungs absorb part of the external environment, and in Buddhist esoteric physiology share with other hollow areas in the mystical symbolism of *shunyata*, 'emptiness'. Although empty, the lungs are potentially complete, full and whole.

Tibetan physiology links the lungs (*lobu*) with the head, heart, solar plexus and sex organs. A network of subtle arteries (*rtsa*) interconnects these five cardinal zones. The centre controlling the lungs lies not within the lungs but in the throat, and an important artery (*thong-rtsa*) carries the impulses from throat to mouth. The energy that is inhaled with each breath is transmuted at the throat centre into the vitalizing charge that gives strength to the human organism.

Books

Huard, Pierre, *La Médecine tibétaine*, Latema, Paris, n.d.
Marcet, W., *A Contribution to the History of the Respiration of Man*, London, 1897.
Williams, C. A. S., *Encyclopedia of Chinese Symbolism and Art Motives*, Julian Press, New York, 1960.

MAN

Man can be considered at several levels of significance. He has a physical body, and an asomatic* or non-material body which includes the soul. Between these two extremes he is in contact with many different dimensions of existence. Mystics, occultists, hermetics, take a transcendental view of man, and express this view in rhapsodic and rapturous terms. In the esoteric concept, the Copernican system did not displace the earth from its central position in the universe, nor did the Darwinian theory shift man from his central place on earth. The human entity still remains the world's centre, and the universe extends from man outwards to all infinity. The Kabbalah says: 'Where you stand there stand all worlds.' And the German poet, Rainer Maria Rilke (d. 1926), adds: 'Where you are there arises a place.'

In his total make-up, man is a microcosm of the universe. He is a transcript in minuscule of the grand script writ across the cosmos, a lesser version of the divine plenum. Yet he reflects not only God, but all nature and the world, and every principle, whether good or evil. As the glory of divinity abides in man, so in him lies the iniquity of Satan. In him is every virtue and every vice. In him all states of heaven and hell. Every human being is linked with some part of the upper and the lower spheres.

In the mind of man lies the consciousness of the cosmos, in his soul the universal essence. Man's will is dynamic throughout the world, and his word is powerful to reach the outer bounds of space. In man's body is contained every shape and every geometrical form, every sign and symbol, with all their inner meanings, potencies and significances. In his system is every means of locomotion and mechanical principle. In him is the universe with all its elements, all numbers, colours, rays; the disposition of the constellations, the traits of the zodiac; the cosmos in all its dimensions and directions, time with all its durations, from immeasurable aeons to incalculable moments. In him are all changes of season, temperatures, and times of coming and going, of existence and becoming, of being and not being. In him are reflected the solstices, the equinoxes, and all the moving panorama of the universe. In him is the eternal flux.

Man is the universal criterion, the canon of proportion for every manifestation (*see* harmonic proportion). He comprises all the energies and substances out of which the universe is fashioned. His body holds all levels of etheric matter, the elements, the potencies. Its workings are in harmony with the mechanism of nature, and it contains every measure and rhythm.

An occult maxim says, 'The cosmos is not great; my body is not small.' The universe is man writ large. As with cosmic man, Adam Kadmon, so in man the microcosm, the earth is present in his flesh, the waters in his bodily fluids, the atmosphere in his vital airs, the fire in his essence. The erogenous zones are correlated to the great crosspoints of the universe, containing the creative impulses that make for cosmic regeneration. Man is male and female within himself, as is woman androgynous in herself. Together they form a united being, linked with the greater whole.

The universe is delicately balanced and the pivot of its equilibrium is provided by man, the *axis mundi,* 'the fulcrum of the world'. A disorder in the microcosm disturbs the macrocosm. An impulse from below reacts on all the spheres. Man's evil infects nature. The life of the human being pulsates to the hidden rhythm of the macrocosm, for man is patterned after the celestial archetype. Therefore everything done by the individual is reflected in the macrocosm, and the higher reality is affected by the acts of man. The laws of the cosmos have been written into man. In other words, man and nature are organized on the same pattern. Know yourself and you will understand the universe. When man explores the universe he is exploring himself, and in understanding himself he begins to understand the universe.

These ideas have been held in many places by many eminent people, who have become deeply aware of the interrelationship between the immanent world of man and the transcendent landscape of the divine world. One of the earliest expressions of the notion occurs in the famous hermetic text known as the Emerald Tablet, which traditionally dates back many thousands of years. One verse of this tablet reads: 'What is below is like what is above, and what is above is like what is below.' The Greeks held the same view, as we find in the words of the celebrated sophist Protagoras (d. 410 BC), 'Man is the measure of all things.' The Chinese summed it up in their own way: 'Man's head is round, and so is the sky; like the earth his feet are square; his five viscera correspond to the five elements; his vertebrae to the fortnights that make up the seasons; his 365 bones to the days of the year.'

Buddha (d. 483 BC) echoed a related idea when he said, 'I proclaim to you that this animated body, no more than one fathom in height, is the dwelling place of the world.' A medieval Hindu text, the *Visvasara Tantra*, teaches: 'What is here is elsewhere. What is not here is nowhere.' The stoic philosopher, Poseidonius (d. 46 BC) of Apamea in Syria, spoke of man as a 'bridge-being', intermediate between two worlds, higher and lower, animal and divine. The kabbalists believed that the tetragrammaton, the four Hebrew letters (*yod, he, vau, he*) that speak God's name, written downwards, form the image of a man, showing that man is God in miniature. According to the *Zohar*, 'As soon as man appeared all was achieved, both in the upper and the lower worlds, for all is contained in man.' Philo Judaeus (d. AD 50) said that man was God in miniature, and also the epitome of nature, the *brachys kosmos* (Gk. 'little world').

The medieval scholastics continued the theme. Albertus Magnus (d. 1280) spoke of man as the *imago dei*, 'image of God', and also as the *imago mundi*, 'image of the universe'. Earlier, Origen (d. 254) had said, 'Know that you are another world in miniature, and that you are the sun, the moon and the stars too.' According to Nicholas of Cusa (d. 1464), the heavens are in the human form and likeness. Pico della Mirandola (d. 1494), Italian renaissance philosopher, wrote, 'God contains in Himself all things because He is their source, and man contains all things because he is their centre.' And in the view of Cornelius Agrippa (d. 1535), 'Man is the most express image of God, and man's nature is the most complete image of the universe.'

In the words of Paracelsus (d. 1541):

> The *spiritus vitae* [life spirit] takes its origin from the *spiritus mundi* [world spirit], and being an emanation of the latter it contains the elements of the cosmos, so the influence of the stars may be seen in the body of man. It is a great thing to consider for once, that out of nothing God made everything, and out of everything he made man. Man is an extract of the firmament, the quintessence of the cosmos, the spark of the divine flame.

The writers of the seventeenth and eighteenth centuries were no less convinced about the matter. 'The human constitution', said Jacob Boehme (d. 1624), 'bears the stamp, seal and signature of the whole mundane order.' According to Robert Fludd (d. 1637), man is the magical mirror of the universe, 'the centre and miracle of the world, a replica of the divine keyboard'. In the view of Nicholas Culpeper (d. 1654), 'Man is the recapitulation of all things, the perfection of the whole work of nature'. And according to Sir Thomas Browne (d. 1682), 'We carry within us the wonders we seek without. There is all Africa and her prodigies within.'

Gottfried Wilhelm Leibniz (d. 1716) held that every individual contains an integral reproduction of the universe. 'Nature', said Emanuel Swedenborg (d. 1772), 'is man in diffusion.' Among the thinkers of this century, the philosopher, Rudolf Eucken (d. 1926), said: 'Man is the meeting point of various stages of reality.' Carl Gustav Jung wrote: 'Our psyche is set up in accord with the structure of the universe.'

Man has been described as a wise, inventive, talking animal. Aristotle in the *Nicomachean Ethics* defines man not as a rational but as a choosing agent, able to make decisions, based on long-term goals which are self-selected. Pico della Mirandola (d. 1494) says of man's glory that it lies in his mutability and free will; his orbit is not fixed like that of the angels or animals, and he can transform himself and become what he wishes. He can be saint or brute, demon or angel, and if he chooses he can withdraw into the secret centre of his own spirit and encounter the solitary darkness of God. 'Who', asks Pico, 'would not admire this chameleon?'

Man is the centre of all mysteries. His thoughts are radiances, creative and dynamic, his actions are a trail of wonders. He is a living talisman, attuned by invisible strings to the greater cosmos, and through the chords of his being the music of the spheres sends forth its celestial diapason. Peter Lombard (d. 1164), bishop of Paris, said: 'Man is made to serve God. The universe is made to serve man. Man is placed at the middle point of the world that he may both serve and be served.'

Man indeed is a supernatural creature, a replica of the divine prototype. In the New Testament he is the citizen of another kingdom, and one of the household of God.

Books

Browne, Sir Thomas, *Religio Medici and Other Works*, L. C Martin (ed.), Oxford University Press, London, 1964.

Butler, J. A. V., *Man is a Microcosm,* Macmillan, London, 1950.

Campbell, Joseph (ed.), *Spiritual Disciplines,* Routledge & Kegan Paul, London, 1960.

Cassirer, Ernest, *The Individual and the Cosmos in Renaissance Philosophy,* Barnes & Noble, New York, 1963.

Conger, G. P., *Theories of Macrocosm and Microcosm in the History of Philosophy,* Russell & Russell, New York, 1922.

Dewar, D., *Man: A Special Creation,* Houldershaw, Southend, 1946.

Hall, M. P., *Man: The Grand Symbol of the Mysteries,* Philosophical Research Society, Los Angeles, 1947.

Harrison, R. J., *Man, the Peculiar Animal,* Penguin, Harmondsworth, 1958.

Jung, C. G., *Memories, Dreams, Reflections,* Collins and Routledge & Kegan Paul, London, 1963.

Lestocq, Hubert, *Secret Man,* Rider, London, 1945.

Needham, Joseph, *Science and Civilisation in China*, Cambridge University Press.

Pachter, Henry, *Paracelsus: Magic Into Science,* Henry Schuman, New York, 1951.

Radhakrishnan, S. and Raju, P. T. (eds), *The Concept of Man,* Allen & Unwin, London, 1960.

Reinhardt, Karl, *Kosmos und Sympathie,* Munich, 1926.

Towers, M. *et al., Naked Ape or Homo Sapiens?* Garnstone Press, London, 1969.

Wind, Edgar, *Pagan Mysteries in the Renaissance*, 2nd edn, Faber, London, 1967.

Wright, J. S., *What is Man?* Paternoster Press, London, 1955.

MASTURBATION

Masturbation is the commonest and most widespread form of self-gratification. It is found among children, adolescents, married and unmarried men and women, and the aged. Most people feel unhappy about having masturbated and are ashamed of it. It places a heavy burden of guilt on all who indulge in it and gives them a deep sense of having committed a sin or done something disgraceful and disgusting. Few adults, even though they know that the habit is universal, like to talk about it, or are willing to confess to it. The fear of undergoing experimental tests in drugs or hypnosis, is often due to a fear that the habit would be exposed.

It was once widely believed that masturbation caused blindness, pimples, a blotchy skin, trembling, a poor memory, epilepsy and insanity. Practised in excess, beyond the needs of natural relief, it is still popularly thought to cause these maladies. Psychologists say that masturbation is often a sign of neurosis, anxiety and fear, and represents an aggression or resentment against someone. In such cases it is a symbolical act of protest against something said or done which one resents, and a form of release from the resulting tensions.

In its more esoteric aspect auto-stimulation with its highly charged sexual feelings and the discharge of vital fluids is connected with procreative power. In ancient Egypt, as recorded in the hieratic papyrus of Nesi Amsu, the god Atum's self-gratification was a creative act. He is made to say: 'I established it in my heart; I copulated with my fist; I joined myself in embrace with my shadow; my heart came into my hand; with pleasure the semen was ejaculated.' By this means the god created the deities Shu and Tefnut.

A great burst of energy accompanies the act of masturbation. Psychic researchers have repeatedly established that the centre of poltergeist activity is often a persistent masturbator, and they believe it possible that the biomagnetic energy drawn by the 'poltergeist' is obtained during the release of sexual tension, when the masturbator reaches his or her climax. Excessive masturbation by adolescents has also been cited as the reason for other unexplained psychic occurrences, which stop when the excess ceases.

Autosexuality is frequently accompanied by fervid erotic fantasy, and the images, reinforced by lust and passion, are believed to actualize for a time as transient thought-forms. They have been described as 'silently wailing spirits', conjured up out of nothing and given an ephemeral existence lasting for a few minutes. In sex magic, however, magicians use these 'offspring of Onan', and cause them to be 'ensouled' by evil entities, so that they actually remain active for periods of several days. Black magicians sometimes employ masturbators for this kind of creative purpose, often in group masturbatory orgies. A form of *modo solito,* 'solitary method' of seminal magic, without manipulation and with flaccid penis, is also practised as a means of augmenting one's psychic powers.

The techniques of sex magic as perfected in Grade VIII of the occult society known as Ordo Templi Orientis, includes the practice of mystical masturbation, the object being to achieve a state of 'eroto-comatose lucidity'. The operator visualizes what he desires, and carries out the procedure.

Aleister Crowley (d. 1947) makes a reference to this when he speaks of the performance of an act *manibus plenis,* 'with full hands'.

Anton Szandor LaVey, priest of Satanism, recommends masturbation as part of a ritual for a woman who desires to increase her sexual awareness and thereby gain power over men.

Books

Alibert, Dr, *The Vices of Love: Self Abuse Among Women,* Medical Library, Paris, n.d.
Budge, E. A. Wallis, *The Hieratic Papyrus of Nesi Amsu,* London, 1891.
Hare, E. H., 'Masturbational Insanity', *Journal of Mental Science,* 1962, 108, 1–25.
LaVey, A. S., *The Compleat Witch,* Dodd, Mead, New York, 1970.
Meagher, J. F. W., *A Study of Masturbation and the Psychosexual Life,* London, n.d.
Menzies, K., *Autoerotic Phenomena in Adolescence,* Lewis, London, 1921.
Rohleder, H., *Die Masturbation,* Berlin, 1899.
Stekel, W., *Auto-erotism,* P. Nevill, London, 1950.
Symonds, J. and Grant, K. (eds). *The Magical Record of the Beast 666* (Aleister Crowley), Duckworth, London, 1972.
Tissot, S. A., *An Essay on Onanism,* Dublin, 1772.

MEDITATION

An aid to mental development, and, according to its advocates, to spiritual advancement and enlightenment, involves a great deal of mental discipline. Some people have a natural aptitude for meditation, but most need to adopt guidelines and follow certain fixed procedures. Meditation is an ordered course in a particular direction aimed at a predetermined goal in a form of self-induced xenophrenia. Throughout the meditative process, even during all the apparently 'unconscious' or trance phases, there is allegedly a continuity of conscious awareness. Meditation can confer genuine benefits, but is not without its pitfalls. The four chief stages in the meditative tradition are briefly outlined below.

(1) *Attention,* the first stage, is said to be like 'preparing to enter the pool of the mind'. It requires an intentness of consciousness, the direction of awareness by an act of will. But because men are constantly beset by irrelevant lures and diverted by transient issues, they need meditative aids, which are provided at this stage. This first phase is known in yoga as *pratyahara,* 'withholding', or the exclusion of distractions from the mind such as sense objects and conceptual notions. In Buddhist meditation one can start by focusing the mind on a simple object such as a bare pole standing upright on the ground. It must be done in a state of 'relaxed attentiveness', with no attempt at analytical thought. When extraneous thoughts arise one must not follow them; they should be disregarded, as bubbles on the surface, and allowed to burst and vanish.

Psychologists point out, however, that rigid, undeviating attention can also be pathological in origin. It is then known as *hyperprosexia* (Gk. *pros,* 'over', *exō,* 'to hold'), a psychotic condition in which the mind takes hold of an idea with unshakeable fixity. This is found in various kinds of mental disorder.

Certain forms of *monoideism* (singleness of idea), as in ceaseless daydreaming; or in erotic, status or power fantasizing; and *monomania*, where the mind is obsessed with a single thought (*idée fixe*), and one keeps reverting to it in speech, are symptomatic of the same pathology. A number of seemingly paranormal faculties have been explained in terms of such hyperprosexia, where the powers of attention, observation and discrimination are at work to an abnormal degree, so that people can apparently see, hear and feel things that are beyond the scope of the average person.

(2) *Concentration,* the next stage, is the ability to centre one's consciousness on a subject without being distracted. It is 'entering the pool of the mind'. In yoga this stage is known as *dharana,* 'holding'. In the Buddhist system the exercise of the previous stage may be advanced to include some such qualification as: think of the same pole, but do not think of a monkey climbing it. The idea of the monkey has now been suggested to the student and he has deliberately to exclude it from consciousness. This is achieved without strain or effort, and in a condition of 'passive concentration'. Great powers accrue from concentration. Sir John Woodroffe (d. 1908), authority on tantrik yoga, wrote that by means of concentration alone, certain yogis are able to kill insects, birds and even larger animals. They can light a fire without flint or matches, by the same means.

The great mathematician and engineer, Archimedes (d. 212 BC) of Syracuse, is supposed to have had extraordinary powers of concentration. The story goes that once deeply absorbed in a problem he unconsciously registered the rise of the water level as he immersed his body in the tub for a bath, and in a flash conceived the idea of an important hydrostatic principle. So profound was his mood that he immediately rushed through the streets crying, 'Eureka! Eureka!' (I have it), quite unaware of the fact that he was still naked. The same genius during the capture of his beloved Syracuse by the Roman general, Marcellus, had been so absorbed in some mathematical diagrams he had drawn in the dust, that he said to a Roman soldier who came too close, 'Do not disturb my circles, fellow', which so annoyed the Roman that he killed him, in spite of specific instructions from Marcellus that the great scholar was not to be touched.

For training in concentration the Neoplatonist philosopher, Plotinus (d. AD 270), recommended mathematics, dialectics and analytical thought. Sufis refer to the middle stages in the meditative process as *fikr* or devotional concentration on higher things. But in all systems it is emphasized that without concentration no progress can be made, for it is by this means alone that the mind learns to become receptive to the messages from the higher planes.

(3) *Contemplation* involves deep internalizing of thought. This stage has been compared to 'diving into the pool of the mind'. Here the degree of mental absorption reaches a kind of trance. All the senses are closed to distracting incoming stimuli: one's consciousness is withdrawn and the mind focused inwards. It is a receptive state and some regard it as the final stage of meditation proper. It continues to be a mental operation, but the man absorbed in contemplation is divested of the ego. In yoga this stage is known

as *dhyana,* 'contemplation', in Pali as *jhana,* in Chinese *ch'an,* and in Japanese *zen.* Plato (d. 347 BC) in his *Symposium* relates how Socrates once remained standing motionless, absorbed in profound meditation, for the space of twenty-four hours. Another story tells of St Thomas Aquinas (d. 1274) who was once so wrapt in meditation on the divine mysteries that he scorched his finger without noticing it.

(4) Many exponents agree that the final stage of the meditative process takes one beyond meditation, and outside the mental plane altogether. One's consciousness is divorced from all empirical content, unmixed with sensation, pathemia or thought. It is a stage of 'mindless awareness', unconnected with any direct cerebral activity. This transcendent state is known by various names. It is the *samadhi,* 'conjoining', of yoga; the *nirvana,* 'extinction', of the Buddhist; the *satori,* 'illumination' of the zen practitioner; the *unio mystica,* 'mystical union', of the western mystic; and the *fan'a,* 'annihilation', of the sufi. It has been described as the exaltation of consciousness to the highest degree, yet recallable to the conscious mind after the experience is over.

The neoplatonist, Iamblichus (d. AD 333), said that the power of contemplation can at times be so great that the soul leaves the body. And indeed others speak of this last stage as a movement of the soul resembling the spiritual ecstasy* achieved by prophets, sages and mystics. It is a kind of rapture, a peak experience of clear and unclouded bliss. It has been referred to as a merging with the Total, Pure, Objective or Cosmic Consciousness, perhaps representing a flicker of the consciousness of God. But many have denied this as presumptuous. The sufis speaking of the final stage in the mystic's progress, which they call *hal,* declare that it cannot ever come solely through man's effort, however assiduously he tries, since it is vouchsafed by God's grace. Hal, they declare, is gifted.

Certain physiological concomitants are associated with the trance state, and in recent years scientists have carried out extensive tests to measure the changes that occur in the body when a person is in a meditative trance. Hindu yogis, zen Buddhist monks, Egyptian fakirs, Voodoo practitioners, African medicine-men and Siberian shamans, have all been subjected to such tests. While the results are not conclusive certain factors do seem to be constant. For instance, it has been found that cardiac activity decreases, the heartbeat is slower than normal, blood pressure falls, the general metabolic rate is reduced. Breathing slows down, and oxygen consumption may be appreciably lower than the minimum necessary to support life. The temperature may be feverish, reaching 39°C. (102°F.), but this is not always so. EEGs indicate that alpha waves (*see* brain waves) predominate.

Properly undertaken there would appear to be much physical and mental benefit in the complete relaxation and tranquillity that many meditative disciplines provide. The bodily energies are restored and the powers of concentration developed. But the effects of meditation go beyond body and mind, and penetrate to the deepest recesses of the human psyche. Most responsible exponents today affirm that meditative exercises should never be undertaken lightly. Buddha laid great emphasis on the need for 'right meditation'.

In the first place the purpose of meditation has to be very clearly determined. Meditating on a practical problem is actually a form of attentive concentration, and can be a useful aid to its solution. Meditating in order to understand oneself and acquire discipline and self-control can be very beneficial if carried out in the proper spirit. Sometimes extravagant promises of personal success are held out to the student as a reward for his effort. But we are warned that any meditation undertaken with the object of obtaining *siddhi* (Sanskrit, 'power'), or gaining wealth, or injuring one's enemies, can do great harm to the practitioner.

Again, the methods of meditation are also very important. The aids adopted, the ritual paraphernalia used, can all serve as pitfalls for the beginner. Meditation on the psychic centres (chakras) can stimulate them and cause them to be needlessly activated. It has been said, 'More men and women have been driven insane through a premature awakening of the forces latent in these centres than most students realize' (Anon., 1935, p. 23). It is also undesirable to meditate on one's guru or preceptor, such as many Hindu systems advocate. Not only does this smack of idolatry, but it can be used by an unscrupulous guru to gain ascendency over a pupil in more ways than one (*see* expersonation).

Experts further warn that nothing should be done to precipitate the meditative state, such as quick methods of inducing xenophrenia, through drugs for example. Some occult systems employ magical designs: the mandala of the Buddhist, the eight trigrams of the *I-Ching*, the kabbalistic tree, the tarot trumps; and also vibratory phonemes or mantras. They may be used in order to effect changes of consciousness, and in some cases to raise thought-forms and elemental entities. These are illusory phenomena arising from false meditation, causing fantasies to emerge from the unconscious mind. They act like poisons in the spiritual system.

Again, meditation, for all the virtues claimed on its behalf, can be negative and meaningless, as many inadvertently confess when they reveal that they 'empty the mind', or 'concentrate on nothingness'. Spiritually, the value of many forms of meditation may be regarded as negligible, and could even be retrograde. Alice Bailey says, 'It is essential to realize that meditation can be very dangerous work.'

Correct meditation avoids esoteric techniques and tricks, concentration on the chakras, the repetition of meaningless syllables, ritual procedures, visualization of the guru. The purest form of meditation, it is said, can only be directed to pure ends and use pure means, and is best achieved by devotion to God. When accompanied by beneficient and positive thoughts for the welfare of others, such meditation has a healing virtue for the soul, and this indeed is what the word originally signified (from Latin, *mederi*, 'to heal').

Meditation that is described as 'getting close to God without humility', and that 'does not ask for guidance' (Anon., 1935, p. 7), might be regarded by many as both arrogant and foolhardy. The personal effort in meditation, without divine grace, can lead one to the shoals. The practitioner can soon be led to believe that he is divine, a self-delusion that is fostered by the autohypnotic repetition of mantras like Aham Brahmasmi (I am God). This leads to antinomianism, the meditator ending up by believing that he is absolved from the requirements of the ethical, moral or religious law, and above spiritual judgment.

Because of the traps that beset the path, theistic religions such as Judaism, Christianity and Islam declare that no method of inner development should be divorced from religion, nor should any method of development be undertaken in a spirit of self-sufficiency. In essence, meditation is humble supplication to God, as a creature to his Creator, in the form of prayer.

Books

Anonymous, *Concentration and Meditation. A Manual of Mind Development*, Buddhist Lodge, London, 1935.
Bailey, Alice, *Letters on Occult Meditation*, Lucis Publishing, New York, 1922.
Bailey, Alice, *From Intellect to Intuition*, Lucis Publishing, New York, 1965.
Benson, H. and Wallace, R. K., 'The Physiology of Meditation', *American Journal of Physiology*, 1971, pp. 221, 795.
Eastcott, Michal J., *The Silent Path: An Introduction to Meditation*, Rider, London, 1969.
Hare, W. L., *Systems of Meditation in Religion*, Philip Allan, London, 1937.
Hittleman, R., *Guide to Yoga Meditation*, Bantam Books, New York, 1969.
Jacobson, Edmund, *Progressive Relaxation*, University of Chicago Press, 1929.
Lounsbery, G. C., *Buddhist Meditation*, Kegan Paul, London, 1935.
Metzner, Ralph, *Maps of Consciousness*, Macmillan, New York, 1971.
Miles, E., *The Power of Concentration*, Methuen, London, 1919.
Naranjo, C. and Ornstein, R. E., *On the Psychology of Meditation*, Viking, New York, 1971.
Rawcliffe, D. H., *The Psychology of the Occult*, Rockliff, London, 1952.
White, J. (ed.), *The Highest State of Consciousness*, Doubleday, New York, 1972.
Wood, Ernest, *Concentration*, Theosophical Publishing House, Adyar, 1950.

MEMORY

The power of retaining, recalling and recognizing previous experience. In its most developed and significant meaning memory is a faculty of the higher intellect. Memory serves as a link with our own past and constitutes an all-important ingredient in the integrative process of our personalities and the recognition of ourselves as individuals. Memory alone forms the link in the continuous flux of perception, and is, according to David Hume (d. 1776), 'the source of personal identity'.

In amnesia or loss of memory, frequently due to injury or shock, one is unable to remember the past, either totally, which is very rare, or partially, where one cannot recall a particular place, time or experience related to a particular set of circumstances usually of a traumatic character. In the form of amnesia known as fugue, 'flight', the victim forgets his name, address, occupation and his personal identity. He has no knowledge of his past, and as a rule disappears from his usual haunts. In other respects he is perfectly normal and his intellect remains unimpaired.

What we consciously remember is obviously only a small part of our total memory, even if we cannot recall it to conscious awareness. We do not remember most of our dreams, nor do we remember countless incidents that have happened to us a few years, a few months, even a few days ago. We do not remember large segments of our youthful experiences, nor much of our childhood, and nothing of our early infancy and prenatality. Speaking of the strange amnesia that blots out much of the first six or eight years of our life, Sigmund Freud said that 'it serves for each individual as a prehistory.'

It has been estimated that in the course of his seventy years of life, an individual, only when awake, receives and perhaps stores fifty trillion bits of information. (A 'bit', short for 'binary digit', is the smallest unit of information for a storage device, like a computer.) Yet no single event in our lives, however insignificant, is ever forgotten, as is suggested by the phenomenon of cryptomnesia (Gk. *kryptos*, 'hidden', *mnēmē*, 'memory'), in which something previously experienced but forgotten is recalled, and now appears as a new experience without awareness of its original source. Religious exaltation, pre-mortem delirium, senility, insanity, high fever, disease, drug states, electrical stimulation of the brain, psychoanalysis, hypnotic trance and other xenophrenic states are among the conditions that often lead to the recall of memories long forgotten and apparently beyond recollection.

How far the human memory can go is still not clear, but *age-regression* suggests that there is virtually no limit to recall. In age-regression one recollects very early periods of one's life, sometimes even the birth trauma. This is important for the psychologist who looks to the period of these early years for certain suppressed memories, which might be the genesis of later mental ills and aberrations. But the mere recollection is not enough; the patient must undergo the process of *abreaction*, during which he re-lives the pathogenic (disease-producing) memories in the same emotional state he originally experienced them and thus works off the unconscious repressed emotions associated with them. Abreaction therapy is akin to the *pathesis* or 'suffered' experience that the candidate had to undergo in the ancient Greek mysteries; or to what Aristotle (d. 322 BC) called *catharsis*, 'purging', which he said was the function of great dramatic tragedy: to relieve the mind of pent-up emotion.

Experts contend that even prenatal events are recorded in the child's memory. The French psychical researcher, Col. Eugène Albert de Rochas (d. 1914), claimed that under hypnosis his subjects went right back through all the phases of their lives to infancy, birth and the foetal period. Indeed some people have claimed to remember their life as an embryo, and in a few instances have allegedly re-lived the sensations caused by sexual intercourse between parents during gestation. An even more fantastic claim was made by a woman who said that she had a consciousness of herself as a tiny speck at the very moment of her conception, that is, when sperm met ovum in her mother's womb. Finally, according to reincarnationists, there is the age-regression that reaches back beyond prenatality to the memory of one's previous incarnation on earth.

Certain scientists believe that our memory is 'material' and registered entirely in the brain. An *engram* is the hypothetical inscription or impress supposedly left on the living cerebral tissue as a result of any excitation caused by the stimuli of experience. Millions of such engrams or neurograms are believed to combine to make up the fabric of physiological memory. Whether engrams are transmitted to progeny and inherited by them like other genetic characteristics is still debated.

The ancient Greeks thought of the mind as a tablet upon which one's personal experiences were inscribed 'like seal on wax'. René Descartes (d. 1650) said that every experience caused the 'animal spirits' to leave a trace on the pores of the brain, and the process of recall was one whereby the pineal gland impelled the animal spirits to seek out the earlier traces in the brain-pores. The English philosopher, John Locke (d. 1704), picking up the Greek idea, compared the mind of a child at birth to a *tabula rasa,* a 'clean slate', upon which the incoming impressions were written as they were received through the senses. Thomas Huxley (d. 1895) maintained that every sensory impression left behind a record in the molecular structure of the brain, in what he called the ideageneous molecules, which formed the basis of memory.

Russian scientists have been particularly interested in establishing a connection between the physical organism and the personality, or the brain-consciousness and character, without any non-material or 'spiritual' factor intervening. After Lenin's death in 1924 Russian surgeons spent two and a half years examining his brain in detail, section by section, in order to learn a little more about him.

American neurophysiologists seem to have demonstrated the possibility of transplanting memory from one brain to another through chemical transference. They suggest that just as DNA (deoxyribonucleic acid) in the cell contains the genetic code with an organism's ancestral memories, RNA (ribonucleic acid) might be the 'memory molecule' serving the memory processes within an organism's own lifetime.

In the early 1960s researchers trained flatworms, which are very primitive organisms, to respond to light. These trained creatures were then pulped and fed to untrained flatworms, and it was found that the untrained creatures acquired the same ability as the trained ones to respond to light. Researchers have also extracted RNA and other brain material from more advanced animals like goldfish, rats and rabbits, after they had been trained to react to certain stimuli. This material was then introduced into the brain of untrained animals, and it was found that the latter acquired the trained reflexes, which they did not possess prior to the experiments.

In the course of experiments in the electrical stimulation of the brain cortex, Dr Wilder Penfield, formerly director of the Montreal Neurological Institute of McGill University, found that when he applied electrodes to various points on the surface of the cortex, patients would re-live forgotten episodes of the past, complete with sights and sounds in perfect time sequence. Penfield's conclusion was that there is a 'ganglionic record' of all past experience within a man's brain, which preserves his perceptions in astonishing detail.

A famous American brain researcher, Karl Lashley, spent the greater part of his career trying to locate the place in the brain where memory might reside. He was unsuccessful and was moved to say in despair that, from the evidence of his research, learning ought to be impossible. According to some theories the memory is not localized in the brain, but is diffused through the whole system of bodily cells, each of which registers engrams. Some psychologists incline to the view that a series of engrams over the generations build up into instincts, race-memories, the collective unconscious, and all the material of the mind in its total range.

Such a theory of several memories, both personal and inherited, could account for many otherwise inexplicable phenomena. Thus, xenoglossis, when people suddenly speak in a language they have never learned, may be a form of cryptomnesia, a hidden remembrance of a language heard in childhood. Certain instances of déjàism, such as *déjà vu* (French, 'already seen') where a person sees something for the first time, yet is convinced that he has seen it before, may be a cryptomnesic experience, or the stirring of an engram inherited from a parent or ancestor who had the original experience. The recall of a past life by the reincarnationist could likewise be the surfacing of a historical encounter undergone by a progenitor. The ancestral, racial or animal past is never lost, and some stimulus may cause it to awaken deep within, and gives us a glimpse of something that we ourselves did not personally experience.

It is to be noted that all such recall is not to be confused with the Platonic concept of *anamnesis*, 'reminiscence'. According to this the soul has experienced in its earlier pre-mundane existence a vision of the great Ideas, such as Truth, Beauty and Goodness, and other archetypal forms, with which it had been familiar. The soul loses this vision at birth, but remembers fragments of it in occasional flashes of 'reminiscence'.

Books

Adams, J. A., *Human Memory*, McGraw-Hill, Maidenhead, 1967.
Calder, Nigel, *The Mind of Man*, BBC, London, 1950.
Grant, Joan and Kelsey, Denys, *Many Lifetimes*, Gollancz, London, 1969.
Gurowitz, Edward M., *The Molecular Basis of Memory*, Prentice-Hall, New York, 1967.
Hunter, I. M. L., *Memory*, Penguin Books, Harmondsworth, 1957.
John, E. R., *Mechanisms of Memory*, Academic Press, London, 1967.
Kimble, Daniel (ed.), *The Anatomy of Memory*, Science & Behavior Books, Palo Alto, California, 1964.
Rochas, Eugène Albert de, *Les Vies successives*, Charcornac, Paris, 1911.
Stevens, L. A., *Explorers of the Brain*, Angus & Robertson, London, 1973.
Vogelin, E., *Anamnesis*, London, 1966.

MENSTRUATION

(Lat. *mensis*, 'month'), the monthly discharge of blood from the uterus, is connected with ovulation, the time when the ovum escapes from the female ovary into the womb. If the ovum meets a spermatozoon, conception takes place, and menstruation does not occur. Aristotle (d. 322 BC) held that during pregnancy the menstrual blood was diverted to form the embryo. Among the terms used for menstruation are: menarche (first menstruation), catamenia, monthlies, menses, periods, courses, 'the curse', flowers (either because of the red colour or from Latin *fluere,* 'to flow'), the recurrence, redness, seed-time, unclean time, visitation.

Menstruation is generally considered an affliction, and women were for long regarded as natural invalids because of their periodical indisposition. Doctors recognize that many women during menstruation are ill at ease, emotionally disturbed, anxious and troubled for no apparent reason. Some feel depressed and even guilty as if from an unconscious regret over a failed pregnancy. They deprecate their physical inferiority, their sex and their genitals, and regard the discharge as a kind of faeces.

In earlier times the female was considered unlucky enough, but her periodical association with dark and evil-smelling blood, exuded from the inmost recesses of her person, made her a veritable symbol of psychic pollution and the embodiment of uncleanliness. It was thought that the aura radiating from her contaminated all who came within the ambit of her influence. It has been said that the reason why the adjectives 'bloody' and 'bleeding' are regarded as indecent, is because of their implied association with menstrual blood.

According to Hippocrates (d. 359 BC) catamenia was essentially a cleansing process or catharsis, but during the process the body became charged with an extremely noxious element that brought peril and blight. Modern physiology confirms that menstruation consists of the disintegrated ovum, 'infertile blood', mucus and dead tissue, and involves the elimination of menotoxins, poisonous substances that accumulate in the body of a woman and appear in her menses, her sweat and other bodily fluids.

In primitive societies menstruating women were subject to special taboos and restrictions, and were usually segregated from the rest of the community. They were forbidden to touch the men's food and weapons and even their own domestic utensils, or to touch fire or bathe in a river or pool in case they polluted the elements. According to Pliny (d. AD 79), the touch of a menstruous woman turned wine into vinegar, caused fruit to rot, blighted crops, and so on. Traces of this belief exist in the west to this day. Sexual contact with a menstruating woman was absolutely forbidden in many parts of the world. It was thought that it would bring injury, disease and weakness to the man, and that the child born out of congress during the menstrual period would be defective physically, mentally and spiritually. Many people in advanced societies today still believe that venereal disease is very easily contracted by coitus with a menstruating woman.

Menstrual blood is regarded as a potent aphrodisiac. Added to a man's drink it was supposed to increase his virile force and arouse him to strange lusts for the woman. Till the eighteenth century it was not unusual in Germany and eastern Europe for a woman to mix some menstrual blood in the food and drink of her husband or lover to kindle the amorous flame. Such blood mixed with wine can, it is believed, madden with love the man drinking it. In alchemy and sex magic it was believed to contain the *elixir rubeus,* 'red elixir', a potent ingredient whose power was increased during the full moon. The connection between the periodical flow of blood and the phases of the moon was noted from earliest times and added a further element of mystery to the phenomenon of menstruation.

It has been suggested that the segregation of menstruating females in a special area reserved for them, and the taboos surrounding their condition, was the foundation of all taboos and initiation rites. Here girls were taught the secrets of the feminine functions, the fertility rituals, the rules of sexual intercourse, ways of preventing conception, love-magic, including the use of herbs and poisons. The secrecy surrounding the mysterious phenomenon of menstruation may have aroused the sex envy of the male and caused him to adopt his own 'mysteries' and initiations, in imitation of the exclusive female rites.

Books

Chadwick, M., *Woman's Periodicity*, Noel Douglass, London, 1933.
Dalton, K., *The Premenstrual Syndrome*, Thomas, Springfield, Illinois, 1967.
Ploss, H. H. and Bartels, M. and P., *Woman*, ed. E. J. Dingwall, vol. I, Heinemann, London, 1935.

MIDRIFF

(Old English *midd*, 'middle'; *hrif*, 'belly'), the middle region of the body, specifically the diaphragm, which is the dome-shaped muscular partition separating the space of the abdomen (occupied by the liver, stomach and intestines) from the thorax (occupied by the lungs and heart). The diaphragm is the chief muscle used in breathing; when air is drawn into the lungs the diaphragm is expanded and flattened.

According to the ancient Greeks, the functions of willing, feeling and thinking are located in this region. Says Grey Walter, 'The Greeks seeking a habitation for the mind could find no better place for it than the midriff, whose rhythmic movements seemed so closey linked with what went on in the mind.'

Above the midriff, it was believed, resided the vapours of the mind, below it the humours of the feelings. The midriff itself was the meeting place of these two currents and often engendered poisons and malignant humours that gave rise to distempers and furors. The Greek word for diaphragm was *phren*, which appears in the English language in words like frenzy, frantic, frenetic, schizophrenia, phrenology, and so on.

The midriff is regarded as a major occult centre, for not only are the actions of the lungs and heart controlled from there, but it sends out pulses to the epigastrium and the navel, whose plexuses generate energy for the harmonious functioning of the esoteric body.

Books

Kürkheim, Karlfried, *Hara: The Vital Centre of Man*, Allen & Unwin, London, 1962.

Onians, R. B., *The Origins of European Thought*, Cambridge University Press, 1951.
Walter, W. Grey, *The Living Brain,* Duckworth, London, 1953.

MILK

The food for the new-born and the sick frequently appears in religious ceremonial as symbolic nourishment for the neophyte, the initiate, the spiritually born-again. The pure whiteness of milk was a matter of considerable wonder to all peoples, and is repeatedly alluded to in the folklore and riddles of the world. The Koran speaks of milk (*laban*) as one of the special gifts of God.

Like blood and wine, milk is one of the great sacramental 'wet elements'. Offerings of two bowls of milk were regularly made in the temples of ancient Egypt, and libations of milk were poured over the 365 offering tables surrounding the tomb of Osiris. Milk was also the divine nourishment of the gods, and periodically the reigning pharaoh, as the representative of the deity, had to be suckled by a goddess or her representative on earth to refresh him and give him strength for his royal duties.

In ancient Greece milk was used in a number of regeneration ceremonies. The Orphics had a rite in which a sacrificial lamb was boiled in its mother's milk, and its flesh then eaten by the celebrants in order to give them new life. An oft-repeated Orphic formula went, 'As a kid I have fallen into the milk.' The meaning here is obscure, though one interpretation suggests that when an Orphic believer died, his soul passed upwards through the Galaxy, that is, the Milky Way, and the phrase may signify not only, 'I am regenerated', but 'I am become a god.' The strict Biblical ban on 'seething a kid in his mother's milk' (Deut. 14:21) was expressly directed against participation in similar pagan rites.

Frequently milk was included among the sacrificial offerings made to the chthonian deities and departed spirits. In the *Aeneid* Virgil (d. 19 BC) says that the spirits of the dead take particular delight in offerings of warm milk and blood. In many such rites milk served as a substitute for blood, since milk was regarded as 'blood filtered through the breast'.

A popular toast at medieval marriage festivities in England used to be the *sillabub* (Old Saxon *salig,* 'blessed', *bub,* 'breast'), originally made with milk, often curdled, wine and sugar. The marriage ring used to be thrown into a pail of sillabub and was fished out by the bride, after which the guests partook of the mixture. Milk and honey together formed a perfect food, and were both regarded as symbols of plenty from very early times.

Among the relics treasured in certain churches in Italy, France, Spain and Germany, are the reputed specimens of the milk from the breast of the Virgin Mary. The great Cistercian abbot, Bernard of Clairvaux (d. 1153), received the favour of nourishment from the milk of Our Lady, and was thereafter called the Mellifluous, 'honey-flowing' or sweet-tongued, because of his remarkable eloquence.

Clement of Alexandria (d. AD 213) spoke of the early Christians as *galactophagoi,* 'milk-drinkers', referring to the 'milk of the word' (1 Pet. 2:2), for as a child is fed on milk so are Christians on the Word. A dissenting Russian sect known as the *Molokane* (Russian, *moloko,* 'milk') which had its origins in the sixteenth century and survived till the Russian Revolution of the twentieth century, were so named because during their ceremonial fast-days they would drink nothing but milk. Milk, they believed, was the purest form of food and gave not only physical but spiritual nourishment. When drinking it they said they were imbibing the true Milk of the Word.

Milk was often prescribed both as a healing remedy and a form of beauty treatment. Milk from a woman's breast reduced redness in the eyes and relieved inflammation. A butter ointment made from it was also good as a healing salve. Pliny (d. AD 79) said that if an ointment made from the milk of a mother and her daughter were rubbed over the eyes it would preserve one permanently from all eye afflictions. Dropped into the ear, woman's milk will cure earache.

In certain parts of South America it is believed that drinking woman's milk will cure rattlesnake poisoning, and in the rural districts of eastern Europe that it will cure tuberculosis. If a dog drinks woman's milk it will never get hydrophobia. A girl using her own mother's milk as a face cleanser will have a wonderful complexion. Like Poppaea (d. AD 65), wife of Nero, who bathed in asses' milk, Beau Brummell (d. 1840), the English arbiter of elegance, was said to have bathed in milk, and so also the dissolute William Douglas (d. 1810) fourth Duke of Queensberry. Human milk drunk by adults is believed to have special powers of rejuvenation.

According to another age-old superstition, a special property resides in human milk, that affects the character of the child or adult who drinks it. The Latin writer, Aulus Gellius (d. AD 180), quotes from ancient authorities to the effect that 'there is the same virtue in the property of the female milk as the male seed.' The English chronicler, Giraldus Cambrensis (d. 1223), tells of 'a sow pigling that sucked a brach [bitch] and when grown up would miraculously hunt all manner of deer as well as an ordinary hound'.

The passion of the mother, it was said, be it temper, jealousy, brooding or melancholy, corrupts the infant, for 'by the ill humours of the mother's milk, the child is easily seasoned and corrupted.' It was equally believed that if a wet-nurse be 'misshapen, unchaste, dishonest, imprudent, drunk, cruel', the child that sucks upon her breast will be so too. Says Robert Burton (d. 1640) in his *Anatomy of Melancholy*, 'All the affections of mind and body are engraved, as it were, into the temperament of the infant by the nurse's milk.'

The cruelty of the Roman emperor, Caligula (d. AD 41), has been attributed to the viciousness of his nurse who anointed her paps with blood. Tiberius (d. AD 37) inherited his drunkenness from his drunken nurse. A child best thrives on the milk of its own mother, and only if it is demanded by nature or by the physician, should the mother 'put out her child to nurse', otherwise it is an outrage against nature. Sir William Paddy, a friend of Robert Fludd (d. 1637) and of Archbishop Laud (d. 1645), maintained that 'the morals of nurses (i.e. wet-nurses) are imbibed by infants with the milk.'

Occasionally the human breasts secrete substances that are not milk at all. Thus, a kind of secretion is sometimes produced from the breasts of male and female infants shortly after birth. This secretion disappears in a few days. Again, during what is known as the 'genital crisis', when a young child, some years before puberty, displays adult physical characteristics, the breasts of girls, as well as boys, may exude a thin fluid, to which some strange qualities are attributed. The 'milk' from the boy is said to be toxic, whereas that of the girl has a highly stimulating effect sexually. The milk sucked by a man from a virgin's breasts, after puberty, is a particularly potent aphrodisiac. Virgin's milk does not flow immediately, but begins only after the process has been repeated regularly for a few weeks.

This latter milk is to be distinguished from the thin yellowish fluid called *colostrum,* or 'witches' milk' which is secreted from a woman's breasts during pregnancy before the birth of her child. Sometimes traces of colostrum persist after childbirth, and if present in large quantities can cause the child to become ill. It is not unknown for pregnant women to give suck to male adults because of the belief that 'witches' milk', like virgin's milk, has remarkable aphrodisiac properties. Such milk is also a rejuvenant. It is recorded that the physicians of the ailing Pope Innocent VIII (d. 1492) tried a kind of blood transfusion, using the blood of three youths, and when that failed, kept him alive for a few days, by making him suck milk from a woman's breasts. Till the middle of the nineteenth century rich old men would sometimes feed themselves by sucking the breasts of hired wet-nurses.

Books

Bourke, J. G., *Scatologic Rites of All Nations*, Lowdermilk, Washington, D.C., 1891.
Eisler, Robert, *Orpheus the Fisher,* J. M. Watkins, London, 1921.
Graves, Robert, *The Crane Bag,* Cassell, London, 1969.
Laurent, E. and Nagour, P., *Magica Sexualis,* Falstaff Press, New York, 1934.
Posener, Georges, *A Dictionary of Egyptian Civilization,* Methuen, London, 1962.
Robbins, R. H., *Encyclopedia of Witchcraft and Demonology,* Peter Nevill, London, 1959.
Rohde, Erwin, *Psyche: The Cult of Souls and Belief in Immortality Among the Greeks,* Kegan Paul, London, 1925.
Walker, Kenneth, *The Circle of Life,* Cape, London, 1942.

MIND

Mind is the factor inherent in and underlying the existence of all ents or things in the universe. In varying degrees it is present everywhere. Consciousness in its broadest sense is sometimes identified with mind. But more specifically, consciousness is a psychological, even a physiological concept, while mind is a purely metaphysical one. Mind is coterminous with the cosmos and is one of the ultimates of the universe. Some psychologists have denied its existence, and dismissed it as a merely nomenclatural convenience, notably Gilbert Ryle (b. 1900) who called mind a 'category mistake'.

Others regard mind as an attribute of existence. 'Mind is the oldest of all things', said the Cambridge Platonist philosopher, Ralph Cudworth (d. 1688), 'it is senior to the elements and the whole corporeal world.' If a thing exists it has mind of a sort. The entry of mind into an ent creates its consciousness. Mind might be compared to the ubiquitous air around us, and consciousness to the air in the lungs.

All ents have mind, but differentiated. The German philosopher, Friedrich von Schelling (d. 1854), said: 'Mind sleeps in stone, dreams in the plant, awakes in the animal, and becomes conscious in man.' This theory of panpsychism (all-mind) received strong advocacy from Gustav Fechner (d. 1887), professor of physics at Leipzig, regarded as the father of experimental psychology, who stated that a kind of psychic life abided not only in animals, but also in plants, and in all so-called inanimate things.

There is a gradation of mind in nature determined by varying degrees of awareness. The potency of mind 'sleeps in stone'. From atoms to galaxies, all ents (units of creation) have a dormant mind-aura. It might be termed an insentient mind with a degree of palaeo-consciousness in a state of 'unawareness'. It manifests in the interior activity of inanimate material things. It inheres in energies, fields and forces, in protyles, particles, atoms, crystals, stones, stars and galaxies.

Higher in the mind-scale we come to the mind that 'dreams in plants'. This exists in the meso-consciousness of elementary protobiological ents like viruses and amoeba, and also fungi, plants and trees. It is characterized by life or vitalic mind, manifesting in metabolism, nutrition, growth, reproduction and decay.

Next comes the mind-consciousness we find in animals, operating by means of organized neuronal elements through the senses and instincts, and in the higher species by 'humanimal' reason. Its vehicle is the nervous system. It exists in the subego of the human being.

Man being composed of material ents possesses the insentient mind of inanimate things. Being alive he has the vitalic mind possessed by the plant kingdom. As a member of the animal world he has a mind operating behind his senses and instincts. As a personality* he has an individual mind, both conscious and unconscious.

Man's personal consciousness is therefore only one side of a many-faceted totality. His present awareness is a narrow band in a vast spectrum of mind, ranging from conscious awareness, through all the grades of xenophrenic states, to the highest reaches of the transcendental self*. He draws on a racial mind inherited from his ancestors (*see* collective unconscious); and something from the cosmic consciousness* occasionally filters into his conscious mind as well, putting him in touch with the infinite dimensions.

William James (d. 1910) said that our normal, waking, rational consciousness was a specialized kind of awareness, and that all about it were other forms of consciousness, entirely different. 'No account of the universe in its totality can be final', he concluded, 'which leaves these other forms of consciousness quite disregarded.'

The purpose of many mystical and occult teachings is to awaken an understanding and give a personal awareness of these higher ranges of mind.

Grades of mind

Plane	Ent or unit	Grade of mind
spiritual: sphere of divine meaning	man (soul* or transcendental self*)	spiritual, universal, objective or cosmic consciousness
astral*: sphere of thought & emotion	man (superego)	astral, supraphysical acerebral, asomatic consciousness, or higher collective unconscious
etheric*: sphere of life and senses	man (ego or personality*)	neo-cortical or human brain-consciousness
etheric (animal)	animal (subego)	humanimal, neuronal, reactive, instinctive, thalamic or ganglionic consciousness
etheric (plant)	plant fungus amoeba virus	vegetal, vitalic, organic, cellular or meso-consciousness
physical	stone crystal molecule atom particle field	material, unaware, inanimate, insentient or palaeo-consciousness

Books

Armstrong, D. M., *A Materialist Theory of Mind*, Werner Laurie, London, 1956.
Beloff, John, *The Existence of Mind*, MacGibbon & Kee, London, 1962.
Broad, C. D., *The Mind and Its Place in Nature*, Kegan Paul, Trench, Trubner, London, 1925.
Hook, Sidney (ed.), *Dimensions of Mind*, New York Universities Press, 1960.
James, William, *The Varieties of Religious Experience*, Longmans Green, London, 1941.
Jung, C. G., *The Structure and Dynamics of the Psyche*, New York, 1960.
Owen, George, *The Universe of the Mind*, Johns Hopkins Press, Baltimore, 1971.
Ryle, Gilbert, *The Concept of Mind*, Hutchinson, London, 1949.

MIND–BODY RELATION

The connection between the neural activity of the brain on the one hand and mental awareness on the other remains the major psychological problem still unsolved. How mind and body react is still unknown. Nerve fibres when excited convey impulses to the brain. But how does the collection of brain cells help in the miracle of 'seeing'? What is it in us that becomes aware when something is presented to the sight? Why does the response in the brain cells produced by the stimulus of light on the retina, not remain merely a mechanical event, without 'mental' overtones? Why does it result in the flow of understanding that makes us appreciate colour and movement? What stimulates our consciousness when we 'think'? Does the nerve stimulus come first, or is it prompted by something? What is this something?

In other words, what is the connection between physiology and psychology; between soma and psyche; between somatic action and psychic light; between the cerebral cortex and consciousness; a nerve impulse and an idea; an electrical reaction in the brain and the awareness of sights and sounds; the electro-chemical phenomena taking place in the neurones and conscious thought; between the stimulation of the brain cells and mystical experience?

According to St Augustine (d. 430) soul and body are not merely two juxtaposed substances put together, but form a unity. The body cannot act on the soul (or mind), and it is the soul that experiences sensation. The body is an occasion for sense experience, an instrument by which the soul is in touch with material things. On the other hand there is the old theory that accounts for mind as a purely bodily function, first advanced by Aristotle (d. 322 BC) and taken over by many other thinkers, including Thomas Hobbes (d. 1679) and in our own century by the Behaviourists. It has formed the basis of all mechanist and 'reductionist' theories. According to the reductionists the workings of both body and so-called 'mind' are explicable entirely in terms of a unified system of mechanics and biology, and it is possible to understand the workings of the mind by a study of the neurons.

According to René Descartes (d. 1650) the mental and physical have two radically different kinds of existence. The physical body is a machine and can not in any way interact with the mind. Animals, said Descartes, are automata or machines, devoid not only of reason but of any kind of consciousness. Descartes reconciled his mind–body dualism by advancing the theory of *interaction,* which asserted a causal influence between mind and body. In the case of man, the body was influenced through the rational soul by a 'concourse of secondary causes', which provided the occasion for mind to experience phenomena. This soul was quite independent of the animal-like body, and was located in the pineal* gland.

One of Descartes' followers, Arnold Geulincx (d. 1669) of Antwerp, put forward the doctrine of *occasionalism,* according to which both body and mind were interactive through a continuous divine intervention on each occasion that an action took place, to produce the corresponding perception in the mind. In other words, that God had so arranged things that when there was a physical noise, the idea of the experience of the noise occurred to the mind. God, he said, caused thoughts of seeing to arise in the mind each time something was presented to the sight, and when the soul wished to move the body, God moved the body for it.

This was one of the earliest theories of what was known as *psychophysical parallelism,* which posits a simple parallel between mind and body. It assumes that there are two entirely independent but concomitant series of events, the one physical and the other mental, which run parallel and which accompany each other, without any causal connection between them.

For the recurrent miracle of occasionalism, Gottfried von Leibniz (d. 1716) substituted the single creative act by which harmony between mind and body was established once and for all. He put forward the hypothesis of *pre-established harmony*, or an absolute synchronism between psychical and physical events. According to this theory God has made each of the two substances from the beginning in such a way that though each follows its own laws, each agrees throughout with the other entirely, as if mutually influenced. He compared the soul and body to two clocks, synchronized by God and working together in unison.

The French materialist philosopher, Julien de Lamettrie (d. 1751), rejected altogether the idea of a soul or mind, and held that there was no ultimate difference between plants, animals and men. In a controversial book he put forward the idea that all living things, including men, were automata, and declared that man himself was nothing more than a machine, governed entirely by the laws of mechanics. This idea was further elaborated by another Frenchman, the physician and materialist philosopher, Pierre Jean Georges Cabanis (d. 1808). Body and soul, he said, are the same thing. Man is just a system of nerves, and he concluded, 'The brain secretes thought just as the liver secretes bile.'

Thomas Huxley (d. 1895) developed the theory of *epiphenomenalism*, which states that consciousness is an epiphenomenon or by-product of nervous processes, and that thought is a mere accompaniment of neural activity. Epiphenomenalism interprets mental processes in terms of physical activity in the brain. Mental processes are just epiphenomena, 'after-showings', or secondary accompaniments that appear after a physical change has taken place. Consciousness is a kind of temporary shadow cast by the brain. A mental event is simply a secondary physical event.

Many modern psychologists and philosophers have also dismissed mind and consciousness, or explained them away in physiological terms. Gilbert Ryle called mind a 'category mistake', and derisively christened the immaterial agent alleged to reside in the human body as the 'ghost in the machine'. There was, he said, no such entity using the cerebral apparatus for producing consciousness.

The brain is known to be affected by toxins, by alterations in the aerial content of the lungs, by changes in the bloodstream, and by the activity of the hormones. The magician, Aleister Crowley (d. 1947), whose theories fluctuated from the materialistic to the occult, held that brain consciousness was entirely the result of brain activity, and that consciousness continued as long as the tissues functioned. Thoughts, he said, accompanied modifications in the cerebral tissue. To illustrate the point he once wrote a story about the conscious experiences that would accompany the slow putrefaction of these tissues.

Today brain physiologists seem to have established by experimental methods the close connection between brain and thought. They claim to have demonstrated that every aspect of our mental and emotional life can be altered not only by disease and hormonal activity, but by surgery, electrical stimulation of the brain (ESB) and chemicals (drugs). Certain key areas of the brain have been mapped and show an intimate connection with physical and mental responses. José Delgado, a Spanish-born scientist at Yale University, implanted electrodes in the brains of men and animals and proved the possibility of controlling emotions by artificial manipulation of the brain. On a visit to Spain he staged a mock bull-fight after first implanting electrodes in the brain of a bull. As the animal charged be brought it to a halt by throwing the switch of a small transmitter. The animal turned meekly away.

But all the arguments and demonstrations have failed to convince the critics. In the animal world, they point out, we find meaningful and intelligent behaviour in lower organisms which have no brain. Insects and species with a ganglionic system achieve results similar to the higher vertebrates with a brain. Birds do not have a cerebral cortex. As far as the mapping of the brain is concerned, it is pointed out that in spite of decades of research the brain is still largely uncharted territory, and our present information still too vague to provide support for any theory of the mind's ultimate dependence on the brain. Besides, although we do not add to our stock of nerve cells after birth, it is known that the substance of the cells undergoes constant change. Like our bodies, our brains are in a state of constant flux. We do not have the same brain material we are born with, nor in fact the same brain material we had a few years ago.

Again, it is known that people have lived normal lives, thinking and acting normally with much of their brains removed or destroyed. The most celebrated case is that of Phineas Gage, an American foreman who met with an accident in 1848 when an explosion during a rock-blasting operation drove an iron rod, four feet long and over an inch thick, diagonally through his left cheek and up through the frontal lobe of the brain and out of the skull. Gage remained conscious while workmen carried him several miles to the road. He sat up in the oxcart that took him home, and walked up a long flight of stairs. He spoke coherently to the doctor who examined him. Gage lived for twelve years with the front of his brain destroyed, and earned his living exhibiting himself and the tamping iron. He suffered no impairment in his thinking or memory processes, although his character was somewhat altered for the worse.

There are medical reports of over 500 experimental cases to prove that large portions of the cerebral cortex (where brain and mind are presumed to meet) may be extirpated or lost, with no appreciable disturbance to the motor, sensory or intellectual functions, and, in the words of Sir Charles Sherrington, 'without the patients noticing difference or change'.

After operations for hemispherectomy in which one entire side of the cerebral hemisphere is removed, patients can talk, walk, sing, play and do arithmetic. If the cerebellum is removed a certain precision in motor co-ordination is lost, and often nothing more. Abscesses of the brain have involved the cerebrum, the cerebellum and other vital areas without this in any perceptible way leading to abnormalities in the lives of the persons concerned. It is a commonplace of medical observation that people whose physical bodies are dying, even when their brain has deteriorated or been destroyed, will suddenly regain their mental faculties, and their sight, hearing and other senses.

Some experts feel that the concept of a disembodied mind is not to be lightly dismissed. If man is an animated body, what animates him? If he is an embodied anima, what is the anima? It would seem that consciousness and brain activity are not identical, nor can every aspect of mind be explained in terms of the cerebral, neural or ganglionic mechanism. Thought is not an activated neuron; consciousness is not the same as a vibrating nerve cell. There is another element.

Mind and body are united by a *tertium quid*, a 'third something', which is the self*. Socrates (d. 399 BC) spoke of the 'secret ties between the body and the soul'. The physicist, John Tyndall (d. 1893), said: 'The passage from the physics of the brain to the corresponding facts of consciousness is unthinkable.' Sigmund Freud (d. 1939) spoke of the 'mysterious leap from mind to body'.

The eminent brain physiologist, Sir John Eccles, concluded after years of research that the brain was an apparatus not for generating conscious activity, but for responding to the conscious activity of some immaterial agent, the mind. Dr Wilder Penfield, Director of the Montreal Neurological Institute of McGill University, speaking in 1950 before an assembly of eminent surgeons at Johns Hopkins Hospital in Baltimore, said, 'What is the real relationship of the brain to the mind? Perhaps we will always be forced to visualize a spiritual element of different essence, capable of controlling the mechanism of the brain.'

Books

Black, Stephen, *Mind and Body*, Kimber, London, 1969.
Campbell, Keith, *Body and Mind*, Anchor Books, New York, 1970.
Delgado, José, *Physical Control of the Mind*, Harper & Row, New York, 1970.
Deutsch, Felix, *On the Mysterious Leap from the Mind to the Body*, Grune & Stratton, New York, 1945.
Eccles, John (ed.), *Brain and Conscious Experience*, Springer Verlag, Berlin and New York, 1966.
Flew, Antony (ed.), *Body, Mind and Death*, Macmillan, London, 1964.
Penfield, W. and Rasmussen, T., *The Cerebral Cortex of Man*, Macmillan, New York, 1950.
Rosenblueth, Arturo, *Mind and Brain: A Philosophy of Science*, MIT Press, Cambridge, Mass., 1970.
Ryle, Gilbert, *The Concept of Mind*, Hutchinson, London, 1949.
Sherrington, Charles, *Man On His Nature*, Cambridge University Press, 2nd edn, 1951.

MORS OSCULI

(Lat. 'the death of the kiss'), an enigmatic term used for an experience of great intensity in which the body suffers a kind of physical death. The precise nature of the experience, though vaguely hinted at in mystical writings, has never been revealed. All that can be said with any certainty is that it is connected with the mystical exaltation of the soul which the righteous man experiences at certain moments. Such occasions cannot be induced or provoked by meditation or prayer, but seem rather to be bestowed on man by an act of grace. It appears to be identified with the *mors justi*, 'the death of the just', a phrase which like the first is left unexplained.

A number of interpretations have been advanced for the experience underlying the use of these strange terms. Thus, it is said that in the supreme passion of religious ecstasy it is possible for the spirit to sever its ties with the physical body, which dies as a result, and this is thought to be the mors osculi. The love of a god for a mortal, or a mortal for a god, brings death to the physical life, but immortality to the spirit: the love of Bacchus for Ariadne, Eros for Psyche, Zeus for Ganymede, Diana for Endymion, all had a fatal outcome for the human partner. A mortal desiring to be united with his god and partaking of eternal bliss cannot attain the union while in the flesh, but must first be freed from the body by death.

One school of Jewish mystics speaks of the mors osculi as the kiss of the Shekinah, the female aspect of divinity. The kabbalists say that the biblical version of the death of Aaron, brother of Moses, deliberately obscures a very profound incident, for when on Mount Hor, called the 'mountain of mountains', Aaron, on God's command, was stripped of his garments (Num. 20:28), it was in order that he might receive the kiss of the Shekinah. From this kiss Aaron, the first high priest of Israel, died, for no person can endure union with the Spirit and survive in mortal form.

The mors osculi has also been given a sexual interpretation, implying the ecstasy that accompanies the rite of exhaustion-magic when the prolonged sexual activity raises one to spiritual heights. Here the point of orgasm is repeatedly reached without emission, resulting in a suspension of normal physiological functions. Thus the mors osculi is 'the death of the man at the moment of the kiss'. Exhaustion mysticism attains this death by mainly sexual means, the goal being a form of sex-death enlightenment, a spiritual and occult ecstasy that lies outside the normal range of human experience. It has been described as a condition of eroto-comatose lucidity, in which one has moments of preternatural vision and spiritual enlightenment of a special kind.

Yet another interpretation equates the mors osculi with the symbolic resurrection of candidates in the death-and-rebirth ceremonies of the ancient mysteries. The ritual death of the initiate was a necessary experience in most great mystery religions, for it is impossible to attain perfection without dying to the more imperfect life. So sacred was the experience said to be, and so far beyond words, that although the Eleusinian mysteries of ancient Greece were carried on for centuries, and hundreds of eminent people were initiated, not one single definite or reliable record has come down to us. Their secret rituals have never been disclosed.

The notion of two deaths was developed in the *Phaedo* of Plato (d. 347 BC) and was further elaborated by the Platonists. But not much factual information can be gleaned from these writings. The biblical passages referring to the second death (e.g. Rev. 2:11) suggest that it was a kind of punishment, and there is little to connect it with the mors osculi, the mors justi, or with the ideas discussed by Plato.

The Old Testament has been scoured by Talmudic scholars and some of them trace a reference to these matters in the apostrophe of Balaam, 'Let me die the death of the righteous' (Num. 23:10), here presumably referring to the mors justi. Another biblical reference is traced in the verse, 'Let him kiss me with the kisses of his mouth' (S. of S. 1:2), rendered in the New English Bible, 'That he may smother me with kisses'.

In Jewish legend it is related that the three companions of the great rabbi, Simon ben Yochai (d. AD 160), were so transported with ecstasy at the mysteries he revealed to them that 'their life went forth in a kiss'; they were wrapped in the expanded veil and carried off by the angels. This was the death of the kiss.

The Judasites, a gnostic sect of the second century AD, who held that Judas was a favoured disciple singled out for a special mission by Christ, believed that the so-called betrayal of Jesus with a kiss was a symbolical prefiguration of the mors osculi that was to be enacted on the Cross.

Pico della Mirandola (d. 1494), setting forth the virtues of the Kabbalah, tells of the kabbalists going into a profound trance and communicating with God through the archangels. Their ecstasy can reach such intensity that the body can accidentally die in the experience. This according to him is the *morte de bacio,* or the death of the kiss. He distinguishes between two deaths: in the first, temporary, death, the released soul may move into the celestial presence and nourish its purified eyes with contemplation of the divine image. But if the soul would more closely possess the Beloved it must die the second death, by which it is completely separated from the body, and be joined with the celestial Beloved in the union of the kiss. Pico continues:

> The learned kabbalists declared that many of the ancient patriarchs died in such a spiritual rapture, that is, they died the death of the kiss, including Abraham, Isaac, Jacob, Moses, Aaron, Elijah. This is what our divine Solomon desired in the Song of Songs.

The Jewish neoplatonist, Judah Abarbanel (d. 1535), in his *Dialoghi d'Amore* which he wrote under the name of Leone Ebreo, speaks of 'the union and copulation with God Most High', which he defines as a spiritual delight perfected in death. He writes,

> Some of those who have attained such a state of union have been unable to continue in its prolonged enjoyment because of the ties of the flesh, but as they reached the limit of life, the soul, in the embrace of God, would abandon the body altogether, and remain conjoined with the Godhead in supreme bliss.

The English mystic, Thomas Vaughan (d. 1666), mentions the experience in his *Magica Adamica* in a cryptic commentary on the dream of Jacob when the patriarch saw the angels ascending and descending a ladder that reached to heaven (Gen. 28:12). Vaughan says: 'It is written of Jacob that he was asleep but this is a mystical speech, for it signifies death, namely that death which the kabbalists call mors osculi, or the death of the kiss, of which I must not speak one syllable.'

Giordano Bruno (d. 1600) in his work *Eroici furori* also refers to this same secret matter, providing no further information of the divine experience.

Jewish scholars of the Hasidic sect in medieval times devoted a great deal of attention to the subject, and also spoke of two kinds of death, but again without revealing any detailed particulars. One of the Hasidic texts reads: 'Our sages declare that there is a kind of death which is as difficult as drawing a rope through a ring set on a tall mast, and there is a death as easy as drawing a hair out of milk, and this is called the death of the kiss.'

Modern sex magicians of course have added their own interpretation to the enigma. In an essay entitled *De Arte Magica* ('On the Magical Art') Aleister Crowley describes a sex-magical rite in which the practitioner is brought by interminably protracted intercourse and repeated orgasms to the point of death – the death of a just man. He writes, 'The most favourable death is that occurring during the orgasm and is called mors justi.'

Books

Buber, Martin, *Tales of the Hasidim: The Early Masters*, Thames & Hudson, London, 1956.
Friedeberg-Seeley, F. and Barnes, J. H., *The Philosophy of Love* (translation of Ebreo's *Dialoghi d'Amore*), Soncino Press, London, 1937.
Myer, Isaac, *Qabbalah. The Philosophical Writings of Avicebron*, Ktav Publishing House, New York, 1970.
Symonds, John, *The Magic of Aleister Crowley*, Frederick Muller, London, 1958.
Waite, A. E., *The Works of Thomas Vaughan*, Redway, London, 1919.
Wind, Edgar, *Pagan Mysteries in the Renaissance*, 2nd edn, Faber, London, 1967.

MOUTH

According to Sigmund Freud (d. 1939) the organization of sexual life during the period when the genital zones (penis and vulva) have not yet assumed the dominating role, has two sensory phases: the oral, with its emphasis on the mouth, through which the world is largely sampled by the infant; and the anal with its emphasis on the anus.

The pregenital phases are usually completed by the age of about six, when the first permanent teeth appear, when toilet training has been completed, when the child gives up its desire for the oral gratification provided by sucking on the breast, pacifier or thumb, and genital primacy has been established.

The lips are the first external organs to form in the foetus, and after birth the sensations received through the mouth when sucking remain a source of pleasurable experience throughout a person's lifetime. All normal adults retain an unconscious memory of the pleasure of the oral stage.

Oral deprivation in infancy creates an urge for continued oral activities: thumb-sucking in later childhood; nail-biting in adolescence. It manifests in a love for sweets and chocolates, in eating and drinking excessively, in a predilection for odours, even unpleasant ones, in an intense need for kissing and oral sexuality beyond the requirements of normal love-making.

Orally arrested persons are mother-fixated or breast-fixated, and tend to seek mother substitutes in their wives, showing a special preference for women with large breasts. In sexuality there is a marked proclivity to perverse forms of oralism. It is also said that orally fixated adults tend to cyclothymia, or alternations in manic-depressive moods, moving from optimism to pessimism, elation to depression, with rather longer periods in the depressive phases.

Books

Abramah, K., *Selected Papers,* Hogarth Press, London, 1927.
Bernfeld, S., *The Psychology of the Infant,* Kegan Paul, London, 1929.
Bloch, Iwan, *Odoratus Sexualis,* Panurge Press, New York, 1934.
Campbell, H. J., *The Pleasure Areas,* Eyre, Methuen, London, 1973.
Freud, Sigmund, *An Outline of Psychoanalysis,* Hogarth Press, London, 1964.

MUTILATION

Mutilation covers a wide range of physical operations performed by human groups in all stages of cultural development. It includes marks and scars made on the skin that do not alter the configuration of any limb, and those that do, constituting an actual mutilation of the shape. It is invariably considered a disgrace to show signs of suffering or pain during the process, which is often carried out as a test of endurance and courage.

Various reasons, apart from mutilation inflicted as a punishment, have been put forward to account for this universal practice. Firstly, aesthetic, since the scars and marks, and their shape, contour, design, may be a form of adornment intended to make the person more attractive. They range from cranial deformation, footbinding and laming, to the removal of bodily hair, the filing of teeth, the piercing of ears, earlobes, nose, lips, or other parts of the face.

Mutilation often serves to increase and accentuate those physical characteristics which are considered beautiful, or to produce them by artificial means. Thus, the arms, legs, or waist may be compressed by the application of tight bandages or metal bands in childhood, which cut deep into the flesh when adult. Among European women the use of tight corsets and tight lacing resulted in fashionable deformation of the torso and hips.

The sex organs figure prominently in many mutilation practices. Castration is the most hazardous, and involves cutting off, or rendering infertile, the genital organs. Castrant practices among males were known throughout the world from earliest times, and were often determined by religious demands, and signified dedication to a deity, usually a Mother Goddess. The term castration applies to both sexes, and in women it refers to the removal or destruction (by crushing) of the ovaries, a usually fatal operation, but which, strangely enough, formed part of the ritual of initiation of certain castrant sects such as the Skoptsi of Russia. Other forms of female mutilation include the circumcision of the outer and inner labia, and clitoridectomy, or excision of the clitoris. The clitoris is an organ of self-gratification in girls who can attain complete satisfaction by stimulating it and therefore do not need the male. Men are jealous of it and insist on its removal.

It is commonly believed in many primitive societies that bodily organs are stimulated and strengthened by the process of torture and the infliction of pain. Such is the reason behind circumcision. Deep wounds are often inflicted to prevent sickness or cure disease. Mental maladies were relieved by trepanning, boring a hole in the skull. Many forms of mutilation, notably pricking and tattooing, are performed to ward off the evil eye, so that they serve as a talisman. A consciousness of guilt and a need to atone for it by inflicting pain on oneself is another reason, which thus makes it a form of self-punishment. Mutilation also constitutes a substitutionary sacrifice to a deity. Circumcision and finger-lopping are alternatives to offering one's life. Sometimes it becomes a votive offering to a deity for favours received or sickness cured. Lesser mutilation may be carried out as a sign of mourning or a memento to a departed friend, which usually takes the form of painful laceration on the face and body.

Scars and marks also help to establish kinship. They make it possible to identify those belonging to the same clan, and there is no feud between tribes tattooed or scarred in the same way. A related idea is that of a blood-exchange between two parties to a contract to establish faith through a blood brotherhood.

Some authorities regard mutilation of the sex organs such as foreskin, breasts, labia, clitoris and other parts of the vulva, and even infibulation (partial stitching of the lips of the sex organs) as a form of transsexing, an attempt to equalize the sexes by taking on some of the characteristics of the opposite sex, or by removing those of one's own sex.

Anthropologists think that the origins of certain tribal marks may ultimately stem from some accidental wound received in battle by the king or chieftain. This relic of adventure or bravery was carefully preserved and imitated, and in time became a symbol of the tribe. It may even be linked with the tribal fetish. The Dahomeyans claimed that a panther was the fetish of their royal family, and all members of the royal family had small parallel scars on the face, numbering from two to five, depending on their status.

Such totemic scars become personal and tribal symbols, and are often marked on the outside of dwellings and on tribal shields. It is said that banners, flags and armorial bearings are survivals of such old totemic tattoos and scars. Such marks may indicate rank, occupation and title. Sometimes they are a distinguishing badge, marking the difference between a superior conquering race and inferior subject races. Conversely they may indicate a servile status and may be marked on slaves to establish possession just as cattle are branded to indicate ownership.

Books

Anonymous, *Praeputii Incisio: A History of Circumcision, Castration, Hermaphroditism and Infibulation*, Panurge Press, New York, 1930.

NAILS

Ashley-Montague, M. F., 'Ritual Mutilation Among Primitive Peoples', *Ciba Symposium*, VIII, 1946.

Bettelheim, Bruno, *Symbolic Wounds*, Thames & Hudson, London, 1955.

Cabanes, Augustine, *The Eroticon: Scientific Marvels of Human Sexuality*, Falstaff Press, New York, 1933.

Davenport, John, *Sexagyma*, p.p., London, 1888.

Dawson, B. E., *Orificial Surgery: Its Philosophy, Application and Technique*, Kansas City, edn of 1925.

Lanval, M., *Les mutilations sexuelles dans les religions anciens et modernes*, Brussels, 1936.

Ploss, H. H. and Bartels, M. and P., *Woman* (ed. by E. J. Dingwall), 3 vols, Heinemann, London, 1935.

NAILS

Nails, like hair, are believed to have a life of their own, which seems to be confirmed by the fact that both continue to grow on a dead person. Again like the hair, the nail clippings were believed to contain the mana or personal emanation of the individual to whom they belonged, and were widely used in magical operations. For instance, a poppet or little wax or wooden model would be made by a sorcerer who then embedded in it in the appropriate place, nails and hair obtained from the victim, and then enlivened the image, after which he pricked or burned it to injure or kill the individual. In many parts of the world cut hair and nails are always carefully disposed of to prevent them from falling into the wrong hands.

Many strange beliefs and practices are connected with the nails. The ancient Egyptians decorated their fingernails to keep off evil spirits and the evil eye. As the hands are in constant motion, the flashing fingernails were thought to frighten off the spirits and deflect the flash of the malicious glance. In China the fingernails of the nobility used to be painted gold to mark their rank; and mandarins allowed their nails to grow to enormous length as an indication that they did no menial work. Later only the nail of the little finger was left uncut. False nails were often clipped on to the fingernails on special occasions.

Because of the age-old connection between the middle finger and the phallus, it was believed in many parts of medieval Europe, that if a man dropped a tiny fragment of nail from that finger into the glass of a woman he desired it would act as an aphrodisiac and inflame her passion. According to a modern belief, nail-dust is a strong emetic, and girls who wish to be temporarily rid of a zealous lover, unobtrusively file their nails over his drink so that the dust falls into it. Drinking it will make him violently sick or sleepy (Wallace, 1967, p. 92).

Divination by 'nail reading', or finding out the state of a person's health and his character from his nails is called onychomancy (Gk. *onyx*, 'nail'). Since they reflect light, nails are also used for scrying, which is done by the scryer staring at the reflection on the thumbnail.

Books

Frazer, J. G., *The Golden Bough*, abr. edn, Macmillan, London, 1922.
Pardo-Castello, V., *Diseases of the Nails*, Baillière, London, 1936.
Radford, E. and M. A., *Encyclopedia of Superstitions*, Rider, London, 1948.
Wallace, C. H., *Witchcraft in the World Today*, Tandem, London, 1967.
Wolff, Charlotte, *The Human Hand*, Methuen, London, 1942.

NECK

The primary transit area for the principal channels connected with breathing, hearing, eating, swallowing, speaking, the activity of the heart, the circulation of the blood. More specifically, it comprises: (a) the pharynx, a channel at the back of the throat with apertures into the nose, middle ear, and mouth; (b) the trachea or windpipe; (c) the oesophagus or gullet for the passage of food and drink; (d) the larynx or voice-box; (e) the vagus nerve; (f) the carotid artery; (g) the jugular vein; and (h) the thyroid gland. The neck is upheld by the cervical vertebrae, and is the seat of the cervical plexus, one of the key plexuses in occult physiology. From earliest times protective pendants, necklaces and strings of beads, as well as elaborate ornamental collars, were worn around the neck to bring good luck and avert the evil eye.

Recent postural studies lay great stress on the proper placement of the neck in our daily activities, and certain unorthodox therapies lay emphasis on the tension and posture of the neck as a cause of neuroses. Matthias Alexander (d. 1955) found that by altering the set of the head and neck on the shoulders he could bring about fundamental psychological changes in the patient.

The neck is an important occult centre. According to the voodoo belief of Haiti, 'the conscious soul is located in the nape of the neck' (Smythies, 1967, p. 296); and those who experience discoincidence during astral projection have said that one of the signs at the onset of the experience is felt like a weight on the back of the neck.

Situated in the neck are the *carotids*, the two great arteries running down each side of the neck, near the ear. Just as the jugular veins, which for a space run almost parallel to the carotids, carry blood from the head down to the heart, so the carotids carry blood from the heart up to the neck and head. The term is said to be derived from the Greek *karos*, 'torpor' or deep sleep, and it was once believed that drowsiness was conveyed to the head through these channels. Any obstruction of the carotid inhibits the heart-rate and interferes with the circulation of the blood to the brain, resulting in cerebral anoxia (oxygen deprivation of the brain). This can cause breathlessness, dizziness, mental confusion, fainting and convulsions. Carotid pressure is said to have been part of a very old technique of producing states of xenophrenia in certain occult rites. Fakirs who practise suspended animation press on their own carotid arteries. Gentle pressure on the carotid of a subject makes him responsive to suggestion, and is still used by hypnotists where a subject has to be hypnotized in a hurry. The technique is extremely dangerous in non-professional hands.

Books

Barlow, Wilfred, *The Alexander Principle*, Gollancz, London, 1973.
Oved, Sah, *The Book of Necklaces*, Arthur Barker, London, 1953.
Schilder, Paul, *The Image and Appearance of the Human Body*, John Wiley, New York, 1964.
Smart, W. A. M. (ed.), *Furneaux's Human Physiology*, Longmans, London, 1960.
Smythies, J. R. (ed.), *Science and ESP*, Routledge & Kegan Paul, London, 1967.

NERVOUS SYSTEM

The nervous system begins to form at a very early period in the development of the embryo. At the time of birth the child has nearly all the nerve cells (neurons) it will ever have, for unlike the other cells* of the body, the nerve cells cannot be replaced. After birth the nerve cells are lost at the rate of several thousand a day, and by the age of seventy just 2 per cent of the total at birth will have been lost.

The nervous system contains several thousand million neurons, which differ from all the other cells in the body. Each neuron is a tiny electrical battery, the outside of the cell is the positive pole, the inside the negative. The brain alone has 20,000 million of these cells, of which 12,000 million are in the cortex. Besides the nerve cells, the brain contains about ten times as many cells which are not nerve cells. These are the *glia* (Gk. 'glue') cells, once regarded as merely filling, insulating, cushioning or nutrient material for the nerve cells, but now thought to be connected with the memory store.

Each nerve cell has several small branches called *dendrites* (Gk. *dendron*, 'tree'), which receive impulses from other nerve cells; and one larger and longer branch called an *axon*, which conducts impulses away from the cell to other cells. Messages in the form of electrical impulses are carried along the cells and the point where the adjacent cells seem to touch is known as a *synapse*. There is a tiny gap (the synaptic gap) at this point between the cells (that is, between the axon of one cell and the dendrites of another cell) which the message must jump across. Each synapse acts as a kind of valve, forcing impulses to flow in one direction. Each synapse is also a decision point of the nervous system, sorting out the thousands of messages being received, inhibiting and blocking the irrelevant ones, directing the others along the proper route. The synapse is the point of uncertainty where a 'choice' is made, and is said to introduce a probabilistic element into a deterministic system. What makes a cell act the way it does and what makes all the millions of cells act harmoniously together has not yet been discovered.

When an electrical impulse reaches a synapse, it has to be transformed temporarily into a chemical impulse, and this is achieved by means of special substances. At the end of the axon the pulse of electricity causes a flood of chemical substances to be released by the brain cells. These chemicals are known as 'transmitter substances', which bridge the synaptic gap between the neurons to excite or inhibit the next neuron in the chain.

The chief transmitters or chemical agents involved in this activity are the following: *Noradrenalin,* an excitatory, essential for the waking state and for fighting; it is very similar to adrenalin, the hormone secreted by the adrenal glands; it activates the sympathetic nervous system (see below). *Serotonin,* an excitatory, involved in sleeping, which seems to be linked to the intellectual faculties, and found especially in the hypothalamus. Schizophrenics seem to have a low serotonin content. This transmitter is associated with *melatonin,* the hormone of the pineal gland. *Acetyl-choline,* an excitatory. It has no direct hormonal equivalent, but it activates the parasympathetic nervous system (see below). *Dopamine,* an excitatory. A drug called *dopa,* related to dopamine, is used in the treatment of Parkinson's disease. *Gamma-amino-butyric acid* (abbreviated GABA), an inhibitory. *Glutamate,* an inhibitory.

In normal brain activity the transmitters that pour into the synaptic gap for the transmission of signals are broken down and removed after they have performed their function, by an enzyme called MAO (mono-amine-oxidase), which turns the transmitter into a substance no longer adapted for signal transmission. It is believed that certain anti-depressant drugs interfere with the neutralizing activity of MAO, and accelerate the work of transmitters. Such MAO-inhibitors, as they are called, cause an increased discharge of noradrenalin or serotonin into the synapses, and provide the characteristic experiences we associate with the intake of cocaine, amphetamine, reserpine, LSD, mescaline, and the Mexican mushroom, some of which indeed are chemically similar to the transmitter substances. Certain drugs, toxins and nerve gases act directly on the synapses, blocking the release of the transmitters.

During depression the release of certain transmitters into the synaptic gap is greatly reduced. But the mere injection of noradrenalin and serotonin into the bloodstream will not help, for the brain resists the indiscriminate entry of toxic or foreign substances circulating in the bloodstream by a kind of blood-brain barrier.

The nervous system is the central communications organization of the individual. It controls thought, feeling and emotion, working like a complex telephone exchange switchboard, or a giant computer, although these do not adequately describe its functions. It is made up of two subdivisions. (1) The *central nervous system* (abbreviated CNS) which includes the brain* and spinal* cord, the latter like a rope as thick as a finger. It is also called the voluntary or somatic nervous system, because it is largely under the control of the will and looks after the conscious bodily functions, all the skeletal or 'striped' muscles, and the motor reflexes. It is primarily concerned with doing, thinking and other waking activities. It is exteroceptive, dealing with stimuli coming from without. It is described as neocortical and human. (2)

The *autonomic nervous system* (ANS) lies mainly outside the CNS, though it is connected to it, and is largely outside the control of the will. It is primarily sense-directed, and controls all the 'smooth' muscles, like the muscles of the heart. It is interoceptive, responding to stimuli arising inside the body, such as temperature change, hunger, fatigue and the 'sleeping' functions. It is described as paleocortical, subcortical and animal. (What is called the peripheral nervous system operates mainly in the nerve end organs and the cranial nerves that issue from the base of the brain.)

The autonomic nervous system is also called the automatic, involuntary, ganglionic, visceral or vegetative nervous system. It is older than the CNS and was the vehicle of the earliest consciousness. Its activities are largely co-ordinated by the thalamus* and hypothalamus. In general it controls the automatic and unconscious reflexes not under the control of the conscious will, like heartbeats, respiration, digestion, various secretions, salivation, lachrymation (the flow of tears), the size of the pupils, glandular activities, ejaculation, body temperature, blushing and uterine activity. The ganglia of the ANS lie on each side of the spinal cord and outside of its bony structure, and its fibres go to most of the organs. In functioning it bypasses the central controlling forces of the brain. It is not normally the product of 'thought'.

The autonomic nervous system itself is divided into two parts. (a) The *sympathetic nervous system*, which responds to the emotions. When sympathetic impulses are uppermost, the heartbeat is accelerated, the pupils of the eye dilate, blood pressure goes up, adrenalin supply is increased and digestive activity inhibited. It is in the ascendant in emergency situations, preparing the organism for fight or flight. The sympathetic nervous system acts by liberating noradrenalin (see above). (b) The *parasympathetic nervous system*, which usually acts in a manner contrary to the sympathetic. When the parasympathetic system is in the ascendant the heartbeat slows down, the pupils contract, and so on. The parasympathetic nervous system acts by liberating acetylcholine (see above).

Certain drugs have a selective effect on the autonomic nervous system. Thus, they may inhibit the sympathetic nerve impulses and induce parasympathetic effects, or vice versa. For example, the drug atropine paralyses the parasympathetic nervous system, so that when it is taken the sympathetic system is in the ascendant, the heart beats faster, the pupils dilate, the blood pressure goes up. Mescaline and LSD also stimulate the sympathetic system, increasing blood pressure, heart-rate and pupil dilation; the hair stands on end, body temperature rises, fatigue is reduced and sleep abolished, and the threshold for simple muscle reflexes and the knee-jerk is lowered.

The autonomic nervous system operates independently of conscious will. The physiological functions are carried on involuntarily and reflexly, that is, they are controlled at lower levels of command in the brain stem. Thus, the 'visceral' feelings of love, hate, fear, flight, are beyond cortical influence. We find this reflected in the language of everyday life: the heart jumps, or melts; sweat breaks out; the breath catches; there is a tingly feeling; one's hair stands on end; one flushes. Over 20,000 reflex paths protect the organism and automatically perform functions without the brain having to make conscious decisions about them. Most reflexes are innate, but many are acquired, as the Russian physiologist, Ivan Pavlov (d. 1936), showed when he created a 'conditioned reflex' in his dogs. Brain-washing is an extension of the conditioned reflex. Autonomic reactions are the basis of the so-called lie-detectors, which detect not lies but changes in the autonomic activity presumed to accompany lying. The autonomic nervous system also underlies psychosomatic sickness, including heart attacks, hypertension, asthma and peptic ulcers.

Although an individual is able to and normally does exercise control over some of the operations under the management of the CNS, the functions under the control of the ANS are entirely automatic, and it has been generally felt that they are best not tampered with. But a number of occult schools, especially the oriental, have evolved exercises which enable even the autonomic functions to be controlled at will. Thus, adepts among the Chinese, Tibetans, Hindus, Moslems, can consciously regulate their heartbeat, respiration, body temperature, pulse rate, sexual secretions, erection, ejaculation, metabolism, kidney action and so on. This control also extends to the peripheral system so that the circulation of the blood can be controlled, and an arm, leg or other part of the body can be warmed or cooled in isolation.

Certain western systems have also been evolved for the same purpose. Thus, in what is called autogenic training, developed for clinical use by the German physician Johannes Schultz in 1910, 'organ exercises' are performed, combined with physical relaxation, mental concentration, autosuggestion and meditation, to induce warmth in certain parts of the body, speed up or decrease heartbeats, and achieve some degree of control over the autonomic functions. Since 1958, experiments in what is called biofeedback and the artificial control of 'brain waves'* have indeed confirmed that it might be possible to learn voluntarily to modify one's blood pressure, alter the electrical patterns of the brain, and relax interior muscles and organs that are normally inaccessible to the will, with the help of the new mechanical devices to guide one.

Books

Adrian, E. D., *Research on the Central Nervous System*, Frome, London, 1936.

Barcroft, H. and Swan, H. J. C., *Sympathetic Control of Human Blood Vessels*, Edward Arnold, London, 1953.

Brazier, Mary, *The Central Nervous System and Behaviour*, Pitman, London, 1959.

Brazier, Mary, *The Electrical Activity of the Nervous System*, 2nd edn, Pitman, London, 1960.

Brown, Langdon, *The Sympathetic Nervous System*, Hodder & Stoughton, London, 1923.

Burn, J. Harold, *The Autonomic Nervous System*, Blackwell, Oxford, 1968.

Burns, B. D., *The Uncertain Nervous System*, Arnold, London, 1968.

Campbell, H. J., *Correlative Physiology of the Nervous System*, Academic Press, London, 1965.

Crosby, E. C. *et al.*, *Correlative Anatomy of the Nervous System*, Macmillan, New York, 1962.

Kuntz, A., *The Autonomic Nervous System*, Lea & Febiger, Philadelphia, 1953.

Langley, J. N., *The Autonomic Nervous System*, Heffer, Cambridge, 1921.

Nathan, Peter, *The Nervous System*, Penguin Books, Harmondsworth, 1969.

Netter, Frank, *The Nervous System*, New Jersey, 1953.
Schultz, J. H. and Luthe, W., *Autogenic Training: A Physiological Approach to Psychotherapy*, Grune & Stratton, New York, 1959.

NOSE

The organ of smell and respiration and to some extent of taste. The earliest faculty that served to guide the movements of the lower vertebrates was their smell-system, and the cerebral hemisphere itself developed out of the primitive olfactory lobe or rhinencephalon, 'nose-brain', once thought to be exclusively concerned with smell, and now known to be connected with emotional responsivity. The rhinencephalon contains an elaborate structure, the hippocampus, situated on the floor of the lateral ventricle of the brain, to which no one has been able to assign any function so far, but which occultists believe may be the 'seat' of the sixth sense.

Smell plays a subtle but important role in kissing and sexual activity, for there is known to be a close connection between the nose and the sexual reflexes. It is a medically established fact that swelling of the nasal spongy tissues and congestion of the nose occur during sexual excitement in human beings. The nasal passages of women swell, and occasionally bleed, during menstruation. In some cases retarded sexual development may be conditioned by nasal disorders; atrophy of the genitals may be due to disease of the olfactory bulbs; loss of smell may result from removal of the ovaries. Wilhelm Fliess (d. 1928), friend and associate of Sigmund Freud, found a relationship between the nose and the female sexual apparatus, and held that certain gynaecological complaints could be cured by cauterizing the appropriate parts of the nose.

There is also believed to be an affinity between the nose and the virile member, and from ancient times it was thought that a large nose was a sign of a large penis. The licentious Joanna (d. 1435), queen of Naples, usually chose her paramours from among those who had large noses. Similarly, a woman with a little nose is believed to have a small vagina. In a number of north European countries, and in England under the law of Canute (d. 1035), the punishment for adultery for both men and women was amputation of the nose, not only to cause disfigurement and loss of physical attractiveness, but also to symbolize punishment for the offending genitals.

Often a man's worth was judged by his nose. Napoleon said that if he wanted a man of courage, initiative and resource he always chose a man with 'plenty of nose'. Charles Darwin records that he was almost excluded from his epoch-making expedition with H.M.S. *Beagle* because the choice depended on a man who was an ardent disciple of the Swiss physiognomist, Johann Kaspar Lavater (d. 1801), and who doubted that anyone with Darwin's nose would have the qualities required to undertake the work of a naturalist on that arduous voyage. 'But', says Darwin, 'I think he was afterwards well satisfied that my nose had spoken falsely.'

The *nostrils* are said to be the external openings of the two polar opposites within the body. The breath does not, as a rule, pass equally through both nostrils at once, and this phenomenon is used in occultism. Depending on such factors as the disposition of the planets in relation to the individual concerned, the time of the day or night, and the state of physical and emotional health at the given moment, the breath will flow through one nostril with greater force than through the other. Ordinarily there is a cycle ranging from two to four hours for the flow from one nostril to be dominant, while the tissues of the other nostril are slightly engorged, after which the flow shifts to the other nostril.

In esoteric physiology the *right* nostril is solar in character, electrical in quality, masculine, hot, fiery-red to the astral sight, affects the sympathetic nervous system, and breathing through it raises the heat of the blood, energizes the body, stimulates the emotions, and excites action and lust. It lends increased ardour to one's physical activities, so that it is better if one breathes through that nostril when one wishes to add force to whatever one is doing, for example, starting a new enterprise.

The *left* nostril is lunar in character, magnetic in quality, feminine, cooling and soothing, pale white to the astral sight, and affects the parasympathetic nervous system, and operates on fantasies and dreams. It stimulates the power of one's mental, artistic and psychic activities, but decreases the emotional force of what one is undertaking, so that it is better to breathe through that nostril when one is angry or emotionally upset.

There are short periods when everyone breathes through both nostrils equally. This is an inauspicious time, and a person in this condition should suspend all important activities and decisions, or trouble will ensue. Accidents and death occur at such times. But it is also a period of psychic power, when paranormal faculties are in the ascendant. Curses uttered while breath is flowing with equal pressure through both nostrils are very effective, but are also detrimental to the curser.

Associated with the nasal organ is the act of *sneezing*, the uncontrollable expulsion of breath induced by a tickling sensation in the nose, although precisely why such a sensation should set off that complicated reaction is not known. Because of its explosive nature the sneeze was invested with many superstitious notions. In the physiological polarities, a sneeze is antagonistic to the hiccup.

The *Problemata* of the Aristotelian corpus regards sneezing, like yawning, shuddering, blushing and other involuntary acts, as having special significance. Its quality and nature are ejective, like the belch, but unlike belching, which comes from the belly, the sneeze comes from the head, the holiest part of man, and is therefore sanctified. The Bible records that when the prophet Elisha restored to life the dead son of the woman of Shunem, the first sign of the child's reanimation was that it sneezed (2 Kgs. 4:35). A common superstition has it that a dying man who sneezes will recover.

There is said to be a direct connection between sneezing and orgasm (Hegeler, 1969, p. 349). The person who is able to have a good, wholehearted sneeze is thought to be able to achieve a thoroughly satisfying orgasm, while the ineffectual sneezer is incapable of a similar experience. It is not possible for the eyes to remain open during a sneeze, and there is a transient loss of consciousness during a sneeze, as there is at the moment of orgasm.

Books

Bedichek, Roy, *The Sense of Smell*, Michael Joseph, London, 1960.

Bloch, Iwan, *Odoratus Sexualis*, Panurge Press, New York, 1934.

Fliess, Wilhelm, *Die Beziehungen zwischen Nase und weiblichen Geschlechtsorganen, in ihrer biologischen Bedeutung dargestellt*, Vienna, 1897.

Hald, P. T., 'The Nose in Literature', *Lancet*, 27 January 1906.

Hegeler, Inge and Sten, *An ABZ of Love*, Neville Spearman & NEL, London, 1969.

McKenzie, D., *Aromatics and the Soul*, Heinemann, London, 1923.

Warwick, E., *Nasology, or Hints Towards a Classification of Noses*, Bentley, London, 1848.

NUDITY

A natural condition in many primitive societies, which assumes significance only when it is practised after clothing becomes a part of the social pattern, and when nudism implies some violation of the normal social conventions. In other words, nudity becomes occultly meaningful when 'undressing' on ceremonial, ritual or festive occasions involves some departure from modesty, tradition or morality.

Ritual nudity may imply the total uncovering of the whole body, or only of the genital area, or the buttocks, or, in the case of women, the breasts. It is generally held that men should in no circumstances show themselves nude, especially to the opposite sex, as this reduces the power of the male organ. Even in primitive societies males take special precautions to protect their private parts from the common gaze. The Bible relates how King David uncovered himself and danced naked before the sacred ark, and when the daughter of Saul saw him she despised him (2 Sam. 6:16).

Female exposure on the other hand has a special significance. The sight of female breasts is believed to be a wonderful charm, and the female sexual organs have immense talismanic virtue, are charged with occult power, and promise the blessings of bountiful fertility and good luck. Female figures with vulva exposed were widely used as amulets in ancient times in Egypt, Greece, Rome, Christian Europe and various other parts of the world. It was believed that bad weather could be mitigated, storm quelled, lightning averted, rain brought down and fertility to the land ensured, by women baring their private organs to the sky and fields, or to the sea.

The term *baubism* is used for the ritual exposure of the female sexual parts, and may ultimately be derived from the Sumerian fertility goddess Bau, a word meaning female pudenda. Images of Bau show her standing with knees bent exposing her vulva. More directly it comes from Baubo, the name of a young woman of Athens who helped the distraught goddess Demeter when the latter was searching for her lost daughter Persephone. Casting about for some way to distract the goddess, Baubo shaved off her pubic hairs, spread her legs apart and exposed her bared genitals to the goddess, who thereupon forgot her troubles for a while, smiled and partook of the wine offered to her.

Ecclesiastical writings of the middle ages distinguished four classes of nudity: (1) *nuditas naturalis,* the natural state of man in his innocence, as with Adam, with primitive people and with children; (2) *nuditas temporalis,* the nudity of circumstances, due to poverty, sickness or circumstances beyond one's control; (3) *nuditas virtualis,* the nudity of virtue, as in sacred love, for example among religious ascetics, and among anchorites, as a sign of contempt for worldly things; (4) *nuditas criminalis,* typified by lust, eroticism and profane love.

Nudity may be practised for practical reasons. For example, it is convenient when exercising. It may be a way of releasing inhibitions, as required in certain religious and fertility rites. It is often a sign of revolt against convention and social standards. The band of Greek philosophers, the Cynics (from *kynos,* 'dog') were so called because they went about like dogs, that is, naked. When the Israelites in the Wilderness worshipped the golden calf, they and their wives and daughters sang, and drank and danced naked (Ex. 32:25). Again, nudity was a sign of decadent luxury and opulence. Rich Egyptians, Greeks and Romans always had beautiful nude and semi-nude women to serve at their feasts and to dance and play the flute for their entertainment.

In the occult view it is believed that the human body is a storehouse of psychic energy and that powerful biomagnetic forces reside within it. These can be stimulated, concentrated and if necessary projected by special methods. There is a strong aura radiating from the naked body. Clothing impedes the free movement of this force, and hinders its release, hence the need for nudity in certain religio-magical rituals and even everyday occasions.

To start with, the sight of a beautiful nude body has positive aphrodisiac virtues which can be used for therapeutic ends. The impotent male is often aroused to marital intercourse by the sight of a nude woman. The presence of a nude female in a room wards off disease. The ancients believed that medicines were more effective when administered to a patient by a beautiful female who was lightly clad, as her healthy aura spread a healing beneficence over the patient. Pliny (d. AD 79) describes a healing ceremony connected with Apollo in which a naked virgin girl administers medicines to a patient who is likewise nude.

Most rites connected with fertility were of course commonly performed in the nude, partly for convenience, since the participants were expected to indulge in intercourse as a sympathetic rite. Similarly, rain-making ceremonies also usually involved nakedness. The Iroquois Indians of north America, for example, used to celebrate an annual Naked Dance in the course of which a man and woman copulated to ensure rain and an abundant harvest.

Divination and prophesying sometimes required nudity on the part of the enquirer or the priest. When Saul prophesied, he 'stripped off his clothes and lay down naked' (1 Sam. 19:24). Even today popular superstition rules that those who wish to know the future must carry out certain rites in the nude. A girl must stand naked before a mirror at midnight to see her future husband.

NUDITY

The psychic radiations from the nude body are believed to create repercussions in the spirit world and help to ward off evil. Spirits are therefore said to be frightened of nudity. Martin Luther (d. 1546) was said to have bared his buttocks* to drive off the devil. There is an ancient belief that exposure of the genitals is an infallible means of thwarting the designs of evil spirits and of exorcizing them.

It is believed that because nudity involves an inversion of the normal course of things, then when something radical is demanded of nature or the gods, some appropriate, radical action is required on man's part to stimulate or coerce the higher powers. Thus we find obscenity also involved in magical nudity.

Even symbolic nudity influences events by some kind of intensive contagion, particularly when associated with a religious rite. We read that Isaiah went about naked for three years in obedience to the command of the Lord, so that through him by a kind of pathemic magic, the Egyptians and Ethiopians might be led away captive, 'naked and barefoot, even with their buttocks uncovered' (Isa. 20:4).

Many religious and cultic rites were practised in the nude. Circumambulation ceremonies around religious shrines frequently took place after the pilgrims had divested themselves of their clothing. Pliny remarks that in religious ceremonies in ancient Britain, the women and girls went about completely nude. Maimonides (d. 1204) recounts that the women of ancient Persia would dance naked at dawn in homage to the sun. In Egypt temple-priests used to divest themselves of their habit before entering the holy of holies. So did the early Babylonian priests, who carried out most of their priestly functions and sacrifices in the naked state.

A number of sects in India, notably the Jains, also practised ritual nudity. The ancient Greeks, who knew of these sects, called them gymnosophists (Gk. *gymnos,* 'naked', *sophos,* 'wise'). In western Europe nudity was practised by various fringe sects such as the Adamites, Eleutherians, those afflicted with the Dancing Mania, the Flagellants, the Anabaptists, the wilder congregation of the Hussites, the early Shakers, the Dukhobors.

In the purely social context the Greeks believed that young men and women should get used to the sight of each other's naked bodies. Greek men and boys frequented the baths, the palaestrae (wrestling places) and gymnasia and the athletic schools quite naked. Plato in his *Laws* suggested that young men and women should carry out gymnastic exercises together in the nude. Spartans encouraged the nude exercise of boys and girls. The Spartan festival of Gymnopaedia, 'naked boys', was celebrated with dances and physical exercises by naked boys. The Cretans too had a nude festival, known as the Apodysia, the Festival of Undressing, during which women undressed themselves in public.

Nudity was useful for making the right selection for marriage, to know what one was getting. This pragmatic view was reflected by Sir Thomas More (d. 1535) who in his *Utopia* recommended that young people should see each other naked before marriage. When Sir William Roper expressed the wish to marry one of More's daughters, More took him to the bedroom where his two daughters lay sleeping and whipped off the blanket. They were on their backs, their smocks up to their armpits. They then turned on their bellies. Having seen both sides of both girls Roper patted the girl of his choice on the buttocks saying, 'Thou art mine'.

It is believed that the contagion of sanctity is more easily transmitted and received by a naked person. Nudity therefore formed part of various initiation ceremonies in secret societies the world over. Not only was the nude state meant to suggest the candidate's rebirth, it also facilitated his receptive power. Originally Christian baptism required that neophytes be nude, and so did the Mithraic initiation.

Nudity or semi-nudity has also been associated with mourning and death rites. As a warning of approaching lamentation Isaiah says, 'Tremble, ye women, strip you and make you bare' (Isa. 32:11). In Attic vase-paintings, women mourners are shown walking naked behind the funeral cortège. In the ancient middle east, when a death occurred, a man would uncover his penis and a woman her rear parts. In medieval Europe during drought, famine, plague, war, or other calamity, men, women and children, young and old, married and unmarried, used to go naked in procession through the streets.

A special significance was also associated with the parade of nude women, either walking, dancing, or riding on horses, a good example of the latter being found in the legend of Lady Godiva who rode naked through the market place of Coventry. In the classical world nude girls and prostitutes accompanied the triumphal processions given in honour of victorious generals or conquering heroes, and danced naked before them. In medieval times the same kind of spectacle was enacted when kings entered a city. Thus when Louis XI made his entry into Paris in 1461, naked women decorated his path. Their beautiful breasts, 'straight, separated, round and firm', greatly pleased the monarch and the populace. Similar scenes took place during the fêtes and triumphs in Holland, Belgium, Italy and other parts of Europe.

In classical times dances, games and plays were often enacted in the nude. The satyrs in the Aristophanic stage always appeared nude. In English medieval plays, especially the Coventry and Chester Mysteries, Adam and Eve before the Fall used to appear quite naked on the stage, while the devil strode on with an exaggerated phallus. At the time of Charles the Bold (d. 1477) and Louis XI (d. 1483), the plays put on at the French courts had nude girls acting in scenes like the Judgment of Paris, and the history of Noah. The German popular carnivals of medieval times were largely nudist affairs.

Mystical writings point out that the initial state of innocence in the Garden of Eden will have to return to each individual's heart before the lost paradise is restored. In the *Gospel of Thomas,* Jesus says, in reply to a disciple's question about when he would come again: 'When you strip yourselves without being ashamed. When you take off your clothes and lay them at your feet like little children and trample on them.'

Books

Clark, Kenneth, *The Nude in Art,* John Murray, London, 1956.
Contenau, G., *La Déesse nue Babylonienne*, Paris, 1914.

Craig, Alec, *The Bibliography of Nudism*, Sun & Health, London, 1954.
Cunnington, C. Willett, *Why Women Wear Clothes*, Faber, London, 1941.
Eden, Adam, *A Vindication of the Reformation on Foot Among the Ladies to Abolish Modesty and Chastity, and Restore the Native Simplicity of Going Naked*, 2nd edn, London, 1775.
Hahn, H., *Demeter und Baubo*, Lübeck, 1896.
Hall, Carrie, *From Hoopskirts to Nudity*, Caldwell, London, 1938.
Langdon-Davies, John, *The Future of Nakedness*, Noel Douglas, London, 1929.
Norwood, C. E., *Nudism in England*, Noel Douglas, London, 1933.
Rickles, N. K., *Exhibitionism*, Lippincott, Philadelphia, 1950.
Scott, George Ryley, *The Common Sense of Nudism*, T. W. Laurie, London, 1934.
Sham, Heinrich, *Naked Humanity, Jubilant Future*, London, 1893.

OPPOSITES

The two facets of a duality, associated by their mutual contrariness, exist throughout nature and the universe. Every ent is interrelated, everything is relative. If a thing exists it has its opposite by virtue of physical, material, pathemic or other relationship. Opposites together form a paradoxical whole. They give existence, meaning and validity to each other, and between them there is a flow that keeps them vitalized and gives them significance.

Opposites are found in philosophy, religion, psychology, physics and other sciences. Many biological and occult opposites are present in the human body. In normal persons these forces are equally balanced; and where they are not, strange things are likely to happen in their immediate vicinity.

The main esoteric opposites as they exist in the human being are tabulated below. Opposites generally, but not necessarily, imply a male-female, positive-negative, yang-yin relationship.

Masculine	Feminine
Eros (love)	Thanatos (death)
life	death
pleasure	pain (opposite evils, according to Speusippus, d. 339 BC)
sympathy	antipathy (*see* pathemia)
love	hate
love	will
joy	sorrow
astral body (vehicle of consciousness and emotions)	etheric body (vehicle of life principle and sensations)

etheric body (magnetic potential)	physical body (electrical potential)
mind	body
pneuma (spirit)	psyche (mind)
psyche (mind)	physis (nature)
spiritus (spirit)	anima (life)
anima (spirit)	persona (personality)
aura	soma
hun (spiritual soul)	p'o (material soul) (Chinese)
conscious	unconscious (*see* dichotomy under Human Types)
animus (unconscious male element in woman)	anima (unconscious female element in man) (C. G. Jung)
animus (in brain)	anima (in heart)
objectivity	subjectivity
extraversion	introversion
intellect	instinct
intellect	senses
reason	emotion
thought	feeling
inference	intuition
argument	experience
talent	genius
schizophrenia	epilepsy
schizophrenia	hysteria
depression	mania
sexuality	anxiety
anabolism (building up)	katabolism (breaking down) (metabolic processes)
ontogeny (individual evolution)	phylogeny (race evolution)
man	woman
vir rubeus ('red man')	mulier candida ('white woman') (in alchemy)
male (positive externally, negative internally)	female (negative externally, positive internally)
zachar ('man')	neqebah ('perforated', i.e. woman) (Hebrew)
adult	child
right side of body (warm)	left side (cool) (Galen)
front right side of body (positive)	rear right side of body (negative)
rear left side of body	front left side of body
back	abdomen
area between shoulder-blades	epigastrium

OPPOSITES

frontal lobe of brain	occipital lobe of brain
frontal bone of skull	occipital bone of skull
back of head	base of spine
cerebrum (electrical)	solar plexus (magnetic) (Gurdjieff)
left cerebral hemisphere	right cerebral hemisphere (*see* cerebrum)
outside of neuron	inside of neuron (*see* nervous system)
brain	heart
brain	base of spine
viscera (yang)	brain (yin)
sahasrara	kundalini (*see* plexus)
pituitary gland	pineal gland
anterior lobe of pituitary (masculine)	posterior lobe of pituitary (feminine)
insulin	adrenalin
central nervous system	autonomic nervous system
sympathetic nervous system	parasympathetic nervous system (*see* nervous system)
spine	sternum (breast bone)
pingala (subtle artery on right side of sushumna)	ida (on the left side of the sushumna) (*see* spine)
eyes	throat (Chinese)
retina of eye	cornea of eye
right nostril	left nostril
lungs	heart
lungs	liver
prana (heart wind)	apana (rectal wind) (Hindu)
hot breath	cold breath
exhalation	inhalation
sneeze	hiccup
heart	abdomen
blood (positive)	breath (negative)
diastole (dilation of the heart)	systole (contraction of the heart)
arterial blood	venous blood
spleen (north)	liver (south)
right kidney	left kidney
fu (hollow, yang organs)	zang (solid, yin organs) (Chinese)
small intestine	heart (Chinese)
large intestine	lungs (Chinese)
gall bladder	liver (Chinese)
stomach	spleen (Chinese)
bladder	kidneys (Chinese)
'triple warmer'	'circulation sex' (Chinese acupuncture)
feet (north)	sex organs (south)
linga (phallus)	yoni (vagina) (Hindu)

breasts (female)	buttocks
lips (female)	labia
testicles	brain
testicles	lungs
semen	breath

Books

See under body *and* man

ORGASM

The climax of sexual union, when the tensions built up during love-making and coital activity are released. Melting and flowing sensations are felt in the genital area and the orgasm itself is experienced as the opening of a dam. A feeling of warmth pervades all parts of the body, which undergoes a series of powerful spasms and pleasurable waves. There is a feeling of a glow within, and, as Alexander Lowen says, 'an overall body sensation of illumination'.

The whole body participates in the complete orgasm, and many authorities feel that physical, mental and psychic health depend on orgastic potency or the capacity for complete surrender during the acme of sexual excitement. Modern researchers state that when the tension of sexual excitement reaches its climax and release at the peak of orgasm, a measurable electrical energy is discharged as a result of the violent muscular contractions.

In the male adult orgasm is accompanied by the ejaculation of semen. Since sperm is not manufactured in the testes until puberty, a small boy can have an orgasm without an ejaculation. Wilhelm Reich (d. 1957) pointed out the distinction between ejaculation and orgasm. Most men feel a weak spasm of pleasure when they 'come off', but seldom experience a genuine orgasm. In fact ejaculation without orgasm is a common experience among civilized men.

According to certain schools of thought, ejaculation, involving as it does the expenditure of semen, is not desirable at every act of intercourse. To begin with the lassitude that follows ejaculation shows that it is enervating and depletes the male of vital energy. Ascetic communities in early Christian times regarded ejaculation as a form of pollution and refrained from all forms of sexual activity, and the encratic groups trained themselves to avoid emission altogether. It is still widely believed that each drop of semen ejaculated is equivalent to the loss of forty drops of blood.

The conservation of semen was highly extolled by eastern occultists, both as a means of toning up body and mind, and of storing and augmenting psychic energy. Chinese, Indian and Arab writers warn against the wasteful loss of seminal fluid, and insist that if the seed is emitted it must be drawn back, and several sex magical techniques, such as acclivity, have been devised for this purpose. The ideal of these schools is prolonged orgasm without ejaculation. The seminal energy stored in the bodies of celibates is believed to exert a magnetic attraction over women. It sends forth a silent and masterful call to the female organ which in turn becomes filled with a strong urge for union with it.

In the female, orgasm is manifested by muscular contractions and the secretion of mucus from the Bartholin glands and elsewhere. Modern authorities make a distinction between vaginal and clitoral orgasm. Many believe that in woman true orgasm can only be of a vaginal nature, when the vagina contracts strongly along its whole length from three to fifteen times, and 'invagination' is accelerated by a strong urge to draw into the womb and absorb the ejaculated semen. Others maintain that all orgasm is ultimately clitoral and that it is most satisfactorily achieved not by direct titillation of the clitoris, but by penile penetration of the vagina, since this affects the whole genital area. Anything large enough to stimulate the vagina pulls down on the labia and thus stimulates the clitoral nerves, and at the same time spreads the sensation over the whole area of the vulva and throughout the interior towards the uterus.

Some authorities maintain that the growing stress on clitoral orgasm today is a panic reaction arising from growing male impotence even among the young and seemingly vigorous. The inadequate male is relieved to hear that despite his inability to have an erection and his tendency to premature ejaculation, he can still satisfy the woman completely by the simple method of clitoral stimulation by hand or mouth. Be that as it may, experts like Wilhelm Reich state that the majority of women in civilized countries suffer from complete absence of vaginal orgasm.

The importance of the clitoris in sex magic is well known to many peoples with a sophisticated sex tradition. The yin force generated by clitoral stimulation is exceedingly, almost painfully acute and pleasurable, and often the taoist or tantrik practitioner did not have to undertake the more arduous task of vaginal intercourse in order to sip his partner's energy, but aroused her by manual stimulation. Depleting a woman of her yin force in this manner was regarded as extremely dangerous, for it deprived her of her normal sexual reflexes, led to perversions, and caused the spiritual degradation of the woman concerned. Occultly speaking, the 'barren' satisfaction of clitoral orgasm was not favourable for the welfare of the woman.

Besides its physiological concomitants, orgasm has its mystical side. At the climax of the sexual act the ego seems to dissolve, and the whole being is surrendered progressively to the animal nature within, to the opposite partner, to the unconscious, and to the whole cosmos. It has been described as a flash of universal awareness in which man and woman find their identification with the cosmic process (*see* sex mysticism).

Chinese taoists said that at the moment of orgasm the partners flowed into the universal essence. Hindu tantriks said that it was a time when ego-consciousness was lost and the self of both partners merged into the universal bliss. Zoroastrians believed that at the moment of climax the man and woman entered into another, holy state of being, so prayers were recited before coitus and during ejaculation. Similarly, a good Muslim is enjoined on first penetration to utter the words, 'In the name of God', and during ejaculation to complete the formula by saying, 'The Merciful, the Compassionate'.

The moment of true orgasm is a moment of mental and physical oblivion, an actual loss of consciousness. In some men the act of intercourse and orgasm resembles a minor attack of epilepsy. Some students of the subject point out the close connection between orgasm and death. Psychologists say that Eros (Love) and Thanatos (Death) are next of kin. Sigmund Freud (d. 1939) spoke of the similarity between the state following complete sexual satisfaction, and dying. In many languages the expressions of love and death are interwoven. The Arabs say that love and death abide in the same tent.

The intense voluptuous contractions of the genitals, the twitchings, convulsions and reflex movements of the whole body at the moment of orgasm have frequently been compared to death throes. Ancient Chinese, Japanese, Sanskrit, Greek and Latin writings record that women reaching orgasm scratch, bite and struggle as if in agony, moan and whimper, and involuntarily cry out, 'Take my life', 'I am dying'. Nearly always their expressions refer to death. Modern sexologists report the same reaction among women today. Women themselves are unable to explain this in their sober moments. As Havelock Ellis (d. 1939) has said, 'Over a large part of nature, but a thin veil divides love from death.'

Books

Bergler, E. *et al.*, *Kinsey's Myth of Female Sexuality*, Grune & Stratton, New York, 1954.
Brecher, Ruth and Edward, *An Analysis of Human Sexual Response*, André Deutsch, London, 1967.
Elkan, E., 'Orgasm Inability in Women', *International Journal of Sexology*, 1951, 4, 243 *et seq.*
Kinsey, A. C. *et al.*, *Sexual Behavior in the Human Female*, Saunders, Philadelphia, 1953.
Koedt, Anne, *The Myth of Vaginal Orgasm*, New England Free Press, 1969.
Lowen, Alexander, *Love and Orgasm*, Mayflower Press, London, 1968.
Malleson, Joan, *Any Wife to Any Husband*, Heinemann, London, 1960.
Masters, W. H. and Johnson, Mrs V., *Human Sexual Response*, Little, Brown, Boston, Mass., 1966.
O'Hare, Hilda, 'Vaginal Versus Clitoral Orgasm', *International Journal of Sexology*, 1951, 4, 243–6.
Reich, Wilhelm, *The Function of the Orgasm*, Panther Books, London, 1968.
Rosenberg, Jack Lee, *Total Orgasm*, Random House, New York, 1973.
Sigusch, V., *Exzitation und Orgasmus bei der Frau*, Stuttgart, 1970.

PARAPERCEPTION

The awareness of phenomena beyond the apparent capabilities of the senses or of the normal conscious processes of reason and judgment. The term covers all those mental and psychical impressions that are not mediated through any sense known to physiology, or through any medium known to science.

Popularly its organ of communication is the so-called *sixth sense* or second sight, which operates in some fourth dimension. Everyone has the faculty of the sixth sense, but usually to a small, barely perceptible degree. The person whose powers are unusual in this respect is known as a sensitive or psychic, that is, sensitive to psychic or paranormal phenomena. More serious students speak of the sixth sense as the psi-faculty, psi-factor or psi-function, named from *psi,* the first letter of the Greek word *psyche,* 'soul'. Various other terms such as extrasensory perception (abbreviated ESP, sometimes confined to the experimental side of paraperception), ultra-perception, paracognition, paranormal cognition, paragnosis (coined by Willem Tenhaeff, professor of parapsychology at Utrecht University), psi-perception, psi-cognition, and so on, are also current.

There are several varieties of paraperception, covering a wide range of experiences involving seeing without eyes, hearing without the auditory sense, knowing without having the means of acquiring the facts and so on. It includes: (1) clairvoyance, seeing things happening elsewhere; (2) clair-audience, hearing voices or sounds not present; (3) telepathy*, commonly known as mind-reading; (4) precognition, or seeing into the future; (5) retrocognition, or a vision of things that have already taken place, in the past; (6) psychometry, or knowing the history of an object by handling or looking at it; (7) radiesthesia or dowsing, finding hidden objects, usually by means of a simple instrument such as a forked rod or pendulum.

The scientific study of paraperception, called *parapsychology,* also known as psychical research or metapsychics, includes the field of psychokinesis* and all other paranormal, occult, psychic and spiritualist phenomena. Because the psi-faculty operates across a distance without discernible connection, sceptics refer to it derisively as telemagic, or magic performed from afar.

Paraperception may be induced by drugs, rituals, hypnosis; or come during dreams, trance or other xenophrenic states. It may be aided by the dowsing rod, the crystal ball or other gadgets. But as a rule paraperception is beyond control, cannot be directed and occurs spontaneously, without warning. It is an unconscious processs experienced as an instinct, an intuitive awareness or a 'feeling in the bones'. What is paraperceived may be vividly seen, heard, felt, although there is nothing to see, hear or feel. It may impinge on one's consciousness with immediacy and full comprehension. The phenomena may be manifested before and witnessed collectively by everyone in a group, or by a few, or only by one or two persons.

Certain conditions favour paraperception. During periods of national crisis, excitement, rejoicing, disaster, war, people living even in remote places in the country, seem to become affected by a tenseness in the atmosphere that conveys to them the realization that something has happened. In the more personal sphere, the psi-faculty seems to be activated in times of unease, anxiety, depression, illness, danger and during the coma that precedes death.

In experimental work it has been found that certain factors help and others hinder ESP. For example: (1) concentration and anxiety on the part of the subject are a hindrance to success; (2) the best results occur at the beginning and the end of a session; (3) interest, belief, enthusiasm and sympathy on the part of all concerned assist in correct scoring, while prejudice, scepticism, fatigue and boredom are inhibitive; (4) soporifics such as barbiturates and alcohol in large quantities reduce the psi-faculty, whereas caffein sometimes raises the score; (5) certain weather and seasonal conditions affect the faculty; it is found, for instance, to diminish in stormy weather; (6) the psi-faculty is not under anyone's control, so that no one can predict before an experiment whether the subject is going to do well; (7) elaborate gadgetry and monotonous repetition of a test tend to inhibit sensitives; (8) sometimes a higher percentage of correct guesses occurs for the card immediately preceding or immediately following the target card; (9) ESP (e.g. telepathy) seems to be associated with alpha waves, as PK with theta waves.

The psi-faculty is probably universal and possessed by all living organisms. In man its operation is always active but not consciously recognized or exercised. It is now established that a great deal of information about our environment, the atmosphere, the earth's magnetism, cosmic changes, distant happenings, coming events, is actually picked up by our bodies, although it seldom reaches our conscious awareness.

Paraperception is strengthened if there is a strong emotional bond or psychic rapport between two people. Similarly, those with a common background, or linked by ties of blood or close association, often think and act 'telepathically'. The paraperceptive faculty is sometimes hereditary. Certain national or racial groups, including pockets of people in advanced countries, usually those who live in rural areas, have this faculty more highly developed. Those who live close to nature often have a keen paraperceptive sense, and have been reputed to send and receive telepathic communications over long distances. People who suffer the loss of one of the normal senses often appear to have the sixth sense highly developed. Children and animals also show evidence of a keen paraperceptive faculty.

No one knows how paraperception operates. Earlier explanations included divine intervention (through prophets), the operation of demons (through sorcerers), or spirits (through mediums). Controlled tests have now virtually ruled out coincidence, guesswork, accident, self-fulfilling prophecies, false observation and fraud. Parapsychologists have further eliminated cryptomnesia, hyperaesthesia, clues picked up from ideomotor movements.

An electromagnetic hypothesis was once adduced to account for paraperception, but laboratory research has demonstrated that there is no evidence of any physical radiation passing from one brain to another during telepathy, as we have, for example, in wireless waves. Already in 1932 Professor Leonid Vasiliev (d. 1966) of Leningrad University found that ESP worked even through a radiation-proof cabin ('Faraday cage') that excluded all electromagnetic radiation. There is therefore no question of a 'mental radio' operating. More recently Dr Alexei Gubko of the Ukrainian Institute of

Psychology admitted that 'most scientists were now inclined to believe that the brain radiates a special, so far unknown, kind of energy that was responsible for telepathy' (Ostrander and Schroeder, 1973, p. 153). Not many years ago the Russians dismissed telepathy and similar manifestations as 'idealistic fiction', but they are now pursuing investigations in this area more assiduously than ever, and have gone far ahead of most other countries. They believe that the facts have now placed an inescapable burden on science to go further in the explanation and understanding of such phenomena.

Books

Beloff, John (ed.), *New Directions in Parapsychology*, Elek, London, 1974.
Ebon, M. (ed.), *Psychic Discoveries by the Russians*, New American Library, New York, 1971.
Hansel, C. E. M., *ESP: A Scientific Evaluation*, Scribner, New York, 1966.
Haynes, Renée, *The Hidden Springs: An Enquiry into ESP*, Hollis & Carter, London, 1961.
Heywood, Rosalind, *The Sixth Sense*, Chatto & Windus, London, 1959.
Ostrander, Sheila and Schroeder, Lynn, *PSI: Psychic Discoveries Behind the Iron Curtain*, Sphere Books, London, 1973.
Rhine, J. B. (ed.), *Progress in Parapsychology*, Parapsychology Press, Durham, North Carolina, 1971.
Ryzl, Milan, *Parapsychology: A Scientific Approach*, Hawthorn, New York, 1970.
Schwarz, Berthold, *A Psychiatrist Looks at ESP*, Signet Books, New York, 1968.
Vasiliev, Leonid L., *Experiments in Mental Suggestion*, Institute for the Study of Mental Images, Church Crookham, Hampshire, 1963.

PATHEMIA

(Gk. *pathos*, 'feeling') is the emotional relationship or tone of feeling subsisting between things. The ents (individual units of creation) constituting the universe are not motivated by purely mechanical factors, the actuating principle behind each of them, the power that determines the outcome of their relationship to other ents, being the hidden pathemic reaction that arises when they come together. Empedocles of Agrigentum (d. 425 BC) spoke of two fundamental powers which set the universe in motion and continued to operate it thereafter – love and hate. These two principles drew things together or drove them apart.

The network of pathemic impulses which links the component parts of the cosmos together is spoken of as *cosmopathy*, the universal tendency inherent in both animate and inanimate nature to react with sympathy, empathy, antipathy, or apathy to a person, thing or situation. In inanimate creation such pathemia underlies all tropisms, by which objects respond to external influences such as the sun, earth, heat, light and water.

A latent pathemia underlies all things, each person or object standing in a natural pathemic relationship to every other. Medieval writers held that when two persons meet their emanations or 'flames' may be friendly or antagonistic. If the flames are broken or thrown back on contact there is suspicion, hatred or discord; if they remain unmoved there is apathy or indifference; if they embrace and merge there is love and friendship.

Every state of existence thus has a 'magical' element in it, for it is in that situation by reason of its pathemic response to its surroundings. Pathemia determines the relationship between any two ents. The relationship may be one of sympathy* or attraction, resulting in union, love, friendship, compassion, compatibility, integration, harmony, concord. If it is one of antipathy or repulsion, we have hostility, hatred, incompatibility, leading to disintegration, disharmony and discord. If it is one of apathy, we have indifference and a state of inertia and neutrality.

Empathy is the imaginative experiencing of another person's emotions. In a literary context it is sometimes called mimpathy (Gk. *mimos*, 'imitator'), the self-identification with another person's condition, especially the contrived or induced empathy of a historian or novelist, that enables him to enter into the feelings of a character or situation he is describing. In German it is rendered as *Nachfühlen*. Great writers often live vicariously through their creations by mimpathizing. Honoré de Balzac (d. 1850), for instance, once met a friend in the street and in a highly strung frame of mind began to speak in mournful tones of the death of his hero, a character in the novel he was writing at the time, as if he were a real person.

When a pathemic bond subsists between two persons, it is known as rapport, which plays a vital role in hypnosis, mediumistic phenomena and telepathic communications.

It is now well established that the emotions have a direct effect on the physical system and the bioflux*. Every strong emotion brings about a change in the neural activity of the brain and disturbances in the blood supply. G. I. Gurdjieff (d. 1949) used to say that a single moment of anger would cost him three pints of blood.

If the body is the cauldron, and thoughts are the ingredients put into the cauldron, then the emotions may be compared to the fuel which brings the mind to its maturity. Scientists believe that it is possible to measure the quantity of electrical current used up by a person while he is experiencing a strong emotion, and it will eventually be possible by physiological processes alone to regulate one's feelings. Be that as it may, no science can measure the love, heartache, pity, tenderness, contentment, sorrow, jealousy, frustration, shame, despair, pride, triumph, hatred, rage, that cause the currents to be set in motion in the first place.

A strong feeling charges the whole body, energizes the mind and colours the soul. It can quite literally reinvigorate, renew, fortify, blight, damage and even cause death. Russian scientists have discovered that the white blood cells, which act as defensive agents in disease, increase in number when the patient feels positive emotions, and that negative emotions counteract healing power. The study of psychosomatics confirms that negative emotions do in fact bring on diseases of various kinds, affect the heart, liver, brain and radically alter the constitution of the physical apparatus. The emotion of faith firmly held and sustained can bring about remarkable cures of body and mind.

Every strong pathemic relationship carries a dynamic charge, which sends out a vibrating current of force and, depending on whether the emotion is friendly or hostile, one of love or hate, the current stimulates corresponding reactions in others, and, what is more important perhaps, in oneself. The emotions carry a quick contagion: one cheerful person can spread joy through a group; one despondent person can plunge a company into gloom.

Albertus Magnus (d. 1280) said that an *excessus affectus* lay behind all magical influences, for the capacity to raise and intensify emotion creates the necessary conditions for genuine magic. During strong emotion, it is said, the threshold of consciousness is lowered and the unconscious and its contents break through to the surface.

The pathemic element in man belongs to the astral body, as distinguished from sensation*, which is experienced by the etheric body. Both the astral and etheric bodies are asomatic*, and the effects arising from their operations remain in the permanent self or soul. The Upanishads say, 'Man is formed of desire; as his desire so his will; as his will so his works; as his works so his destiny.'

Each person creates and lives in his own pathemic atmosphere, and his love, serenity, compassion, jealousy, greed, lust, fear, anger, hatred, pride, all contribute to determine his fate. The control of the emotions is therefore one of the primary aims of many ethical systems. The main purpose of existence on earth is believed to be the building up of a healthy and positive pathemic attitude, which is one of love and sympathy, for this leaves a beneficial impress on the soul, and by this the individual will be judged. According to Emanuel Swedenborg (d. 1772), the function of purgatory is the exhaustion of impulses and desires from the personal ego. The sufis say that if we do not resolve discord within ourselves on earth, paradise itself will not make us happy.

Books

Arnold, M. B., *Emotion and Personality*, 2 vols, Columbia University Press, 1960.
Bain, Alexander, *The Emotions and Will*, Longmans, Green, London, 1875.
Bell, Charles, *The Anatomy and Philosophy of Expression*, London, 1806.
Falconer, William, *A Dissertation on the Influence of the Passions Upon the Disorders of the Body*, London, 1778.
Gellhorn, E. and Loofbourrow, G. N., *Emotions and Emotional Disorders*, Harper & Row, New York, 1963.
Hufeland, Friedrich, *Über Sympathie*, Weimar, 1811.
Knapp, P. (ed.), *Expression of Emotions in Man*, International Universities Press, New York, 1963.
Liddell, H. S., *Emotional Hazards in Animals and Man*, Thomas, Springfield, Illinois, 1956.
Plutchik, R., *The Emotions: Facts, Theories and a New Model*, Random House, New York, 1962.
Pribram, K. H. (ed.), *Mood States and Mind*, Penguin Books, Harmondsworth, 1969.
Reinhardt, Karl, *Kosmos und Sympathie*, Munich, 1926.
Scheler, Max, *The Nature of Sympathy*, Routledge & Kegan Paul, London, 1954.
Weidlich, Theodor, *Die Sympathie in der antiken Literatur*, Stuttgart, 1894.

PENIS

The derivation of this word is obscure and is variously said to originate (1) from *penis*, the Latin word for tail; (2) from the Latin *penus*, an interior room in the Roman house where food and provisions were stored, the same word being used for the innermost sanctuary in the temple of Venus; the word had a secondary meaning of vagina, so penis was what penetrated it; (3) from Penates, the household gods to whom a special domestic sanctuary was dedicated; (4) from the Latin *penitus,* signifying 'deep within', the penis being the only part of the human male that could effectively reach and probe the *penetralia,* 'insides' of the female.

A related word, *phallus*, has an anthropological rather than an anatomical connotation. It is believed to be of Semitic origin, probably from the Phoenician *palas,* which also had the meaning of 'pressing into' or 'breaking through'. The Hebrew *palah* means to split or cleave. In Sanskrit *phal* means to burst or rend. The root persists as *palus,*Latin for post, and *pfahl,* in German a stake, and the English *pole.* Alternative terms are *membrum virile,* 'the virile or manly member', and the Sanskrit *linga* (or lingam).

Among the colloquial English synonymns for the penis are: bone, cock, cod, Dick, ding, horn, John Thomas (or J.T.), knob, mentule, priap, prick, prong, root, thing, wick. Terms like private parts, genitals, sex organs, pudenda, may be used for either sex, depending on the context. The descriptive epithets for penis are endless: the long-necked, the hairy one, the impudent, the weeper, the one-eyed, the short arm, the middle leg, the trouser snake, yo-yo, junior, silent flute, night-stick, dingle-dangle, joy-stick, Cupid's torch, tree of life, butter knife, gravy-giver, lady's lollipop, Old Slimy, root of evil, ransacker, pusher, searcher, housebreaker, tearer. Some psychologists hold the view that the male fear of the *vagina* dentata*, or 'toothed vulva', has its counterpart in the female fear of the *penis aculeatus,* 'pointed penis', which pierces and tears her. Many names given to it also suggest various instruments: rod, tool, stick, prod, hammer, pole, hose, pipe, handle, pintle, verge.

The average length of the erect penis varies from four to six inches, the diameter at the base being about 1½ inches. The human penis is quite small as compared with the dimensions of other animals in proportion to their size. Thus, the boar has a penis 1½ feet long; the stallion 2½ feet; the bull 3 feet; the elephant 5 feet; the blue whale 8 feet. Nothing yet known can enlarge the size of the penis without permanently damaging it. The proportions of the human penis are entirely an individual matter. Its size does not depend on race, and the belief that the Negro or Arab has a penis larger than normal is absolutely legendary.

According to the Hindu science of phallimancy, or divination by the phallus, the man with a very long penis will be wretchedly poor; he who has a very thick penis will always be in distress; the possessor of a thin and lean penis will be very lucky; and the man whose linga is short will be a raja (Burton, 1963, p. 199).

In primitive societies the penis is often regarded as being endowed with a life and intelligence of its own, particularly because of the mystery connected with erection*, which is often beyond the control of the man. A number of tribal legends tell of a certain class of men, like the Trickster of the American Indians, who can take off their phallus and carry it around in a box. The

Rhodesian Ba-Ila believed that the penis is the dwelling place of an animal which controlled it. Chinese taoists listed the penis as one of the six sense organs, the others being the eyes, nose, ears, tongue and mind, and said that it operated in an entirely different sphere from the other organs.

In European medieval tradition Satan had control over the penis. The *Malleus Maleficarum* (1486), the famous witchcraft manual, says: 'The power of the devil lies in the privy parts of men.' It was the devil's organ, and the devil and his demon company who attended the sabbat had enormous phalluses, rough and scaly, often bifurcated so as to penetrate both vagina and anus at the same time. According to medieval demonologists the devil had the power of despoiling the male body of its appendage, either by giving the owner the illusion of deprivation so that he could not feel or see his member in its proper place, or by actually taking it away to store in a repository he had for the purpose. The existence of such 'treasuries' is mentioned in the *Malleus Maleficarum* and other writings on witchcraft.

Reginald Scot (d. 1599) states that among the diverse atrocities committed by witches was that of depriving men of their members, which they used to collect in great numbers, twenty or thirty together, and secrete them in the nests of birds or shut them up in boxes where they would move about like living things, and would be fed on oats and corn. They would then be distributed to male members of a coven who either lacked their own, or were impotent, or whose organs were not up to the standard required at their ceremonies. The *Malleus Maleficarum* says of these unique repositories that 'they have been seen by many and it is a matter of common report', but prudently adds that it is said to be done by illusion induced by the devil, 'for the senses of those who see them are deluded, and the organ of vision confused.'

One story, also from Scot's work, relates how a young man discovered after fornication that as a result of a ligature put on him by a sorcerer he had become emasculated. He went to a witch with his problem and she told him to climb a certain tree and help himself from a nest in which he would find several organs. Accordingly he climbed the tree and from the living treasury selected the biggest and heaviest specimen he could find, whereupon the witch told him that he could take any one he liked except that one, because that was reserved for the parish priest. 'This', said Scot, 'is no jest, for it is given credence by judges who passed sentence of death upon those who knew of this great treasure chest.'

Because it was the source of such intense pleasure, because it was the sacred organ of generation, because it seemed to be endowed with a life and will of its own, the phallus was accorded great reverence. The practice of penis-kissing, for instance, is of very ancient origin. In primitive communities kissing the penis of a chief was believed to cure disease and give one strength. Barren women were especially helped if they kissed the fecund organ of a male. Wall mentions that among the Druses of Syria the sheikh grants audience on special days to women who wish to kiss his phallus. In other places women kiss the member of a priest. In Europe the Templars, and witches at the sabbat, were both said to follow this ritual.

Goldberg speaks of the priests of Canara (India) who at certain times go naked down the streets ringing bells so that women could perform the religious duty of kissing their sacred member. If during the operation the penis ejects, the mouth is applied and the life-bearing fluid sipped. It has been observed that as a rule in the case of holy men no amount of excitement stimulates erection. Modern observation suggests that this state of apathy is brought about by the habitual use of weights which are tied to the organ and soon render it permanently flaccid.

From the earliest times nature and natural objects were invested with a sexual symbolism, and a great deal of sex worship centred around the phallus. Although the female vulva did receive homage, it was primarily the penis, the erect phallus, that was the special object of devotion. Traces of phallic symbolism are found in tree-worship, pole-worship, stone-worship, snake-worship and so on. The *jed* column of Osiris was also a phallic monument. Wandering in the wilderness the Israelites noted and occasionally imitated the sex-worship of the Canaanites, joining in worshipping a stone column called the *asherah*.

Among the many symbols of the phallus are: the line, stick, rod, sceptre, spear, sword, dagger, candle, plough (the field or furrow being female), the tongue of a bell (the bell itself is feminine), the pulpit (the altar being female), fingers, toes, fish, serpent, tortoise (because of its long retractable neck). Also all tall conical upright things like pillars, posts, maypoles, tree-trunks, crosses, obelisks, monoliths, pyramids, towers, spires, campaniles, minarets, upright stones, rocks, hills.

The phallus has a philosophical and occult as well as a mystical significance. Arthur Schopenhauer (d. 1860) held that the genitals were the real focus of the will, and the opposite pole of the brain. Aleister Crowley (d. 1947) wrote, 'The phallus is the physiological basis of the Oversoul.' The psychoanalyst, Phyllis Greenacre, uses the term 'penis awe', to describe the feelings certain people get at the sight of a penis. Some have even described it as being surrounded by a halo.

Books

Burton, Richard (ed.), *The Ananga Ranga of Kalyana Malla*, Kimber, London, 1963.

Davenport, John, *Sexagyma*, p.p., London, 1888.

De Ropp, Robert, *Sex Energy*, Jonathan Cape, London, 1970.

Goldberg, B. Z., *The Sacred Fire: The Story of Sex in Religion*, Jarrolds, London, 1931.

Greenacre, Phyllis, 'Penis Awe and Its Relation to Penis Envy', in R. M. Loewenstein (ed.), *Drives, Affects and Behavior*. International Universities Press, New York, 1953.

Simons, G. L., *A History of Sex*, New English Library, London, 1970.

Summers, Mongatue (ed.), *Malleus Maleficarum*, Pushkin Press, London, 1951.

Wall, O. A., *Sex and Sex Worship*, Kimpton, London, 1919.

Williamson, H. R. (ed.), *Discoverie of Witchcraft* (by Reginald Scot), Carbondale, S. Illinois, 1964.

PERCEPTION

Perception is the apprehension of objects that impinge on the senses. More briefly, it is the organization of sensory data. More simply, it is the mental reaction to a stimulus, the process by which something brought to the notice of the senses* is recognized and identified for what it is, as when something hard, black, cylindrical, smooth is recognized as a pen. Perceptions may be experienced through any of the sense organs: they may be visual (seeing), auditory (hearing), tactile (touching), gustatory (tasting), or olfactory (smelling). The person who perceives is known as the percipient, and the object perceived is the percept, although the term percept is more correctly confined to the mental modifications that accompany the act of perceiving.

The inability to attach meaning to sensory perception is termed *agnosia.* In this condition the act of perception cannot be completed, so that a person, although able to see an object, is unable to recognize its nature. Agnosia is found in certain types of nervous disease and insanity. It is also possible for one's perceptions to alter under the influence of drugs, hypnosis, intense expectation, hope, fear, or diseases of the sensory organs. Besides this, there are certain kinds of false or mistaken perceptions which result in delusions.

Metaphysically, several interesting problems arise in considering perception, the following among them: (a) is the object that we believe we perceive actually there? (b) is the object as we perceive it, the object as it really exists? (c) are perceptions to be understood only within the context of the senses and reason? Eminent thinkers have expressed the view that all perception involves a degree of clairvoyance; (d) is paraperception* possible, that is, the perception of things without the use of the known physical senses?

Books

Adrian, E. D., *The Physical Basis of Perception,* Oxford University Press, London, 1953.
Armstrong, D. M., *Perception and the Physical World,* Routledge & Kegan Paul, London, 1961.
Bach, Marcus, *The Power of Perception*, Doubleday, New York, 1966.
Boring, E. G., *Sensation and Perception in the History of Psychology,* Appleton-Century, New York, 1942.
Brain, W. R., *Mind, Perception and Science,* Blackwell, Oxford, 1951.
Broadbent, D. E., *Perception and Communication,* Pergamon, London, 1958.
Dixon, N. F., *Subliminal Perception: The Nature of a Controversy,* McGraw-Hill, London, 1971.
Hamlyn, D. W., *Sensation and Perception,* Routledge & Kegan Paul, London, 1961.
Hirst, R. J., *Problems of Perception,* Allen & Unwin, London, 1959.
Huxley, Aldous, *The Doors of Perception,* Chatto & Windus, London, 1954.
Lean, M., *Sense Perception and Matter,* Routledge & Kegan Paul, London, 1953.
Moncrieff, M. M., *The Clairvoyant Theory of Perception,* Faber, London, 1951.
Smith, K. and Smith, W., *Perception and Motion,* Sanders, Philadelphia, 1962.
Smythies, J. R., *An Analysis of Perception,* Routledge & Kegan Paul, London, 1956.
Vernon, M. D., *The Psychology of Perception,* Penguin Books, Harmondsworth, 1962.

PERINEUM

The small area in the human body lying at the junction of the thighs, between the sex organs and the anus. It is situated at the midpoint of the body, in the crotch of dichotomous man, being placed 'between the up and the down, the right and the left, the front and the back' (Walker, 1974, p. 40). It is an important occult platform, the polar opposite of the bregma, and one of the most significant locations in the body. As a plexus the perineum is more important in the male than the female, being the inner or hidden root of the penis. Its position in the male corresponds, in the woman's body, to where the yoni or female sex organs are situated, and hence in Hinduism the perineum is called the 'yoni-place'. It is sometimes identified with the Hindu chakra called the *muladhara*, 'root-foundation', the home of the kundalini*, and described as the root of sensual pleasure.

The perineum plays an important part in Chinese and Hindu systems of sex-magic. It is known in Chinese occult physiology as *ch'ing tao*, 'spirit way', and is regarded as the seat of very powerful forces. At the moment of ejaculation either the man or the woman presses the man's perineum firmly with two fingers, so that the semen that would normally be ejaculated and so escape, is intrajaculated, and taken within the body. According to modern physiologists what actually happens is that the semen is diverted into the bladder, where it is later voided at the next urination, but according to taoists and tantriks the semen becomes 'etherialized', and what is diverted into the bladder is merely the gross seminal residue of the testes, and not the subtle quintessence of the semen, which is made to ascend by certain secret processes into the region of the head.

The practice of pre-ejaculatory perineal pressure, medically known as coitus obstructus, or coitus saxonicus, was long known to the native peoples of Africa, north and south America, and Australia. It is used as a means of birth control by Persians, Turks, Armenians, and to a lesser extent by Europeans and Americans. With a partially impotent person, a firm pressure on this area by the woman during intercourse, can help in maintaining erection.

Books

Leadbeater, C. W., *The Centres of Force and the Serpent of Fire*, Theosophical Publishing, London, 1910.
Narayanandi, Swami, *The Primal Power*, Prasad, Rishikesh, 1950.
Rele, V. G., *The Mysterious Kundalini*, Taraporevala, Bombay, 1927.
Walker, Benjamin, *Beyond the Body*, Routledge & Kegan Paul,London, 1974.

PERSONALITY

(Etruscan, *phersu*, 'mask'), the outward manifestation of the transient self, made up of the individual's social, empirical, external, workaday behaviour. The personality represents the superficial accretions of the man through life, his status in society, the image he presents to the world. It is an individual, born in a certain country, in a certain cultural environment, of certain parents, having a certain name, possessing certain characteristic features. Mentally, it depends on inherited talent and education. Physically it lies in limbs and organs, many of which can today be changed or replaced by prostheses or transplants, and is made up of cells and tissues which constantly fluctuate, and all of which will eventually vanish with the dissolution following death. It is not part of the permanent self.

The personality is an aspect of the ego, and is what outwardly distinguishes one person from another. As the subego is related to the unconscious, so the ego or personality is related to the conscious mind or waking behaviour. The ego is the agent, the brain the medium and consciousness the effect. The personality is integrated and made coherent by memory, which registers on the brain as engrams. It receives knowledge of the external world through the senses, and is capable of reason and judgment. It is the cerebral, logical, causal self; the self on the earth-plane. In certain circumstances it can be possessed, dispossessed, depersonalized and expersonated, so that the distinction between the I (the self) and the It (the rest of the world) becomes blurred and overshadowed.

Through the personality we play a role, and so dominant is its power that role-playing pervades all our thoughts and actions. But the personality is quite a superficial thing, and will in time be shed after we die, as an actor casts off his mask and costume when he has played his part. Progress of the self is not possible as long as the personality is dominant. The personality has to be surrendered to the higher self. The personality is not immortal; it is an incidental experiment for the self*, which will go on to other grades of experience. The personality has no lasting existence. It is a phantom entity, varying from day to day, and changing with mood, emotion and thought. In this sense it has no existence. The personality or ego is the agent of our illusion in the world of phenomena.

Buddhists speak of the personality as an aggregate of five skandhas, five discontinuous psycho-physical elements, namely: (1) the physical body; (2) the senses; (3) reason; (4) will; and (5) consciousness. The medieval church theologians distinguished between the what (*quid*) and the who (*quis*) of a man. The what was his intrinsic, essential and permanent self, and the who his transient personality. Those who believe in an after-life point out that in the next world it matters little who you are. But it matters a great deal what you are. Human evolution might be seen as the advancement of the self from personality to spirit, from ego to essence.

Books

Allport, G., *Personality: A Psychological Interpretation*, Holt, New York, 1937.

Cummins, Geraldine, *Beyond Human Personality*, Nicholson & Watson, London, 1935.

Eysenck, H. J., *Dimensions of Personality*, Routledge & Kegan Paul, London, 1947.

Fairburn, W. R. D., *Psychoanalytic Studies of Personality*, Tavistock Publications, London, 1952.

Greenacre, P., *Trauma, Growth and Personality*, Hogarth Press, London, 1953.

Guntrip, H., *Personality Structure and Human Integration*, Hogarth Press, London, 1961.

Knipe, H. and Maclay, G., *The Dominant Man: The Mystique of Personality and Prestige*, Souvenir Press, London, 1972.

Mottram, V. H., *The Physical Basis of Personality*, Penguin Books, Harmondsworth, 1944.

Murphy, Gardner, *Personality*, Harper & Row, New York, 1947.
Storr, A., *The Integrity of Personality*, Heinemann, London, 1960.
Tyrrell, G. N. M., *The Personality of Man*, Penguin Books, Harmondsworth, 1947.

PHYSIOTAXIS

The 'natural arrangement' of the parts of an organism, the relationship of the various patterns they form, the functions to which they are adapted as a result of this arrangement, and their mutual interconnections. Evidence of physiotaxis abounds in nature. It is seen for instance in the movement of electrons in molecules, the order of the planets and constellations, the movement of the spheres; in the pattern of cells in a tissue, the arrangement of angles in a crystal, the direction and curve of diffusion of a spiral, the design of the shell of a mollusc, of scales on a fish; in the location of the roots, trunk and branches of a tree; in the disposition of whorls in the petals of a flower, in the placement of leaves on a stem, of veins in a leaf. In its esoteric aspect it is best studied in the architecture of the bony and muscular structure, and the arrangement of the organs and limbs in the human body.

One division of human physiotaxis relates to the front-and-rear aspects. The more important organs are situated in the front, and it is the front that gives and receives love and sympathy and that symbolizes union and social relationships. The back separates one from others, and is turned on those one hates, despises or rejects. It has less sensation than the front and is provided with thicker and heavier muscles. It bears the burdens. Another is the right-and-left aspects, or laterality*, which provides a separate branch of study. In this context the posture* of the human being acquires great meaning. Man is the only creature that stands foursquare to the world, and in this erect position the placement of his organs and limbs shows their relative pre-eminence.

Also playing an important part in the physiotaxis of the body* is the longitudinal flow of vital forces from head to feet and back. This vertical flow is important for physical and mental health, but is interrupted by horizontal blocking bands of tension, which Wilhelm Reich (d. 1957) called armouring. These inhibiting bands are located in the region of (1) the forehead and eyes; (2) the neck and shoulders; (3) chest and heart; (4) diaphragm, waist and small of the back; and (5) pelvic area.

It has also been pointed out that as we ascend from the feet upwards we notice that the organs of the superior function are located higher up. The feet, which perform the 'pedestrian' function of locomotion, are situated lowest of all. The anus is relegated to the rear, and is further 'lowered' to the ground during evacuation. The genitals, essential as they are for procreation, are of medium significance in the spiritual scale. Some people interpret the proximity of the organs of generation and excretion as symbolic of the inferior status accorded to sexual activity. The abdominal viscera, which nourish and sustain the physical framework, occupy the middle front. The heart and lungs, responsible for vitality, are placed above them. The head, the centre of consciousness, crowns all. In the brain too, the higher faculties are located in the front and top cerebral areas, the more primitive at the back.

The hands* are the only part of the body that can move freely from low (the feet) to high (above the head). According to evolutionists, one of the most important consequences of the upright position assumed by man was the freeing of his hands, so that his forelimbs were emancipated from locomotors to manipulators, and man became *homo faber*, 'man the maker', able to use tools and fashion things for himself. It also involved a new positioning of the skull in relation to the spine, removing the necessity for bulky masticatory organs, and so left room for the enlargement of the brain.

Books

Lartigues, Alfred, *Biodynamique générale*, Paris, 1930.
McCulloch, W. S., *Finality and Form*, Springfield, Illinois, 1958.
Pettigrew, J. B., *Design in Nature*, Longmans, London, 1908.
Reich, W., *Selected Writings of Wilhelm Reich*, Noonday, New York, 1961.
Thompson, D'Arcy Wentworth, *On Growth and Form*, abr. edn, Cambridge University Press, 1961.

PINEAL GLAND

An endocrine gland, so named because of its pine-cone shape; alternatively called the conarium (Gk. *konos*, 'cone'). About the size of a grain of puffed rice, the gland is attached to the midbrain, situated at the base of the brain, roughly between the cerebellum and the thalamus. It contains tiny granules of what have been called brain-sand, and also a pigment similar to that in the retina of the eye.

Biologically, the pineal gland, which responds to light, is regarded by modern science as an evolutionary relic of a third eye, a structure that exists in certain lizards, of which one class still survives in New Zealand. Occultists believe that the pineal gland is in fact the seat of the third eye*, and although its position is farther back than where the third eye is traditionally believed to be, it is said that in adepts it moves forward at the end of an invisible stalk like a sensitive antenna, and appears in the centre of the forehead, where it is visible to those who are perceptive in such matters.

The ancients regarded the pineal gland as the 'seat of the soul'. Herophilus (fl. 300 BC), the Greek anatomist who founded the medical school of Alexandria, described the pineal as a 'sphincter which regulates the flow of thought'. The French philosopher, René Descartes (d. 1650), maintained that there was a non-spatial mind infusing the body through the brain, and suggested the pineal gland as the point of contact between mind and matter. It was, he said, the abode of the sidereal spirit in man, the organ through which the divine spirit exercised its function.

Occultists point out that the position of the pineal gland is directly posterior to the extremity of the mysterious third ventricle, which controls reason and judgment. This is in accord with the early belief that the pineal guided the flow of vital spirits through the ventricles*. When the pineal gland is regenerated or stimulated by occult exercises, even the ordinary man becomes endowed with supra-physical vision.

Physicians today are still unaware of the precise function of the pineal gland. It produces a hormone called melatonin, which seems to react to darkness and may be involved in the regulation of circadian biorhythms* connected with our response to the alternation of day and night. Melatonin in turn influences the brain cells using serotonin, involved in the sleep mechanism (*see* nervous system).

The pineal gland is larger in children than in adults, more developed in women than in men. Sir Alexander Cannon says that his own study at post mortem examinations confirms that the pineal gland is larger in mediums. It is known that tumours of the area tend to produce sexual precocity and paralysis of the eyeball, among other symptoms. Removal of the pineal causes enlargement of the ovaries, and removal of the testicles enlargement of the pineal.

A modern biologist has said that if ecstasy has any biochemical basis it is becoming increasingly difficult to avoid the conclusion that 'the substances controlling both its sexual and transcendental manifestations are probably manufactured in the pineal gland' (Bleibtreu, 1968, p. 78).

Books

Bleibtreu, John N., *The Parable of the Beast*, Gollancz, London, 1968.
Cannon, Alexander, *The Power Within*, Rider, London, 1950.
Kitay, J. I. and Altschule, M. D., *The Pineal Gland: A Review of the Physiologic Literature*, Harvard University Press, 1954.
Tilney, F. and Warren, L. F., 'The Morphology and Evolutionary Significance of the Pineal Body', *American Anatomical Memoirs*, 1919, 9, 257.
Wurtman, R. J. *et al.*, *The Pineal*, Academic Press, New York, 1969.

PITUITARY

(Lat. *pituita*, 'phlegm'), also known as the hypophysis, is the most important of the endocrine* glands, formed during the early stages of foetal development from a downgrowth of the brain. This tiny gland, about the size of a pea, is situated at the base of the brain, roughly above the roof of the mouth and behind the bridge of the nose. It has two main components, the anterior and posterior lobes, regarded as occult opposites*, which between them secrete at least nine known hormones of highly complex functions. Despite its minute size the pituitary is the master gland of the body; it exercises control over many of the other glands and was once descriptively called 'the conductor of the endocrine orchestra'. There is some historical evidence to suggest that the turning of the tide in the career of Napoleon was partly due to pituitary failure.

In human typology the individual dominated by the anterior pituitary has masculine characteristics. He has a strong physical frame, long bones, a rugged face, prominent nose, resolute jaw, large hands and feet and large teeth. He is capable of great self-control and discipline, is forceful and determined, and possesses high qualities of leadership. Example: Abraham Lincoln. The individual dominated by the anterior pituitary has feminine qualities, tends to be short and is often stout and paunchy. Temperamentally unstable, he has scant body hair, is sensitive and emotional, and tends to cyclothymia or cycles of optimism, followed by moods of depression, though on the whole he tends to be cheerful, gay and tolerant. He has strong leanings to poetry, music and the arts. Example: Frédéric Chopin.

The occult importance of the pituitary gland was recognized from very early times. It was believed to be the centre for the reception and distribution of ros* or celestial dew absorbed from the pneumosphere. Physiologically it is known that certain serous liquids from the cerebrum descend into the third ventricle* that lies near the base of the brain. The pituitary is closely connected both with the third ventricle, and with the diencephalon (thalamus* and hypothalamus) lying around and beneath the third ventricle. From a cavity in the underside of the third ventricle there opens a funnel-shaped duct called the infundibulum, which continues down past the diencephalon and terminates in the pituitary.

Medieval physiologists believed that the vitalizing ros, transmuted into materiality in the third ventricle, trickled down the funnel into the pituitary and thence to the nose, palate and mouth in the form of phlegm (*see* humoralism). The word phlegm itself derives from the Greek *phlegma,* which is translated in Latin as *pituita,* whence comes the name of the pituitary gland.

Occultists say that most of the vitality of the ros is dispersed and adulterated by the time it reaches the mouth, although the fluids of the tongue, cheeks and mouth are impregnated with its vapours so that some of its power is retained in the saliva*.

In the esoteric plexal system the pituitary gland is specifically associated with the crown plexus*.

Books

See under endocrine glands

PLEXUS

(Lat. 'network'), physiologically an intricate criss-crossing of nerves and blood vessels, is applied in occultism to any one of a number of focal points where the subtle body meets the physical body (*see* subtle arteries). Each plexus is a generator of pneumic energy; it concentrates bioflux and emanates its subtle power, and is responsible for the distribution of etheric force to the sense organs. The plexus has been called 'an opening on the macrocosm', since it provides a way to superconscious experience, each plexus contributing its own kind of experience. Collectively the plexuses fill the body with the subtle effluvia of cosmic energy and vivify the psyche.

There are many plexuses in the human body extending from the scalp to the soles. But the major plexuses in all esoteric systems are situated within the 'undivided body', that is, the trunk, excluding the arms and legs, arranged along an axis extending from the top of the head to the root of the spine, and between three and eight in number, around the nervous system (brain and spine), the blood system (heart) and the sex system (sex organs).

There is said to be an intimate interconnection between the centres of the plexal system, each invigorating and charging the others. Power rises upward from the lowest plexus to the crown of the head, as in the case of the kundalini*; or energy seeps down from the top, materializing in the ros*, the ineffable celestial dew. In eastern schools the crown plexus and the root plexus are defined in terms of male and female potencies, whose conjugation is celebrated as a kind of mystical union which bestows great benefactions on the practitioner. By awakening these centres of force, either by meditation or yogic exercises, man acquires power on the astral plane. He becomes the master of his subtle body much as a gymnast becomes master of his physical body.

The plexuses were known to many of the early cultures, although there are some discrepancies concerning their number and location. The priest physicians of ancient Egypt believed that the human body was served by thirty-six 'subtle arteries' called *metu* which sent energy to various organs and rose to the surface of the skin at specific points where they joined the physical system. This idea was borrowed by the peoples of the ancient middle east.

In the Chinese taoist system, the yang and yin (the male and female principles diffused throughout the universe) are concentrated in the human body in three secret centres known as *tan t'ien*, 'fields of cinnabar', or 'fallow fields' located (1) in the middle of the forehead; (2) in the heart*; and (3) in the hypogastrium. In Chinese esoteric physiology an invisible cavity called *ni-wan* is situated in the crown of the head. It opens into the *nao* or brain which is connected by an invisible funnel-like organ to the spiritual world, and this organ receives the forces from that world. The nao is the seat of yin or female energy, and this energy unites with the fire-force in the root of the spine to produce spinal marrow through which vitality is communicated to the rest of the body.

In the Tibetan theory the major centres of the plexal system are situated in the brain, throat, heart, solar plexus and sex organs, and their presence is already discernible as a vein as fine as a hair during the fifth week of the embryo's life, with circular enlargements at the five centres. The Japanese theory resembles the Chinese but lays greater emphasis on the *ḥara* or *tanden*, situated below the navel in the hypogastric region. Physical culture and breathing exercises can activate it.

In Hindu esotericism the plexus is called a *chakra*, 'wheel', and the theory concerning them is the most richly elaborated and complex of all. There are seven main chakras, ranging from the basal plexus which houses the serpent-like kundalini, to the thousand-petalled sahasrara at the crown of the head. The result of their union is the creation of a heavenly ambrosia, which feeds the subtle body. This wonderful substance 'coalesces in the form of a fluffy ball about the size of a pea and can be made to ascend and descend rapidly time after time' (Blofeld, 1970, p. 235).

In the Maya tradition, preserved in the *Popol Vuh* of the Kiché Indians of Guatemala, there are references to 'air tubes' along the spine, that bear a great resemblance to the Hindu plexal system. Rivière thinks that the Hindu kundalini is represented by Hurakan, the tempest god of the Mayas, and that the Maya plexuses are symbolized by animals which closely correspond to the theriomorphic deities met with in the Hindu descriptions of the chakras. The Aztecs of Mexico had a similar scheme which they may have acquired from the Mayas.

Ancient Greek writings contain passages betokening an acquaintance with a system of hidden centres within the body, which scholars think was derived from ancient Egypt. From Greece the teaching passed on to the neoplatonists, and ultimately found its way into the eastern orthodox church, where it occurs in the teachings of the Hesychast monks of the middle east from the eleventh century. The latter laid great emphasis on quietude (Gk. *hesychia*, 'stillness') and interior prayer, and their disciplines included certain respiratory exercises with concentration on the plexuses. Six plexuses are mentioned, namely: (1) the space between the eyebrows; (2) the throat; (3) heart; (4) solar plexus; (5) sex organs; and (6) anus. The last two were later discarded as inimical to the Christian tradition, but the others were used in their prayer-rhythms and in meditation.

The kabbalists of the middle ages treated the occult centres in the human body as miniature replicas of the points situated along the central pillar (spine) of the tree of the sefiroth (symbolizing Adam Kadmon, or cosmic man). They named four such centres, each in one of the four worlds as follows: (1) the head plexus, equivalent to Kether, situated in Atziluth the world of emanation; (2) the heart plexus, equivalent to Tifareth, situated in Briah the world of creation; (3) the navel plexus, equivalent to Yesod, situated in Yetzirah the world of formation; and (4) the sexual plexus, equivalent to Malkuth, situated in Assiah the world of matter.

The sufis inherited their concept of the plexuses from ancient Mesopotamia, but incorporated new features from their contemporaries both east and west. Their plexuses were situated in the forehead, throat, heart and navel, the latter being the most important. Their meditative practices included turning the tongue up and back against the roof of the mouth, assuming occult bodily postures, breathing exercises, intoning mystic syllables and concentration on the navel.

In medieval Europe certain followers of the neoplatonists wrote scattered accounts about the subtle centres, but it was Paracelsus (d. 1541) who revived interest in the subject. He spoke of the *astrum* (Lat. 'star'), a focal point in the human body through which sidereal and planetary forces operated in man. His disposition of these astrums is almost identical with the major plexuses as we know them today. He believed that at the time of a person's birth the heavenly bodies engrave their impressions on the astrums and these determine his character, health and destiny. Through these astrums, Paracelsus declared, 'the heavens work in us'.

The following is a brief descriptive list of the major plexuses as found in most systems of esoteric physiology.

Crown plexus, also the bregmic or ventricular plexus. Hindu, sahasrara. Chinese ni-wan. Situated in the crown of the head, it is in close association with the thalamus*, the bregma and the third ventricle*. Associated endocrine gland: pituitary*. Associated skeletal area: top of skull, specifically the bregma.

Brow plexus, also the glabellic or pineal plexus. Hindu, ajna. Chinese: one of the three 'fields of cinnabar', and 'the mysterious pass between the eyes'. Situated in the region of the glabella, a small elevation on the forehead, between and slightly above the line of the eyebrows. It marks the location of the 'third eye' (*see* 'eye'). Associated endocrine gland: pineal*. Associated skeletal area: the front of the skull, specifically the glabella.

Pharyngeal plexus, also the laryngeal or cervical plexus. Hindu: vishuddha. Situated near the region where the spinal column meets the medulla oblongata. Involves the whole region of the neck*, pharynx, throat, larynx (voice-box). Associated endocrine gland: thyroid. Associated skeletal area: the seven cervical vertebrae, specifically the first or Atlas.

Cardiac plexus, also the thoracic plexus. Hindu, anahata. Chinese: one of the three 'fields of cinnabar'. Situated in the thorax, the region of the heart (Gk. *kardia*) and lungs. Associated endocrine gland: thymus. Associated skeletal area: the six upper bones of the twelve thoracic vertebrae, specifically the first thoracic.

Epigastric plexus, also the solar or coeliac plexus, it is sometimes included in the umbilical plexus (see below). Situated in the epigastrium*. Associated endocrine gland: adrenals. Associated skeletal area: the six lower bones of the twelve thoracic vertebrae, specifically the ninth thoracic.

Umbilical plexus, also the lumbar plexus. Hindu: manipura. Situated in the region of the navel, it extends from the lower part of the epigastrium to the upper part of the hypogastrium. If the middle of the closed fist is placed over the navel, the fist will roughly show the extent of the plexus. Associated endocrine gland: pancreas. Associated skeletal area: the five lumbar vertebrae.

Hypogastric plexus, also the sacral or prostatic plexus. Hindu: svadishthana. Chinese: one of the three 'fields of cinnabar'. Japanese: tanden or hara (belly), situated 'three finger-breadths below the navel'. The hypogastric plexus is sometimes identified with the umbilical plexus. Situation: in the hypogastrium (from the Greek, 'below the stomach'), it extends from about two inches below the navel line, to the line of the pubic hair. Associated gland: prostate (in males only). Associated skeletal area: the five sacral vertebrae.

Perineal plexus, also the root, base, basal or coccygeal plexus. Hindu: muladhara. Situated in the perineum*, between the sex organs and anus, and the site of the kundalini fire-force. Associated endocrine glands: the gonads or sex glands (ovaries and testes) producing gametes or sex cells (ova and sperm). Associated skeletal area: the four bones of the coccyx.

Books

Blofeld, John, *The Way of Power,* Allen & Unwin, London, 1970.
Kürkheim, Karlfried, *Hara: The Vital Centre of Man,* Allen & Unwin, London, 1962.
Leadbeater, C. W., *The Centres of Force and the Serpent of Fire,* Theosophical Publishing, London, 1910.
Leadbeater, C. W., *The Chakras,* Theosophical Publishing, Madras, 1938.
Meyendorff, Jean, *Saint Grégoire Palamas et la mystique orthodoxe,* Paris, 1959.
Narayanandi, Swami, *The Primal Power in Man,* Rishikesh, India, 1950.
Rivière, J. Marquès, *Tantrik Yoga: Hindu and Tibetan,* Weiser, New York, 1970.
Walker, Benjamin, *Hindu World: An Encyclopedic Survey of Hinduism,* 2 vols, Allen & Unwin, London, 1962.

PNEUMA

(Gk. 'breath', 'energy', 'life'), the vitalizing element contained in the aerial environment, which is taken in along with the air inhaled. Occultists say that just as the physical body subsists on the atmosphere, the etheric body needs the vital element in the pneumosphere or cosmic ether.

In occultism breath is a cosmic energy, the secret life-principle of the universe. Just as the body makes use of the essential qualities in food and from these nourishing elements forms blood, bone, muscle, nerve and tissue, so breath is converted into the vital elements needed to sustain respiration, blood circulation, cardiac and cerebral activity and other physiological functions.

The aerial substance taken into the lungs differs considerably from what is breathed out, just as food differs from faeces. Physiologists state that the lungs inhale oxygen and exhale carbon dioxide, but to occultists there is another substance absorbed by the body more refined than oxygen. This is the pneuma, which acts directly on the etheric body. When a man dies he is said to expire, that is, his pneuma leaves him. There is air, including oxygen in his body, but no pneuma, for the etheric body has left.

The fact that there is a close connection between breath and soul is reflected in a number of ancient languages, in their word for breath: the Greek *pneuma,* the Sanskrit *prana,* the Hebrew *ruah,* the Arabic *ruh,* the Chinese *ch'i,* the Latin *spiritus,* mean both 'breath' and 'soul'.

The pneuma contains a vitality which is diffused through the lungs by the subtle arteries, but each living being processes the energy in a way appropriate to its own species. The human body utilizes the pneuma inhaled into the lungs for its particular needs. It is a powerful agent of transformation and adepts are said literally to subsist on air alone, because they know how to store and direct the energy.

Hippocrates (d. 359 BC) thought that the pneuma was the source of intelligence and feeling, and that via the lungs the power of cognition was distributed to the brain and the power of feeling to the heart. In all esoteric systems pneuma was regarded as the fusing, transforming, canalizing, directing and activating agent of the body and brain. It is the pneuma that 'pushes' the blood along the blood vessels and the other fluxes along the nerves and subtle arteries. It is the pneuma that is responsible for the physiological and mental processes, aiding every faculty and activity, from digestion to thought.

According to the Tibetan school the bodily air (Tibetan *lung*) is responsible for the birth and development of the child at every stage of its growth. After birth the breath becomes localized and sealed in various parts of the body to perform its various functions. For example, one kind of breath has its seat in the heart and directs the vital activities of the body, one in the anus directs digestion, and one in the navel is responsible for etheric life.

In Hindu esoteric physiology the pneuma is likewise metamorphosed in the body to perform various functions, each under the control of a specialized kind of 'wind'. These five winds are responsible for (1) respiration; (2) excretion, erection, ejaculation, sneezing, coughing; (3) digestion, eructation, retching, hiccuping; (4) speech, blinking, closing the eyes, yawning; and (5) causing the circulation or movement of all the elements to the various organs of the body.

After being inhaled and utilized the breath of the human being when exhaled is imbued not only with the waste products of the respiratory process, but also with a subtle charge of power, characteristic of the person concerned. The immediate environment of each person is therefore filled with pneumic exhalations which may favourably or harmfully affect those near by. Certain people send forth very powerful emanations of their energy, and living for some time in their presence can be very beneficial. To some extent each living thing has its special pneumic environment. This forms the basis of pneumopathy, or healing by breathing in the pneumosphere of such an environment.

The personal exhalation of an individual, varies considerably in different circumstances. Tibetan physiology speaks of the *lung,* 'air', being different even at different times of the day. There are variations in pneumic discharge during running, walking, swimming, coition, eating, drinking, resting, drowsiness, sleep, trance. But pneumic discharge varies not only with physical activity, but also with the emotions, whether of pleasure, fear, anger, joy. Every mood has its own breath, which can be rough or smooth, cutting or healing, burning or cooling, chafing or soothing.

Breath-magic* makes special use of sex-breath, the hot breath of desire. During the sexual act the breath of love differs from the breath of lust; the breath of intercourse from that of orgasm.

POSTURE

Books

See under respiration

POSTURE

Posture is the attitude assumed by the body, usually more or less static, and thus to be distinguished from gesture*, which involves movement. As a living form posture can assume the character and potency of a dynamic symbol, directly relating the physical world to the spiritual. The physiotaxis* or arrangement of the limbs and organs of the human body is regarded as particularly adapted to the linking of the two worlds through bodily postures.

A posture, according to occultism, is the shape of an energy, and any posture assumed by the body is a force pattern. The Hindu god Shiva was said to have brought the 8,400,000 species of living things into existence by merely assuming the forms he thought up for them. By spreading his arms out he created the eagle; by going on all fours and projecting his nose he created the elephant.

In ritual activity and in times of emotional stress, postures become a focus of concentrated power and a channel through which power is projected. Every posture deliberately assumed for ritual, religious or sexual purposes is a source of magical potency. 'A form of vibratory energy rises spontaneously from such operations just as vapour steams up from a tropical marsh in summer' (Walker, 1970, p. 59).

The functioning priest with his hands raised in benediction, the witch-doctor pointing a bone at a victim, the Druid priest standing on one leg while uttering a curse, the prostration of the devotee during prayer, are all channels or conductors of power. The postures of copulation are regarded as occult forms. All postures of the human body during such occasions are moulds into which supraphysical forces are poured, and channels through which human energy may be directed outwards.

The body, inert and quiescent, has a mystic power, which activity dissipates. Immobility is one variation of ascetic stability, and may manifest in such things as staring fixedly at objects, remaining immobile in the face of provocation or threat as part of a discipline or an exercise in indifference or non-involvement. Ascetics often assume certain fixed positions for prolonged periods. Various forms of spontaneous and induced trance are characterized by catalepsy.

The schizophrenic will go into a state of stupor and catatonia during which time he is quite immobile, and not responsive to any outside stimulus, and he can keep his limbs for hours in the most uncomfortable postures. Many of the poses are bizarre in the extreme, and their significance is obscure, but it is possible that a study of them may yield a meaning. They seem to be the nearest one can get to a pure position of the human frame motivated entirely from the interior psyche, unrelated to getting a response from the outside world, and hence may give one a glimpse of archetypal patterns in a vital context. Some of these postures resemble the more extravagant asanas practised by exponents of yoga.

Books

DeJong, Herman H., *Experimental Catatonia*, Baltimore, 1945.
Guillaume, Paul., *La Psychologie de la forme*, Paris, 1937.
Lamb, Warren, *Posture and Gesture*, Duckworth, London, 1965.
Lartigues, Alfred, *Biodynamique générale*, Paris, 1930.
Peladan, J., *Les Idées et les formes*, Paris, 1901.
Walker, Benjamin, *Sex and the Supernatural*, Macdonald, London, 1970.
Wolff, Charlotte, *A Psychology of Gesture*, Methuen, London, 1945.

PREGNANCY

Pregnancy or gestation, the condition of being with child, begins with conception and normally ends with childbirth.

Conception is the fertilization of the ovum by the sperm, marking the commencement of the formation of the foetus*. Modern researchers have tried to discover whether any relationship exists between conception and such factors as the disposition of the stars, the position and phase of the moon, the sunspot periods, cosmic radiation and other cosmobiological factors.

Dr Eugen Jonas of Poszony, Czechoslovakia, a biologist and gynaecologist, is perhaps the foremost authority in this line of research. Going back to the writings of the ancient Egyptians, Greeks, Hebrews and Indians, he became convinced that there was a close connection between astrological factors and conception. In the course of his career Jonas personally studied several thousand cases of fertility, infertility, pregnancy, abortion, miscarriage and abnormal births, particularly with relation to astrological factors. He came to the conclusion that the disposition of the heavenly bodies that prevails when a girl is born, and certain other cosmological, particularly lunar, factors, determine (1) her future ability to conceive; (2) the sex of the embryo; and (3) the viability of the foetus. In 1968 the Czech government, after much opposition to his unorthodox beliefs, founded the Astra Research Centre for Planned Parenthood in Nitra, where the work continues.

Childbirth or parturition relates to the experience of the mother in giving birth to her child, and is distinguished from birth*, which covers the experience of the child itself. Parturition is universally regarded as a portentous time, since a new soul is brought into the world. Till modern obstetrical practice made puerperal death negligible, this period was always regarded as one of great danger for mother and child, and many strange practices were observed to ensure safe delivery.

Childbirth begins with travail, the pains accompanying the rhythmic contractions of the muscular walls of the womb and the dilation of the cervix or neck of the uterus. The contractions increase in strength and when the uterus finally pushes out the baby, it is, as Watson says, 'with a force strong enough to break an obstetrician's finger'.

Labour pains are often avoided today by the use of anaesthetics. But some doctors feel that it is not desirable for either mother or child that travail should be avoided. According to them, children born by caesarean section, having missed the stimulation of the normal and energetic contractions of the mother, eventually show retardation in speech and manual dexterity, and may become more emotionally jumpy, anxious and shy than other children. It seems that the child needs the apparently 'psychical' impulses that are impressed upon it during its passage out of the maternal womb. The mother too should not be denied the feeling of satisfaction and the overall exhilaration that comes from the knowledge that she has been completely responsible for the birth of her baby.

During the formation of the foetus, a mass of tissue called the placenta develops inside the wall of the womb, and it is joined to the foetus by a cord for purposes of nutrition. This connecting cord, called the umbilical cord, navel cord or navel string, is a slender rope-like structure containing veins and arteries through which blood passes to and from the placenta. Both foetus and placenta originate in the same cell.

When the child is expelled from the womb at birth it is still connected by the umbilical cord, which therefore has to be cut. The placenta, along with the remaining portion of the cut umbilical cord, is expelled from the uterus about ten minutes after the child. This is called the afterbirth or secundine. The stump of the cord, that is, the piece which is left on the child's body and is marked by a scar called the navel, withers and falls off itself in about four or five days.

Many mammals eat the placenta after the birth of their young, and it is believed that in earlier times human beings always did the same thing. The word placenta comes from the Greek *plakous*, meaning 'flat cake', and the German word is *Mutterkuchen*, 'mother cake', terms which are thought to indicate the once prevalent custom of injesting the placenta. Until a century ago many chemist shops in Europe dispensed dried placenta as a regular item. It is of interest to note that in modern medicine human placentas are processed into gamma globulin, a life-saving protein which when injected into a patient raises the 'antibody' level and enables the human body to fight invading viruses. The Philippines export about 230,000 placentas to the USA every year for the manufacture of gamma globulin.

The period that begins with travail and ends when all the procreative organs affected by pregnancy and delivery have returned to their normal shape and position after the birth of the child is known as the puerperium. It usually lasts for about one month and was once almost universally regarded as an unclean period. The lochia or mucus discharge from the genitals during the puerperium was held to be almost as defiling as menstruation.

Books

Blondel, J., *The Power of the Imagination on Pregnant Women and Its Effect on the Foetus*, Strasbourg, 1750.

Cole, F. J., *Early Theories of Sexual Generation*, Clarendon Press, Oxford, 1930.

Flanagan, Geraldine, *The First Nine Months of Life*, Heinemann, London, 1963.

Gebhard, P. H. *et al.*, *Pregnancy, Birth and Abortion*, Harper, New York, 1958.

Meyer, A. W., *The Rise of Embryology*, Stanford University Press, 1939.
Montague, A., *Prenatal Influences*, Thomas, Springfield, Illinois, 1962.
Ostrander, Sheila and Schroeder, Lynn, *PSI: Psychic Discoveries Behind the Iron Curtain*, Sphere Books, London, 1973.
Read, G. D., *Revelation of Childbirth*, Heinemann, London, 1973.
Watson, Lyall, *Supernature*, Hodder & Stoughton, London, 1973.
Witkowski, G. J. A., *Histoire des accouchements chez tous les peuples*, Paris, 1887.

PSYCHOKINESIS

('Mind movement') abbreviated 'PK', the term applied to the paranormal phenomenon of telekinesis ('distance movement'), cryptokinesis ('hidden movement') or telergy ('afar action'), where objects are moved or influenced by the power of thought, is a manifestation of what is popularly called 'mind over matter'. Broadly, PK covers all instances of paranormal action, as in physical mediumship, poltergeist manifestations, psychic photography and paranormal healing.

The Persian philosopher, Avicenna (d. 1037), believed that there exists in the human mind a certain power capable of altering the position and even the nature of objects. Paracelsus (d. 1541) claimed, 'It is possible for me without help from my body and without a sword but by the power of fervent thought alone, to injure another person.' Francis Bacon (d. 1626), in his *Sylva Sylvarum* published a year after his death, suggested that human imagination has objective force and can cause movement. He referred in this connection to the 'casting of dice'. And indeed some gamblers believe that when they are in the proper frame of mind they can control the throw of dice.

It is said that some people who possess this gift are able to influence matter and material activity at a distance, without physical means, merely by willing. For example, the magician, Aleister Crowley (d. 1947), was said to have put out a candle at ten paces by willing it to go out. In the course of numerous experiments conducted by Dr J. B. Rhine at Duke University, Durham, North Carolina, and other researchers, subjects have tried by mental concentration to make dice fall with the desired face up, or to will a matchstick to shift its position when laid on a table.

From 1965 a group of Soviet scientists have been conducting experiments with a Leningrad housewife, Nelya Mikhailova, who can allegedly move wineglasses, apples, bread, without touching them. She is also said to have successfully separated the white from the yolk of an egg immersed in a tank of water at a distance of ten feet from her. Russian and Czech scientists are at present exploring the possibilities of collecting and storing the biomagnetic energy radiating from human beings in specially moulded generators, from where it could be directed to effect changes in the physical environment. It is thought likely that such psychokinetic energy may be generated in the atmosphere by supercharged adolescents, and it is perhaps this that manifests in poltergeist activity. One tentative hypothesis is that psychokinetic energy works by exerting a neutralizing influence on gravity. A French scientist claims that through PK human beings can even influence the rate of radioactive decay.

A revival of interest in PK has been started as a result of experimental investigation into the powers allegedly possessed by an Israeli wonderworker, Yuri Geller (b. 1946), who can apparently make things appear and disappear, translocate objects, stop clocks and bend spoons and other metal objects by holding them or by simply waving his hand over them.

In experimental PK tests, as in all tests in paraperception, it has been found that mood, keenness, alertness, belief and other positive psychological factors play an important part in a successful outcome. Another fact that has so far emerged from electroencephalographic data is that PK seems to be associated with theta waves, as telepathy is with alpha waves.

The application of mental power and parapsychological methods to technology is also envisaged, the goal being the mental control of automobiles, ships, aircraft and spaceships. Researchers think it not improbable that the development of parapsychology will one day direct civilization on an entirely new course.

Books

McConnell, R. A., 'Wishing With Dice', *Journal of Experimental Psychology*, 1955, 50, 269.

Ostrander, Sheila and Schroeder, Lynn, *PSI: Psychic Discoveries Behind the Iron Curtain*, Sphere Books, London, 1973.

Pratt, J. G., 'Target Preferences in PK Tests with Dice', *Journal of Parapsychology*, 1947, 11, 26.

Rhine, Louisa E., *Mind Over Matter*, Macmillan, London, 1970.

Schmidt, H., 'Mental Influence on Random Events', *New Scientist*, 1971, 50, 757.

Schwab, F., *Teleplasm and Telekinesis*, USA, 1923.

Steiger, B., *ESP: Your Sixth Sense*, Aware Books, New York, 1966.

Taylor, John, *Superminds*, Macmillan, London, 1975.

PSYCHOSOMATICS

Psychosomatics studies the influence of thought and the emotions on the body, especially in causing physical and mental disorders. Many diseases are known to be psychogenic, 'mind-originated', resulting mainly from disturbances of the autonomic nervous system. There is but one step from the psychic to the somatic. Psychological factors play a paramount role in physiological functions. The body is not a machine that can be understood in terms of physiology, physics and chemistry alone. Many organic diseases develop from observable changes in the organs and tissues that have an emotional origin.

Sigmund Freud (d. 1939) showed that when our emotions do not or cannot find expression and relief through normal channels, that is, when they are repressed and excluded from proper discharge, they often become the cause of chronic mental and physical disorders which manifest in tension and hysterical symptoms. But Georg Groddeck (d. 1934), the father of psychosomatic medicine, concluded from his own vast experience, that the ability to make oneself ill in order to serve a purpose was not confined to the hysteric. Every man has this ability and each uses it 'to an extent beyond comprehension'.

Imagination* has a most insidious influence on the physical system. It works its secret effects on our bodies, and is probably the strongest ingredient in all miraculous cures. When a person is moved by emotion, observable changes take place in the electrical activity of his nervous system, that affect the glandular, enzymatic and bacterial activity in the body. Strong negative emotions such as hate and jealousy generate actual poisons by causing an excess of endocrine secretions to be pumped into the bloodstream.

Whereas love suffuses the whole body with a vitalizing glow, brings a sparkle to the eyes and beauty to the cheeks, rage fills the body with chemically toxic substances that tend to dry the tissues, change the colour of the skin, cause palpitations, sap the energy and paralyse the will. Aristotle (d. 322 BC) said, 'The mind has the same command over the body as the master over the slave.'

This is now a well-recognized fact in medicine. To illustrate: a mother who sees a heavy, sharp-edged piece of metal narrowly missing her child's neck, receives such a shock that a red circle appears around her neck and remains swollen for hours. An invalid father seeing his son on the point of being run over by a car, leaps out of his wheelchair and dashes out to save him.

There is an old occult adage: as the mind so the form. That is, the mind can shape. Thinking about an action can be not only ideodynamic*, producing imperceptible reflexes required to do it, but also the reactions in the internal organs that normally accompany it. Even hearing about someone eating a slice of sour lime can set the teeth on edge and start the saliva flowing. Bad news received shortly after a meal can bring on vomiting or indigestion. A strong emotion can produce hormonal changes.

Our colloquial expressions reflect an understanding of how the mind affects the body. We say that something makes a person's flesh creep; one can get hot under the collar; people get white with fear; look pale as death; boil with rage; sweat it out (this last illustrates the disagreeable tension of anxiety). The 'hot seat' is figuratively occupied by a person under a great deal of stress. Turning on the heat suggests making a person uncomfortable. A person is 'on the hook', when he is in a helpless and unpleasant predicament.

A prominent British communist unable to bear the 'sight' of what was happening when the Russians invaded Hungary in 1956 actually suffered a temporary loss of his sight. Dermatologists have reported cases of people who, because of a feeling of guilt for some reason, developed weals on the buttocks, as if to punish themselves.

Everyone knows the devastating consequences of abandoning the mind to the uncontrolled obsession of a single overpowering emotion, be it jealousy, envy, anger, hatred, lust or greed. They are universally condemned as causing a spiritual blight and seriously affecting the moral condition of the victim who is in the grip of these shattering passions. Even the more passive mental conditions arising from unrequited love, loneliness, homesickness, anxiety, grief, fear, frustration, have a deeply disturbing effect that can drive one to insanity.

Our simplest emotional reactions are reflected in physiological changes. This process is now a securely established scientific fact. Depression brings insomnia and loss of appetite; nervousness can cause vomiting and difficulty in swallowing; shame results in blushing; sorrow in weeping; amusement in laughter; sadness in sighing; anger in higher blood pressure and tremors; fear in palpitations, pallor, horripilation (gooseflesh).

Guilt, especially when it arises from having sacrificed a moral or religious principle, takes strange shapes, as in the phenomenon known as 'symptom conversion'. Thus, if migraine springs from a guilt complex, its relief may be followed by an eruption of eczema or other malady, as if to continue the punishment. Similarly when ulcerative colitis is healed a mental disorder may follow. Related to this is 'symptom migration', when pain or some trouble which is made to disappear in one place reappears elsewhere. Thus psoriasis may jump from arms to legs, or settle in some almost 'symbolic' part of the body.

Mental and emotional stress may manifest in almost any form of disease. Emotional factors have been held responsible for cancer and tuberculosis. A German psychiatrist proved that quite a few diseases are due to 'competition and the feverish pursuit of wealth and social position', which build up unbearable tensions in the mind. Even accidents may have an emotional cause, and the accident-prone are often unconsciously motivated to seek punishment or desire to escape from an intolerable situation.

The following brief list gives an idea of the wide range of illnesses to which a psychosomatic origin has been attributed. Colds often follow slights, humiliations and disappointments. Nietzsche once said, 'Contentment preserves one even from catching cold. Has a woman who knows that she is well dressed ever caught a cold? No, not even when she had scarcely a rag to her back.' Skin diseases, itches, rashes, eczema, urticaria, dermatitis, acne, warts, pruritus, allergies, may indicate impatience, guilt, hostility, erotic impulses. The skin* has been described as 'an organ of emotional expression'. The four cardinal symptoms of changes in the skin surface: rubor (redness), tumor (swelling), calor (warmth), and dolor (pain) often reflect mental states.

Headache and migraine are mainly emotional in origin, resulting from suppressed hostile impulses, sexual frustration, resentments. Peptic ulcers come from tension and responsibility; the so-called 'three-ulcer executive' is a highly paid administrator with worrying problems. Peptic ulcer is said to develop from a tussle between the infantile desire for dependence and love, and an adult desire for independence and success, which may conflict with love. Heart disease and high blood pressure have many causes, for any emotion can affect that organ. Anxiety, tension, anger, if continued for any length of time, can cause actual organic lesions.

Intestinal and digestive troubles like diarrhoea, constipation, colitis, indigestion, are frequently due to emotional disturbances like anxiety and depression. Respiratory disease may be due to tension, fear, threat to one's security or love. Asthma, which is essentially an inability to exhale or breathe out, is associated with the childish habit of breath-holding by obstinate children. It may be a form of protest or a sign of one who seeks protection. Tuberculosis has been called a psychosomatic disease. Inflammatory diseases and fevers without apparent cause are the expression of inflamed mental conditions. The distempers of the body externalize those of the mind. Rheumatism and arthritis stem from rebellion against restrictive influences. Menstrual and uterine troubles are often emotional in origin, resulting from fear of pregnancy, loss of love, jealousy.

Books

Alexander, Franz, *Psychosomatic Medicine*, Allen & Unwin, London, 1952.
Barlow, W., *Modern Trends in Psychosomatic Medicine*, Butterworth, London, 1954.
Cannon, W. B., *Bodily Changes in Pain, Hunger, Fear and Rage*, 2nd edn, Appleton, New York, 1929.
Dunbar, H. F., *Emotions and Bodily Changes*, 3rd edn, Columbia University Press, New York, 1947.
Groddeck, Georg W., *The Unknown Self*, Vision Press, London, 1951.
Hill, O., *Psychosomatic Medicine*, Butterworth, London, 1970.
Ludwig, A. O., *Psychosomatic Aspects of Gynaecological Disorders*, Oxford University Press, London, 1969.
Pierloot, R., *Recent Researchers in Psychosomatics*, Wiley, London, 1971.
Simon, A. (ed.), *The Physiology of the Emotions*, C. C. Thomas, Chicago, 1961.
Tuke, Daniel Hack, *Influence of the Mind upon the Body*, 2 vols, London, 1884.
Weiss, E. and English, O. S., *Psychosomatic Medicine*, 2nd edn, Saunders, Philadelphia, 1949.
Wengraf, Fritz, *Psychosomatic Approach to Gynaecology and Obstetrics*, Thomas, Springfield, 1953.
Wolf, Harold, *Stress and Disease*, Thomas, Springfield, 1953.

PULSE

The rhythmical throb of blood in the arteries as it is transmitted by the beating of the heart, can be felt by pressing the finger-tips at various points on the body, such as the temples, nose, neck, behind the ears, the armpits, wrists, thumbs, groins, genitals, anus, ankles. The normal pulse rate is 70 to 72 beats a minute for men; 78 to 82 for women; 100 to 120 for children and infants.

The pulse rate rises following physical exercise, emotional excitement, chronic infections and the intake of certain drugs. An abnormally rapid heartbeat and fast pulse rate of over 120 per minute is known as *tachycardia* (Gk. *tachys*, 'swift', *kardia*, 'heart'), and this may rise to as much as 250 to 270 beats a minute, a condition that can become fatal if unchecked. During certain xenophrenic states such as mediumistic trance, possession and epilepsy, the pulse rate increases to about 130 beats per minute in the case of female mediums, and to 230 beats in the case of male shamans, and even higher in those 'possessed'. Cases of thanatomania are often characterized by tachycardia, when the pulse races so fast that it beats the victim to death.

The opposite condition is known as *brachycardia* (Gk. *brachys*, 'short'), when there is an abnormally slow heartbeat, with a pulse rate of 60 per minute or less. It is normally found in the aged, in convalescents, adolescents and in athletes, and is a symptom in brain tumour, uraemia and certain other diseases.

PULSE

The pulse is a remarkable indicator not only of the physical condition but of the state of mind and emotional balance as well. The ancient Egyptians referred to the pulse as 'the voice of the heart'. The Greeks said that 'physicians can tell the thoughts of the heart from the state of the pulse.' All animals with hearts have a pulse beat, but it is the human pulse above all others that is believed to be in tune with the divine stream. Robert Fludd (d. 1637), the English physician and mystic, described the pulse as the audible effect of the operation of the divine life breathed into Adam by God, and 'a reflection of that divine harmony with which God has clothed the spheres'.

In China, examination of the pulse has been the chief diagnostic method from earliest times. The pulse is taken at the wrist in the usual manner, but the physician seeks to establish rapport with the inner processes of the body and to read the subtle signals sent by the pulse. In some Chinese systems, as in acupuncture, the pulses in the right and left hands and wrists are divided into six zones, making a total of twelve pulses. The first pulse is on the first phalange of the thumb; the second at the root of the thumb; the third at the ball of the thumb; and three, the distal (outer), middle, and proximal (nearer), one after the other on the wrist. Each pulse can show up to twenty-seven variations, and from a thorough examination of the pulse alone an accurate diagnosis can allegedly be made.

In the Tibetan system of diagnosis, which has been borrowed in part from the Chinese, the physician feels the pulse one inch from the wrist joint, using his index, middle and ring fingers. The physician must keep his fingers in line close to one another but not touching. Pressure should be varied in order to obtain the precise information required. The tip of each finger of the physician is moved slightly from one side to the other, since each of the two sides provides information about different organs. The information is transmitted to the subtle body of the physician through the *rtsa* or subtle arteries of the patient.

Tibetan doctors use the right hand to feel the patient's left pulse, and the left hand to feel the patient's right pulse. The information is as follows. (a) From the right hand of the doctor, examining the patient's left wrist: the right side of the tip of the doctor's index finger will show the condition of the patient's heart; left side of index finger, the large intestine; right side of middle finger, spleen; left side of middle finger, stomach; right side of ring finger, kidneys; left side of ring finger, seminal vessels. (b) From the left hand of the doctor, examining the patient's right wrist: the right side of the tip of the doctor's index finger will show the condition of the patient's lungs; left side of index finger, small intestine; right side of middle finger, liver; left side of middle finger, gall bladder; right side of ring finger, rectum; left side of ring finger, bladder.

In many parts of the middle east and India a somewhat similar system of diagnosis by the pulse is widely practised. Called the *nabbazi* system, it is based in the main on principles laid down by the Greeks, although the Moslems greatly developed it. Every major human ailment is supposed to have its own distinctive pulse, but long training and experience are required before the physician can become sensitive enough to recognize the exact kind of flutter indicating a particular disease. The real expert is regarded as divinely inspired, for the final result comes to him almost in a trance state.

In most of these systems the pulse is taken mainly at the wrist, but supplementary information is obtained by feeling the pulse of the liver, kidneys, brain and other parts of the body, by pressure on special points known to the physician. Many other factors are taken into account, besides the pulse rate: the depth of the vibration, whether superficial or profound; whether hard or soft, hollow or full, relaxed or excited; the 'language' in which it speaks; its flutter and periodicity; the cycles of its undulation. A comparison is also made between the pulses of the right and left arms. It is good if the right arm has a more rapid and vigorous rate than the left, because this is a sign of good health.

In general a very weak pulse is said to indicate depletion of vital energy; a small thin pulse, insufficiency of will to use the available vital energy; a small, hard and 'pointed' pulse, suggests spasticity and contractures of some organ, or mental or emotional withdrawal; soft and strong, suggests inflammation; full, hard and taut, hypertension and neurasthenia; overflowing, full and large, excess and the need to be bled. In the Indian system the pulses are classified as serpent-like, leech-like, crow-like, quail-like, and frog-like, and the characteristics of these animals indicate the nature of the disease.

The parts of the body where the pulse can be felt, such as the neck, groins, wrists, ankles, were believed to be especially susceptible to the invasion of psychic forces, and precautions were taken to protect these sensitive areas. The elaborate ornaments of antiquity, like the necklace, wristlet, girdle and phallocrypt, often decorated with potent gems, were originally talismanic devices to keep off the evil eye, ward off hostile entities and preserve the wearer.

Books

Ghalioungui, Paul, *Magic and Medical Science in Ancient Egypt,* Hodder & Stoughton, London, 1963.
Kutumbiah, P., *Ancient Indian Medicine,* Madras, 1962.
Rechung, Lama, *Tibetan Medicine,* Wellcome Institute, London, 1973.

RAPPORT

Rapport is the reciprocal pathemic relationship that subsists between two persons so that one thinks and feels as the other does. Originally the term was confined in meaning to the 'magnetic relation', experimentally induced, between a magnetizer and his patient, that is, the communion of thought and feeling between hypnotist and subject, that was believed to be established by personal contact, insufflation and command, and brought about by the projection of the magnetic fluid of the operator on to the magnetic fluid of the subject. Thus under hypnosis the subject becomes receptive to suggestions from the hypnotist and accepts commands from him.

The term has since been extended to cover all forms of related sympathetic connection between such parties as a medium and his control, the sender of a telepathic message and the recipient, mother and child, lover and beloved. Also between man and animal, and even man and an inanimate object. It includes the intimate co-existence of feeling between two persons known as empathy (in German, *Einfühlung*), which enables one to enter imaginatively into another person's state of mind and experience his feelings.

Rapport is often characterized by *symplastia,* where the relationship is strong enough for the one to influence not only the thoughts and feelings, but also the actions and material appearance of the other, sometimes to the extent where one party can be made to bear on his own body the imprint of what is being done or felt by the other. Thus, a hypnotic subject, insensible to any stimulus applied to his own body, can be made to respond to a stimulus applied to the hypnotist, so that if the hypnotist is pricked the subject feels the pain. Dr E. Azam, a French physician, found that under hypnosis one of his patients could taste substances that Dr Azam put into his own mouth. There have been interesting hypnotic experiments when sensations were transferred by appropriate suggestions from a hypnotized person to a dummy made of putty, with whom he had previously been put in symplastic rapport. For example, hair may be cut from the subject and fixed firmly to the dummy, and when the hair on the dummy is pulled the subject cries out. Such exteriorization of sensibility is sometimes explained by astral projection. Some early magnetizers (hypnotists) have recorded that a magnetized person shares the sensations of the operator and experiences during the trance what the magnetizer is doing. In one case the subject while lying in trance followed the magnetizer into town and correctly described what he saw.

Symplastic rapport is occasionally seen in materialization seances. Thus, if the ectoplasm emanating from a medium is injured, the medium suffers pain. If an injury is inflicted upon a body materialized at a seance, the injury will be reproduced with faithful accuracy on the same part of the medium's body. It has sometimes been found that if chalk is rubbed on a materialized hand, a corresponding mark appears, after the hand has vanished, on the hand of the medium. It is known that a medium remains in close rapport with the spirit form manifested during a seance, and it has been noticed that when objects are being moved at a distance the medium herself carries out imitative gestures on a lesser scale. Thus, while a musical instrument is being played by invisible hands at one end of the room, the hands of the entranced medium are seen carrying out tiny motions simulating the movements that would be necessary to make the instrument play (*see* ideodynamics).

There is believed to be an intimate rapport between a man's physical body and his astral form when the two are out of coincidence. In the phenomenon of repercussion any damage inflicted on the astral body is reproduced in the physical body, a fact known to black magicians who try to injure their enemies by damaging their astral bodies during sleep or astral projection. Occultists find a symplastic relationship between the wolf form assumed by the lycanthropic sorcerer and his physical body, so that a wound inflicted on the animal will be found duplicated by sympathetic repercussion on the body of the man who assumed the wolf form.

Many kinds of symplastic rapport are set up by imitation, contagion, sympathy or other channels of interrelationship. Thus, a witch is believed to induce, by means of magical rites, a symplastic rapport between a wax poppet and the person she wishes to injure. Then by pricking the poppet with a pin she can cause harm to the victim. In one type of magic the sorcerer holds up a large leaf and makes his pupil identify himself with it. The master smooths out the leaf, as though he were soothing the pupil; he caresses it, and talks to it, strokes it, and then with a sudden violent movement crushes it. The student grimaces with pain, and feels subdued, humiliated, docile and crushed, and becomes thereafter, subservient to the sorcerer's will.

A deeply religious man may have a symplastic rapport with the object of his devotions, as St Francis (d. 1226) and other stigmatics who received on their bodies the marks of Christ's wounds. A devout Moslem has an almost idolatrous veneration for the Koran and will feel any injury done to it.

Books

Hull, C. L., *Hypnosis and Suggestibility*, Appleton-Century, New York, 1933.

Moll, A., *Hypnotism: Including a Study of the Chief Points of Psychotherapeutics and Occultism*, London, 1909.

Muldoon, Sylvan J. and Carrington, H., *The Projection of the Astral Body*, Rider, London, 1929.

Scheler, Max, *The Nature of Sympathy*, Routledge & Kegan Paul, London, 1954.

Schrenck-Notzing, A. von, *The Phenomena of Materializations*, Kegan Paul, London, 1920.

REASON

Reason is the faculty of mind whereby ideas are analysed and synthesized. In his *Phaedrus*, Plato (d. 347 BC) represents reason as the charioteer, with two horses representing the moral and concupiscent elements in the nature of man. It has occasionally been invested with an almost divine status. The German idealist philosopher, G. W. F. Hegel (d. 1831), described God as Cosmic Reason seated on the throne of the universe. Reason, he said, 'was the very pulse of cosmic life'. According to him, 'the real is the rational, and the rational is the real.' But in the end he was forced to concede that nature was too weak to exhibit reason everywhere, and that 'much is accidental and wholly without meaning.'

At the animal level reason is the mental faculty of consciously linking ideas, discovering the relationship between things and drawing inferences. It is a faculty of the cerebral cortex and reaches its highest development in the human being. Man has been defined as a rational animal. Rationality (Lat. *ratio,* 'calculation') emphasizes the supremacy of reason, and of reason's handmaidens, logic and mathematics, and of reason's offspring, the sciences. These, according to Martin Luther (d. 1546), are the bastard progeny of 'the harlot, Reason'.

It is impossible to be completely rational, nor can reason be self-sufficient. Rational enquiry is, to use the phrase of Immanuel Kant (d. 1804), 'an infinite task'. If reason were the way to truth we should all be arriving at identical conclusions, and even behaving alike. We reason as we desire to reason, and there are numberless unconscious motives that sway our reason. Moreover, our thoughts are influenced by our heredity, environment, prejudices, self-interests, feelings, passions and other intangible determinants, all of which distort our thinking and motivate our actions. The promptings of the heart, the urges of the viscera and the sex organs are at critical times more powerful than the calculations of the cerebral cortex. In times of great joy, in states of ecstasy, in adversity, depression, panic, we cease to reason. Blaise Pascal (d. 1662) said, 'The heart has reasons of which the head has no knowledge', and he concluded that 'the supreme achievement of reason is to know that there are limits to reason'.

Reason develops at the expense of instinct, intuition and natural comprehension. Reason is deductive and Cartesian. It is often in opposition to religion, revelation, the numinous and the occult. Reason is no basis for moral or ethical principles, for, if we try, we could find valid reasons for justifying promiscuity, murder, sexual perversion, incest, adultery and even cannibalism.

Reason, it has been pointed out, is not equipped to understand the reality and pattern of the universe, and much else besides. Reason cannot explain 'without a remainder' and it is this inexplicable residue, inaccessible to our reason, that constitutes one of the most significant factors in our lives. The beauty, complexity and subtlety of the real world surpass the instruments of science and the intellect to measure, and the powers of reason to comprehend.

The human reason is adapted primarily for practical ends. We cannot by means of this instrument penetrate to reality. Besides which, we have no absolute justification for assuming that Reality, the world 'out there', or even Nature, are rational and conform to the rules of logic or science. For all we know, chance is as much responsible for human progress as reason. Serious students of the subject have averred that the universe is basically irrational and not amenable to the postulates of logical comprehension.

Books

Cohen, M. R., *Reason and Nature: An Essay on the Meaning of Scientific Method,* Free Press, New York, 1931.

Crawshay-Williams, Rupert, *The Comforts of Unreason,* Kegan Paul, Trench, Trubner, London, 1947.

Dodds, E. R., *The Greeks and the Irrational,* Cambridge University Press, 1951.

Gilson, E., *Reason and Revelation in the Middle Ages,* Scribners, London, 1938.

Hock, Alfred, *Reason and Genius,* New York, 1960.

Hogben, Lancelot, *The Retreat from Reason,* Allen & Unwin, London, 1937.

Merleau-Ponty, Maurice, *Sense and Non-Sense*, Evanston, Illinois, 1964.
Rignano, E., *The Psychology of Reasoning*, Kegan Paul, Trench, Trubner, London, 1923.
Taton, R., *Reason and Chance in Scientific Discovery*, Hutchinson, London, 1957.

REM SLEEP

REM sleep, or sleep accompanied by REMs (rapid eye movements), is the phase when the eyes under the closed lids move about rapidly, as though the sleeper were watching something. Such REMs seem to suggest that the sleeper is at the time engrossed in some interior concentration and involved in some emotional experience, as if he were watching a play.

The phenomenon began to be studied in 1953 and since then a series of experiments have been conducted with the EEG (electroencephalograph, which registers brain activity), the EOG (electro-oculograph, eye movements), the ECG (electrocardiograph, heart activity), and other biotelemetrical aids. All the evidence indicates that during the REM phase the sleeper is usually having a dream. REM sleep is also known as paradoxical sleep as opposed to ordinary or orthodox sleep.

In contrast to the synchronized slow-wave EEG patterns of orthodox sleep, paradoxical sleep is characterized by desynchronized, more rapid and erratic waves, more characteristic of 'waking' than sleeping. The chief findings as revealed by experimental research are summarized below.

Cats, dogs and other animals studied show regular REM periods of sleep. They have also been recorded in unborn animals. A rhythm identical to the REM cycle is observed in unborn children and subsequently in newborn babies. They have been observed in the congenitally blind, although in this case they decrease with age, so that congenitally blind adults manifest REMs to a considerably lesser degree than people who can see.

REMs are a regular part of the sleep process. They usually begin at an early stage of the sleep cycle, but not normally in the first cycle. Almost invariably REMs are associated with dreaming. REM phases are short during the early stages of sleep, and become longer towards the end. Dreaming is highest between the fourth and seventh hours of sleep. Almost everyone can remember his dream when awakened during an REM phase, because his dream is fresh in his mind, but very few can remember their dreams when awakened ten minutes or so after the eye movements have ceased.

On the average the human adult has a dream once every 90 minutes. Each dream lasts from 10 to 30 minutes. The first dream normally starts after about one hour of non-dreaming sleep. In the course of an average 7 or 8 hours' sleep, the adult has between 3 to 5 REM episodes. Consequently, during a normal night's sleep between one or two hours are spent in dreaming. The average person has over 1,000 dreams a year, the vast majority of them forgotten.

REM sleep is followed by non-REM sleep (abbreviated NREM), which is orthodox sleep, and is dreamless. After each REM phase the sleeper stirs and turns, and continues to be restless until the next REM phase begins.

Certain physiological phenomena accompany the REM or dream phase: (a) the body becomes quite still; (b) many of the muscles are relaxed during REMs, or lose their reflexes; (c) in particular the muscles of the throat and neck become relaxed; the head of a person in dreamless sleep in a chair rests lightly on the chair back, but when the REM phase supervenes his head slumps forward or sideways; (d) compared with the regular heartbeat of orthodox sleep, the heartbeat of paradoxical sleep is irregular; (e) REM sleep is deeper, so that it is harder to awaken a person when he is dreaming than when he is not; (f) among males, even children, REMs are regularly associated with penile erection; among females with vaginal moistening; (g) people who habitually snore, stop or considerably reduce their snoring during an REM phase; (h) there are often very small movements, such as twitching and grimacing, during REMs, like miniaturized mimetic actions (*see* ideo-dynamics); (i) during REMs both eyes move together, that is, in the same direction, whereas this is not so during dreamless sleep, when the eyes, if they move at all, do not move in unison; (j) in the dream phase there is an increase not only in ocular but in cerebral and autonomic activity, accompanied by pronounced irregularities in pulse and respiration rates, and blood pressure. Usually the pulse accelerates, blood pressure rises, breathing becomes shallow, irregular and rapid.

Certain tentative conclusions have been arrived at as a result of experiments in dream laboratories. It seems that paradoxical (rapid-wave, REM or dreaming) sleep is necessary for the development of the brain; and orthodox (slow-wave, NREM or dreamless) sleep for physical development. The human brain grows most rapidly in the month before birth, and premature babies spend more time in REM than normal babies, as if to allow their brains to make up on growth. Children and adults who are learning new things have more REM activity while they sleep. A senile person has very brief periods of REM sleep and his brain shrivels up.

It would seem that each of us has a normal dream rhythm, the regular periodicity of which is necessary for our mental health and well-being. If a person is allowed to sleep but is awakened each time his REMs start, that is, when he is dreaming, he will make progressively quicker and quicker attempts, when he falls asleep again, to start dreaming. The more a man is deprived of paradoxical sleep (i.e. dreams) the more he tries to dream; he tries to catch up not so much on his sleep as on his dreams.

Drugs have an effect both on REM states and sleep. Alcohol, tranquillizers (notably reserpine), amphetamines, barbiturates, tend to reduce the normal REM span. Such dream-depressants have ill effects on mood and behaviour, and in time bring about hallucinations and xenophrenic states. The connection between these drugs and dream deprivation could perhaps to some degree account for the psychotic symptoms of drug addicts and the mentally afflicted. Certain mental conditions such as over-anxiety, worry, tension, also reduce REM (dreaming) sleep. It has been noted that dream suppression often accompanies mental illness. If a person is deprived of his dream sequences, either as a result of drugs, or because of mental strain, he develops symptoms of agitation, nervousness and depression. The frustrated psyche tries to break through during the waking moments in snatches of sleep and micro-dreams. Extended dream deprivation will lead to serious mental disturbance and ultimately to psychoses and insanity.

Books
See under dreams *and* sleep

RESPIRATION

Respiration is governed by the respiratory centre in the medulla of the brain. In the course of centuries many different cultural groups have evolved esoteric breathing methods, some of extreme complexity, all allegedly conferring magical power or curative benefits. The Egyptians, Mesopotamians, Chinese and Hindus, the Gnostics of Alexandria, the Christians of the middle east and the Muhammadans, are among those who have made a distinctive contribution to the subject. In all these respiratory systems the nature and quality of the air breathed in is of particular importance.

Zen stresses that correct breathing is hindered by striving for it, that breathing should be a spontaneous and natural process, the simple 'letting in and out of air'. But few occult schools would follow this advice, and most breathing techniques involve complicated exercises with several factors taken into account to acquire proficiency in them. In the yogic system, called *pranayama* or 'breath-way', a number of subsidiary practices accompany the exercises, including the intoning of vibratory phonemes (mantras), ritual positioning of hands (mudras), and control of the anal sphincter. In taoism there is the accumulation, purification and ingestion of saliva, the direction of the interior winds, the rolling of the eyes a fixed number of times from left to right and from right to left.

Each respiration involves (1) inhalation*; (2) breath-retention*; (3) exhalation*; and (4) holding the breath after exhalation. In many cases formulae are worked out giving the timing in seconds of each operation in sequence, with its particular benefits listed. A wonderful restorative formula is 3-5-7-9.

Breathing is believed to have a biodynamic polarity, depending on the nostril through which it is performed, and on the rhythm of inspiration (negative-feminine) and expiration (positive-masculine). The reflexes accompanying breathing are also controlled. In a relaxed state, abdominal or diaphragmatic breathing is natural; when the breath is drawn in, the belly expands, and on exhalation it contracts. This process is reversed in one type of exercise, so that the belly expands with exhalation, and contracts with inhalation.

Various occult schools have classified the different kinds of breathing, based on (1) the alternating rhythm of in and out breaths; (2) the rate or speed, whether slow or rapid, calculated at so many breaths per minute; (3) the depth of breath, whether deep or shallow. Air may be breathed out in a single gasp or blow, which again may be prolonged or sudden; it may be smooth or jerky, or done with a humming, voiced or whistling sound. The manner of respiration also includes variations of purposeful coughing, snoring, yawning, hiccuping, eructation or belching, sneezing, and in some schools is even connected with breaking wind (*see* flatus).

The permutations and combinations of all these factors make the science of breath control one of extreme complexity. Each variation has its own value and gives its characteristic powers. The subject has never been fully set down in writing. Biodynamic breathing involves the lips, nose, throat, stomach, diaphragm, lungs, brain, heart and sex organs, and in fact the whole body, from the toes and heels to the crown of the head.

Changes in the speed and depth of breathing influence the heart rate and blood pressure, alter the oxygen, carbon dioxide, acid, alkali, lactate and calcium content of the blood, and affect the efficiency of the brain. Anoxia (deficiency of oxygen in the tissues) and anoxaemia (deficiency of oxygen in the blood) are forms of oxygen starvation producing asphyxic symptoms, buzzing in the head, muscular inco-ordination, deterioration of vision, vertigo, blackouts, sweating, unstable emotions, loss of judgment, hallucinations and other xenophrenic states.

Rapid breathing or prolonged deep breathing (overbreathing, hyperventilation, hyperpnea or polypnea) result in blowing off too much carbon dioxide (CO_2). Such loss of carbon dioxide produces tetany, muscle rigidity, stupor, cataleptic coma. It is a method frequently used by witch-doctors to go into a trance. Furthermore fast breathing can produce a degree of anaesthesia and thus reduce susceptibility to pain (*see* eupnea). By contrast, *slow* breathing, as in meditation, increases the CO_2 content of the lungs and blood, and cuts down the amount of oxygen reaching the brain. Anoxaemia increases as trance deepens, causing the brain to accelerate to get more oxygen. This is said to produce the faster alpha rhythms that are associated with meditation. Prolonged *suspension* of breath leads to a high concentration of carbon dioxide in the blood and to CO_2 intoxication, causing a 'carbon-dioxide induced trance'. It promotes the emergence of visionary and mystical experiences, and hallucinations.

Indeed, breathing has some extraordinary qualities. Everyone can breathe hot and cold in a single exhalation. Breathing can both cool and heat the body. Breath inhaled through the mouth is cold, through the nose, warm. Breath may be sipped by rounding the mouth, and moving the tongue in and out and sipping the air, the icy draught that is felt along the tongue is believed to cool the system. Sipping is only one of several cooling methods. Controlled breathing also warms the body both internally and externally, when a peculiar kind of perspiration appears on the surface of the skin. The Chinese speak of a class of magicians who use breath control to regulate their body temperature, producing winter or summer conditions within their bodies at will. The Tibetan practice of tummo teaches an ancient breathing method to heat the body in midwinter. Medical annals also record a few rare instances of people whose breath is so hot that it can apparently ignite things (*see* insufflation).

Breath control is said further to counteract the pull of gravitation and has been invoked to explain levitation phenomena. The effect of certain kinds of rhythmical breathing is an apparent loss of weight and an involuntary movement of the body. Extreme lightness at will is among the siddhis (supranormal powers) claimed by yogis. Albert von Schrenck-Notzing (d. 1929), German physician and pioneer psychical researcher, reported the case of a young man who levitated himself twenty-seven times after following a certain respiratory system. Breath control also underlies the secret of the lungom adepts, the Tibetan marathon-walkers who seem to tread on air as they cross the countryside.

One of the recognized methods of increasing occult power is systematic breathing. This may be practised singly or in unison with others. Many mystics and psychics feel that their powers are intimately associated with breathing. Trance and other xenophrenic states are induced by respiratory techniques. Breath is used for healing by insufflation, as well as for sending forth curses. Tibetan mystics believe that one can change the level of one's consciousness by changing the rate and method of breathing. Following a similar idea the English-born American mystic, Thomas Lake Harris (d. 1906), evolved his own system of 'archnatural respiration', and his disciple, the Scotsman Laurence Oliphant (d. 1888), taught a method of conspiration*, which he called sympneumata. Both these are essentially forms of breath-magic.

Experts point out that tampering with one's respiratory system by trying out breathing techniques can be a dangerous thing. The famous scientist and founder of eugenics, Sir Francis Galton (d. 1911), while experimenting with the mental control of respiration, suddenly found that the automatic function had fallen into abeyance, and had to spend three anxious days breathing in and out by conscious effort and will power until the automatic rhythm was restored.

Besides such physical hazards, the indiscriminate practice of breathing exercises can open up the interior senses to sights and sounds that are normally closed to them. The practitioner will then start seeing strange movements from the corner of his eye, experience unknown presences, hear strange whispers or whistling sounds that soon become formulated into comprehensible articulations of words and sentences that cannot be controlled or stopped.

The famous occultist, Alice Bailey, writes that she received many hundreds of letters from desperate people asking for help in serious trouble brought on by imprudently following the advice of teachers. She adds that nothing can be done for some of these persons, and they end up in sanatoria for the unbalanced or asylums for the insane.

George Gurdjieff (d. 1949) warned his pupils of the risks involved in breathing techniques taught in certain schools and felt that great harm could come from them. Because of this, Gurdjieff's followers have also advised against their practice.

Books

Bailey, Alice, *From Intellect to Intuition*, Lucis Press, New York, 1965.

Ewing, A. H., 'The Hindu Conceptions of the Functions of Breath', *Journal of the American Oriental Society*, 1901, 22.
Haldane, J. S., *Respiration*, Oxford University Press, London, 1935.
Kürkheim, Karlfried, *Hara: The Vital Centre of Man*, Allen & Unwin, London, 1962.
Marcet, W., *A Contribution to the History of the Respiration of Man*, Churchill, London, 1897.
Regardie, Israel, *Art of True Healing*, Helios Books, Toddington, 1964.
Sherrington, Charles, *Man on His Nature*, Cambridge University Press, 2nd edn, 1951.
Sivananda, Swami, *The Science of Pranayama*, Rishikesh, 1960.

ROS

(Latin, 'dew'), a subtle fluid that seeps downward from one of the ventricles* of the brain, into the body. It is spoken of variously as divine elixir, nectar of life, liquid flame, brain dew, dew of the sages, crystalline dew, exalted tincture, heavenly luminous water, *liquor vitae* or 'water of life', *liquor amni* or 'amniotic fluid' of the brain-foetus.

There are a number of references in a varied literature to the strange moisture that fills a crevice of the brain, drips slowly downward and gives mystical illumination. In the Bible the lover says to his beloved, 'Open to me my sister, my love, for my head is filled with dew' (S. of S. 5:2), a verse that is often given a symbolical interpretation. Homer refers to the 'immortal fluid' that drips from the back of the head and helps to preserve the body from corruption.

In Hindu esoteric physiology, the *sahasrara*, the lotus of a thousand petals, is the most important plexus in the human body, situated just above the crown of the head. It is the vessel for the etheric ambrosia of immortality, which constantly drips down and materializes in the cranium in liquid form. Some of it flows down through the spinal cord and enters the testicles where it fulfils a generative function, but most of it is dissipated and lost. The objective of certain yogic disciplines is to discover this nectar, absorb it and thus reinvigorate the body, or to unite the etheric-force of the sahasrara, with its polar opposite, the fire-force of the kundalini*, and thus 'live for ever'. In taoist yoga, vitality and spirit produce an ambrosia in the *nao* or brain, known as *kan lu,* which drips via the mouth into the body and nourishes the immortal seed.

A kabbalistic treatise called *The Book of Concealment* describes the head of Macroprosopon, 'great countenance', or God, being filled with crystalline dew. In the cavity of the cranium of Macroprosopon lies hidden 'the aerial wisdom which is nowhere known'. Kabbalists teach secret ways of drawing down the celestial fluid into the Microprosopon, 'lesser countenance', or man, so that it might be used for his benefit. By the downflowing of this dew the dead are said to be raised up in the life to come.

In medieval times ros was sometimes equated with *pituita* (*see* humoralism). Medieval physiologists believed that certain serous fluids were drained from the ventricles and carried by way of the infundibulum, or 'funnel' of the third ventricle, into the pituitary gland, and then through the nares (nasal cavities) and fauces (back of the nose) into the palate and mouth.

In alchemical literature the cranium was made by God to catch the soul, which is sometimes symbolized by the ros or dew. The dew (soul) drips perpetually into the vessel (cranium), a process equated with celestial mercury and the crucible used in making the philosopher's stone. In some cases human ingredients such as blood, urine, faeces, were added in order to effect the alchemical transmutation. Since these 'sulphur elements' were required to be mixed with 'mercury elements' found in semen, semen was equated with celestial mercury in its gross form.

Some rosicrucian societies derive the first part of their name from this same celestial ros, referring to themselves as Fratres Roris Coctis, 'Brethren of the Fiery Dew'. A few claimed to know its mystery, which was to be sought in the connection between the ros (semen) and the cross (phallus). Semen in fact constituted the creative and regenerative energy of the universe.

The Swedish mystic, Emanuel Swedenborg (d. 1772), spoke of the ros as 'the highly refined alcohol of animal nature that is utterly beyond the ken of our senses', and said that it transmitted to the pituitary a genuine and fresh spirit of its own.

Books

Jung, C. G., *Alchemical Studies*, Routledge & Kegan Paul, London, 1968.
Onians, R. B., *The Origins of European Thought*, Cambridge University Press, 1951.
Singer, C., *Vesalius on the Human Brain*, Oxford University Press, London, 1942.
Swedenborg, Emanuel, *The Brain Considered Anatomically, Physiologically and Philosophically* (ed. R. L. Tafle), Speirs, London, 1887.
Zuckermann, Solly, *Beyond the Ivory Tower*, Weidenfeld & Nicolson, London, 1970.

SALIVA

In occult terms, saliva is the quintessence of the bodily fluids mixed with the psychic emanations from the heart and head, and one of the most potent effluvia in the world. Depending on circumstances it has the properties of the water of life, a deadly poison, and an antidote to poisons and other evils.

Spitting is universally believed to be a prophylactic against witchcraft, fascination, the evil eye and spells. Many country people spit over the shoulder when they see a lame or cross-eyed man or woman, or anyone who has the reputation of being a witch, in order to avert the bad luck associated with them. It is considered advisable to spit on a new or beautiful possession to deflect the look of any envious person who might covet it; and to spit three times to the side if one praises one's own possessions, in order to mitigate the spiritual retribution that follows hubris.

Such token spitting also brings good luck. Shopkeepers often spit on the first money, which is called *handsel,* taken at the start of the day's business, to keep the money flowing in. Anglers in many parts of Europe still spit on their hooks before casting their lines. Spitting on a new-born child brings it good fortune. In England and Scotland the parson at the christening used to (and in some places still does) moisten with his saliva the nostrils and ears of the child. Formal kissing of one's own hand in certain forms of eastern greeting, and blowing kisses in western countries, are variations of salivating for good luck.

Pliny (d. AD 79) averred that in pugilistic encounters it aggravated the force of the punch if one spat on one's hands first. The same superstition is prevalent today: when men start a fight they instinctively spit on their hands. So also when starting a difficult task of any nature, first spit on the hands and rub them together or blow on them.

Spittle has great power, both in preventing and healing various diseases. One's own saliva is universally recognized as possessing curative properties for one's own wounds. On the analogy that animals heal their wounds by licking them, one can heal one's own and someone else's hurt by the same means. Thus, licking a wart, birthmark or mole, or moistening it with saliva is said to remove it in time. A mother kisses the place where the child is hurt.

Saliva was thought to be especially good for eye diseases. Pliny reports that when applied each morning as an eye salve it cures ophthalmia. The Bible records Christ curing blindness by anointing the eyes with clay and spittle (John 9:6).

But saliva could also act as a poison. Its virtue and virulence were well known to the ancient Egyptians, and the Sumerians. In the Sumerian language the word for spittle is *kassapu,* which also means sorcerer and poison. This ancient association might have some basis in fact. Present-day experiments show that enzymes present in the saliva liberate polypeptides from the blood protein. Says Dr Harold Burn, 'It is evident that human saliva has some of the qualities of snake venom, which contains similar enzymes.'

In Australia the aboriginal magician moistens his finger-tip with saliva, then advances towards his victim, pointing the loaded finger at him uttering curses, with terrible effect. Even in more advanced societies it is believed that a curse is rendered more potent if one wets one's forefinger and points it at the victim. Also, that a poppet stroked with a saliva-moistened finger will increase the pain of the victim.

A close connection subsists between the emotions and one's state of health, and the condition of one's saliva. The jealous woman, the hungry beggar, the swain making love, the soldier petrified with fear and panic, the mother tenderly nursing her infant all exude different varieties of saliva. What is called 'fasting spittle', or the spittle of a fasting man, was supposed to be extremely poisonous, but it also had certain healing virtues. Spittle charged with anger is very injurious to others, and one is advised to keep out of the range of an angry man or woman so that droplets of their saliva as they rave and shout do not bespatter one.

Saliva plays an important part in oriental sex magic, but it has to be thoroughly purified before use. Taoist rejuvenatory magic devotes a great deal of time to purifying the saliva first. This is done by adopting a strict diet, especially avoiding the five harsh grains (rice, millet, wheat, barley and beans – though lists vary), by special breathing exercises, and drinking 'mountain dew'. The eating of sialagogic (saliva inducing) substances such as lemons is prohibited. During the 'little tour' in taoist respiration the tongue is pressed up and back along the roof of the mouth, a small quantity of breath is passed to the back of the throat, and the breath-impregnated saliva is swallowed. According to taoist masters, breath and saliva are so full of nourishment that the adept requires nothing else to sustain him.

Books

Burn, Harold, *Drugs, Medicines and Man*, Allen & Unwin, London, 1962.

Cannon, Walter B., *The Wisdom of the Body*, Kegan Paul, Trench, Trubner, rev. edn, London, 1939.

Crombie, J. E., 'The Saliva Superstition', *The International Folk-Lore Congress*, London, 1891.

Mensignac, C. de, *Recherches ethnographiques sur la salive et le crachat*, Bordeaux, 1892.

Nicolson, Frank W., 'The Saliva Superstition in Classical Literature', *Harvard Studies in Classical Philology*, 1897, 8, 23–40.

SCATOLOGY

(Gk. *skatos*, 'filth', 'dung') is the study relating to the substances discharged from the body. Although applied specifically to faeces and urine, it also covers all solids, liquids, and gases emanating from the body that are generally regarded as unclean or unpleasant. They include *egesta*, like dung, urine, mucus, tears and matter from the eyes, pus and snot, or discharge from the nose, cerumen or wax from the ears, saliva from the mouth, phlegm from the throat, vomit, sweat, menstrual blood; the caul, secundine, lochia and afterbirth; *exuviae*, such as skin-scales, including dandruff and scurf, and scourings from the body; hair, nails, and tartar from the teeth; calculi and other stones found in the body; tumours and other excrescences; *effluvia* or body gases, such as belches from the stomach, flatus from the bowels, bad breath and body odour; also worms, lice and any parasites found in or on the body. In some contexts it also covers blood, milk, flesh, bones, teeth, skin, fat, heart, gall-bladder and other parts or fragments of the body.

The Egyptians, Greeks, Romans and other ancient peoples had deities of the natural functions and the egesta, and all things associated with them. The Canaanite god, Beelzebub, was a Lord of Dung, and another god, Belphegor, used to be offered the excretions of the rectum and bladder as an act of homage. The Aztecs had a dung-goddess named Tlazolteotl, who also presided over carnal love and childbirth. The Roman deity, Stercutius, lord of stercus or dung, was associated with agriculture and later identified with Saturn. The Hindu goddess of cowdung was Karishni, a form of the mother goddess, Lakshmi, who presided over wealth. In some parts of southern India at religious ceremonies, the worshippers, both male and female, would make water and evacuate on the idol dedicated to ordure.

The material world and the human condition have often been compared with excrement. Man himself emerges from a near-dung environment. 'We are born', said St Augustine (d. 430), 'between urine and faeces.' Till the beginning of the sixteenth century the pope at his consecration had to sit in public on what was known as the *sedes stercoraria,* 'dung chair', and use it for the purpose intended, while the papal choir sang Psalm 113 (or 112 in the Vulgate), the seventh verse of which reads, 'He raiseth up the poor from his vileness, and lifteth the needy out of the dunghill', in order to remind him that he was after all a mortal man. The custom was abolished by Pope Leo X (d. 1521).

Dung and urine have played a significant part in religion, magic and the occult. There is believed to be a great mystery, only partly known, about the properties of human and animal excreta, and early writers were loud in acclaiming their virtues. Different species pass different kinds of stool, and by examining a sample of coprolite, the remains of fossil dung, an expert can tell the species of animal that passed it. The tiger is not by nature like the cow: their shape, skin, limbs, disposition and character differ, and so too must they differ in their inward make-up and in the internal secretions they manufacture. Their excreta are conditioned by their respective temperaments and therefore hide in their congelations much of the secret chemistry of their different natures.

Today it is known that the bacteria living in all animal bodies release their excretory products into the faeces and urine which are therefore rich in antibiotic substances, and that every animal produces different antibiotic substances (Thorwald, 1962, p. 86). Human excrement and urine, subject to the magical alchemy of the individual character, and passing through the stations of the inner organs, diluted by the digestive juices, heated by the furnace of the vital parts and tempered by the internal winds, is believed to be a product of very mystical significance.

Scatological substances have been employed in all communities for a wide variety of purposes. They are of course valuable fertilizers for the soil. They are used in medicine and magic, when they may be consumed as they are; made into or mixed with broths, wines and other liquids; dried and sprinkled into food or used as a snuff; mixed with herbs and oils; made into pills and swallowed; applied to the afflicted parts like a plaster, ointment or balm. They are also used in amulets and talismans, charms and counter-charms; for making aphrodisiacs, love potions and fertility drinks; in necrophilic rites and black magical operations. Weapons anointed with scatological substances make the warrior invincible. Dung and urine are prominent in puberty and death-and-birth rites and mourning ceremonies.

The use of urine in sacramental functions from ancient times suggests that it was regarded as a blood-substitute. G. R. Scott believes that there are strong reasons for thinking that 'the original holy water consisted of human urine'. Urine was drunk and continues to be drunk both in primitive and civilized societies. Women in childbirth drank the urine of their husbands to hasten delivery. They were given a draught of their own urine for hysteria. Even today in parts of rural England urine is drunk to prevent boils and carbuncles, a cupful being taken each morning (Rawcliffe, 1959, p. 213). Urine was prescribed for malaria till the end of the last century in Europe. A drink of one's own urine was said to be a specific cure for snake bite and gravel.

In point of fact urine is known to have many wonderful properties. It is restorative, purgative, stimulating, tonic, intoxicant and purifying. The presence of ammonia in it neutralizes acids and may be good for acid-forming diseases. At the time of its liberation it is virtually free from bacteria and has been used as a disinfectant for wounds in the battlefield. Lye-tea made of human urine and lime-water was once a popular remedy for colds in Europe.

Many valuable chemicals utilized by the body pass through the urinary system with their potency only slightly diminished. The shamans of certain Siberian tribes, during their sacred rites in which a trance-like state was induced by eating mushrooms, drank one another's urine because it still contained the trance-inducing drug. Similarly, when penicillin was first clinically tried out in 1941 on certain patients, the substance was afterwards extracted from their urine and used again owing to the short supply of the wonder drug at the time.

Drinking urine was long believed to increase the virility of the male, a belief that may have been substantiated by Dr Butenandt's discovery in 1931 that male urine contains the active male hormone, androsterone.

Books

Bloch, Iwan, *Odoratus Sexualis,* Panurge Press, New York, 1934.
Bourke, J. G., *Scatologic Rites of All Nations,* Lowdermilk, Washington, D.C., 1891.
Dare, Paul, *Indian Underworld,* Rider, London, 1938.
McLaughlin, Terence, *Coprophilia or A Peck of Dirt,* Cassell, London, 1971.
Rawcliffe, D. H., *Illusions and Delusions of the Supernatural and the Occult,* Dover, New York, 1959.
Rosebury, Theodor, *Life on Man,* Paladin, London, 1972.
Scott, G. R., *The History of Corporal Punishment,* Laurie, London, 1939.
Smith, Anthony, *The Body,* Allen & Unwin, London, 1968.
Thorwald, Jürgen, *Science and Secrets of Early Medicine,* Thames & Hudson, London, 1962.

SELF

The metaphysical agent underlying an individual's subjective experiences as an evolving entity. For centuries philosophers have tried to account for the cohering, integrating and organizing factor behind the individual, without having to postulate a Self, but this has proved difficult, and indeed impossible. Gilbert Ryle (b. 1900) said that 'gratuitous mystification begins from the moment we start to peer around for beings named by our pronouns'; but say the philosophers, that is what the self is. It is the I, the Me, the You.

The self uses brain and body as a mechanism. It is the controlling factor, the central directorate, the continuing element. The self generates thought, and is the thinker behind the thinking process. It is the *moi central* (Fr. 'central me'), the innermost core of the individual. It is the entity of the asomatic* elements, and perhaps the seat or envelope of the soul. St Augustine (d. 430) said: 'I cannot totally grasp all that I am. But where is that part of the mind which I do not know? Is it outside me? As this question strikes me I am overcome with wonder and almost stupor.'

In more practical terms the self has been described as a psychic totality, including the conscious and unconscious, the permanent identifying element underlying a hierarchy of three grades as follows, whose boundaries fluctuate constantly.

(1) The *subego,* the primitive, instinctive, animal, natural, sense-aware underself; the *id* of Friedrich Nietzsche (d. 1900), which Sigmund Freud took over; the Mr Hyde in the Jekyll-Hyde twosome, and the shadow side of the self. We are animals in this, our lower nature. It is the obscure and chaotic part of the personality; the autonomic, hypoconscious, subpersonal, brain-stem self. In occultism it is part of the etheric body.

(2) The *ego* is what Freud called 'the organized part of the id'. It is the emotional, 'socialized', thinking and feeling personality*; the cerebral self, guided largely by the conscious* mind. As the subego is related to the hypoconscious, the ego is related to the conscious, empirical or awake self. In occultism it is part of the astral body.

(3) The *superego* is opposed to the animal or natural impulses, and as such it is the censor, the voice of conscience, the keeper of the religious and moral code. In this sense, as the ego is the organized part of the subego, so, according to Freud, the superego is the organized part of the ego. Its particular function has usually been regarded as one of progressive development. The French writer, Leon Daudet (d. 1942), son of the novelist Alphonse Daudet, speaks of two entities, the ego (*moi*), and the self (*soi*), and says that the life drama is the struggle between the two. The highest human endeavour would imply the evolution of the self from ego to Absolute.

The self is not a structural concept but a dynamic one; a process as well as a pattern. In the occult sense the concept of the higher self is one that goes beyond the Freudian superego. The higher self is not a 'socialized' self, but the creative, choosing and aspiring psyche, endowed with supraconsciousness, and in this sense is known as the true, transcendental or noumenal self, the self of faith and the higher reason. It is asomatic, acerebral, arational, acausal and symbolic. It can exist outside the body, and in fact survives the physical, etheric and astral bodies, to continue its existence in another sphere, and has been identified with the soul*.

Eminent thinkers from earliest times have said that a knowledge of this essential self and its development should be our chief concern. 'Know thyself', said Solon of Athens (d. 558 BC). But knowing yourself leads to the next and most difficult step: being yourself. The Hasidic rabbi, Zusya (d. 1800), said before his death, 'In the coming world, they will not ask me why I was not Moses, or Abraham. But they will ask me why I was not Zusya.' The final lesson of the sages is therefore (1) knowing the essential self, and

(2) becoming that self, a truth that the poet Pindar (d. 443 BC) summarized in the precept: 'Become what thou art.'

Books

Alexander, F. M., *The Use of the Self*, Methuen, London, 1932.
Allport, G., *Personality: A Psychological Interpretation*, Holt, New York, 1937.
Cummins, Geraldine, *Beyond Human Personality*, Nicholson & Watson, London, 1935.
Fairburn, W. R. D., *Psychoanalytic Studies of the Personality*, Tavistock Publications, London, 1952.
Freud, Sigmund, *The Ego and the Id*, Hogarth Press, London, 1961.
Guntrip, H., *Personality Structure and Human Interaction*, Hogarth Press, London, 1961.
Jung, C. G., *The Undiscovered Self*, Little, Brown, Boston, 1958.
Laing, R. D., *The Self and Others*, Tavistock Publications, London, 1961.
Newland, C., *Myself and I*, New English Library, London, 1965.
Ryle, Gilbert, *The Concept of Mind*, Hutchinson, London, 1949.
Shoemaker, S., *Self-Knowledge and Self-Identity*, Cornell University Press, Ithaca, New York, 1969.
Storr, A., *The Integrity of Personality*, Heinemann, London, 1960.
Symonds, P. M., *The Ego and the Self*, Appleton-Century-Crofts, New York, 1951.
Sypher, Wylie, *Loss of the Self in Modern Literature and Art*, Random House, New York, 1964.
Tyrrell, G. N. M., *The Personality of Man*, Penguin Books, Harmondsworth, 1947.

SEMEN

(Lat. 'seed'), the thick, whitish fluid, containing sperm cells, which is ejaculated by the male during orgasm. Unlike the female ovaries which have all their eggs at birth, the male testes do not manufacture sperm until puberty, when they start producing millions. At each ejaculation approximately 200 to 400 million spermatozoa are ejected, of which one sperm may successfully reach the female ovum. Spermatozoa have a short life, and if still in the vagina after an hour they cease to move; if they reach the uterus they may survive for twenty-four hours. In symbolism semen is sometimes represented as a serpent, and the ovum as an egg, and the figure of a serpent entwined around an egg represents generation.

How sperm comes into existence was a question that greatly exercised the ancients. The Egyptians believed that semen was generated in the heart, since the god Atum said of the vital effluence, 'I established it in my heart.' In the *Brihadaranyaka Upanishad* the question is asked, 'On what is semen based?' and the answer is given, 'On the heart'. The Ionic philosopher, Anaxagoras (d. 428 BC), held that semen developed from a drop that came from the male brain, and a text attributed to Aristotle (d. 322 BC) mentions that semen is drawn from the spinal marrow. Democritus (d. 361 BC) maintained that semen was produced from all parts of the human body. Some two thousand years later the English mystic, Robert Fludd (d. 1637), wrote that this precious fluid was created from all the different components of the microprosopon, an idea further developed by the rosicrucians (*see* ros).

According to the Talmud, the food eaten by men is converted into semen, taking about seven weeks to complete the process. With women the food is turned into an igneous fluid that comes with the menstrual flow, and which is itself converted in a pregnant woman into certain substances for nourishing the child.

According to the Tibetans, sperm is formed in seven days from the food eaten. The first day is taken up with digestion. On the second day the retained part of the food becomes blood, then on successive days it becomes flesh, fat, bone, marrow, and finally sperm. One drop of semen has the value of forty-nine drops of blood. This sperm is diffused throughout the body and undergoes further stages of refinement. The most subtle part, called *mdang,* is lodged in the heart, and the reproductive part goes to the testicles. During intercourse the gross sperm heated by the mdang is emitted to produce the child. Tibetan adepts have evolved special techniques by which the gross sperm-energy can be used to generate internal bodily heat and other physical powers. But it is only the mdang that can give immortality.

In the Hindu view too semen is the occult end-product of digestion, and food successively becomes chyle, blood, flesh, marrow and semen, but the process is longer, taking one full lunar month. After a period of 330 days semen becomes *ojas,* a fluidic energy that spreads throughout the body, and is described as white and oily. In other esoteric traditions the male seed is sometimes conceived of as oily. The *Zohar* says that in the testes are gathered all the oil, the dignity and strength of the male from the whole body. The idea of the seed as oil may explain the practice in some places of anointing kings with a substance containing sperm, as a begetting and bestowal of new divine life.

In esoteric theory semen consists of (1) the *liquor vitae,* 'fluid of life', containing the physical seed which it nourishes within the body of the male, and (2) the *aura seminalis,* or super-physical essence, which has a 'fiery' nature. Pythagoras (d. 500 BC) held that semen was an immaterial thing, like a thought, or a flame, which 'ignited' the female seed, and the idea of the fire-quality of the semen was upheld by many other early thinkers. Semen was widely believed to be the materialization of a kind of fire, and was sometimes described as a vital fire-fluid. At the coronation of the pharaohs of ancient Egypt, a mystical fluid called *sa,* the invisible semen of the god Ra, magically infiltrated into the veins of the pharaoh during the ceremony, filling him with a flame-like quality that gave him majesty, dignity and divine power. Robert Fludd wrote that semen had a twofold character, an external, visible substance, and an invisible flame-like principle descending from above. Since semen was produced as the result of 'burning' passion and 'raging' lust, the word for burning was sometimes used for the seed and seminal fluid, like the English *spunk,* which signifies spark or flame. As already stated, the fire-force is used by Tibetan magicians as a means of generating heat in the body, in the rite of tummo.

The potency of semen, or its fire-force, is infinitely subtle, and is distributed all over the male body. During sexual excitement it is drawn down into the condensing and expulsive apparatus of the body, from where it is forcibly ejected along with the visible semen. According to the Talmud the seed is sacred because it receives its life from a divine flame. It must be deposited within the receptacle of the duly consecrated wife whose body is sanctified for the purpose; she absorbs what she needs, the rest is rendered harmless. Sperm is perfected in the wife, but is defiled in all unlawful activity involving adultery, incest, concubinage, intercourse with virgins; and the progeny of such intercourse carry an inheritance of sin.

Early and medieval church authorities, notably St Augustine (d. 430) and Thomas Aquinas (d. 1274), believed that the devil and his minions were able to collect human seed from the man and transmit it to human females. The semen was collected either by female elementals called succubi, who received the male sperm during intercourse, or was taken after the male had emitted his seed in 'infertile' acts such as sodomy, self-abuse and bestiality. Night emissions, arising from a natural superfluity of humours, do not have the same degree of generative virtue, so the devil does not make much use of them. Semen thus collected by demon hosts is used by the devil to impregnate a woman through the intermediary of an incubus or male elemental. The view of the Franciscan friar, Ludovico Maria Sinistrari (d. 1701), about the corrupting effect of this intermediation is thought to have relevance to contemporary discussions on artificial insemination whether by the sperm of the husband or an outside donor.

Semen was believed to have very strong magnetic properties, and by adding it to a philtre a lover could inflame his mistress. Consequently it was prized as an aphrodisiac. Even when deposited in the vagina during normal intercourse it could still act to increase the desire of the female. The *Brihadaranyaka Upanishad* describes a rite for arousing the woman's love so that she might feel a greater passion for the man. He is enjoined to introduce his member in hers, join mouth to mouth, caress her genitals, and while rubbing the area he should address his semen thus: 'You take your origin in every limb, you are generated in the heart, you are condensed from the internal organs; drive mad this woman and this her vagina, like a doe wounded by a poisoned arrow.'

The ill effects on the female denied the opportunity of receiving semen during sexual intercourse, has seldom been more lugubriously expressed than by the herbalist and astrologer, Ebenezer Sibly (c. 1770):

> Powerful indeed is the effect of the seminal fluid when suddenly mingled, and in great quantity, with the fluids of the female. In the eye of common observation the sallow and inanimate female, by coitus, often becomes plump and robust, beautiful and active, whilst the widow, or married woman, deprived of commerce with her husband, gradually returns to the imperfections and peculiarities of a single life; and the ancient virgin, all her life deprived of this animating effluvium, is generally consumed with infirmity, ill temper or disease. It is well known too, that the want of coition at the time of life when nature seems to require it, lays the foundation of many disorders in females.
>
> In the vernal season, or juvenal spring of life, every tube and vessel appertaining to the genital system, being now filled with a procreative liquor, excites in the female a powerful irritation of the parts, strongly soliciting

> the means of discharging their load by venereal embraces. These from prudential motives being often necessarily denied, the prolific tinctures seize upon the stomach and viscera, obstruct and vitiate the catamenta, choke and clog the vessels, whereby the venal, arterial, and nervous fluids become stagnant, and a leucophlegmatia, or white flabby dropsical tumour, pervades the whole body and quickly devotes the unhappy patient to the arms of death.

The expenditure of semen was sometimes regarded as a good thing, and sometimes as a great evil. Retaining it by refraining from intercourse or other sexual activity was supposed to have a deleterious effect on the organism of the male. Duns Scotus (d. 1308), the great medieval schoolman, held that semen too long hoarded turned to poison, causing giddiness and clouding the sight. The release of semen was a natural process and assisted in the healthy flow of the other bodily fluids. The Catalonian physician, Arnold of Villanova (d. 1312), recommended the daily ejection of semen either manually or in intercourse. Some scholars regarded semen as the end product, even the waste product, of an excess of humours and emphasized the need for getting rid of it at regular intervals.

On the other hand there were many who valued the semen as a magical fluid to be conserved at all costs, and considered that its emission in any manner resulted in a diminution of a person's very mana (*see* encratism).

Books

Cole, F. J., *Early Theories of Sexual Generation*, Clarendon Press, Oxford, 1930.
Ellis, Havelock, *Studies in the Psychology of Sex*, Random House, New York, 1936.
Meyer, A. W., *The Rise of Embryology*, Stanford University Press, 1939.
Rechung, Lama, *Tibetan Medicine*, Wellcome Trust, London, 1973.
Röer, E., *The Brihadaranyaka Upanishad*, Theosophical Publishing House, Adyar, Madras, 1931.
Sinistrari, L. M., *Demonality, or Incubi and Succubi* (ed. by Montague Summers), Fortune Press, London, 1927.
Smith, Anthony, *The Body*, Allen & Unwin, London, 1968.
Wall, O. A., *Sex and Sex Worship*, Kimpton, London, 1919.

SENESCENCE

Senescence or the condition of old age is a time of strange occult changes. In the strictest sense the process of getting old begins at birth, and is faster in young people than in old. At the age of seven the blood vessels already begin to show signs of hardening. The human body reaches a state of its fullest vigour at the age of twelve. It has still to grow in physical size and intelligence, but at this age it is less likely to die than at any other. Younger, it is more vulnerable; older, it is already on the decline in terms of resistance and vitality.

The biological study of ageing is known as *gerontology* (Greek, *geron*, 'old man'), and the care of the elderly as geriatrics. It is an interesting fact that no one as yet knows the reason for senescence. Men have tried in the past to make deductions from the observation of animals, but of this study of beasts, Francis Bacon (d. 1626) said in his *Historia Vitae et Mortis* ('History of Life and Death'), 'Knowledge is slender, observation negligent, tradition fabulous.' The carp and pike, formerly believed to live for one or two centuries, do not in fact live longer than 30 or 40 years. Large tortoises do live over 100 years, but man himself is not far behind; he is still one of the longest lived of all creatures.

Very little is known about the ageing process, and medical science has so far found nothing to prolong life beyond the Biblical span of three score years and ten; it has only enabled more people to reach this span. Furthermore, it is not merely a long life that is sought, but also the health and vitality to appreciate it. When the Greek Tithonus, beloved of the goddess Aurora, asked her for immortality, he forgot to ask for eternal youth as well, and like all mortals he became old and decrepit. The gods in pity changed him into a grasshopper. Gulliver, in Jonathan Swift's tale (1726), came across the people called Struldbrugs, who could not die, but just went on getting older and weaker and crazier and were a nuisance to everyone.

Again, no one knows the cause of progeria, a rare disease in which a child becomes prematurely old, and displays wrinkling of the skin, hardening of the arteries and other symptoms, to become a wizened and aged dwarf.

There is an eternal and elemental conflict between youth and age. Youth is the abundant springtime of life, when we are the favourites of Nature the Prodigal; in old age we are the pensioners of Nature the Miser. Youth can perform, but does not know. Age knows, but is unable to perform. Youth feels that age represents the dead past, the done-with, and like other obsolete things the old too should be out of the way, and not obstructing the view with their presence.

Physically and mentally the old are a nuisance, a menace, an encumbrance. In many primitive societies the old were abandoned or killed when they ceased to be useful members of the tribe. The Scythians regarded death passively awaited because of old age, as dishonourable, and those who were too old for the nomadic life committed suicide by burning themselves alive. Fire, they believed, would be contaminated if it did not receive the human sacrifice still breathing.

The primitive tribes of ancient Germany also slew their aged kinsfolk. German legend preserves the memory of such ritual killings in the Rhineland districts. The Byzantine historian, Procopius (d. AD 565), relates that the Heruli, a Germanic tribe, used to stab to death those who were too old or sick to be useful. Albertus Magnus (d. AD 1280) records that the custom of killing off the aged was prevalent within the borders of Saxony and Poland even in his day.

Among the Buriats of Siberia men and women of advanced age used to be dispatched with all due ceremony. They were dressed in their finest raiment, taken to a special seat of honour where they participated in a wild drinking party, and were then quietly strangled. The Yakuts thought it disgraceful if their aged parents died a natural death, for it was believed that an evil spirit would eat the soul of the deceased. Besides, if they became too decrepit they would be unfit for life in the next world. Till the beginning of the present century elderly or infirm parents were buried alive or left to die of hunger, after preliminary rites and festivities.

Most preliterate communities, if they did not go so far, treated their old folk with scant regard. The old were a burden both to the householder and to the community and were woefully neglected.

A strange nemesis seems to overtake the old. The old man, who in his youth represented force and virility, now becomes a symbol of decay and weakness. The old woman, who in her youth was a vision of beauty and allure, is now a wizened old hag. The once beautiful mouth is now filled with decaying teeth or is toothless, the head is balding or hairless, the skin hangs in ugly folds. 'Fear old age', said Plato, 'for it does not come alone.' Greek, Roman and medieval writers sometimes spoke in very unsympathetic tones about men in their dotage. They were both foul without and evil within. Blind, deaf, doddering, slobbering, incontinent, with frame shrunk, the body ravaged, sexual desire extinct or contrary to nature, the vitality ebbing, they are hateful to children, contemptible to women and without friends or companions. The bitter twilight of life is filled with envy and empty frustration. Dull of wit, feeble of memory, deprived of reason, morose, troubled, fretful, hard to please, miserly, egotistic, intolerant, they represent the human animal at its lowest.

But there is another side to this picture. In as many communities the old were and still are respected and even revered. The fifth commandment specifically enjoins a man to honour his father and mother, and the Jews, for instance, generally adhere strictly to this injunction.

From the occult viewpoint a particular virtue resides in the aged. The old are endowed with a powerful mana. Psychic energy is said to increase with advancing age, and an old person's curse or blessing is more effective than a young person's. They are a tangible connection with the ancestral world and constitute a link with the authentic past. Their thoughts and dreams are fed from the profound well-springs of the unconscious, the archetypal mind that is the repository of the collective, tribal or ancestral consciousness, and the ancient wisdom of humanity.

It seems that the barrier between the material and spiritual worlds becomes attenuated in the old, and much that is of great importance comes to their understanding. The physical stage past, the intellectual stage transcended, they are in a position to receive intuitively the wisdom from the supernal realms. In all communities they constitute the patriarchs, lawgivers, high priests, legislators, senators, statesmen.

Among the early Chinese the man of forty was entitled to grow a moustache as a symbol of his maturity. And only a man of sixty could grow a full beard. No one was allowed to be taught and to practise taoist 'seminal' disciplines, that is, breath-semen techniques, until he was at least forty years old. Likewise, certain kabbalistic teachings associated with the merkabah or chariot mysticism of the book of Ezekiel could not be communicated to a person until he had reached the age of forty.

The deeper secrets were not confided to him until ten more years had passed.

In Hinduism it is said that the life-flame of the aged, uncontaminated by the frets of living, burns with a bluish flame, and close contact with the old revivifies the young. The old cannot vampirize, but in fact give off a subtle emanation that strengthens the deeps of the soul. This idea is put forward to explain gerontophilia, or 'aged-loving', the desire, including sexual desire, that a younger person has for an older, and the vitalizing power that supposedly rejuvenates young people through contact with the old. Young women are rendered more beautiful, and young men more attractive after periodical association, including sexual intercourse, with older persons.

Since old people are past the period of their own sex, they become in this post-reproductive stage, a third asexual gender, but at the same time they share the magical characteristics of the androgyne, being as it were both sexes in one.

Like the dying, the aged are in close proximity with the other dimension and with the mysteries of death.

Books

Carlisle, Anthony, *An Essay on the Disorders of Old Age and on the Means of Prolonging Human Life,* London, 1818.

Comfort, Alex, *Ageing: The Biology of Senescence,* Routledge & Kegan Paul, London, 1956.

Comfort, Alex, *The Process of Ageing,* Weidenfeld & Nicolson, London, 1965.

Cowdry, E. V. (ed.), *Problems of Ageing,* William & Wilkins, Baltimore, 1942.

De Ropp, R., *Man Against Ageing,* Gollancz, London, 1960.

Hall, G. S., *Senescence,* Appleton, London, 1922.

Hoch, P. H. and Zubin, J. (eds), *Psychology of Aging,* Grune & Stratton, New York, 1961.

Kaplan, O. J. (ed.), *Mental Disease in Later Life,* Stanford University Press, 1956.

Koty, John, *Die Behandlung der Alten und Kranken bei den Naturvölkern,* Stuttgart, 1934.

Richardson, Bessie, *Old Age Among the Greeks,* Johns Hopkins Press, Baltimore, 1933.

Simmons, Leo, *The Role of the Aged in Primitive Society,* Yale University Press, New Haven, 1945.

Strehler, B. L., *Time, Cells and Ageing,* Academic Press, New York, 1962.

Vischer, A. L., *Old Age, Its Compensations and Rewards,* Allen & Unwin, London, 1949.

Walker, Kenneth, *Commentary on Age,* Jonathan Cape, London, 1952.

SENSES

The means by which the stimulus of physical events is experienced, the experience itself being the *sensation.* For instance, light waves strike the retina of the eye, cause an electrical disturbance, which is communicated to the brain by special sensory nerves, and by some mysterious process this is converted into the meaningful patterns that we experience as 'seeing'.

The senses convey sensations of sight, hearing, taste, smell, touch and feeling. In addition, psychologists speak of kinaesthesis (Gk. *kineo,* 'to move'; *aisthanomai,* 'to feel') or muscular sensations of movement and equilibrium;

of coenaesthesis, or sensations of internal activity in general, such as the heartbeat, digestion, etc.; and of other senses that enable us to distinguish pain and pleasure; temperature (heat and cold); pressure (deep, light, tickling).

The English philosopher, Thomas Hobbes (d. 1679), was the founder of modern 'sensationalism', the theory that all knowledge is derived from sensation. But according to some researchers, sense impressions are essential not only for our understanding of the material environment in which we live, but for our very consciousness. A case is on record of a boy with cutaneous anaesthesia, a nervous disease, which had destroyed all tactile sensation, all hearing and the sight of one eye. Apart from the feeble links of taste and smell the boy's sole contact with the outside world was through the remaining eye. He would immediately go to sleep when the other, seeing, eye was closed.

The recognition and identifying of data through the senses constitutes perception*, which is analysed by reason. And it is by means of the senses and reason alone that we build up our conception of the universe. St Thomas Aquinas (d. 1274) declared that 'it is natural to man to reach the intelligibilia through the sensibilia, because all our knowledge has its beginning in the senses.'

But whether the senses are in fact capable of bringing us a perception of things as they really exist has been debated for centuries. Plato (d. 347 BC) in his *Phaedo,* discussing the acquirement of pure knowledge, speculates whether sight and hearing have any truth in them, and whether they enable us to perceive (see and hear) anything accurately. Socrates points out that when the soul tries to consider anything in company with the body, it is deceived by it. Only in thought or by absolute reason, when the soul leaves the body, can it reach towards reality.

Some scientists feel that it is the function of the senses and brain to filter the flood of impressions that surround us, and that they keep out more than they admit to our cognizance. Our sense impressions represent only a narrow band of a vast spectrum. The human eye is sensitive to only a limited range of light waves between red and violet, and the difference between a few thousandths of a millimetre in wavelength makes the difference between visible and invisible. Similarly the human ear can register only a small segment of the field of frequency, and cannot distinguish electromagnetic waves, which must first be converted into sound waves by electronic apparatus.

In theory, the dimension that could be revealed by any single sense is virtually limitless. Even as they exist the senses are extremely refined. Quinine can be tasted by a man in a concentration of one part in two million, and the stink produced by a skunk can be smelt by a man in a concentration of one part in 30,000 million. Marcel Proust (d. 1922) said that the only true voyage consists, not in travelling through a hundred different countries with the same pair of eyes, but seeing the same land through a hundred different pairs of eyes. A vast and varying panorama would be unfolded in observing the same thing from varying viewpoints, under different emotional situations and with different experiences. We could, of course, never bear the full impact of all the impressions that might be presented to our sight with full understanding and with all intensity.

Though the senses are capable of extreme sensitivity, they can also supply the wrong kind of information as a result of defects in the sensory system. A wide terminology has emerged from a study of such anomalies. Thus, a heightening of the sensory faculties is called *hyperaesthesia*; an insensitivity to pain is *anaesthesia*; where the sense feelings are perverted to the extent that sensations are misinterpreted, misplaced or abnormally felt, we have *paraesthesia,* the symptoms of which include tingling, numbness, pins and needles; where the senses are mixed up or transposed we have *synaesthesia*; where there is a multiplication of sensations we have *polyaesthesia*, so that a stimulus applied to one part of the body is felt in other parts of the body as well. Where a sensation is felt elsewhere than at the place stimulated we have *alloaesthesia* (or allachaesthesia). Where the sensation is felt in the symmetrically opposite side of the body we have *allochiry.* These strange quirks of the senses are usually the result of nervous disorders, hysteria and 'possession'. They may also be induced by hypnotic suggestion.

In scholastic terms the senses not only deceive, but constitute a moral snare. The delight of beautiful things, and sensual and sexual gratification, can eventually lead one astray or into a spiritual dead end. St Augustine (d. 430) held that the devil uses the senses to corrupt man. 'He insinuates himself in sensuous forms; he adapts himself to colours; attaches himself to sounds; abides in perfumes and flavours; lurks in conversation; and clogs the channels of understanding.'

Although we have more than five senses, we still traditionally speak of only five: sight, hearing, touch, taste and smell. But besides the senses that give us an awareness of physical things, we are also said to possess a kind of ultra-sense, popularly called the 'sixth sense'. The perception of things outside the range of the normal senses, presumably through the sixth sense, is the province of paraperception*.

Among the ancient Greeks the sensory feelings were thought to be controlled by the *thumos* or 'sensing soul', residing in the *phren* (Gk. 'diaphragm'). The concept of thumos (thymus) is said to be derived from the steam arising from the fresh blood of a sacrifice. In occultism the senses are based in the asomatic* element known as the etheric body, which is coterminous with life. This perishes with the death of the physical body, although its effects remain in the non-permanent (astral) part of the soul.

Books

Adrian, E. D., *The Basis of Sensation,* Christophers, London, 1928.
Barlow, H. B., *Symposium on Sensory Communication,* Wiley, New York, 1961.
Boring, E. G., *Sensation and Perception in the History of Experimental Psychology,* Appleton-Century, New York, 1942.
Buddenbrock, W., *The Senses,* University of Michigan Press, 1958.
Geldard, F. A., *The Human Senses,* Wiley, New York, 1953.
Hamlyn, D. W., *Sensation and Perception,* Routledge & Kegan Paul, London, 1961.
Schilder, Paul, *The Image and Appearance of the Human Body,* Wiley, New York, 1964.
Wolters, A. W. P., *The Evidence of Our Senses,* Methuen, London, 1933.

SENSORY DEPRIVATION

Sensory deprivation or the denial of sensory stimulation to an individual can lead to many strange mental and physical effects. In the 1950s a number of experiments in SD (sensory deprivation) were begun at McGill, Princeton and other universities in which volunteers were isolated in a 'black room', a small completely light-proof, sound-proof and constant-temperature cubicle, where all normal sights and sounds were missing, to test their reactions to silence, solitude and restricted movement. Food and toilet requisites were provided, and there was a panic button in case the subject wished to be released.

It was generally found that most subjects soon went to sleep in the extreme darkness and silence. But when they awoke they had difficulty in keeping their minds occupied. The idea that one can use the opportunity provided to think deeply and solve problems was generally found to be fallacious. The situation was not conducive to solving problems. In some cases the subject was unable to maintain a consistent line of thought, since ideas that came would quickly evaporate. In other cases some quite innocuous idea would arise in the mind and intrude itself so insistently upon the consciousness that the subject, unable to shake it off and finding it unendurable, would press the panic button.

The maximum period of confinement that anyone could stand was four days. Most panicked within forty-eight hours. Contrary to expectation it was found that people of high intelligence were less able to tolerate SD than those of lower intelligence. If at any stage a slight stimulus was introduced into the cell it gave unbelievable pleasure; a subject who would normally demand loud music and dazzling colours, would be ecstatically happy to see a dim ray of light and hear even the faintest trace of sound. Their brains, it seemed, hungered for stimulation.

In the black room, where all external sounds are excluded from reaching him, the subject will still hear noises and feel movements from his own heart, lungs and the rest of his body. He will hear the blood coursing through the blood vessels near the ear, hear his own breathing, and his stomach and intestinal rumblings. He will become conscious of the pressure of his body on the bed if he is lying down, on the floor if he is standing, and of other muscles in any movement he makes. Almost all subjects lose weight, although there is plenty to eat and they do no exercise. After the experiment their reactions are slowed down and their sensitivity to pain increased.

Depending on the degree of SD and on the temperament of the volunteer, the experiments revealed that at some stage the subjects invariably began to suffer from a marked intellectual and emotional deterioration. Time duration was distorted, orientation faulty, rational judgment seriously impaired. Sensitivity and emotional distress became acute, and amenability to suggestion very marked. Auditory and visual hallucinations were common. In a different context it would seem that this is analogous to the situation where a radar operator begins to see pips that are not there, a long-distance truck driver stops for hitch-hikers who do not exist, a mountaineer hears voices of phantom companions. Prisoners are ready for brain-washing in similar circumstances.

In still more restrictive stages of SD the mental deterioration produces symptoms comparable to those of advanced drug addiction or madness. The subject hears distant music, threatening and menacing voices, sees flashes of light, coloured lines, geometrical patterns. Familiar objects undergo strange distortions and he sees things that are not there in reality. Figures and apparitions appear and act out strange performances. In some cases the phenomena take on a mystical aspect. He may have a sense of bilocation, of being in two places at the same time. He may have a feeling that he has two heads, or that he is depersonalized. His inner perceptions seem to be sharpened and clairvoyance and clairaudience come into play. Some subjects even have experiences of partial or total astral projection, often rising above the place of confinement, and seeing themselves as they lie or sit below. Sometimes they drift outside and away.

These experiments, taken together with the experiences of people like arctic explorers, Himalayan climbers, balloonists, solo flyers, who have found themselves in situations of stimulus-starvation, have led psychologists to the following conclusions. Sensory deprivation reduces intellectual capacity. A certain level of stimulation is essential for the normal functioning of the brain; it keeps the brain active, fresh and alert. A change of stimulation also contributes to a person's well-being, for his proper perception of and his efficient response to the outside world. A man cannot endure monotonous and tedious activity for long, no matter how good it is. He becomes bored, loses interest in what he is doing and looks for change. If a man were totally deprived of all sensory stimulation (a difficult if not impossible task) his brain would cease to function, or would compensate by creating hallucinations.

Since these first experiments were conducted, an even nearer approach to total SD has been achieved in laboratory tests. Today subjects are temporarily blinded and deafened; their limbs immobilized; their bodies encased in yielding material and then immersed in lukewarm water to achieve neutral buoyancy. As near as possible they are deprived of any sense impressions that might reach them directly through the senses. Under these circumstances confusion in most cases is almost immediate. The sense of disorientation, depersonalization, loss of identity and mental blankness, creates panic within a few minutes. In a short time the subject loses control over his own mind and his thinking faculties. He has no point of reference within himself, still less with the outside world. He becomes only a speck of consciousness isolated from everything else in the world.

Other experimenters, however, notably Dr John Lilly, have not found these effects in their own case. Dr Lilly concludes that external sensory stimulation is not necessary for keeping awake. He reported a sense of heightened awareness and increased sensory experience. At the same time he had the feeling that other people, whom he could hear, see and feel, had joined him in his dark isolation. There were also periods when he went through lucid dream sequences, although he was awake.

But in spite of this evidence to the contrary the majority of psychologists believe that sense impressions, even passive ones, are necessary for the existence of life itself, and if these are not present, hallucinations are substituted for them. We could live without food for days, without breath for minutes, but, according to Dr Daly King, in the complete absense of passive sensory impressions, no human being could survive beyond the duration of a fraction of a second.

Books

Burney, C., *Solitary Confinement*, Coward-McCann, New York, 1952.
Campbell, H. J., *The Pleasure Areas*, Eyre Methuen, London, 1973.
King, C. Daly, *The States of Human Consciousness*, University Books, New York, 1963.
Lilly, John C., *The Centre of the Cyclone*, Calder & Boyars, London, 1973.
Schultz, D. P., *Sensory Restriction*, Academic Press, New York, 1965.
Solomon, Philip *et al.*, *Sensory Deprivation*, Harvard University Press, Cambridge, Mass., 1961.
Vernon, Jack, *Inside the Black Room*, Penguin Books, Harmondsworth, 1966.
Zubek, J. P. (ed.), *Sensory Deprivation: Fifteen Years of Research*, Appleton-Century-Crofts, New York, 1969.

SEX MAGIC

Sex magic utilizes the biomagnetic energy generated by sexual arousal and sexual activity for magical ends, as a rule for selfish or evil purposes, and is thus to be distinguished from sex mysticism*. It usually involves a ceremonial rite, when the generated sex force is concentrated by a magical operation, trapped and augmented, to create a whirlpool of occult power.

As soon as the sex urge is aroused in man or woman, an invisible force is set in motion in the psychic sphere around them. Since the sexual act is immediately concerned with the process of creating a new life, it has powerful repercussions in the astral planes. Prolonged erethism alone can be used as a source of power. The result of sexual arousal, action and climax, is a mental as well as magical exaltation, which becomes a focus of creative energy. In this state the unconscious mind is manifesting but the participants are both physically and spiritually blinded, and in the normal sex act the sex-force is consumed in the activity itself and then dissipated after orgasm.

Few are able to utilize or are even aware of the immense power arising from such a situation. Magical forces can be generated in all forms of sexuality, and every act resulting in arousal can be used in sex magic. Autosexual activity or masturbation* produces a specific kind of perverse power, which may be directed to magical ends if one knows how. Heterosexual* activity, that is, between opposite sexes, is the least harmful source of power if performed with one's lawful spouse. But it acquires a more sinister quality in cases of adultery, rape, incest, or even fornication involving an unmarried person. In homosexual activity a still more powerful but perverse current is set up, where two evil streams of force, finding no fruitful outlet, can be generated and used for a magical ritual. Additional homosexual perversions such as mutual masturbation or acts of oral sex set up further dark and turbulent currents very difficult to control. Bestiality can also be used for creating elemental monsters, but their control is only within the powers of the most adept black magicians.

Group sexual activity quickens the forces of generation to a considerable degree. Primitives are aware of the tremendous potency inherent in group orgies, and seasonally indulge in sex rites to give fertility to the soil, to their cattle and their women folk. In black magical societies where group sex is practised, the leader himself does not necessarily participate, but harnesses the sexual energy released by the participants, especially during moments of climax, and directs it along specific occult channels by methods known to him.

Finally, occultists point out that while each sex deviation creates its own kind of power, the different postures assumed by the individual, couple or group concerned gives it its own magical emphasis, and this should be taken into account in determining the manner in which the activity is to be conducted.

The history of sex magic goes back to very early times, and has a widespread diffusion. In China taoists employed sex magic for the attainment of magical powers, for achieving control over the elements, and for the purposes of rejuvenation. It was regarded as a method of nourishing life by tapping the yang and yin elements, the transcendental cosmic forces that become immanent in the male *ching* (or *tsing*), 'semen'; and in the gynergic force in the female, and in her *khuai,* 'orgasm'. A great deal of this lore reached India and influenced the sex magical practices of the tantriks. The Tibetans borrowed from China and India and added it to their own traditional lore of Bon. Omar Garrison tells of an order of Tibetan nuns who had spies among the general populace on the lookout for vigorous young men who were kidnapped and hidden in remote convents, 'where they are held in thrall and used as a source of psychic galvanism for various occult practices'. The Tibetan dugpa sect kidnap women for the same purpose.

The practitioners of the middle east had their own sex magical traditions that were elaborately cultivated in Persia and North Africa. It was from Arab and Indian experts that western students acquired the art, which was brought to ritual form in such societies as the Ordo Templi Orientis, abbreviated OTO, Aleister Crowley (d. 1947) tried many experiments in sex magic, some of which he recorded in his book entitled *Rex de Arte Magica,* 'the King (i.e. Crowley) on the Great Art'.

Most of these involve meditation and breathing exercises, combined with methods of 'increasing, purifying, energizing and enriching the semen', and absorbing its subtle essence, in order to increase one's psycho-magnetic potency and put one in touch with elemental entities. It demands proficiency in the art of prolonged erection, in the control of ejaculation or coitus prolongatus, in coitus reservatus, intrajaculation, acclivity, and as a final test, congressus subtilis, or intercourse with invisible astral beings, especially demon entities.

Books

Blofeld, John, *The Secret and the Sublime: Taoist Mysteries and Magic,* Allen & Unwin, London, 1973.

Crowley, Aleister, *The Magical Record of the Beast 666,* ed. by J. Symonds and K. Grant, Duckworth, London, 1972.

SEX MYSTICISM

Garrison, Omar, *Tantra: The Yoga of Sex,* Academy Editions, London, 1972.
Howard, C., *Sex and Religion,* Williams & Norgate, London, 1925.
Laurent, E. and Nagour, P., *Magica Sexualis*, Falstaff Press, New York, 1934.
Tabori, Paul and Raphael, Phyllis, *Beyond the Senses,* Souvenir Press, London, 1971.
Underwood, Peter, *Into the Occult,* Harrap, London, 1972.
Walker, Benjamin, *Sex and the Supernatural,* Macdonald, London, 1970.

SEX MYSTICISM

Sex mysticism arises from the consciousness of the sacred or religious character of sexual life and activity. It is to be distinguished from the Platonic or Pauline concept of spiritual love between two persons of the opposite sex in which sex plays no perceptible part; and from sex worship in which sex deities and the sex organs or their symbolical representations receive actual homage; and also from sex magic, which is usually black magic stemming from sexual activity.

The philosophy of sex mysticism has a wide basis. God is creative and so is coition, therefore sexual intercourse has an element of the divine and partakes of the nature of a sacramental act. Sexual intercourse becomes a form of worship. Furthermore, the sexual act was believed to be amenable to a spiritualizing process. The animality inherent in male-female union could be transcended and the sex act raised to a high level of sanctification amounting to a divine experience.

Chinese taoists and Hindu tantriks, both of whom used sex for magical purposes, also believed that sex could be sanctified and elevated into a divine rite. The taoists held that the act of intercourse, correctly performed, brought down into the microcosmic world of the pairing couple the greater potencies inherent in the cosmic yin and yang. The Hindu Upanishads compare the union of the religious mystic with the godhead, to the shared delight of man and woman in sexual union who 'lose consciousness of what is without and what is within'. In the words of the *Taittreya Upanishad*, 'God dwells as light in the stars, as procreative power in the sperm, and as pleasure in sex.'

In Hindu sex mysticism the act of intercourse is accorded the status of a sacrificial rite. The woman is the temple, her hips and haunches the sacrificial area, the mons veneris the altar, the pubic hairs the sacred grass, the moist labia the press for the extraction of the soma juice, the yellow vulva the prepared fuel, the red-tipped phallus the ember. The lust of intercourse is compared to the smoke of the sacrifice, penetration to the sacred chants, voluptuousness to sparks, movement to the friction producing the heat, orgasm to the living flame, semen to the oblation offered to the deities.

The gnostic teachers often equated sexual union with union with the divine. A gnostic text (c. AD 200) says that the sex act is the fulfilment of a cosmic mystery and adds that at the moment the male seed springs forth and the woman receives the strength from the male, they both receive the vitality from the heavens. The act of intercourse brings into the minds of the man and woman the experience of the grandeur and glory of the cosmos. The neoplatonists sometimes spoke of carnal love as a prefiguration of divine love. Plotinus (d. AD 270) wrote:

> Those to whom the divine passion is unknown, may get an idea of it from the passions on earth. Yet on earth our love is only a courtship of shadows that pass and change, but our soul's beloved is elsewhere who is ours to enjoy by true possession.

According to the Talmud, the sexual act is a profound mystery, to be treated almost as a ritual act. The kabbalists also regarded intercourse as a means of attaining spiritual enlightenment, and a method of linking the heavenly and earthly spheres. The whole world in fact was sustained by the sex act being performed somewhere or other by men and women, and if at any time the act was not being carried out the whole world would start to dissolve like a salt castle immersed in a running stream.

Even Christian saints and mystics drew a parallel between the union of male and female and the universal spirit. According to Bernard of Clairvaux (d. 1153), all higher love and even the love of man for God begins first with *concupiscentia,* for this is the natural impulse of every creature for its own perfection.

> Since we are carnal and born of fleshly concupiscence, needs must that our desire or love begin from the flesh, and if it be governed by right order, going forward by degrees under the guidance of grace, it will at last be consummated in the spirit.

In medieval Europe a number of sects advocated the doctrine of sex sanctification. Such were the Adamites, the Eleutherians, the Kissing Sects, as well as little groups like the Prato nuns and others. They held that for unredeemed man, those who formed the great mass of mankind, the sexual urge was a natural and physical urge like hunger, but for regenerate man it was a mystery and a sacrament, and although the sensual element was present in part, it was essentially suprasensual and mystical. Men and women who obey only their animal instincts during the sex act are not susceptible to any kind of spiritual or moral elevation.

Thus a small sect in Cambrai, France, who came under a Free Spirit movement in about 1410, put into practice their ideas of sanctifying the sexual act. They were tried by the authorities in 1411 and accused, among other things, of teaching that 'the natural sexual act could be performed in such a manner that it was likened in effect and value to a prayer in God's sight.'

Cornelius Agrippa (d. 1535), occultist, kabbalist and scholar of great erudition, said that coition was an act of the highest solemnity, full of magical endowment. It was a sacrament at which all nature assisted and in which the whole of man was employed, no matter how brutally, ignorantly or blindly it was performed.

The Spanish antiquary, orientalist and mystical writer Benito Arias Montanus (d. 1598), also known as 'Aratus', wrote:

> As the physical union of male and female leads to the fruit from the composition of each, so the interior and secret association of male and female, is the copulation of male and female soul, and is appointed for the production of fitting fruit of the divine life.

The English mystic, Thomas Vaughan (d. 1666), wrote:

> Marriage is a comment of life, a mere hieroglyphic or outward representation of our inward vital composition. For life is nothing else but a union of male and female principles, and he that perfectly knows this secret knows the mysteries of marriage – both spiritual and natural – and how he ought to use a wife. Matrimony is no ordinary trivial business but in a moderate sense sacramental. It is a visible sign of our invisible union with Christ. If the thing signified be so reverend, the signature is no contemptible agent.

Love and marriage and the union of counterparts are the mystical signs of the connection between human and celestial love. And the mystics of all ages stress how important these are. Nor are modern advocates wanting for this point of view. Alexander Lowen says, 'The great mystery of life is sexual love.' He remarks that during orgasm there is 'an overall body sensation of illumination'. Psychology confirms that a satisfactory sexual union can effect a transformation of consciousness, annihilating the duality of the participants, and enabling them to reach a state of superconsciousness.

Books

Cohn, N., *The Pursuit of the Millennium*, Secker & Warburg, London, 1957.
Fränger, Wilhelm, *The Millennium of Hieronymous Bosch*, Faber, London, 1952.
Lowen, Alexander, *Love and Orgasm*, Granada, London, 1971.
Mann, Charles, *Spiritual Sex Life*, Orange, New Jersey, 1902.
Steiger, Brad, *Sex and the Supernatural*, Lancer, New York, 1968.
Wind, Edgar, *Pagan Mysteries in the Renaissance*, Faber, London, 1967.

SEXUAL PERVERSION

Sexual perversion, or to use a milder term, sexual deviation, can take many forms. If the norm for sexual intercourse is taken as male-female, face-to-face, penis-vagina congress, then in varying degrees deviation is almost universal. Deviations become sins, offences against nature and crimes against society, only in relation to the moral or religious standards that might be violated by their perpetration.

Thus there are transgressions against social or religious law such as fornication (intercourse before or outside marriage), adultery (intercourse with another than the lawful spouse), rape, incest, polygamy. Sexual activities like coitus interruptus, coitus obstructus, coitus reservatus, coitus in public, can also be treated as perverse. The abnormal period of the emergence of sexual expression, when it is either too early or too late, may be a deviation from an accepted norm. Sexophobia or fear of sex, the absense of the sex drive, the suppression of the libidinous instinct leading to sex abstinence, if not perverse in themselves, may lead to perversion. There may be purely physical reasons for perversions, such as hormonal imbalance, or structural abnormality of the genital organs. A pathological increase in sexual desire leading to an urge for constant and recurrent satisfaction, as in satyriasis and nymphomania, are both forms of erotomania, which is also a perversion.

Attempts have been made to classify the recognized perversions in various ways. For example, sexual familiarity with one's own sex, or homosexuality (sodomy and lesbianism); or with an immature person (pedophilia or pederasty); with a very old person (gerontophilia); with animals (bestiality); with corpses (necrophilia); with elementals and demons (congressus subtilis). Sexual satisfaction by means of the secondary appurtenances of sex, as in fetishism, is also a perversion. So is pornography, or reading and writing of sexual matters; and coprolalia or erotolalia, listening to or saying dirty words.

Various kinds of self-satisfaction include such acts as masturbation; voyeurism or watching others; exhibitionism or showing oneself to others. The 'vessel' used may be perverse, as in anal intercourse, oral intercourse, and sexual stimulation by means of the breasts, thighs, armpits or parts of the body other than the sex organs. The use of artificial devices like the dildo or artificial phallus; or the female doll, used by men. There is also the sexual satisfaction that comes from inflicting pain (sadism) and from receiving pain (masochism).

A small number of deviations, including sodomy, are common to all societies, but most of them emerge in advanced and degenerate cultures. They represent a disease of civilization, resulting from early and continuous sexual stimulation, increasing nervous tension, over-excitation of the sexual centres. The facility with which normal sexual satisfaction is obtained leads to jaded sensibilities that need special stimulation to reach the desired end.

From the occult point of view all sexual activity generates a kind of energy vortex, beneficent in legitimate sexual activity, and malignant in perverse. Abnormal sexual activity not only attracts undesirable entities, but engenders forces that are harmful. The nature of the act, the type and number of participants, the way in which the act is performed, the postures, all determine the character of the created entity, and the 'colour', strength and duration of its energy. Each kind of act actualizes different potencies, and each kind is believed to draw into its ambit a phantom after its own kind. The solitary act differs from the dual, and the latter from a group orgy or one involving a non-human partner.

The performance of sexual acts which are condemned by the orthodox religions creates cross-currents of turbulent energy and charges the atmosphere with envenomed flashes. In general, the more heinous the sin, the more malignant and powerful the force created through the intermediary of the offending participants. Aleister Crowley (d. 1947), an expert in the matter, pointed out that abnormal acts of love attracted or excited spirits, incubi and demons.

Certain ancient sects like the Nabateans of Mesopotamia used to perform perverse intercourse whenever they wished to raise a perverse power. Thus, when they grafted one plant to another, which was an act contrary to nature, they dramatized the process by getting a young girl to bend down and insert the graft while at the same moment a man performed the act of sodomy on her person.

Homosexuality, or sexual indulgence between members of the same sex, commonly refers only to sexual activity between two males, as distinguished from lesbianism. It is known variously as uranism, pederasty, sotadism, sodomy, buggery. It plays a part in sex magic and is believed to provide a special kind of force not obtainable in heterosexual relationships. It augments the potencies found in maleness but has a perverse quality. It is commonly practised among black magicians to raise a charge of power for instantaneous utilization.

Lesbianism, or homosexuality among women, is practised because of fear, hatred or disgust of the male sex; lack of sexual satisfaction from heterosexual intercourse; dissatisfaction with marriage; fear of childbirth and pregnancy; lack of opportunity for heterosexual relationship; a desire for raising power in sex magic rites. In early and medieval legend mention is made of certain sororities where lesbianism was practised for occult purposes. Sanskrit writings speak of the semi-historical queendom of Oddiyana whose ravishing beauties disdained the services of men, except for procreation. They followed a secret cult of sexual magic which involved perverse methods of obtaining orgasm by variations of lesbian practice.

Oralism of different kinds may take a perverse form. Thus, in cunnilingus a person explores the female genital zone with his tongue; similarly, in penilingus or fellatio a person applies the mouth to the male organ. The coital posture known as gamahucher involves both types of oralism together. Oralism is not unusual in sex magical rites. Aleister Crowley (d. 1947) records time and again how with a certain objective in mind he performed rites of sex magic while 'licking the cunt' of his partner. Tantrik practitioners advise that before intercourse the man should touch the vulvar cleft of his partner with his mouth, for such contact between two 'opposite' areas sets in motion a great cycle of power which the tantrik can use to energize himself. Chinese taoists regard cunnilingus as an effective method of making a woman release her yin energy, which he then absorbs direct into his mouth.

Bestiality or carnal intercourse between human beings and animals is as old as the domestication of beasts, and men and women from earliest times have tried to satisfy their sexual urges on the bodies of domestic and pet animals. In their book on Hebrew myths, Graves and Patai write that in the Jewish tradition Adam had intercourse with the beasts before the creation of Eve. Greek, Roman, Egyptian, Hindu and other mythologies have stories of gods and mortals indulging in this form of sexuality. In certain cults dedicated to Isis, both priest and priestess performed the rite with the temple animals. The custom of ritual bestiality prevailed in many parts of the ancient world.

More unusual types of bestiality are sometimes practised in order to acquire magical power or material success. Congress with crocodiles, for instance, was practised in ancient Egypt as part of divine worship. During intercourse with her mate the female crocodile turns over on her back while the mate mounts her, and she can only resume her normal position with great difficulty. Richard Burton (d. 1890) quotes a French traveller's account of bestiality he witnessed among the fellahin of Egypt. The men, taking advantage of the female crocodile's helpless position, drive off the male and 'supplant him in this frightful intercourse'. This congress, adds Burton, is believed to be 'the sovereignest for rising to rank and riches'.

Books

Allen, Clifford, *The Sexual Perversions and Abnormalities*, Oxford University Press, London, 1951.

Burton, Sir Richard, *Love, War and Fancy* (ed. by Kenneth Walker), Kimber, London, 1964.

Caprio, F. S., *Female Homosexuality*, Grove Press, New York, 1954.

Crowley, Aleister, *The Magical Record of the Beast 666* (ed. by J. Symonds and K. Grant), Duckworth, London, 1972.

Dodson, V. and S., *A Study of Deviate Sexual Fantasies*, Publishers Export Co., San Diego, California, 1968.

Gillette, Paul, *Psychodynamics of Unconventional Sexual Behavior and Unusual Sexual Practices*, Holloway House, Los Angeles, 1966.

Graves, Robert and Patai, Raphael, *Hebrew Myths: The Book of Genesis*, Cassell, London, 1964.

Hirchfield, Magnus, *Sexual Anomalies and Perversions*, Francis Aldor, London, 1944.

Kraft-Ebing, Richard von, *Psychopathia Sexualis*, Putnam, New York, 1965.

Masters, R. E. L., *The Hidden World of Erotica: An Objective Re-examination of Perverse Sex Practices in Different Cultures*, Lyrebird Press, London, 1973.

Rickles, N. K., *Exhibitionism*, Lippincott, Philadelphia, 1950.

Storr, Anthony, *Sexual Deviation*, Penguin Books, Harmondsworth, 1964.

SKIN

The largest organ of the body, weighs about five pounds and has an area of approximately seventeen square feet. It contains about two million glands whose length would total eight miles, and it can hold about one quarter of the body's total blood supply. It is the area of direct contact with the material environment, but at the same time insulates us from the outside world, forming a defensive coat against insects and germs. In the Chinese system of healing known as acupuncture the skin is believed to be interconnected by means of the subtle arteries to the internal organs of the body.

The skin is an important organ of excretion, getting rid of poisonous waste products in the form of sweat, and regulating the temperature of the body, thus to some extent assisting the function of the kidneys. To a small degree it is also respiratory, supplementing the work of the lungs. In frogs and certain other animals the skin plays a major role in respiration.

The colour of the skin varies considerably, ranging from almost pure white to almost pure black, depending on the amount of pigment or colouring substance found in certain cells of the epidermis. If the skin is exposed to sunlight or X-rays, or is affected by some chronic skin disease, more pigment (melanin) is produced, and darkening, freckles, bronzing or pigmented patches result. The surface of the skin is raised in ridges, which are especially well marked in the tips of the fingers, and responsible for fingerprints.

Common skin blemishes include the birthmark or naevus, usually in the form of a red or purple 'port-wine stain' or 'strawberry-mark' found on the skin of infants and allegedly due to the strong desire of the mother for something, like strawberries, during pregnancy; the wart, a small hard growth which is sometimes infectious; and the mole, a small skin tumour containing the brown colouring matter of the skin, and usually raised. Skin eruptions, itching, and skin diseases may be due to either physical or emotional causes, and the skin can therefore also be regarded as a true mirror of the internal state of an individual, reflecting thc condition of the heart, brain, stomach, blood, spleen, as well as the emotions.

It is clear that the skin is not an inert envelope encasing the body, but a dynamic organ. Dr Logan Clendening described it as 'one of the most interesting and mystic of structures' (Schifferes, 1959, p. 479). The tumults of the mind and the storms of the soul are recorded on its surface, and often manifest in uncontrollable blushing, sweating, flushing, pallor. The complexion and appearance of the skin are influenced by the nervous system, so that shame, anger, fear, excitement, can cause it to become pale, red, mottled, flushed, patchy, pasty. Saints dwelling on the crucifixion of Christ develop stigmata, the marks of Christ's wounds.

In all ages and in all communities the skin was subjected to an extraordinary amount of mutilation, scarification, tattooing, flagellation and other processes, whether in the cause of beauty or for purposes of identification, self-mortification or healing. These processes were often linked with tribal blood-rites, head-hunting, scalping, shaving the head, circumcision (some forms of which involved skinning the penis) and other kinds of sacrifice or punishment. Flaying or skinning was another form of ritual or religious interference with the body. This was usually done on the dead victim, but in special circumstances even when the victim was alive. Both human and animal skins (fur and hide) were used in occult and religious rites, often to suggest a renewal or rebirth. In nature, the prototype of this renewal is found in the sloughing of the snake's skin.

Human skin has talismanic virtues. Girdles of human skin were believed to help women in labour. Human tallow and the light diffused through lampshades made of human skin were said to be excellent for the eyes and complexion.

Books

Brand, John, *Popular Antiquities of Great Britain,* London, ed. 1872.

Lanval, M., *Les Mutilations sexuelles dans les religions anciens et modernes*, Brussels, 1936.

Lewis, T., *The Blood Vessels of the Human Skin and Their Responses,* Shaw, London, 1927.

Moss, Louis, *Acupuncture and You,* Paul Elek, London, 1972.

Obermeyer, M. E., *Psychocutaneous Medicine,* Thomas, Springfield, Illinois, 1955.

Schifferes, Justus J., *Schifferes' Family Medical Encyclopedia,* Permabooks, New York, 1959.

Sinclair, D. C., *Cutaneous Sensation,* Oxford University Press, 1967.

Wittkower, E. D. and Russell, B., *Emotional Factors in Skin Disease,* Hoeber, New York, 1953.

SLEEP

Sleep, like its accompaniment, dreaming*, is one of the great mysteries of life. During sleep our awareness of practical things withdraws, and a totally different mental life supervenes. Normally, up to eight hours sleep in every twenty-four is sufficient for the average adult. Some people can do with much less, and a few rare individuals apparently do not sleep at all, but recover their energies in short bursts of microsleep that last a few seconds at a time. On the other extreme there are a few cases of people who, as a result of accident or illness, have 'slept' for months, even years.

Recent experiments have shown that: (a) the average length of a night's sleep is seven and a half hours; (b) the duration remains constant from the age of thirty to eighty years; (c) girls sleep more than boys; (d) a sleeping adult in tossing and turning makes about forty major movements during the night; (e) body temperature, blood pressure, muscle tension, the production of blood sugar, urine, digestive juices and saliva are reduced during sleep; (f) carbon dioxide pressure in the lungs is decreased; (g) thoracic respiration replaces the normal abdominal breathing of the waking state; (h) consciousness sinks to a low level, and the brain waves, as shown by EEGs, gradually expand from quick wavelets of ten per second (alpha waves), to lazy rollers at the rate of four per second (delta waves).

Sleep is ushered in by the initial phase of drowsiness called *hypnagogia,* during which there is a shimmering of consciousness, a feeling of relaxation, a desire to let the body 'collapse', and a tendency to yawn, no one knows why. Although a precursor of sleep, yawning does not occur during sleep itself. In the middle of the yawn there is said to be a simultaneous two-way movement of air, and as the air is exhaled and inhaled at the same time, two kinds of breath are exchanged. Students of astral projection speak of hypnagogia as the condition immediately preceding discoincidence of the astral double, when the astral body slides, and sometimes jerks, out of alignment with the physical body. This stage is often accompanied by a sudden spasm known as the myoclonus. Though compared to a miniature epileptic seizure, the myoclonic jerk is quite normal and lasts for only a fraction of a second. Sometimes the sleeper lets out a sudden grunt as his body is momentarily convulsed.

During sleep a cyclic pattern of activity and consciousness has been observed. First, a short phase of oblivion; second REMs* (rapid eye movements) and dreams; third, dreams cease and the body moves and adjusts itself; fourth, a phase of very deep and dreamless sleep. There may be between three to five such cycles lasting ninety minutes, and as the night progresses the length of the phases alters, the last phase, in particular, getting progressively shorter.

Man is a night sleeper and has been so for countless generations, and this tendency to sleep at night is inbuilt in him. But the increasing pressures and varied activities of modern life are beginning to disrupt the sleep habits of a great many people the world over, whether as a result of late-night socializing, of night travel, or of round-the-clock work by aircrews, night-shift workers, telegraph operators, newsmen and others. The crossing of time-zones during jet flights, when the blood sugar and temperature are at their lowest, is known to cause mental disorientation and erratic judgment.

The time for sleep is regulated by a built-in 'local time' of the body itself, intimately connected with the internal bodily mechanisms and the metabolic processes established over thousands of years. Many of the physiological concomitants of sleep, therefore, such as the drop in body temperature and in blood sugar, continue to take place at the habitual time of sleep, whether the person is actually asleep or not. The long-term effects of the disruption and the consequent disharmony of the physical and psychological rhythms are at present being studied. It is to be noted that the overall sleep patterns even of those who are not subjected to the particular pressures that necessitate night working and night travel are gradually being affected as well. Child psychologists say that sleep is replacing eating as a source of parental anxiety.

There are many unanswered questions about sleep, and no satisfactory explanation has been forthcoming to solve them. One third of our lives is spent in sleep. By the biblical age of threescore years and ten, we will have spent over twenty years in sleep. No one knows precisely why we sleep, although a number of hypotheses have been advanced to account for it. Sleep is said to be due to fatigue of the muscular tissues or nerve fibres of the body. Perhaps the fatigued cells create acids and toxic products that have a soporific effect, like a drug, and these hypnotoxins induce sleep. Some researchers believe that the need for sleep is to be sought in dreams, and that we sleep because we must dream. Occultists explain sleep as the regular and normal discoincidence of the astral body. During sleep the astral gently moves away from the physical and takes a 'breather' in the astral planes, recharging itself and the body, with cosmic energy. 'Sleep,' said Arthur Schopenhauer (d. 1860), 'is to the individual what winding is to the clock.'

Sleep appears to be a foretaste of death. Even the preparations we make before sleep are reminiscent of the final departure. After a preliminary ritual of washing and changing into loose shroud-like garments, we lie down, cover our bodies with what might be our winding-sheets, turn our eyes upwards, reach a condition of physical immobility, and pass into a death-like trance. Tertullian (d. AD 230) said, 'Sleep is a kind of temporary death, in which the soul leaves the body.' In his *Religio Medici* Sir Thomas Browne (d. 1682) wrote:

> Sleep is a death, whereby we live in a middle moderating point between life and death, and so like death, I dare not trust it without my prayers and a half adieu unto the world, and take my farewell in a colloquy with God, after which I close my eyes in security, content to take my leave of him and sleep unto the resurrection.

Books

Foulkes, David, *The Psychology of Sleep*, Scribner, New York, 1966.
Giles, L., *Sleep*, Bobbs-Merrill, New York, 1938.
Hartmann, Ernest (ed.), *Sleep and Dreaming*, Churchill, London, 1970.
Kleitman, Nathaniel, *Sleep and Wakefulness as Alternating Phases in the Cycle of Existence*, Chicago University Press, 1963.
Koella, W. P., *Sleep: Its Nature and Physiological Organization*, Thomas, Springfield, Illinois, 1967.
Laing, A. M., *The Sleep Book*, Muller, London, 1948.
Luce, G. G. and Segal, J., *Sleep*, Heinemann, London, 1967.
Macnish, Robert, *The Philosophy of Sleep*, Glasgow, 1830.
Murray, E., *Sleep, Dreams and Arousal*, Appleton, New York, 1965.
Oswald, Ian, *Sleep*, Penguin Books, Harmondsworth, 1966.
Priestley, J. B., *The Shapes of Sleep*, Heinemann, London, 1962.
Stopes, Marie, *Sleep*, Chatto & Windus, London, 1956.
Wolstenholme, G. E. W. and O'Connor, M. (eds), *The Nature of Sleep*, Churchill, London, 1960.

SOUL

Soul, or Spirit, a term having many connotations and used in varying contexts. The concept of soul is *sui generis*, in a class by itself, and cannot be derived from any other field of empirical knowledge. It is independent of any substrate, and not restricted by physical conditions like space, time or causality. It is non-material, non-physical, non-cerebral. It cannot be compared with life, mind, emotions, instincts, or any of the other asomatic elements that make up the human being. It is not the personality, which is the ephemeral, transient and changeable part of the self, nor is it limited in scope to the individual's mental capacity. While no sexual element can be attached to the soul, it is described, in the way that God is, as androgynous, and all-encompassing in its attributes.

Aristotle (d. 322 BC) defined the soul as the 'form of the body', a concept which St Thomas Aquinas (d. 1274) accepted. It is the spiritual nucleus and the inmost centre of man's being, permanent and immortal. 'It seems to me', says St Augustine, 'that the soul is a certain kind of principle, sharing in reason, and fitted to use and rule the body.' Regarded as the transcendent or noumenal self, it is a religious concept, as the etheric and astral bodies are occult concepts. It is governed by spiritual law.

The soul is sometimes regarded as having pre-existed, because it had its being in God, before its earthly sojourn. It is the God-element within man, a fragment of the Divine, a spark of the Absolute. Plato (d. 347 BC) in his *Timaeus* spoke of the soul entering from a world of Being into a world of Becoming. The neoplatonist philosopher, Plotinus (d. AD 270), in the *Enneads* spoke of the soul as a stranger on earth, having 'fallen' into matter from a world without space and time. Another neoplatonist, Proclus (d. 485), referred to the soul as an incorporeal, indestructible, self-animating principle, having a temporary activity in matter and an eternal existence in the immortal realms.

Men through the ages have spoken in rhapsodic terms about the soul.

'Whatever road you may explore', said Heraclitus (d. 475 BC), 'you will not reach the limits of the soul, for the soul has no limits.' In the words of the Upanishads, 'It is not born, does not die, is not the consequent of any cause, is everlasting, self-existent, imperishable, ancient.' Meister Eckhart (d. 1327), scholar and mystic, wrote, 'There is a spirit in man, untouched by time and flesh, flowing from God, itself wholly spiritual. It is free of all names and void of all forms. It is one and simple, as God is one and simple.' C. G. Jung (d. 1961) in his later years spoke of the soul as 'the greatest of all cosmic miracles'.

The soul is sometimes regarded as an indwelling monitor. It has been equated with the conscience and symbolized in the figure of the genius within, prompting us to do the right, and reproaching us when we stray from the path. It is also a passive watcher, a recording angel, witnessing and setting down our good and bad deeds. The Upanishads liken the personality and the soul to two birds both occupying the same tree: one bird, the personal self, pecks greedily at the fruit, while the other, the higher self or soul, does nothing, but just looks on.

The soul tends to God, and the inherent aspiration of the soul is expressed in the Latin phrase, *anima naturalita religiosa,* 'the soul is by nature religious'; which Tertullian (d. 230) interpreted to mean, *anima naturalita christiana,* 'the soul is naturally Christian'. The purpose of life is so to order one's actions that they are in accord with the highest ideals of the soul. In the final prayer that ends his *Phaedrus,* Plato says, 'Give me beauty of the inward soul; and may the outward and the inward man be one.'

The soul's operation even in the practical world is seen in the larger spiritual dimension for which we yearn in our everyday conscious states: in our various intellectual and social ideals; our moral aspirations; our admiration for things that are true and good; our appreciation for beauty; our longing for self-improvement and perfection. All these represent the impulse of the soul Godward.

On a physical analogy the soul is a 'field' containing the thoughts, memories and ideas formed during one's lifetime. Each person is responsible for his own fragment of God entrusted to him. When the individual dies his bodily functions come to a standstill and by degrees the physical and etheric systems perish. But a nucleus of the self survives death, and this consists of the astral body and the soul. The new being thinks and feels, and remembers its past bodily experiences, and has a separate continuing existence on a different level in the next world. According to Immanuel Kant (d. 1804), 'The form matrix which contains the sum total of all inner experience of the individual may be conceived of as the soul.' On the analogy of the other asomatic bodies, the soul could be called 'the body of meaning'.

The soul, in the words of the neoplatonists, is 'restored to life' only after death of the body. There are higher powers that decide (The Judgment) the allocation of the soul in the next spheres. It continues, with the astral, to learn, by vivid experience in the varying grades of 'hells' and 'purgatories', the shortcomings of its earthly apprenticeship. The Greek writer, Plutarch (d. AD 120), who was an initiate into the mysteries and also a hierophant in a temple, declared: 'Whatever others might say, that when the spirit is freed from the flesh it does not suffer punishment nor is conscious, I know better than to believe them.'

According to the reincarnationists, the soul comes back to earth in another body; the reincarnated man has a different astral but the same soul. Others contend that the doctrine of reincarnation is true, but only in the sense of transmigration. The soul does not return to earth, but goes on to other spheres, migrating from level to level towards ultimate perfection.

The soul is the permanent ground, the continuing ent of each individual, which works in the interest of a real life for the self in another world. After its term in purgatory the soul has further experiences necessary for its advancement. Goethe (d. 1832) said, 'The thought of death leaves me in perfect peace, for I am firmly convinced that our soul is indestructible and moves on from eternity to eternity.' Briefly, we go from earth to a new sphere, perhaps many new spheres, perfecting ourselves at each rebirth till we enter the final Reality which is God.

Some occultists maintain that immortality is not to be taken for granted. The soul is the immortal medium that is loaned to man to give him a chance of earning immortality for himself. If he fails he personally is extinguished, and the soul returns to God for future allocation to another individual.

Books

Bailey, Alice, *The Soul and Its Mechanism,* New York, 1930.

Baraduc, Hippolyte, *The Human Soul,* Paris, 1913.

Brandon, S. G. F., *Man and His Destiny in the Great Religions,* Manchester University Press, 1962.

Burnet, J., *The Socratic Doctrine of the Soul,* Oxford University Press, 1916.

Crawley, A. E., *The Idea of the Soul,* Black, London, 1909.

Eliade, Mircea, *Yoga, Immortality and Freedom,* Routledge & Kegan Paul, London, 1958.

Hulcrantz, A., *Conceptions of the Soul among North American Indians,* New York, 1953.

Johnson, A. R., *The Vitality of the Individual in the Thought of Ancient Israel,* Verry, New York, 1949.

Jung, C. G., *The Soul and Death,* Routledge & Kegan Paul, London, 1960.

Lys, D., *Nèphèsh,* Paris, 1959.

Rohde, Erwin, *Psyche: the Cult of the Soul and Belief in Immortality Among the Greeks,* 8th edn, Kegan Paul, Trench, Trubner, London, 1925.

White, Victor, *Soul and Psyche,* Collins, London, 1960.

SPINE

The spine (vertebral column) in man, is made up of thirty-three segments that are generally counted in five groups, as follows: (1) *cervical,* seven vertebrae making up the bones of the neck; the first cervical vertebra is appropriately called the *atlas* as it supports the head; (2) *thoracic,* or dorsal, twelve bones attached to the ribs, completing the rib-cage and making up the trunk bones; (3) *lumbar,* five bones in the small of the back or loins; (4) *sacral,* five bones in the rump, lying between the two haunch bones, and forming the back wall of the pelvis; in the adult these are fused together into a triangular bone called the sacrum (see below); (5) *coccygeal,* four small bones forming the coccyx (Gk. *kokkux,* 'cuckoo'), so named from its supposed resemblance to the shape of a cuckoo's bill. The coccygeal vertebrae correspond to the root of the tail in animals.

The vertebral column encloses the spinal cord, a basic part of the nervous system*. Its importance in the life and vital functions of man was recognized by all peoples. The early Indo-Europeans believed that the soul of man, which they likened to a fire or flame, was fed on the cerebro-spinal marrow. In occultism the sixth ventricle* extends throughout the cord and expands above into the fourth ventricle. The Greek physician, Galen (d. AD 201), who served several Roman emperors, said that injury to the spinal cord between the first and second vertebrae caused instantaneous death; between the third and fourth vertebrae produced an arrest of breathing; below the sixth vertebra it gave rise to paralysis of the chest muscles; injury lower down caused paralysis of the lower limbs, bladder and intestines.

In ancient religious symbolism the backbone was variously referred to as a road, a ladder, a serpent, a rod, a tree. The spine was a replica in the human body of the primal cosmic tree, and the brain, as its efflorescence, corresponded to the expanse of heaven. In ancient Thrace and Macedonia people thought that the backbone of a dead person turned in time into a snake.

The Egyptians believed that the sperm comes from the spine, and the hieroglyph 'ded' stood, among other things, for the spinal column or the sacrum of the god Osiris. In the mystery cult of Abydos the sacral bone was set up on a pillar, and upon this the head of Osiris was placed, after which the god declared, 'I have made myself whole and complete.'

In Hindu esoteric physiology the spinal column has an astral counterpart in what is known as the *brahmadanda,* 'rod of Brahma', an invisible shaft which starts from a place between the anus and the tail-bone, and proceeds upwards along the spine to the base of the skull. Within this shaft is the *sushumna,* 'pleasing', the largest of the subtle arteries of the body.

According to the Chinese system an exceedingly fine tube starts at the sacral extremity and goes up the spine and enters the skull, and is connected with a reservoir of marrow called *t'ung te* situated at the back of the head. The Tibetans took over this notion and added a refinement by introducing a system of *bu-gu-chan* veins which branch out of the spinal column and then loop back again forming a network of tiny channels filled with vapour-like essence. This system of veins is responsible for vitalizing the blood, semen and other 'wet' elements of the body.

In occult physiology the most important bone in the body is the *sacrum* (Lat. *sacer,* 'sacred'), the holy bone. It had a role of special significance in many systems of divination by the bones of the body, in religious rites, in sacrificial ceremonies. It was commonly believed to contain the immortal part of the body and to be directly connected with the spirit realm. In the western tradition this was the bone kissed at the witches' sabbat.

Semitic peoples have a tradition that there exists in every man a tiny bone that cannot be seen or felt, cannot be burned or otherwise destroyed, never rots or perishes, and is lodged in the sacrum. At death this invisible, indestructible, incombustible, imponderable, impalpable, atomic bone-particle will remain incorrupt in the earth, and when the time of resurrection comes it will form the 'seed' around which a new body will be built, the body that will proceed to the last judgment and to its final destiny in heaven or hell.

Formerly, Jews believed that when they died this bone, which they called *luz* (or luez), would find a resting place in the Holy Land, and that if a Jew was buried far away, the luz would travel underground or find some means of getting to the sacred soil. If the bone was eaten *en route* by a bird or animal it would not be absorbed into the system but passed out. Muslims too believe in the existence of this bone, which they call *al ajb*, 'the curious', a tiny fragment around which the resurrection-body will take shape.

In medieval Europe a number of popular beliefs were associated with the spine. Thus, a man possessed of an unusually large spine, such as a hunchback, was thought to be endowed with almost talismanic power. Hence an old form of address for a hunchback was 'My Lord'. To touch a hunchback brought good luck, and to touch and wish at the same time ensured that the wish would come true. The expression 'to have a hunch', implying prescience about a matter, derives from a belief in the precognitive faculty inherent in the hunch of a hunchback.

Books

Garrison, F. H., 'The Bone Called Luz', *New York Medical Journal*, 1910, 92, 149–52.

Hall, Manly Palmer, *Man the Grand Symbol of the Mysteries*, Philosophical Research Society, 5th edn, Los Angeles, 1947.

Smith, Anthony, *The Body*, Allen & Unwin, London, 1968.

Williams, C. A. S., *Encyclopedia of Chinese Symbolism and Art Motives*, Julian Press, New York, 1960.

SUBTLE ARTERIES

It has long been held by many ancient peoples that there exists in the human body a hidden connection between the internal organs and certain parts on the body's surface, and that this connection is maintained by a system of subtle arteries.

In the system of physiology developed by the ancient Egyptians the human body was believed to be served by thirty-six channels called *metu* which, starting from the head, flowed to the major organs and limbs of the body, each part receiving the energy from two metu, as follows: the eyes, nose, ears, mouth, shoulders, arms, hands, heart, lungs, spleen, liver, testicles, phallus, bladder, rectum, hips, legs and feet. From these distribution centres the energy was redistributed by smaller arteries all over the body, and the various parts of the body were in this manner subtly connected.

The breathing action of the lungs and the beating of the heart urged the flow of these subtle emanations or vital essences of air, blood, semen and nourishment, from one part of the body to another, to be diffused throughout the physical organism. In addition, these invisible arteries also carried the subtle essences of mucus,excrement and bodily impurities,as well as the *vehedu*, 'pain-substances', which caused aches, inflammations, fevers and diseases. The vehedu were engendered within the body, but could also enter it from outside.

The metu, along with the lesser arteries through which the vital forces were conducted, formed a network, interconnecting different parts of the body with the surface of the skin, and cures of deep-seated organs were attempted by treatment of the relevant skin area.

In Hindu physiology the arteries of the subtle or etheric body are called *nadi* (Sanskrit, 'tube') which ramify, not from a central area but from various plexuses*, such as the diaphragm, the perineum, the heart and the head. Each of the 101 major nadis branch out into lesser nadis and these in turn to still lesser ones, making a total of more than 700 million nadis, along which the life-giving currents are believed to flow.

In Chinese medical theory the vital bipolar yang-yin energy that is everywhere diffused in the universe flows through the body in the form of a vitalizing breath called *ch'i,* Here too it is thought that the vital elements are distributed through twelve (or fourteen) major channels or meridians, assisted by thousands of lesser arteries.

According to the Tibetan system the subtle body is nourished by a network of *rtsa,* 'veins', which carry the essence of the fluids and airs that are required for the vitality and the preservation of the body. In its grosser form one class of rtsa is visible as the blood vessels, and the movement of blood within the rtsa is responsible for the pulse*.

Because of the connection that was believed to exist between an internal organ and the outside of the body, many ancient healing systems diagnosed disorders of deep-seated organs by manual examination or palpation of the body surface, and also took particular note of various blemishes, moles, beauty spots, pimples, wrinkles and other skin conditions and diseases. Chinese, Korean, Japanese and other Far Eastern healers, for example, believed that a mole on the wing of the nose indicated a disturbance of the large intestine, and a defect on the lobe of the ear, of the small intestine.

Similarly, the treatment of disease in a particular organ was effected by touching, stimulating or administering remedies to a part of the body surface sometimes remote from the organ concerned. Thus in ancient Egypt where the *metu* theory prevailed, eye diseases were treated by dropping medicinal oils into the ears, heart troubles by enemas, and lung afflictions by applying curative salves to the soles of the feet.

The taoists, who elaborated the Chinese doctrine of meridians as an aid to sex-magical rites, found that pressure on a certain part of the middle finger, while the other fingers were bent in a certain way, would cause an erection, and pressure on a point at the corner of the chin would prevent the emission of semen. Again, pressing a point located along the leg about a span above the heel, would diminish a man's sexual potency.

In India there are specialists in this type of therapy, who with their knowledge of the nadis and chakras can stop a headache by massaging one of the ribs, or relieve asthma by pressing a point behind the ears, or cure constipation by tapping the navel. This knowledge resides in families and is handed down as a family secret.

The discovery that there exists an interconnection between an internal organ and some surface area of the body, apparently unconnected with it, may have been made accidentally, perhaps in battle, where it may have been found that an arrow striking one part of the body, adversely affected or cured some malady in another part. This may have been confirmed by the observation that during certain illnesses some specific area of the body becomes more tender than others. Doctors are aware that a pain in the shoulder-blade may indicate trouble in the gall-bladder, pain in the left arm may be a sign of heart disease.

All healing systems based on the theory of the subtle arteries carried out therapy by pressure, irritation, massage, stimulation or 'feeding' of the part believed to be connected with the diseased organ. Similar notions are also found in a number of later physiological systems, all of which may be summarized as below.

(1) There exists within the etheric double, between twelve to thirty-six major arteries or channels, which branch off into a system of lesser and lesser 'arteries' and 'capillaries', ramifying through the whole body.

(2) The subtle nutritive potencies of breath, blood, warmth, and 'life force' are conveyed through this network of channels and arteries to all parts of the body.

(3) At certain intervals along these arteries are situated tiny nodes or points of interconnection.

(4) Each node is a nexus of invisible 'nerves' and is directly connected with a particular part of the body, or organ, or part of an organ, whose functioning it controls.

(5) Hundreds of these invisible nodes, each scarcely larger than a pinhead, are located along the skin and subcutaneous tissues.

(6) There is a hidden connection between internal organs and some outward point on the body's surface located in the vicinity of its governing node. The physical organ and the node are the two 'poles' which provide the means of diagnosis and cure of diseases.

(7) A knowledge of these nodes, their precise location, and the organs they govern is therefore essential for anyone practising healing by such methods as Chinese acupuncture or Hindu sri-vidya.

(8) The channels, arteries and nodes of the subtle body do not follow any paths known to western anatomy, are not only invisible to the naked eye but undetectable by scientific instruments, and are not to be identified with the nervous, venous, arterial, vascular or lymphatic systems. The location of nodes is not amenable to textbook classification.

(9) How and where to find the node, and above all what treatment to apply to it, were secrets transmitted to those who had the required degree of sensitivity. For the node was actually a psychic point, and its presence made itself felt to the right practitioner and this came either through practice and the development of very sensitive fingers, or by a sort of sixth sense.

Books

Brockbank, William, *Ancient Therapeutic Arts*, Heinemann, London, 1945.
Clements, F. E., *Primitive Concepts of Disease*, Berkeley, California, 1932.
Chalioungui, P., *Magic and Medical Science in Ancient Egypt*, Hodder & Stoughton, London, 1963.
Gordon, B. L., *Medicine Throughout Antiquity*, Davis, Philadelphia, 1949.
Rechung, Lama, *Tibetan Medicine*, Wellcome Institute, London, 1973.
Skitter, M., *Chakras in Hindu Esoteric Physiology*, Calcutta, 1936.
Thorwald, Jürgen, *Science and Secrets of Early Medicine*, Thames & Hudson, London, 1962.
Veith, Ilza, *The Yellow Emperor's Classic of Internal Medicine*, Williams & Wilkins, Baltimore, 1949.
Zimmer, Henry, *Hindu Medicine*, Johns Hopkins University Press, Baltimore, 1948.

SUGGESTION

A comprehensive term for a process by which ideas and impulses are introduced into the mind, creating a tendency to believe in them without rational or critical thought. Suggestion lies at the root of our upbringing and education; it can account for many of our likes and dislikes, and our prejudices, and may be a decisive factor in the formation of our character. As a result of suggestion we tend to conform to our social circle in dress, habit and behaviour.

Waking suggestions are in constant operation. The contagion of a yawn is practically irresistible. Few can read a medical book without getting morbid ideas themselves. Laughter, coughing, clearing the throat, can spread from one person to another. Watching or hearing someone vomiting will often induce nausea in others. People are at all times subjected to a barrage of suggestions or ideas presented to them in everyday life and activity. Newspapers, advertisements, commercial propaganda, fashion displays, political campaigns, books, magazines, films, radio and television are today's principal media through which suggestions are incessantly implanted.

Apart from these, parents, friends, teachers, superiors, leaders and other agents also make a substantial contribution to the fund of suggestions that determine a person's way of life. In all cases, authority, confidence, status, fame (good or bad), age, experience, rank, a commanding presence, 'hypnotic' eyes, a resonant voice, a gift for words, help considerably in increasing an agent's power of suggestion. The shaman and the sorcerer rely as much on these gifts to bend a subject to their will, as does the dictator in the political arena.

Furthermore, suggestion can be operative in groups, so that if one person has a hallucinatory experience such as a vision, a number of others may soon have it too. On a larger scale mass suggestion is frequently found in an atmosphere of heightened emotional expectation, mental strain and tension, as seen in crusades, religious revivals, mass social movements, and these often rise to a considerable pitch, becoming virtually psychic epidemics, like the flagellation and dancing manias of the middle ages, the violent passion of political rallies and public demonstrations, and other outbreaks of mob hysteria.

Suggestions may be made directly or indirectly, to the conscious or unconscious mind, by word, gesture, picture or symbol. They are most effective when they touch upon one's personal appearance, desires (especially love emotions), hopes, fears, beliefs, family or security. They are reinforced by repetition.

Suggestions may be made doubly effective through hypnosis, which has been described as a method of inducing an increased state of suggestibility. During hypnosis a suggestion may be made to be acted out immediately, or at some later period after the hypnotic trance is over. The latter is then known as a post-hypnotic suggestion.

Auto-suggestion (also called self-hypnosis) is achieved by the person repeating a short affirmative suggestion to himself, preferably just before going to sleep and immediately on waking up, and sometimes during the day. The French physician, Émile Coué (d. 1926), offered an all-purpose formula that was to be repeated to oneself over and over again: 'Every day in every way I am getting better and better.' Concentration, suggestive evocation, rhythmic movements, may all be employed to assist auto-hypnosis, and often precede such supra-normal feats as fire-walking, in which a trance-like state is first induced in the participant.

Again, suggestions are an important arm of politics, well exemplified in the communist technique of brain-washing, where threats, intimidation, coercion, insomnolence, torture, alternating with cajolery, kindness and sympathy are used to confuse and break down a person's mental resistance. After the brain-washing the victim becomes amenable to indoctrination, and is prepared to confess to any crime or reveal any secret. Brain-washing is also referred to as 'induced political psychosis', 'menticide' or 'conditioning'.

Suggestibility, or the readiness to accept suggestion, varies considerably with different individuals. From a study of hypnosis it has been found that almost any person can be hypnotized, except imbeciles and the hopelessly insane. Hysterics are either very easy or very difficult to put under hypnosis. Cyclothymes or manic-depressives are more suggestible than schizophrenics. Primitive people, anaemic persons, the uneducated, men *en masse* are more credulous, and therefore also more suggestible. But it is not true that those who are susceptible to hypnosis are necessarily of low intelligence, submissive, gullible, have feeble will power, or lack emotional stability. Nervous excitement or fear of being hypnotized makes a person less amenable. The susceptibility of a person to hypnosis is increased if he has been previously hypnotized. Suggestibility is also increased by fatigue, strong emotion, drugs, hysteria. Willing subjects are easier to hypnotize, the unwilling or resisting very difficult.

There is no difference in the suggestibility of males and females. The social position of a person does not influence his suggestibility. Children above the age of three are more suggestible than adults. The age of seven has been found to be the time of maximum suggestibility, decreasing till the age of sixteen, and thereafter remaining constant. Suggestions (including hypnosis) can be induced at a distance by speaking through a telephone or over the radio or on television, and even by letter. Some believe it is possible to hypnotize animals and induce in them the state known as cateplexy.

The study of suggestion reveals the seemingly inexhaustible potentialities of body and mind, especially as seen in hypnosis. It would appear that the mental capacity and physical strength and endurance of the human being are far greater than is generally realized. By suggestion men have brought on sickness in themselves and in others, given them disease and mental illness, as is often found in psychosomatic sickness. It is possible for a man to suggest himself to death. Xenophrenic states of all kinds can be brought about by suggestion, and hallucinations and delusions presented as real. States akin to clairvoyance and paraperception can be brought about under hypnosis, and it would seem possible to regress back in time and to look ahead into the future during states induced by suggestion.

Under hypnosis the body can be made to feel pain and react as if to pain, without cause. Thus, by suggesting that a cold metal applied to his arm is actually hot, a man will wince, and blisters will appear on his arm. Or a hot metal can be applied to the skin without pain being felt then or afterwards, and the blisters which form will show no sign of inflammation and will heal rapidly. The Scottish magnetizer (earlier name for hypnotist) and surgeon, James Esdaile (d. 1859), performed hundreds of major and countless minor operations on patients without anaesthetics and by means of suggestion alone. Another Scottish magnetizer, James Braid (d. 1850), noted how a weakling who could not lift a weight of twenty pounds with both hands could, when hypnotized, easily raise with his little finger a weight of thirty pounds. Under hypnosis a person can inhale deeply a bottle of ammonia without spluttering or coughing; he can become drunk on water; his body can become cataleptic, a condition impossible for him to assume during wakefulness; he can revive lost memories and the remembrance of past incidents not normally accessible to recall, even from his earliest childhood and infancy. He can be induced to states of laughter and tears, show outstanding dramatic flair and powers of impersonation. He can diagnose his own ailments and prescribe for them, and can be cured of bad habits and neurotic states. Menstruation, lactation, micturition, bowel action, can all be affected by suggestion. Body temperature can be raised or lowered, the temperature of the two hands may be made to differ, one being warm the other cold.

Suggestion can create many states or manifestations found in hysteria, like analgesia (loss of pain sensation), topoalgia (sensation of pain without cause), euphoria (abnormal feeling of elation and happiness), hyperaesthesia (a heightening of the sense faculties), hyperacuity of the powers of observation and attention. It can also account for many supposedly occult and supernatural phenomena such as the stigmata, automatism, and the feats of shamans, witch-doctors and voodoo priests.

Books

Baudouin, A. Charles, *Suggestion and Autosuggestion*, Allen & Unwin, London, 1922.
Bernheim, H., *De la suggestion*, 2nd edn, Paris, 1887.

Castiglioni, A., *Adventures of the Mind*, New York, 1946.
Frank, J. D., *Persuasion and Healing*, Oxford University Press, London, 1961.
Hadfield, J. A., 'The Influence of Suggestion on Body Temperature', *Lancet*, 1920, I, p. 68 *et seq.*
Hull, C. L., *Hypnosis and Suggestibility*, Appleton-Century, New York, 1933.
Meerloo, J. A. M., *The Rape of the Mind: The Psychology of Thought Control*, Grosset & Dunlap, New York, 1956.
Sargant, W., *Battle for the Mind*, Pan Books, London, 1957.
Siddis, Boris, *The Psychology of Suggestion*, New York, 1898.
Tuckey, C. L., *Treatment by Hypnotism and Suggestion*, 6th edn., Baillière, London, 1913.
Vasiliev, Leonid L., *Experiments in Mental Suggestion*, Gally Hill Press, Church Crookham, England, 1963.
Winn, R. (ed.), *Psychotherapy in the Soviet Union*, Grove Press, New York, 1961.

SWEAT

Sweat is secreted by tiny glands, two to three million of them, that are distributed over the skin. Sweating regulates the temperature of the body and this is controlled by the medulla of the brain. Like urine, sweat is an excretion and is constantly being exuded by the pores. Even when the body is inactive, over a pint of sweat is lost through evaporation every day. The activity of the sweat glands is influenced by the nervous system; and shame, fright, trepidation, panic, all increase perspiration.

Many diseases have a characteristic odour, due to differences in the smell of the sweat exuded, and the trained nose of the physician can often help in their diagnosis: there are the odours of tuberculosis, syphilis, rheumatism, uraemia, scurvy, typhoid, cholera, smallpox and diphtheria. The kind of sweat exuded during different emotions and different activities also varies. The sweat of anger differs from that of happiness, the sweat of love from that of fear. Sweat can be coloured by different kidney and blood conditions and a person's sweat may have a blue or even reddish tint. The exudation of red sweat from the palms of the hands has occasionally been mistaken for religious stigmata.

Created as it is from the heat of the living flesh, and arising from the inmost depths of the body, sweat is believed to be charged with power. It is thought to be able to generate a kind of magical heat, and sweating for magical ends is commonly undergone in many parts of the world. In Indian occultism it is achieved through asceticism, celibacy, breathing exercises and special stances. North American shamans make use of sweating cabinets to induce violent perspiration and so generate magical fire. Creative and magical generation of heat was also practised among the early Indo-Europeans, and the sweat that was formed as a result of such heat was thought to have very special properties.

Sweat has many healing, rejuvenating, aphrodisiacal and other virtues. Among the ancient Hebrews it was believed that the odour of or contact with the perspiration of virgins helped to promote youthfulness in the aged. In Rome the sweat and dust removed by strigils or scrapers from the dirty bodies of the gladiators was collected, mixed with oil and sold as *rhypos,* which was applied to the genitals to confer on them some of the prowess of the athletes.

The odour of sweat has an erotic appeal at certain times, and can arouse sexual desire in the opposite sex. The passion of Henry IV (d. 1610) of France for the beautiful Gabrielle d'Estrées is said to have arisen when he dried his forehead with her handkerchief during a ball. The course of the seducer can be made easier by taking advantage of the heady effects of sweat. Laurent relates how a lusty young peasant employed the device of letting his chosen victims smell a handkerchief that had been allowed to lie under his armpit during a fast moving dance. In northern Germany the belief was current till recently that the beloved must follow the wish of her lover if he gives her an apple to eat after it has been impregnated with the odour of his armpit.

Sexual excitement produces its own kind of sweat, created by the heat of the sexual organs. In Roman mythology the god Conisalus presided over the perspiration of copulating couples.

Books

Bloch, Iwan, *Odoratus Sexualis,* Panurge Press, New York, 1934.
Laurent, E. and Nagouri, P., *Magica Sexualis,* Falstaff Press, New York, 1934.
Onians, R. B., *The Origins of European Thought,* Cambridge University Press, 1951.

SYMPATHY

The affinity that subsists between one thing and another, is one of the basic factors governing the operation of the universe, for it underlies the coherence and concord of animate and inanimate nature. Sympathy is the connecting link between all interrelated things. In ancient and medieval theory the stars and planets influence one another and everything else through forces based on pathemic* alliances that determine how they shall mutually operate one with the other.

According to the learned Jesuit kabbalist, Athanasius Kircher (c. 1680), the attraction and repulsion that is universally observed among things depends on the magnetism that interpenetrates the whole cosmos. Sympathy is responsible for the law of attraction by which bodies tend to gravitate towards one another, and by which distant stars shed their beneficence upon the earth.

Early thinkers explained the phenomena of weight and the fall of bodies by the theory that the core of the earth is sympathetic towards all material objects and tends to draw them downwards. The upward motion of fire and smoke, on the other hand, are due to their sympathy with the sky. Iron is sympathetically drawn to the magnet. Tropism, or the tendency of an organism to move in a particular direction – the roots downwards, the leaves upwards – reflects the same law of sympathy operating in the animate world. The sunflower faithfully turns its gaze to the sun; the acacia opens its petals at daybreak and closes them at dusk; the nightshade loves the night-time and the moonlight, all because of sympathetic alliances. Among themselves plants have their own occult affinities: the vine is in harmony with the olive tree; the ranunculus feels an affection for the water-lily; the rue for the fig.

Astrology, which is based on the same principle, believes that persons born under certain configurations of the heavenly bodies that are in harmonious aspect, will themselves be attracted to each other. Marsilio Ficino (d. 1499), platonist and physician, ascribed the attraction between friends to synastry, because they were both born under the 'same star'.

The universal magnetism that is everywhere in operation brings two persons into sympathy, and this is further strengthened or modified by the nature and temperament of the people in question. The attraction of friend for friend, of lover for beloved, of parents for children, of men for animals, were all said to have a foundation in the law of sympathy. Such a sympathy also strengthens the telepathic* bond between two persons. The scholastic philosopher, William of Auvergne (d. 1249), tells of a woman who could feel the presence of the man she loved when he was two miles away.

In quality, sympathy is an expansive and outward moving force; it enlarges the soul of the person who is under its influence.

> Sympathy or compassion [wrote the English mystic, Robert Fludd (d. 1637)] proceedeth from a certain dilation of spirits in two or more particulars, or an emitting of their internal beams of life or essence, positively or benignly, from the centre unto the circumference, making a concord between two homogenial natures. Contrariwise, antipathy, by contracting the beams moveth after an opposite manner.

Sympathy may be established and emphasized by: (1) physical resemblance, which is often revealed by a 'signature', or distinctive mark; (2) similarity of substance, since things made of the same material are intrinsically related; all things made of wood are bound together; brother and sister are likewise in mutual affinity; (3) causality, that is, cause and effect, are related, for example, a creator and his creation, an artist and his work, a murderer and his victim, a wound and the sword that caused it; (4) sound or vibration, so that to utter a sound is to evoke the thing signified by it; to pronounce a name is to become sympathetically linked with what is named; (5) imitation, so that a mimetic action establishes a kinship with the original activity; (6) contagion, or intimate physical contact, that links one thing with another by invisible bonds thereafter; (7) thought and feeling, so that concentration, devotion, prayer, desire, hatred, jealousy, are means of establishing a link with their object.

The practical application for magical purposes of the principles of interrelation, as found in the doctrine of sympathy, is known as sympathetic magic, also called imitative, contagious, mimetic or homoeopathic magic. Sympathetic magic reaches its culmination in the making of poppets or wax images to represent a person one wishes to injure.

Books
See under pathemia

TASTE

The sensation by which the flavour and quality of a thing is perceived, depends on the receptor cells called taste-buds, situated in the tongue and certain other parts of the palate and mouth. It is closely related to the sense of smell. The four principal kinds of taste are sweet, sour, salt and bitter, though some classifications add a fifth, pungent, and still others a sixth, astringent.

Great stress is laid on taste in Chinese and Indian medical treatises. The earliest such treatise in China, the *N'ei Ching,* attributed to the Yellow Emperor, Huang Ti (c. 2600 BC), speaks of the importance of maintaining the harmony of the five tastes (acid, sweet, salt, bitter, pungent) for sex potency and enjoyment. Hindu medical texts speak of the curative value of the different tastes, either singly or in combination.

In the medieval western tradition the four tastes (bitter, sour, salt, sweet) were associated with the four humours*, and were sometimes schematically represented at the four faces of a tetrahedron or the four corners of a square, and their relationships worked out. To this, occultists gave further elaborations on esoteric lines.

The taste of *sweet* is mostly confined to the tip of the tongue. According to Chinese and Hindu medicine, sweet things increase phlegm, chyle and flesh, appease thirst and hunger, and in excess cause flatulence and mental depression. The *sour* or acid taste is appreciated from the sides of the tongue; sourness increases salivation and appetite and improves the digestion. In excess it causes heartburn and reduces the procreative juices. The taste of *salt* stimulates digestion and purifies the blood. In excess saltiness causes headache and convulsions. Things that are *bitter* are sensed from the back of the tongue; they stimulate the appetite, clear the complexion, reduce body heat. In excess bitter foods make the stomach insensitive and the spleen dry. A *pungent* taste is not a pure taste, but results from one or more of the four basic tastes, combined with the sharp burning sensation felt on eating such things as hot pickles, chillies and spiced condiments. Pungent foods provoke the appetite, lessen corpulence, purify the blood, clear the head. In excess they cause the face to become drawn. Similarly, the *astringent* taste is not pure, but results from the styptic and contractile effect of certain substances on the tongue and mouth. Astringent foods augment the action of the other tastes.

Taste is closely connected with certain psychological conditions, and a predilection for particular tastes may indicate abnormalities. Perversions of taste occur in pregnancy, hysteria and insanity. The loss of taste, known as *ageusia,* may indicate a mental deficiency of some kind, but may also result from dryness of the tongue, injury to the taste buds or the taste area in the brain.

Books

Sastri, B., *The Medical Lore of the Ancient Hindus,* Madras, 1901.
Veith, Ilza, *The Yellow Emperor's Classic of Internal Medicine.* Williams & Wilkins, Baltimore, 1949.

TEARS

Tears are regarded as potent drops, not far behind blood in occult significance. Man is the only animal that sheds tears as a result of deep emotion. Tears may form in the eyes of a dog, horse, monkey or other animal, but they probably have nothing to do with their feelings. Crocodile tears are of course mythical. Babies do not usually cry with tears until they are about six weeks old. According to a European superstition current in the middle ages, a witch could not shed tears.

The tears of exalted or holy personages are said to have great healing and restorative virtues. The shortest verse in the Bible, 'Jesus wept' (John 11:35), is believed to signify the outpouring of divine love and benevolent power through Christ that was necessary to raise Lazarus from the dead. The tears of the sinner are efficacious for his salvation. Springing from an awareness of wrong-doing and a desire for repentance, they cause the fruits of conversion to sprout in the heart and are a prerequisite for redemption.

Tears, whether of joy or sadness, accompany every important event in life. The infant cries, or is made to cry by slapping, at birth, and whether tears flow or not they are presumed to be present. Some parents clandestinely pinch their children at baptism, in order to cause the auspicious tears to flow. It is regarded as an unlucky sign in many communities if a bride does not cry at some stage of the marriage ceremony, or during consummation. This betokens her maidenly modesty, arouses the ardour of the spouse, ensures fertility, and is essential for her future welfare. In some parts of Europe it is considered proper for the bride to cry if her marriage is to be a happy one. Hence the saying, 'She who does not cry before, must cry after.'

Death, of course, is almost universally a time for shedding tears, as part of the lamentation accompanying mourning. Even where there is no real sorrow, the ritual of weeping must be observed. In some parts of Scotland doors and windows used to be marked with tadpole-like drawings to show that tears were being shed in the house on the death of a loved one. Till a generation ago Persian and Indian mourners used to cry into tear bottles which were then stored away.

When a person is moved by strong emotion, his heart is suffused with heaviness, his breath chokes him and he often breaks out into an involuntary sob. The whole face responds to the feeling, the muscles contract, the blood vessels in the eyes become engorged and the eyes fill with tears. After weeping, according to the medieval physicians, the collected humours are flushed from the system, the body is relieved of an oppressive weight, and the spirit feels lighter. Tears clear the eyes, nose, lungs, heart, brain, mind and soul, and give us a different view of the world.

Tears and weeping, being the outward expression of deep distress, are a powerful means of evoking a response of sympathy from others, of softening their hearts and influencing their feelings, and have contributed to a large extent to the development of man as a kindly and compassionate being.

Books

Campbell, H., 'The Therapeutical Aspects of Talking, Shouting, Singing, Laughing, Crying, Sighing and Yawning', *Lancet*, 1897, 2, 140–2.
Darwin, Charles, *Expression of Emotion in Man and Animals*, Murray, London, 1877.
Dunbar, F., *Emotions and Bodily Changes*, Columbia University Press, New York, 1954.
Montagu, Ashley, *Man in Process*, Mentor, New York, 1962.
Scheler, Max, *The Nature of Sympathy*, Routledge & Kegan Paul, London, 1954.

TEETH

Normally a child is born toothless, and it was inevitably regarded as a sign of devilish ancestry or disposition to come into the world equipped with teeth. Cutting the upper teeth first was likewise an inauspicious sign.

It is widely believed in many parts of the world that children's milk teeth should be carefully disposed of when they fall out. They have to be buried with suitable ceremony. In some places newly fallen teeth are placed near a rat-hole in order that the child's teeth might grow as sharp, firm and brilliant as the rat's. In tribal societies any tooth that has fallen out, whether a child's or an adult's, is carefully concealed lest it fall into the hands of a sorcerer, who might work evil magic with it.

In many primitive communities the teeth are subjected to various kinds of mutilation or interference at initiation ceremonies. Thus, in Australia the teeth, usually the two lower incisors, are knocked out, or two or more teeth broken, by means of wooden wedges and a stone. The people of Madagascar make their teeth as sharp as a shark's by filing them to fine points. In Indochina, Java and Indonesia, the teeth are indelibly stained with a kind of black lacquer, or otherwise artificially discoloured.

Like bones, teeth are virtually indestructible by natural means, and they have been worn as talismans in all parts of the world, including Europe and America. It was popularly believed in Europe that if the first tooth shed by a child were worn by a woman around her waist she would be protected from all uterine troubles. Also that a tooth taken from a skull and worn as an amulet around the neck cured migraine and toothache. The pulverized teeth of an executed criminal were excellent for the restoration of lost virility.

The ancient Greeks believed that widely spaced teeth permitted the inflow of soul-stuff and vital energy into the body, and that a person with such teeth received more strength from his surroundings and possessed greater erotic power than others.

Books

Fauchard, P., *The Surgeon Dentist: A Treatise on the Teeth,* 1746; Butterworth, London, edn of 1946.

Lufkin, A. W., *A History of Dentistry,* 2nd edn, Henry Kimpton, London, 1948.

Radford, E. and M. A., *Encyclopedia of Superstitions,* 2nd edn, Rider, London, 1961.

TELEPATHY

(Lit. 'far-feeling'), a term coined by the psychical researcher, F. W. H. Myers (d. 1901), for the direct awareness by one person of what is in the mind of another, by means other than the known sensory channels. This awareness may be one of images, thoughts, feelings or mental states; it may not be formulated in words, although words may be received.

The faculty is a form of paraperception*, and is known by a number of other names, such as telesthesia, 'far-feeling', also coined by Myers; cryptesthesia, 'hidden feeling', coined by Professor Charles Richet (d. 1935); clairsentience, 'clear-feeling'; thought or mind-reading; thought transference. The term telepathy is usually confined to spontaneous communication between one mind and another, in contrast to ESP (extra-sensory perception), which is the experimental study of this and other paranormal phenomena.

Telepathy is not modified by distance or time. As a rule a telepathic impression received by one person coincides with the moment it actually occurs to the other person, but it may also precede or follow it. Thus, a mother may receive a telepathic impression of her son dying in a distant land, and it is later found that the time of his death coincided with the time she received the message. But in the case of precognitive telepathy, the impression may be received days before the occurrence.

Medieval writers postulated a 'sense of nature' which enables a person to enter into the feelings of others. The scholastic philosopher, William of Auvergne (d. 1249), described it as a sublimer sense than any human apprehension, and nobler and more akin to prophecy. By means of this sense one could discern the presence of a burgher or a felon, a virgin or a harlot. He quotes the case of a woman who could feel the approach of a man she loved when he was still two miles away.

Johannes Trithemius (d. 1516), German occultist and adept at telepathy, declared:

> I am able to communicate my thoughts a hundred miles away to a person who knows the art, and can do this without writing, words or signs. It can be made as clear and explicit as may be required, and that by natural means without the aid of spirits or any other kind of superstition.

Paracelsus (d. 1541) wrote, 'By the magic power of the will a person on this side of the sea may make a person on the other side know what he is thinking.' And again, 'It is possible when two natures are in harmony, for one to understand the feelings that move the other, though the latter be separated by hundreds of miles.'

It is often difficult to draw a line between telepathy and clairvoyance, 'clear-seeing', or perceiving objects or events by paranormal perception, without the aid of the eyes, since what is 'seen', or indeed any existing piece of information in the mind of one person, can theoretically be 'picked up' from the mind of another person by a sensitive. Even facts known only to a deceased person and brought to light subsequently by a sensitive have been attributed to telepathy. This is so because all such data, though known only to the deceased while he was alive, might have been unconsciously transmitted by him to a person now living, and this in turn picked up from the mind of the latter by the psychic. Information forgotten and lost for centuries might in this manner be preserved as a result of such unconscious telepathic storage by individuals in successive generations, and then suddenly recovered by being picked up at some time by somebody and thus brought to light.

But the hypothesis of mind-tapping on this scale presents even greater problems for the sceptic, and is even more far-fetched than the explanation that telepathy and other paranormal faculties are simply a psychic gift, or a more highly developed faculty that in a lesser degree is possessed by all.

In the light of recent research it has been suggested that thought is a form of energy which has 'field' properties that are within the scope of scientific research. EEG tests in the USA and USSR further suggest that a perfect synchronicity of alpha rhythms or brain waves* is maintained by both parties during transmission.

Books

Carington, Whately, *Telepathy: An Outline of its Facts, Theory and Implications*, Methuen, London, 1945.

Ehrenwald, H. J., *Telepathy and Medical Psychology*, Norton, New York, 1948.

Garrett, Eileen, *Telepathy: In Search of a Lost Faculty*, New York, Garrett-Helix, 1941.

Heywood, R., *Telepathy and Allied Phenomena*, Psychical Research Society, London, 1948.

Moncrieff, M. M., *The Clairvoyant Theory of Perception*, Faber, London, 1951.

Puharich, Andrija, *Beyond Telepathy*, Darton, Longman & Todd, 1962.

Tischner, Rudolph, *Telepathy and Clairvoyance*, Kegan Paul, London, 1925.

Ullmann, M. and Krippner, S., *Dream Studies and Telepathy*, Parapsychology Foundation, New York, 1970.

Warcollier, R., *Experiments in Telepathy*, Allen & Unwin, London, 1939.

TESTICLES

The male sexual glands are responsible for producing male hormones and sperm cells, a process continuing till comparatively old age. These glands consist of two 'balls', contained within a bag called the scrotum. Just as the penis is said to correspond to the vagina, so the testicles have been compared to the ovaries, and the scrotum to the womb. In Shakespeare's time the word for scrotum was *cod,* derived from an Old English word meaning 'womb'. Among the synonyms for testicles are: bollocks, balls, cobblers, cod (also for penis), cullions, eggs, knockers (also for female breasts), marbles, nuts, orchis, pounders, secrets, stones, testes.

As the most intimate part of his body, the testes are the ultimate badge of a man's virility and the test of his worth as a male. The absence of testicles or their excision by castration removes the essential maleness of a man. Hence the possession of a penis, but especially of the testicles, was a prerequisite for the priesthood in many religions, and anyone who did not possess these tokens of perfect manhood was, in Jewish law for instance, forbidden to enter 'the congregation of the Lord' (Deut. 23:1). The Chinese spoke of the testicles as *yin-nang*, 'secret pouch', and regarded them as being in the care of the deities in the highest heaven.

No pope could be elected to the papal office who lacked testicles, and his eligibility was accordingly tested in the specially built Porphyry Chair, a model of which can be seen in the Louvre, in Paris. The pope, it is said, would sit on the horseshoe-shaped seat and a cardinal, after checking by manual examination, would proclaim, 'Testiculos habet et bene pendentes' (He has testicles and they hang well) (Smith, 1968, p. 77).

Being the repository of man's seed, the testicles were regarded as so sacred that in Jewish law if a woman, even to save her husband who was fighting with another man, took hold of the 'secret parts' of the adversary, her hand was to be cut off (Deut. 25:12). In many ancient communities injury to a person's testicles could result in the execution of the man responsible.

The words 'testimony' and 'testament', signifying a solemn bond or pledge, are derived from the word 'testicle', because in earlier days people covered the testicles with the hand when they made a solemn avowal. When Abraham desired his servant to take an oath he told him to 'put thy hand under my thigh' (Gen. 24:2), a euphemism for 'over my testicles'.

In Latin the word *testis* is used to mean both witness and testicles, and the early Romans, like the Jews, took oaths with hands placed on their testes. This custom survived in northern Europe till at least the tenth century. An article of the law made by Olaf the Good for the province of Wales in England stated that a violated woman prosecuting her ravisher had to take an oath with one hand on the relics of a saint, and her left hand holding the testicles of the accused (Dulaure, 1930, p. 142).

As oaths were taken on the testes, so a curse was put on a man by the curser touching his own testicles and pronouncing the curse. Such a curse was said to be infallible but replete with ill-effects for the curser, who 'destroyed his own generation' thereby. Similarly, any statement or action could be brought to nought by a man touching his own testicles and uttering an expletive synonym for the testes. The modern expression 'Balls!', suggesting that something is dismissible or beneath contempt, is a relic of a curse of this kind. Similarly the word anathema, for a ritual curse, comes from the Greek *ana-tithemi*, 'to place upon', words which were once accompanied by the placing of the hands on the speaker's testicles.

The secret parts played a role in the symbolism of Greek tragedy, the coryphaeus or leader of the chorus representing the glans (Gk. *koryphē*, 'head') of the penis, and the orchestra representing the testicles (Gk. *orchis*) of the god Dionysus, patron deity of rustic Greek drama. The testicles of deities and heroes were productive of many valiant mortals whose exploits fill the pages of mythology. Most twins are associated with testicles.

It is known that two kinds of sperm exist, one that produces the male embryo when united with the ovum, and one that produces the female embryo. The ancients believed that the right testicle, which is higher placed than the left, produced the male seed, and that males were begotten from the right side of the woman; the left testicle of the male and the left side of the woman produced females. The Hebrew name Benjamin signifies 'son of my right hand', i.e. right testicle (*see* laterality).

Keeping a cool head is reputedly linked with keeping the testicles cool, and displaying the phlegmatic imperturbability of the male, in contrast to the agitation of the female. It is said that coolness of testicles, though tending to cause baldness, increases male fertility, and that rats can be made infertile by wrapping their scrotal sacs in cotton wool. For the same reason the kilt, worn by the Scots, allowing free movement and access of fresh air, is said to make for virility, as compared with the constricting trousers.

Like other suspended objects (the bell, the hanged man) the testes symbolize communion between heaven and earth.

Books

Dulaure, J. A., *The Gods of Generation*, Panurge Press, New York, edn of 1930.
Hannay, J. B., *Sex Symbolism in Religion*, Religious Evolution Research Society, London, 1922.
Humana, Charles and Wu, Wang, *The Ying-Yang: The Chinese Way of Love*, Tandem, London, 1971.
Smith, Anthony, *The Body*, Allen & Unwin, London, 1968.
Wall, O. A., *Sex and Sex Worship*, Kimpton, London, 1919.

THALAMUS

A small but important portion of the brain substance, which, along with the hypothalamus lying immediately beneath it, is embedded in the lower interior part of the brain. Since both lie between the front and back of the brain they are together termed the diencephalon (Gk. *dis*, 'between', *egkephalos*, 'brain'), the interbrain or tweenbrain. The diencephalon is common to all creatures in the evolutionary scale from frogs to men, and hence is included in what is known as the primitive or old brain.

The ancients guessed that these tiny adjuncts were of supreme significance, while medieval physicians attributed almost miraculous qualities to them. The name itself derives from the Greek *thalamos*, 'chamber', meaning the inner bridal chamber in the temple where the hierogamy or mystical marriage of the representatives of the god and goddess was performed.

The thalamus lies on either side of the third ventricle*, and among other things it seems to regulate the idea that a person has of his own body, so that if parts of the thalamus are destroyed or damaged, then the body feels deformed in some way, or bigger, smaller, or heavier than usual.

The hypothalamus is as small as a lump of sugar and is linked with the limbic system of the brain*. It also seems to be the site where the appestat or appetite-controlling element of the individual is located. Part of the hypothalamus constitutes the lower wall of the third ventricle, and it is connected with the infundibulum, which was thought to funnel the transmuted ros* or cerebral fluid into the pituitary* gland hanging by a thin stalk from the base of the hypothalamus.

Modern brain research confirms that these deep-seated primitive regions of the brain play a crucial part in human welfare. Jointly they constitute the centre of the autonomic nervous system, co-ordinating the sympathetic and parasympathetic functions. Some psychologists suggest that the collective unconscious operates from the thalamus. It is also the seat of the instinctual emotions concerned with 'feeling tone', which lends emotional colouring to all psychic processes.

Together the thalamus and hypothalamus, wholly or in part, regulate such involuntary processes as: the heart rate, blood pressure, blood sugar level; the release of adrenal hormones; body temperature; sexual activity and the cycle of the reproductive system; raw emotions like rage; the urine balance of the kidneys; water metabolism and thirst; digestion and appetite; sleeping and waking.

Books

Hess, W. R., *The Functional Organization of the Diencephalon*, Grune & Stratton, New York, 1957.

Lassek, A. M., *The Human Brain: From Primitive to Modern*, Blackwell Scientific Publications, Oxford, 1957.

Poynter, F. N. L. (ed.), *The History and Philosophy of the Brain and Its Functions*, Blackwell, Oxford, 1958.

Walker, A. E., *The Primate Thalamus*, Chicago University Press, 1938.

THOUGHT

Thought is the innermost expression of the human spirit, the whispering of the ego, the mind in action, directed consciousness. It stimulates brain activity and is accompanied by certain molecular movements in the cerebral cortex and the nervous system, producing measurable electrical vibrations. At the same time there is a tendency in thought to seek expression in unconscious movement as revealed in the study of ideodynamics*. A thought does not necessarily consist of words, but rather of a psychic glow, which may or may not be expressed in words.

The elements that go into the thought process are the will*, which provides the impulse for all thinking and activity; the imagination and visualization that enable it to take shape; the pathemic* or emotional content that kindles and colours it; and faith that sustains it. Paracelsus (d. 1541) believed that 'all the wonders of magic are performed by will, imagination and faith.'

According to occultists, the thoughts of individuals determine the kind of psychic 'atmosphere' they live in, and it is therefore essential that the thoughts one holds in mind should be salutary and wholesome in character, otherwise they will prove injurious to the astral body, and through the astral to the physical body. Positive and courageous thoughts create a healthy aura and attract beneficent influences, and thoughts of kindness and sympathy attract similar sentiments from others. By allowing the mind to dwell on depressing and anxious thoughts we create the very conditions we wish to avoid. In the Bible, Job, cursing his fate, exclaims, 'The thing I greatly feared is come upon me' (Job 3:25). It is an established psychosomatic* axiom that thought can cause physical symptoms of distressing maladies and even bring on the disease itself.

Every thought generates a series of radiating and vibratory impulses that have psychic and ultimately physical properties, so that any thought held firmly in the mind over a period of time accumulates energy. Psychoanalysts speak of a *cathexis* (Gk. 'holding'), the accumulation of psychic energy which invests a particular idea. Cathexis is said to be high when a man feels strongly, concentrates hard and imagines vividly. It builds up like an electric battery which constantly seeks to discharge itself, in other words, to find expression and fulfilment. In the case of hatred the cathected energy seeks an outlet in aggression; in a humorous situation, in laughter; in an amorous build-up, in caresses and intercourse. The Arab philosopher, Avicenna (d. 1037), said, 'When ideas and beliefs become firmly fixed in the soul, they necessarily must exist in reality.'

Thought can be sustained, focused, concentrated and projected by prayer, meditation, suggestion, ritual and incantation. It can be transmitted over a distance, as in telepathy*, and turned on people like a ray of power. Satanists and black witches claim that in the course of their training they are taught the secret practice of killing birds in flight by projecting a malicious thought beam at them. Raynor Johnson tells of an Australian friend, Ambrose Pratt, who in the course of meditation accidentally stumbled across a 'power of mind' which could be used to kill. Deciding to put his discovery to the test he stood before a monkeys' cage at the zoo one day, and projected the force at a small animal. Its death followed quickly. Pratt never discussed the matter beyond relating the incident to Johnson, and said that so far as he was concerned the knowledge would die with him.

Recent scientific experiments in psychokinesis* have shown that the emanative power of controlled thought can produce molecular changes in water, and cause objects to move as if propelled by some material force. Thought, according to these findings, would appear to have a concrete character, thus confirming the old occult adage that 'Thoughts are things.' Besides this, clearly defined thoughts are believed to become clothed in an ephemeral elemental essence which under certain circumstances can assume astral substantiality as detached thought-forms* that carry on a temporary independent existence.

What is known as 'group thought'* involves the combined mental energy of several people directed to a specific objective.

Books

Aveling, F., *Directing Mental Energy*, University of London Press, 1927.
Besant, Annie, *Thought Power*, Theosophical Publishing, London, 1903.
Bruner, Jerome S., *A Study of Thinking*, John Wiley, New York, 1956.
Freud, Sigmund, *An Outline of Psychoanalysis*, Hogarth Press, London, 1964.
Groddeck, Georg W., *The Unknown Self*, Vision Press, London, 1951.
Hampshire, S., *Thought and Action*, Chatto & Windus, London, 1959.
Johnson, Raynor C., *The Light and the Gate*, Hodder & Stoughton, London, 1964.
McKellar, Peter, *Imagination and Thinking: A Psychological Analysis*, Basic Books, New York, 1957.
Ostrander, Sheila and Schroeder, Lynn, *PSI: Psychic Discoveries Behind the Iron Curtain*, Sphere Books, London, 1973.
Rapaport, D., *Organization and Pathology of Thought*, Columbia University Press, 1951.
Vinacke, C. E., *The Psychology of Thinking*, McGraw-Hill, New York, 1952.
Wallas, G., *The Art of Thought*, Harcourt Brace, New York, 1926.

THOUGHT-FORM

An astral ent created as a result of concentrated thought. Occultists believe that a thought is not merely an intellectual operation confined to the interior of the skull, but a form of energy that leaves a definite impression on the ether. Every thought produces a radiating vibration or thought wave, which becomes clothed in an ideoplastic elemental essence and has a transient existence on the astral plane.

Mostly these ideoplastic forms are lightly constituted, lacking in energy, and have a very tenuous form, disintegrating almost as soon as they are born and leaving no lasting impression. They may be perceived by sensitives as a feeble glimmer and do not go beyond the aura of the person who generates them, and soon dissolve and vanish like tiny wisps of smoke.

Thoughts that are charged with emotion, on the other hand, such as the passions of love, hatred, jealousy and vengeance, have a longer term of life. The thought energy that is generated by strong feelings can arise like vapour from the mind, assume a shape and split off from the thinker, coloured by his emotions. Any thought strongly held over a period of time accumulates that much more energy and has a correspondingly longer life.

Persistent brooding over a subject may therefore create substantial thought-forms, which hover over the creator and, if unhappy, can cause deep depression. A strong imagination is particularly creative. Charles Dickens (d. 1870) was so absorbed in his characters that they appeared to him and followed him around, and he used to complain that they literally haunted him (Fodor, 1933, p. 382).

Searing thoughts engendered by violence may linger for months, even years, and give the so-called psychic 'atmosphere' to certain localities such as the scenes of murder and suicide and tragic disasters, where the aura may be strong enough for them to be reproduced as apparitions. Phantom armies and ghostly cavalry that are seen in places where great battles were once fought may be the residual thought-forms of long ago.

Countless entities are thus said to be swirling about on the astral plane, some transient, some more obdurate. The thoughts of men beget astral potencies and the man thinking such progeny into existence is responsible for them and accountable for their conduct. An envious wish can create a twisted black shape that will continue its noxious existence if not quenched. Jealousy, rage and hate become terrible monsters. These forms, it is believed, can influence the weak-minded to the point of obsession. Good wishes, prayers for the welfare of others are powerful creations for good. The prayers of a mother for her son can create an angelic entity that will turn him aside from his evil ways. Positive thought-forms are known to be more powerful than negative ones.

From the beginning of time the evil thoughts of men and women have charged the atmosphere around with a deep depression. According to the occultist, Alice Bailey, 'A gigantic thought-form hovers over the entire human family', and she believed that it was the duty of all those who had the strength for it to work towards dissipating the swirling fog in order to help mankind. The inexplicable dread, depression and angst that seem to be universally prevalent today are the result of the passions of greed and lust that seem to be emanating from people everywhere in progressively stronger waves.

A different kind of thought-form can be built up by special occult training and discipline. It then becomes the product of deliberate mental effort. In tantrism the ability to make thought-forms is referred to as *kriya shakti*, 'creative power'. Tibetan magicians have their own magical techniques as a result of which phantom beings called tulpas are called forth. The magician moulds the universal ideoplastic medium or cosmic ether, coagulating it into images and shapes. Such a form conceived by the magician is built up and held by concentrated effort, visualized by his imagination, vitalized by his emotions and sustained by his will. Once it becomes visible it is periodically strengthened and recharged by ritual and sacrifice. Occasionally such an entity can be clothed in a denser vehicle and lead an independent existence, and can allegedly even exist as a human simulacrum.

The most evil of all thought-forms are those that are deliberately created during certain practices involving sex magic and blood sacrifice.

Books

Bailey, Alice, *A Teatise on Cosmic Fire*, 3rd edn, Lucis, New York, 1944.

Besant, Annie and Leadbeater, C. W., *Thoughtforms*, Theosophical Publishing House, Adyar, Madras, 1921.

David-Neel, Alexandra, *With Mystics and Magicians in Tibet*, Penguin Books, Harmondsworth, 1936.

Fodor, Nandor, *Encyclopedia of Psychic Science*, Arthurs Press, London, 1933.

Fortune, Dion, *Psychic Self Defence*, Aquarian Press, London, 1952.

Joire, Paul, *Psychical and Supernormal Phenomena,* Rider, London, 1966.
Walker, Benjamin, *Sex and the Supernatural,* Macdonald, London, 1970.

TONGUE

The organ of speech and taste. It is often regarded as a lying entity, concealing what is in the mind. The Bible frequently mentions the tongue as an organ of mischief, vanity and deceitfulness. The Nubians believe the tip of the tongue to be the seat of all curses and evil wishes. The retroflexing of the tongue, turning it up and back against the roof of the mouth, is a sign of tension, and scriptural references to the tongue cleaving to the roof of the mouth or palate usually indicate silence, dumbness, thirst or penance.

The tongue is a sexual organ. Medieval anatomists equating the parts of the face with the different parts of the body compared the tongue to the penis. The tongue plays an active part in the kiss, in erotic licking of the body of the partner, and in oralism. Sticking out the tongue is a sign of mockery, signifying the 'exposure' of the sex organs. Representations of deities with their tongues lolling out express the passive aspect of an ithyphallic figure. In certain religious penances the tongue is cut or pierced to show the abnegation of sexual activity for a certain period. As a sacrifice to the gods, the Mayas would mutilate the tongue by passing through it a cord set with thorns.

In taoist respiratory techniques the practitioner turns his tongue up and back arching it as far back as he can along the roof of the mouth. Taoists also resort to the technique as a means of increasing the flow of saliva* which they regard as a very important fluid. The related yogic practice of *khechari,* 'void-moving', consists of turning the tongue up and back towards the gullet in order to block the nasal passages that open into the mouth, so that the ros* or immortal dew from the cranium does not seep down and get dissipated, but is used and absorbed by the yogi himself. To assist in the attainment of this feat, the frenum or membranous tissue is cut and the tongue lengthened by regular pulling over a period of six to twelve months till it is long enough, when outside the mouth, to touch the point between the eyebrows. It is part of an intrajaculation procedure in sex-magic.

In certain goetic operations such as the Bon rite of *rolangs,* 'corpse-raising', and the Hindu necromantic working of the *nīla-sādhana,* 'black rite', a cadaver is imbued with a momentary semblance of life and its tongue bitten off as it cries out. Among the secret forest rites of the Tlingits in Alaska is one in which the novice shaman goes into a forest after the death of an older magician and waits for the appearance of an otter or other animal whose tongue he wrenches off and eats, in order to acquire the magical powers of the deceased shaman, for it is in the tongue of the animal that the old preceptor takes up his temporary abode.

Books

Crawley, Ernest, *Oath, Curse, and Blessing,* Watts, London, 1934.

David-Neel, Alexandra, *With Mystics and Magicians in Tibet*, Penguin Books, Harmondsworth, 1936.
Walker, Benjamin, *Hindu World*, 2 vols, Allen & Unwin, London, 1968.
Windstedt, R. O., *The Malay Magician*, Routledge & Kegan Paul, London, 1951.

TOUCH

The feeling that is communicated by the sensory nerves of the skin surface in various parts of the body. Apart from what we call touch proper, the sense of touch borders on our perception of pressure, of heat and cold, of pain and pleasure, of position and movement. In occult terms physical contact with a person or thing brings their two auras into juxtaposition. If two objects agree (pathemically, astrologically, electrically) they are in sympathy or in rapport, they harmonize, love and get along together. If the two auras remain unresponsive they are apathetic or indifferent. If they repel then antipathy, animosity, disharmony and hatred arise.

The areas through which these feelings are most actively communicated are the hands, especially the fingertips, the genital organs, and the erogenous zones, although any physical proximity communicates the sensation of touch. It is believed that a considerable biomagnetic exchange takes place in touching and that a strong emanation of bioflux* flows from the touching agent to the one touched, or from the latter to the former.

Inanimate objects can also receive, store and communicate this magnetism. Clothes, furniture, gems, jewels, acquire an aura, good or bad depending on the touch-empathy of the person wearing or using them. Statues of gods were often touched because it was believed that the magical power inherent in them would flow from them to the toucher. So also, consecrated lamps, rings and talismans must be touched, rubbed or worn, to draw out their magical power.

Touch therefore is believed to communicate an auric contagion (a word that is derived from the Latin *tangere*, 'to touch') that might be good or bad. High-caste Hindus never allowed their bodies to be touched by others, and to the present day many of them do not shake hands by way of greeting in order to avoid possible psychic contamination. For this reason a large segment of low-caste peoples in India used to be classed as Untouchables, because contact with them, according to the higher castes, resulted in impurity.

On the other hand touch also communicates feelings of agreement and solidarity. Politicians are aware that personal contact establishes a commitment, and that a friendly handshake at the right time is often a vote in the ballot box. But personal contact has many deeper overtones. According to Sigmund Freud (d. 1939), touching is 'the beginning of every act of possession, of every attempt to make use of a person or thing'. Holding hands, kissing, cuddling, are all preludes to the final act of sexual intercourse, which represents the highest degree of bodily contact possible between two human beings.

Faith-healing of course greatly relies on touch. According to the early 'magnetizers', the magnetic aura was transmitted from the healer to the patient by means of hand passes and the laying on of hands. One of the greatest exponents of touch-healing in the British Isles was the Irishman, Valentine Greatrakes (d. 1683), who was summoned to the court of Charles II to display his 'sanative contagion' to the king. Many eminent people of his day who were his patients testified to the extraordinary gift of healing that lay in his hands. But such power is by no means always beneficial. What is known as malicious magnetism can just as easily be communicated by touch, and was once reputed to cause hysteria, epilepsy, palsy and fainting fits.

It is further believed to be possible to convey power by a deliberate act of implacing the hands on the body of another or on oneself. In Hindu meditative ritual certain mantras are uttered while the hand is placed on certain parts of the body to implant the psychic essence of the manṭra on those parts. When the guru does this to communicate enlightenment, a marked change of personality in the pupil is believed to take place as a result.

On another level, farmers, zoo-keepers, biologists and veterinarians note that the licking and nuzzling of the young by their mothers is an important factor in the development of young animals. It improves their growth rate, feeding abilities, locomotor powers, and behavioural reactions. The growing animals are unfearful in stress, they show no aggression, and can learn better.

Similarly, it is an established psychological fact that infants have a deep need which is satisfied by feeling the warmth of the mother's body, and being cuddled, fondled and petted often. Failure to satisfy this need results in the child becoming emotionally warped.

The study of premature children and those born after caesarean section, where they have not been subjected to the natural prolonged and energetic stimulation of the mother's uterine contractions, shows that they tend to suffer in later life. Apparently the vigorous pressures of the mother on the child's body at the time of birth in some subtle way moulds the character of the child.

Babies who are taken away from their mothers immediately after birth and are not periodically fondled and lovingly spoken to are affected in their behavioural development. When in the 1920s the paediatrician, Dr J. Brenneman, insisted that every baby in his ward in New York's Belvue Hospital should be picked up and handled for a while every day, it was followed by a remarkable decrease in infant mortality.

For the same reason too, breast-feeding is preferable to bottle-feeding. More of the baby's face comes in contact with the warmth and smoothness of the mother's breast and this is important for the proper development of its respiratory functions. Extensive surveys have shown incontrovertibly that children fed artificially have a higher incidence of problems involving the development of facial bones and teeth as well as certain emotional problems, than breast-fed children.

This need for the comforting touch not only in the lives of children but also of adults is now being increasingly realized, and various attempts are being made to introduce a kind of touch therapy to break down deep-seated inhibitions. Such for instance is the Esalen movement, started in California.

The theory is that communication between men and women is largely confined to sight and speech, while the important area of touch, which plays so great a part in increasing a person's total awareness, is largely neglected. In some 'encounter' groups people remain silent, are often blindfolded or meet in darkened rooms, and communicate only by touch; they hold hands, touch each other's face, hair, legs. In certain other touching cults greater intimacy of touching between the sexes is permitted, and partners are exchanged frequently so that the sexual response, when aroused, is allegedly 'diffused'. A number of such practices are carried out in close association with Sauna baths and Swedish massage.

Books

Barnett, Michael, *People Not Psychiatry,* Allen & Unwin, London, 1973.
Bowskill, Derek, *Person to Person,* Allen & Unwin, London, 1973.
Gustaitis, Rasa, *Turning On,* Weidenfeld & Nicolson, London, 1969.
Howard, Jane, *Please Touch: A Guided Tour of the Human Potential Movement,* McGraw-Hill, New York, 1970.
Montague, Ashley, *Touching,* Columbia University Press, 1971.
Morris, Desmond, *Intimate Behaviour,* Cape, London, 1971.
Napier, John, *The Roots of Mankind,* Allen & Unwin, London, 1970.
Perls, Fritz, *Gestalt Therapy Verbatim,* Lafayette, California, 1969.

TRANSPOWERING

Also called impowering, is the transmission of spiritual or occult insight, which is tantamount to power, from one person to another, usually from master to pupil. It does not necessarily mean the communication of theoretical knowledge, but rather the bestowal of a secret teaching or mystic illumination.

Actually the basic potential or the dormant ember lies within man, only awaiting evocation to burst into flame. As fire lies potential in firewood and remains invisible unless kindled, so the light in man is hidden unless inflamed by spiritual inspiration or by the rite of transpowering. It is an age-old method by which power is bequeathed in a master-disciple succession from generation to generation. To use another simile, as one lights other candles from one burning candle, so the teacher transmits the teaching from heart to heart and illumines others.

Power may be transmitted by word of mouth, such as by whispering a mystic phoneme or meaningful phrase to the recipient; or by breathing upon him (*see* insufflation). It may be communicated in a rite involving aspersion or besprinkling, or even by the impact of a sudden blow or by a loud shout. It may be achieved by various meditative techniques. The master may touch the disciple's head with his hands, as in the 'laying on of hands', or with his own head. Sometimes a mild electric shock is felt by the recipient from the crown of the head to the tip of the spine and the extremities.

Occultly speaking, the rite cleanses the mind and spirit of obstructions, clears the psychic channels, gives insight and understanding, confers power, reveals secret doctrines that cannot be expressed in words, and generally quickens the spirit and prepares the way for illumination. It may form part of an initiation ceremony to the astral planes, permitting the pupil to enter upon advanced practices.

The rite of transpowering is very ancient and known to most religious and occult circles. In Plato's *Symposium* Socrates says, 'How I wish that wisdom could be infused by touch, out of the fuller into the emptier man, as water runs through wool out of a fuller cup into an emptier one.' But it is known that he was not serious when he spoke thus, for he possessed the secret.

Several medieval European mystics apparently discovered their own methods of transpowering, but wrote little about it. Among them, the Catalan priest, Raymond Lully (d. 1315), who said that he had the means of filling even the fool with understanding. The hermetic philosopher, Ludovico Lazarelli (d. 1502), held that the hermetic experience could be transmitted in a miraculous way, similar to Christ's inspiration of his disciples. The speculative thinker and martyr, Giordano Bruno (d. 1600), believed that he could convert the whole world to a single religion by a direct method of awakening the slumbering soul, which he could instantly impart to his disciples, and they to theirs, and so on. But he also felt that the world was not yet ready for the revelation and the time not ripe for the use of this method, and so allowed the secret to die with him.

Books

Bailey, Alice, *Initiation, Human and Solar*, Lucis, New York, 1922.
Blofield, John, *The Way of Power*, Allen & Unwin, London, 1970.
Nicholson, R. A., *Studies in Islamic Mysticism*, Cambridge University Press, 1921.
Stevenson, S., *The Rites of the Twice-born*, Oxford University Press, London, 1920.
Waite, A. E., *Raymond Lully, Illuminated Doctor*, Rider, London, 1922.
Walker, D. P., *Spiritual and Demonic Magic from Ficino to Campanella*, University of London Press, 1958.

UNCONSCIOUS

The term generally used for the state of non-awareness that supervenes when a person is asleep, drugged, drunk, in a trance, coma, faint or other condition of unconsciousness*. Psychologists also refer to the unconscious as the unaware part of the waking mind lying submerged below the threshold of consciousness, which is capable of being brought to consciousness by an effort of memory; in this sense it is equivalent to the subliminal, preconscious, or subconscious mind. (The term subconscious, popularly used, is avoided in psychoanalysis.) But more exactly the unconscious is not normally at the direction of the will, and special methods are required to gain access to it.

The 'discovery' of the unconscious by modern psychologists has been compared to the maritime discoveries of the Renaissance in the sudden opening up of new horizons for the study of the human mind. But this was actually a rediscovery, or a colonizing of land already discovered, for many significant elements about the unconscious were known earlier, both to ancient and medieval scholars. Aristotle (d. 322 BC) and Aquinas (d. 1274) both emphasized the non-conscious as a source of mental events, and since the middle ages scholars have continued to point to supra-conscious factors that seem to operate in human affairs, especially through individuals of exceptional gifts. The psyche, it was stated, was not exclusively or even primarily conscious, since the mind receives a large inflow of material from external, 'unconscious' sources.

In the middle of the last century the German physiologist, physician and artist, Karl Gustav Carus (d. 1869), said: 'The key to the understanding of conscious life can only be found in the realm of the unconscious.' And he went on to say that an important means of human growth was 'making the unconscious conscious'. The psychologist, Eugen Bleuler (d. 1939), coined the term *Tiefenpsychologie,* 'depth psychology', which is the psychology of the 'deeps' of the mind, in other words, the psychology of the unconscious, a study of which is actually many centuries old. But it was Sigmund Freud (d. 1939) more than anyone else who systematized the subject and plumbed the depths of the unconscious mind.

According to Freudian psychologists, the unconscious is the repressed part of the mind, and the storehouse of certain experiences, especially of childhood, largely inaccessible to remembrance, which can be recalled only by accident, hypnosis or the special techniques of psychoanalysis. Freud speaks of the unconscious as the *id,* the dark and practically unknown basement lumber room of the mind, in which are housed our primitive, instinctive and animal urges, most of them of a sexual nature. The vision of the prophet Ezekiel who sees, beyond the inner court of the sanctuary of Jerusalem, 'every form of creeping things and abominable beasts and all the idols, portrayed upon the wall round about' (Ezek. 8:10), has been compared to this part of the unconscious.

Carl Gustav Jung (d. 1961) spoke of a personal unconscious, a vast, groping chaos of memories, vaguely intuitive, poetic, instinctive and mystic. Symbols, not words, he said, and paradoxes, not reasoned statements, are the language of the unconscious. Also, whatever the sex of the individual happens to be, the unconscious is of the opposite sex. Thus, the unconscious of man, known as the *anima,* is the female element in him; that of the woman is the *animus,* the male element in her. In other words the male is consciously male and unconsciously female; the female consciously female and unconsciously male. In addition to the personal unconscious, Jung also spoke of the 'collective unconscious'*, a storehouse of race memories.

Against the background of insights both ancient and modern it would seem that the unconscious consists of many elements. It is made up of the personal experiences of the individual from his conception on, like the unconscious of Freud. It is also the sum total of memories and experiences of parents and ancestors and the human race, like the collective unconscious of Jung. According to other authorities it includes the all-pervading mental element in the universe, the 'cosmic consciousness*', some of which filters into each individual. The unconscious is both personal and universal. It forms a link between self and the world, the personality and the environment, the seen and unseen, past and present, the physical and the spiritual.

The conscious mind is ego-centred, individual and limited in scope; the unconscious mind is all-embracing, ranging far beyond the ego. The unconscious mind has an oceanic expanse, as compared with the tiny inshore pool that constitutes the conscious mind. The unconscious is the dynamic part of the personality and perhaps represents our essential nature, and is the ultimately motivating aspect of the self. Dreams, fantasies, inspiration, paraperception, have been ascribed to the unconscious. The unconscious functions in terms of archetypal and naturalistic images, symbols and concepts. It is ceaselessly operative, unresting, sleepless, is never fatigued, never forgets. It is unfettered by time and space, and is unfathomable, immeasurable and infinite. In fact it is godlike. The unconscious is a reflection of the whole of nature, a partial revelation of our participation in the universal mind. Freud spoke of the unconscious as 'the part of us that is so much nearer the divine than our own poor consciousness'.

Direct knowledge of the unconscious or dormant mind is not possible, for as soon as it enters the consciousness it ceases to be unconscious and changes its character and symbolism. An understanding of this symbolism is therefore a key to the understanding of the unconscious mind of man. Among the many disguises that conceal the motivations of the unconscious, a number have been analysed by psychologists in an effort to plumb the depths of the mind.

One of them is called *parapraxis* (Gk. 'contra-action') where a person reveals his unconscious intentions or thoughts by such things as forgetfulness (memory blocking), small accidents, mistakes and miscalculations, misplacing articles, slips of the tongue and pen and other such 'Freudian errors'. Freud described such mechanisms of unconscious influence on our behaviour as the 'psychopathology of everyday life'. Similarly, the kind of jokes one tells, or laughs at, or does not laugh at, the puns one makes, the kind of doodles one draws, or odd words one writes while thinking about something else, are all like bubbles that rise to the surface from the depths of the mind.

Psychologists have also devised what are called projective tests in which a subject has to interpret roughly sketched pictures or amorphous shapes; from his description a diagnosis is made of his intelligence, personality and fantasy life. In the Rorschach inkblot test a subject has to describe the pattern or shape he sees in a series of symmetrical inkblots. There is also the Thematic Apperception Test (TAT) of Henry Murray and his colleagues, where a series of drawings is presented to a subject and he is asked to tell a story about each. The story discloses his strong and weak qualities, his fears and aspirations. In a related test a patient is asked to enter an imaginary house and describe the interior. He is asked in particular to enter the basement or the attic, open an old trunk or dusty book and say what he sees. This will provide an excellent insight into the person's deeper psyche.

Expressions of sympathy, condemnation, like and dislike, love and hate, may indicate something contrary to the actual words uttered. Thus, overprotestation can reveal a great deal, as when wild antisemitism might signify one's own hidden Jewish ancestry. Hand gestures and other movements, the expressions on the face and other outward signs, most of which are involuntary, often betray unconscious motivations and tensions. Many forms of divination and 'character reading' skilfully attribute meaning to such signs. Similarly, intuitions, premonitions, instinctive antipathies or loves, and unaccountable feelings and hunches, are also important pointers to hidden meaning.

The responses of an individual in discussion or talk, from the dialectic method of Socrates to the give and take of ordinary conversation, are revealing to the thinking person. Sometimes questions might be asked deliberately to provoke or probe, but a less obvious approach is often more effective. Alfred Adler (d. 1937), ex-disciple of Freud, who founded his own 'individual psychology', used to ask each patient, 'Supposing you did not have this ailment, what would you do?'

In what is known as free association, which was once the hallmark of the psychoanalyst, a person is encouraged to talk, without being interrupted, about anything that comes to mind. His train of thought, it is believed, will ultimately lead to unconscious motivations, fears or wishes coming to light, which the analyst then tracks down.

Related to this is the word association test, when a selection of carefully chosen words is addressed to the subject, who responds with the first word that occurs to him. Not only is this word analysed, but any hesitations in responding are also noted. This method, first devised by Sir Francis Galton (d. 1911), was perfected by the experimental psychologist, Wilhelm Wundt (d. 1920), and used by C. G. Jung and other psychologists.

The revelations arising from xenophrenic states also provide ample evidence of what lies in the deeps of the mind. Thus, Freud called dreams* the *via regia,* 'royal way', to the unconscious. Hypnosis, LSD and other drug states, mediumship, automatism, afford further insights full of interest to the depth psychologist.

Books

Carus, Karl Gustav, *Psyche*, Jena, 1848 (edn of 1926).

Edmunds, H. Tudor, *Psychism and the Unconscious Mind,* Theosophical Publishing, London, 1968.

Ellenberger, Henri F., *The Discovery of the Unconscious,* Allen Lane, The Penguin Press, London, 1970.

Freud, Sigmund, *On Creativity and the Unconscious,* Harper, New York, 1958.

Freud, Sigmund, *The Psychopathology of Everyday Life,* Hogarth Press, London, 1960.

Geley, Gustave, *From the Unconscious to the Conscious,* Collins, London, 1925.

Groddeck, Georg, *Exploring the Unconscious,* Daniel, London, 1933.

Hartmann, Eduard von, *Philosophy of the Unconscious,* Kegan Paul, London, 1931.

Kent, Caron, *The Puzzled Body: A New Approach to the Unconscious*, Vision Press, London 1969.
Lyttleton, Edith, *Our Superconscious Mind*, Philip Allan, London, 1933.
MacIntyre, A. C., *The Unconscious*, Routledge & Kegan Paul, London, 1958.
Prince, Morton, *The Unconscious*, Macmillan, New York, 1914.
Rivers, W. H. R., *Instinct and the Unconscious*, Cambridge University Press, 1920.
Walker, K., *The Unconscious Mind*, Arrow Books, London, 1961.
White, Victor, *God and the Unconscious*, Harvill Press, London, 1952.
Whyte, Lancelot Law, *The Unconscious Before Freud*, Tavistock Books, London, 1962.

UNCONSCIOUSNESS

Unconsciousness is the mental condition during which a person is unaware of events. It covers a wide range of xenophrenic* states, including sleep, coma, syncope, blackouts and 'fits'. *Coma* is a state of deep unconsciousness, in which a person does not react to stimuli and does not wake if pinched or shaken. *Apoplexy* or stroke is a loss of consciousness with some paralysis, usually resulting from a damaged blood vessel in the brain. *Syncope*, commonly known as fainting or swooning, is due to a diminished blood supply to the brain. A *blackout* is a sudden and transient period of unconsciousness.

The brain is an electrical apparatus, with a positive and negative polarity, and any interference with this polarity will result in a loss of consciousness. Among the physical causes of unconsciousness are pressure on the brain, cerebral poisoning, brain tumour, fracture or injury to the skull, and even a sharp jolt to the brain. This latter served as the basis for a crude form of anaesthesia in ancient Egypt. Before a surgical operation the patient was given a few smart taps with a leather-covered mallet until he became unconscious. The treatment was repeated if he showed signs of coming round.

There may be coma in very severe cases of influenza, malaria, sleeping sickness and uraemia. Alcohol, opium, barbiturates and other drugs also lead to unconsciousness if taken in excess. Epilepsy, narcolepsy and related nervous diseases are accompanied by blackouts, and unconsciousness is sometimes a concomitant of shock, strong emotion and violent passion. In severe stupor, as in manic depressive insanity, the patient's unresponsiveness to his surroundings may approach a condition similar to unconsciousness. Deep meditation* and certain states of mystical trance also make a person oblivious of his surroundings. Although common fainting spells result from a temporary lack of blood supply to the brain, it has been observed that during trances which result in increased psychical activity, the flow of blood to the brain is sometimes greater than normal.

Several important questions are still unanswered about unconsciousness. One interesting problem is whether the state of consciousness is resumed with or without recall of what happened during the unconscious phase. Unconsciousness with recall occurs in trance and profound meditation; with semi-recall during sleep; without recall during dreamless sleep, coma, stupor, sopor, drunkenness, drug-states, fainting. But some authorities believe that unconscousness can never be complete. They doubt whether there does indeed exist a state of true unconsciousness at all. They maintain that total unconsciousness does not occur till after death, when the Self has permanently left the body. The mind is always conscious, even in unconscious states, but often does not remember what has happened on return to consciousness.

According to this theory cerebral and psychical activity continues during all periods of so-called unconsciousness. When we sleep, we have dreams. In delirium we mutter to ourselves, sometimes quite coherently. Somnambulists behave with apparent consciousness of what they are doing. When unconscious under hypnosis the subject understands and obeys orders. Yogis of long experience can remember what has been said while they were in deep trance. Gay Luce remarks that 'many surgeons have been chagrined to discover that patients in deep anaesthesia have recalled conversations over their bodies on the operating table.'

Books

Abramson, H. (ed.), *Problems of Consciousness*, J. Macy Foundation, New York, 1950.
Adrian, E. *et al.*, *Brain Mechanisms and Consciousness*, Blackwell, Oxford, 1954.
Eccles, J. C. (ed.), *The Brain and Conscious Experience*, Springer, Heidelberg, 1966.
Luce, Gay, *Body Time*, Temple Smith, London, 1972.
Miller, J. G., *Unconsciousness*, Chapman & Hall, London, 1942.
Neumann, Erich, *The Origins and History of Consciousness*, Routledge & Kegan Paul, London, 1954.
Tart, Charles T., *Altered States of Consciousness*, Wiley, New York, 1969.
Walker, Benjamin, *Beyond the Body*, Routledge & Kegan Paul, 1974.
Wavell, Stewart *et al.*, *Trances*, Allen & Unwin, London, 1966.

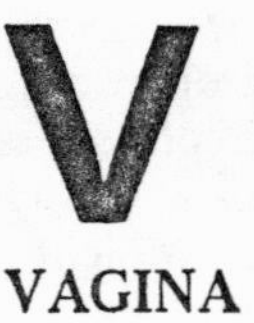

VAGINA

The passage of the female sexual organ from labia to uterus that receives the male penis during coition. The vagina in a state of virginity is sometimes closed by a membrane called the hymen, which breaks when penetration is effected for the first time. In the normal state the vagina is between three to four inches long, but under sexual stimulation can stretch to accommodate a penis of seven inches or more. In women the back of the vaginal wall is the front wall of the anus, and there is a great deal of sensory interplay between anus and vagina during intercourse.

The walls of the vagina are endowed with a very poor nervous system and most of the interior is insensitive, but the vagina responds at a deeper level to the total feeling of the body. Two sets of muscles serve the vagina, the sphincter or constrictor cunni, which opens and closes the entrance, and the levator, which contracts and relaxes the passage itself in an upward and downward movement. Hindu sexologists say that a woman has twenty muscles more than man, five each in her two breasts and the remaining ten in her vagina, some of them forming part of the etheric body. There was a special method of developing these muscles, which was practised, together with breathing exercises and anal contractions, by the women of many communities in China, India, Arabia and North Africa.

Throughout the child-bearing period of a woman's life, gentle and spontaneous rhythmic contractions are said to take place in the floor of her vagina every eight to ten minutes. They start near the cervix at the opening of the uterus and move towards the outer labia at a uniform rhythmic rate. After the menopause these contractions cease.

Quite frequently during intromission of the penis, the vagina seems to receive and draw the male organ with a kind of pulling motion; the muscles contract in forceful spasms and give the impression of sucking in the phallus. This process, called invagination, is exploited by magicians during sex-magical rites. But the esoteric art of absorbing the semen-energy is regarded as the female counterpart of oli technques (*see* acclivity) in oriental sex magic, and not desirable for the male. In Hindu tradition it was said to be taught by magician-priestesses in lesbian centres such as Oddiyana somewhere in the northwest of India. Tantrik experts regard normal intercourse with a woman who has strong invaginatory impulses as extremely depleting, since she absorbs the vital essence of the male. For this reason, in order to counteract the effects of such female vampirism, oli techniques need to be used.

The natural process of invagination, as well as the deep-seated fear that some men have of the opposite sex and sexual intercourse, is probably responsible for the curious belief in the *vagina dentata*, or 'toothed vulva'. Like the womb the vagina is thought to have an existence of its own. This notion is common to certain primitive peoples who think that the vagina of a woman is like some beast of prey, possessing fangs, and waiting to bite off and engorge the male member that penetrates it. The early Jews spoke of the vagina as *beth shenayim*, 'toothed place', and stressed the need for vigilance while entering.

In advanced societies as well the idea of the lurking menace of the vagina appears in art and literature in symbolic form, and is one of the characteristic fantasies of misogyny. The vagina is a destructive orifice and a devirilizing element in the feminine structure, and sexual intercourse results in a kind of castration. Woman then becomes the devouring female, the vulva incarnate.

Books

Burton, Richard, *Love, War and Fancy*, ed. by Kenneth Walker, Kimber, London, 1964.
Freud, Sigmund, *An Outline of Psychoanalysis*, W. W. Norton, New York, 1933.
Freud, Sigmund, *New Introductory Lectures on Psychoanalysis*, Hogarth Press, London, 1964.
Hays, H. R., *The Dangerous Sex: The Myth of Feminine Evil*, Methuen, London, 1966.
Kinsey, Alfred C. *et al.*, *Sexual Behavior in the Human Female*, W. B. Saunders, Philadelphia, 1953.

Koedt, Anne, *The Myth of Vaginal Orgasm,* New England Free Press, 1969.
Stern, Karl, *The Flight From Woman*, Allen & Unwin, London, 1965.
Vaerting, M., *The Dominant Sex*, Allen & Unwin, London, 1923.
Walker, Benjamin, *Sex and the Supernatural*, Harper & Row, New York, 1973.

VENTRICLES

('Little stomach'), one of the several hollow areas in the brain. The ventricles are filled with cerebro-spinal fluid, whose composition is like blood without the red and white cells. This fluid is an internal circulatory system for the brain, and was earlier regarded as the reservoir of the vital spirits.

Occultists recognize seven ventricles: the first and second laterals, the third in the middle, the fourth at the back connected with the medulla, the insignificant fifth, the tubular sixth which descends the whole spinal cord and is sometimes identified with the sushumna of Hindu physiology, and the symbolic seventh which is the cavern of the skull itself. Madame Blavatsky (d. 1891) said that each of these seven cavities is filled with an invisible and intangible etheric fluid, and each has its own colour and its own consciousness.

For the most part the ancients concerned themselves with only three ventricles. According to Alexander Neckham (d. 1217), who collated the data available in his time, the three functions of the human intellect were located in three ventricles, and his account of them was accepted as authoritative for over two centuries. In the earlier works of Albertus Magnus (d. 1280) the three cavities are represented by three circles of equal size filling the entire cranium, in accordance with Neckham's view, as given below.

(1) The *anterior* ventricle, in the left and right sides of the forebrain, comprising the two vaguely wing-shaped laterals and considered as one, is situated about three inches behind the forehead. It is hot and dry, controls *imaginatio,* that is, imagination and fancy, and governs all mechanical arts, architecture and painting.

(2) The *median* ventricle, situated in the middle brain, is the third ventricle of physiology, midway between the forebrain and occiput. Hot and moist, it controls *ratio,* reason, cogitation, judgment, and governs the natural sciences, medicine and politics. Physiologically, the lowest part of the third ventricle is called the *infundibulum* (Lat. 'funnel'), connected with the hypothalamus. It was believed that the serous liquid or ros* from the cerebrum descended through the funnel into the pituitary gland. Both the pituitary and pineal glands are directly connected with the third ventricle.

(3) The *posterior* ventricle, probably the fourth ventricle of the physiologists, is in the rear of the brain in the region of the cerebellum. Cold and dry, it controls *mens,* mind and memory. It governs divine secrets, angelology, theology.

Many ancient and medieval physicians regarded these empty spaces, which they referred to as concavities, caves, cells or hollows, as the abode of spiritual 'harmonies' and as the location of the life force and soul-energy in man. Disciples of the schools of Galen (d. AD 201) and Avicenna (d. 1037) assigned no organs to the 'spirits' or vital centres, but said that they dwelt in the ventricles. It was thought that forces from the celestial spheres penetrated directly into the skull, and in the ventricles communicated with the soul, and their messages were passed through the medulla oblongata down the spinal cord to the sense organs.

Leonardo da Vinci (d. 1519) regarded the ventricles of the brain as one of the three great ventricular systems of the body, the others being in the heart and the reproductive organs. Andreas Vesalius (d. 1564), the anatomist, thought of the ventricles as receiving air that is breathed in, and from it forming 'animal spirits' which in turn produced thought, sensation and movement. William Harvey (d. 1657), discoverer of the circulation of the blood, said that the ventricles of the brain were designed to draw off cerebral excrement.

One main ventricle in the head, differently named by different authorities, was believed to be constantly creating and secreting a crystalline dew known as ros, which slowly seeped down into the body.

Books

Eckstein, Gustav, *The Body Has a Head*, Collins, London, 1971.

Hall, Manly P., *Man: The Grand Symbol of the Mysteries*, Philosophical Research Society, 5th edn, Los Angeles, 1947.

Lassek, A. M., *The Human Brain: From Primitive to Modern*, Blackwell Scientific Publications, Oxford, 1957.

Poynter, F. N. L. (ed.), *The History and Philosophy of the Brain and its Functions*, Blackwell, Oxford, 1958.

Singer, C., *Vesalius on the Human Brain*, Oxford University Press, London, 1942.

Walker, D. P., 'The Astral Body in Renaissance Medicine', *Journal of the Warburg and Courtauld Institutes*, 1958, 21, pp. 119ff.

VIRGINITY

Virginity is the state of not having had experience of sexual intercourse. In many communities virginity is valued in the marriage market because it is a proof of virtue, it is a promise of continued chastity after marriage, and gives assurance that the children of one's marriage will be legitimate.

In folk etymology the word 'virgin' comes from *vir* (Latin, 'man') and *gynē* (Greek, 'woman'), a man-woman or androgyne, a complete person. A virgin has the whole potential of the total original human being. The true virgin is unique, and can be recognized by her behaviour, her voice, her walk, her looks, the shape of her breasts, her urine, her smell and various other characteristics.

Because of their purity virgins were often entrusted with special sacred duties in temples, like the Vestal Virgins of ancient Rome, who had charge of the sacred fires. Because of their innocence they were also regarded as having great occult virtues, and for this reason were encouraged in many cults. They were believed to have strong psychic powers and were trained as mediums and oracles. The sibyl, pythia and high priestess in ancient times was usually a virgin.

Countless powers were attributed to virgins in the middle ages. Savage beasts became tame in their presence, and lightning was averted, and storms and raging seas calmed.

Contact with a virgin had strong rejuvenative powers, and the practice of consorting with virgin girls in the hope of restoring youth and regaining lost virility has been prevalent from very early times. In addition, it was once widely believed, and still is in some quarters, that a virgin had the power to cure the 'diseases of Venus', hence dissolute rakes with syphilis and gonorrhoea would seek out virgins to seduce, in order to cure themselves.

The chief mark of the virgin girl is the hymen, a thin, semi-circular membrane found in the lower part of the entrance to the vagina. A *virgo intacta,* an intact virgin, complete with hymen, was highly extolled among many ancient peoples, and still is in some contemporary cultures. With the Jews and Arabs, and in several European countries till a century or so ago, proof of an intact hymen had to be provided before marriage could be confirmed. For example, the bedclothes with the marks of the blood would be exhibited to the guests or the members of the family.

The act of taking the virginity of a girl is known as defloration. Where the hymen is present defloration ruptures it and causes bleeding. For the girl it is an end (of maidenhood) and a beginning (of womanhood, and perhaps motherhood), the transition 'from maiden-flower to fruit-mother'. The Greeks facetiously spoke of defloration as the act of turning an omicron (small 'o', the fifteenth letter of the Greek alphabet) into an omega (large 'O', the last letter).

According to an earlier belief the act of defloration, whether with or without the girl's consent, caused psychic injury to both parties, and special measures were taken to ward off the dangers believed to accompany the act. Sometimes the task was left to a person with a strong mana, like a king, seigneur or priest, who was powerful enough to withstand the charge. A husband, who was sanctified by the rite of a religious marriage, was also immunized against the impact, and neither he nor his wife suffered any psychic consequences.

The Hindu sage, Shvetaketu, said that a promiscuous society that disregarded the sanctity of the virgin knot and allowed virgins to be violated before marriage, removed the protective barriers against the invasion of destructive spiritual forces, and thus brought disaster to the nation.

Some occultists also believe that at the moment of defloration a powerful impulse of psychic energy is released. To the black magician the force emanating from defloration is as potent as a bent bow. A virgin in this view represents an untapped source of occult energy, and in one secret sex rite he deflowers a girl, and uses the spark that flashes forth to empower his magical operation. Thereafter she is of no more use to him than the husk of a shelled peanut.

Books

Braddock, Joseph, *The Bridal Bed,* Robert Hale, London, 1960.

Cabanes, Augustine, *The Eroticon*, Falstaff Press, New York, 1933.
Magee, Martin, *Virginity*, Monarch Books, Derby, Connecticut, 1963.
Wall, O. A., *Sex and Sex Worship*, Kimpton, London, 1919.
Worsfold, T. C., *The History of the Vestal Virgins of Rome*, Rider, London, 1934.

VISCERA

A generic term used for the organs situated within the chest and abdomen, including the heart, lungs and digestive organs – stomach, liver, spleen, intestines and kidneys.

The *stomach* receives and assimilates substances in the form of food to sustain the physical organism. It is sensitive to a variety of conditions, physical as well as emotional. Emergencies of a serious nature are not infrequently heralded by a 'stomach ache', and these may not necessarily be connected with the stomach at all. Anatomists have called the stomach 'the greatest liar in the anatomy', because it reacts, by pains of various kinds, to diseases in other parts of the body that have little or nothing to do with the stomach itself. But in Chinese esoteric physiology the stomach (*wei*) was regarded as the seat of learning and the truth centre of the body.

The *liver,* the largest gland in the body, manufactures bile, which it passes to the gall-bladder. The liver performs several other functions as a storeroom and clearing house of the body. Like many lower animal species the liver has the power to rebuild itself. According to medical experts, even when masses as large as 80 per cent are removed, it rebuilds to its old contours. A fabulous number of liver cells regenerate within a day, and even within an hour.

Hippocrates (d. 359 BC) believed that the veins started from the liver, which like the heart had a beat of its own. An excess of darker blood in the venous stream gave rise to certain unseemly aspirations, and only when purified by the heart did these assume a more seemly aspect.

According to Galen (d. AD 201), digested food was directed from the human gut to the liver where it was processed to make *natural spirits.* The liver passed the natural spirits to the right side of the heart for conversion into *vital spirits.* The latter were then pumped up with arterial blood to the ventricles of the brain and became converted into *animal spirits.* The animal spirits were the source of nervous energy, and supplied the energy via the pneumatic network, to the nerves and muscles, where they motivated mechanical action.

Liver, brain and breath are closely connected. The position, and to some extent the shape and size of the liver at any moment, as well as the cerebral condition, are determined by one's breathing. When a deep breath is taken the diaphragm is pressed down, the liver descends, the brain shrinks; when breath is exhaled the diaphragm rises, so does the liver, and the brain expands.

Lying under the liver is the pear-shaped *gall-bladder,* which stores and concentrates bile. The bile (or gall) is passed to the intestines where it aids the digestive processes by dissolving fats. It is extremely bitter to the taste. Hippocrates knew bile as *cholē,* which gave its name to cholera, and was responsible for the choleric temperament in the Greek humoral* system. Astrologically bile is under the influence of the constellation Scorpio and the planet Mars.

In Chinese occult physiology bile was regarded as a powerful elixir, and the gall-bladders of fallen warriors and executed criminals of known audacity were emptied of their bile and rice steeped in it, which was then eaten to obtain hardihood, endurance and courage. Inca kings of ancient Peru after a serious illness would be rubbed over by specialist priests with gall and blood taken from human victims to infuse new strength into their body.

The *spleen,* a 5-inch gland situated in the upper left side of the abdomen, is sometimes classed with the ductless glands as it has an internal secretion which it pours direct into the blood stream. The exact purpose of this gland still remains something of a mystery, as yet not fully understood, but its importance is often stressed by occultists and students of esoteric physiology.

The rosicrucian mystic, Max Heindel (d. 1919), stated that the vital energy of the cosmos is absorbed by the etheric body 'through the etheric counterpart of the spleen', from which centre it is diffused along the nerves, providing the body with an electrical impulse. Theosophists regard the spleen as 'the vehicle of the etheric double'. Madame Blavatsky (d. 1891) held that the etheric double lies curled up in the spleen, which is also the seat of the prana or vital breath, and it is from this centre that the vital force is circulated.

In the view of Alice Bailey the spleen is the physical receiving point of what is called 'solar breath' which enters the body through the cranium. She says, 'There is a close connection between the spleen and the top of the head in connection with the etheric body'.

Those who have experienced astral projection list the spleen as one of the points from which the astral body leaves the physical body in exteriorization.

The *intestines,* or alimentary canal, begin from the exit of the stomach and end in the rectum and anus, altogether about twenty-five feet in length. It is the part of the body mainly responsible for absorbing the nourishment from the food eaten, and excreting the residue. It has been said that we eat with the small intestine, the first part of the canal, and drink with the large intestine, the latter part, since solids are absorbed mainly by the former and fluids by the latter. In Chinese esoteric physiology the small intestine is connected with the heart, and the large with the lungs.

In western systems generally the intestines are the seat of pertinacity, determination, doggedness and courage, hence the man possessing these qualities is regarded as having 'guts'. The same organs also respresent the innermost core of man, and are invoked as an intensive, as when Oliver Cromwell (d. 1658) wrote, 'I beseech you, in the bowels of Christ, think it possible you may be mistaken.'

The intestines are to the emotional system what the brains are to the intellectual. Both have convolutions; both are fed, the brain through the eyes, ears and nose, the intestines through the mouth. Both eliminate their waste products, the brain in the form of the humoral element, phlegm, the intestines in the form of excreta.

Books

Bailey, Alice, *A Treatise on Cosmic Fire*, Lucis Publishing, 3rd edn, New York, 1944.

Hall, Manly P., *Man, The Grand Symbol of the Mysteries*, Philosophical Research Society, Los Angeles, 1947.

Heindel, Max, *The Rosicrucian Cosmo-Conception*, Rosicrucian Fellowship, Los Angeles, 1911.

Rechung, Lama, *Tibetan Medicine*, Wellcome Institute, London, 1973.

Williams, C. A. S., *Encylopedia of Chinese Symbolism*, Julian Press, New York, 1960.

VULVA

The female zone in its external aspect. More descriptive epithets have been coined for the vulva in the various languages of the world than for any other part of the human body. One scholar recorded 111 distinct names for the female genitals in the Old German tongue alone.

The original syllable or root-word for the vulva in the Mediterranean world was *cu* or *cwe*. The Egyptian word *ka-t* was used both for the female sex organs, including the vagina, and for mother. The Sanskrit word is *yoni*, but the alternative word *kunti* was also used in contexts signifying the female principle or the wife of a deity. The name is related to Cynthus (Kunthus), Greek goddess of fecundity.

The Greek words are *kteis* and *konnos*. The Latin equivalents include: *cunnus* (from the Greek), *concha* (conch), *navis* (boat), *porca* (sow), *pudenda muliebris* ('sex parts of the female'), *sinus* (cavity), *sulcus* (furrow), *tubus* (tube), *vesica* (bladder). Other terms are *kvithe* (Teutonic), *qitbus* (Gothic), *cwithe* (Old English, also meaning 'womb'), *cunte* or *counte* (Old Middle English), *queynte* (in Chaucer's *The Miller's Tale*). Modern terms are cunt, cunny, quiff, quim (from Celtic *cwn*, cleft or valley), twat. Descriptive epithets of course abound: blind alley, crack, Cupid's highway, cocklane, cockpit, carnal part, hole, loveland, pussy, slit, star over the garter, tender part, and so on.

The vulva covers the whole external sexual region, extending from the pubic area to the anus. It includes the *pubes* and *mons veneris*, 'mount of Venus', marked by a triangular covering of hair; the *labia majora* or outer lips, which do not play any significant part in sex, anthropology or occultism; the *nymphae* or *labia minora*, the inner lips; the *clitoris*, at the upper end of the labia minora (*see* orgasm), which swell and protrude under sexual excitement; the urinary *meatus*, the orifice of the urethra lying below the clitoris; the *vestibule*, which the Talmudists spoke of as the outer room, the entrance to the vaginal orifice; the *hymen*, a thin membrane covering the entrance to the vagina, usually found in virgins. The vagina*, the opening and passage leading from the inner lips to the womb, and the womb* or uterus, the place where the fertilized egg grows into the child, are also often included.

The fear that a girl might obtain satisfaction by herself before marriage, and, after marriage, by someone other than her lawful husband, has led to considerable tampering with the vulva in many parts of the world. The vulva was regarded as the most intimate part of the woman, and a man's proprietary rights over his womenfolk were assured by safeguarding it from assault either by herself or by others. The chastity of daughters and wives was maintained, and the honour of families protected by occlusion (closure) of the vulva by various means such as infibulation (stitching), or by clitoridectomy (excision of the clitoris), circumcision (excision of the labia) and the chastity belt.

The word vulva has a root meaning signifying a revolving or circular motion, and in occultism the vulva is conceived of as a talismanic vortex, a whirling life force that concentrates a fiery essence. Hence the once common practice of baubism, or the exposure by women of their private parts. The sex organs are invested with a deep occult significance, and in different peoples, depending on their religious beliefs, the pictorial, sculptural or symbolical representation of the vulva may inspire awe, fear, horror, or be a symbol of good luck and divine beneficence. The ancient Egyptian talisman called *thet,* known as the girdle or buckle of Isis, is actually the conventional symbol for the vulva of the goddess. This thet amulet was commonly made of some red stone and assured the wearer the protection of the blood of Isis, probably the menstrual blood of the goddess.

Among the objects used as female symbols in religion and mythology, or regarded as symbolizing the female vulva in the human psyche, are the following: all round and oval objects, the circle, the triangle on its apex (the pubes), rings, all holed things and apertures, caves, clefts in rocks, doors, windows, arches, niches, chests and boxes, boats, gates and entrances, wells and springs, hollows and fissures, cups, vases, bowls (e.g. the *argha* or yoni-shaped vessel of the Hindus), cradles, the altar, the nave, gardens, groves (the *asherah* of the Bible), the sycamore, fig, lotus in bud (the virgin), lotus in bloom (the yawning labia of the productive woman), cowries, shells (especially the conch), fish, *vesica pisces* (literally, 'fish bladder'), the *mandorla* (Italian, 'almond'), or oval standing on one end.

Books

Anonymous, *Praeputii Incisio: A History of Circumcision, Infibulation &c,* Panurge Press, New York, 1930.

Budge, E. A. Wallis, *Amulets and Superstitions,* Oxford University Press, London, 1930.

Ploss, H. H. and Bartels, M. and P., *Woman* (ed. E. J. Dingwall), vol. 1, Heinemann, London, 1935.

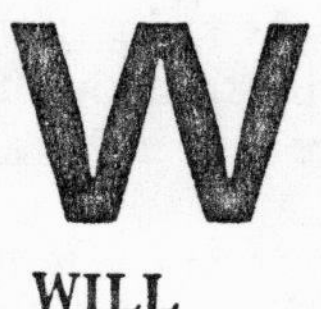

WILL

Will is the faculty of determining and controlling the activity of body and mind, and constitutes the motive power that gives purpose and direction to all phenomena. Joseph Glanvill (d. 1680), the theologian, said: 'Who knoweth the mysteries of the Will with its vigour? For God is but a great will pervading all things by nature of its intentness. Man doth not yield himself to the angels nor to death utterly, save only through the weakness of his feeble will.' The German philosopher, Arthur Schopenhauer (d. 1860), in his masterpiece, *The World as Will and Idea* (1819), defined Will as primary, universal and creative, and spoke of it as the active aspect of nature, as compared with Idea which was secondary and receptive.

In man, will is manifested as the agent of survival, and all activity starts with an act of volition or willing. But on a higher level will is more than a choice between alternatives, and can be directed with purposeful concentration to a particular end and serve as a powerful instrument for one's advancement. The average person, however, is a weak and vacillating creature little able to combine fixity of purpose with undeviating resolution. He is indolent in his thoughts and tepid in his desires, and cannot generate a will strong enough to help him gain his ends. He does not will, but just vaguely desires things and weakly wishes for them, making no effort to gird his loins and bend his mind to achieve what he wants. He is discouraged by trifling setbacks and petty annoyances and gives up trying at the first assault on his comforts.

Occultists stress that the training of the will is the prelude to all power. Self-indulgence, self-assertion, boasting, idle gossip and chatter, excuses and alibis, attenuate the spirit and erode the will. As far as possible these must be avoided. Every opportunity should be taken to exercise the will by seeking to perform those tedious and difficult acts involving sacrifice and even suffering so that one is disciplined to rise superior to one's physical environment. Self-restraint, renunciation, physical austerities, all these charge the body and mind with power easily drawn upon when needed. The French mage, Eliphas Levi (d. 1875), said: 'By perseverance the powers of the body can be developed to an amazing extent. It is the same with the powers of the mind. Would you learn to govern yourself and the other? Then learn how to will!'

The power of a clearly formulated and long-sustained will, concentrated on a single purpose, whatever it be, is difficult to overrate. The human will is one of the most powerful occult forces known, and all obstacles recede before it. Paracelsus (d. 1541) said, 'The will of man is a most powerful agent. The human spirit is so great that no man can express it.' Will implies intention, purpose, determination and faith. It begins with the certitude of finishing successfully. It calls to its aid thought, imagination and feeling. It does not admit of mental laziness or untidiness. On the contrary it entails exertion, vigilance and self-denial and can prove painful and wearisome. But once set in motion it can become a tremendous force that by some hidden energy moves others as if by a hypnotic power, and sweeps out of the way obstacles that would normally be regarded as insurmountable.

But there is a strange paradox and a hidden danger in its operation, for an act of will raises a counter-suggestion to resist. So those who do not will in the proper manner get results, on the principle of 'reversed effect', that are contrary to what they intended. The motto of the Utopian abbaye of

Thélème on the banks of the Loire near Paris, founded by Gargantua, the hero of the great satirical epic by François Rabelais (d. 1553), was, *Fay ce que voudras,* and this in its English form, Do what thou wilt, formed the credo of the magician, Aleister Crowley (d. 1947). But according to an ancient occult formulation it is of vital importance to know one's own will; only after that does the great dogma become applicable. Without this precedent knowledge all such willing runs into the quicksands and ends in the wilderness.

The religious teaching is that although a man has a will of his own, his primary act of will lies in the surrender of his will to God: 'Not my will, but thine, be done' (Luke 22:42). Or, as St Augustine (d. 430) expressed it, *Dilige, et fac quod vis,* 'Love, and do what you will', for if a man love God, everything is willable, and everything is permissible, for then he cannot will wrong.

Books

Aveling, F., *Directing Mental Energy*, University of London Press, 1927.
Bain, Alexander, *The Emotions and Will*, Longmans Green, London, 1875.
Besant, Annie, *Thought Power*, Theosophical Publishing, London, 1903.
Farber, Leslie H., *The Ways of the Will: Essays Towards a Psychology and Psychopathology of Will*, Constable, London, 1966.
May, Rollo, *Love and Will*, Souvenir Press, London, 1970.
Rhine, Louisa E., *Mind Over Matter*, Macmillan, London, 1970.
Schopenhauer, Arthur, *The World as Will and Idea*, London, 1905.

WISH

The fervent expression of a desire is one of the great occult forces, a powerful weapon known from timeless antiquity in myth and legend, folklore and fairy-tale, religion and black magic. Depending on the status of the wisher, the nature of its expression, the solemnity of the utterance, and the intensity of the emotion, every wish is fulfillable. All forms of expressed intention may be termed wishes in the occult sense, including physical actions which express anger or affection, and hence are linked with the field of sound, gesture, and pathemic intensity.

Wishes may take the form of blessings, oaths, curses, exorcisms, excommunications, prayers, benedictions, spells and charms. The blessing or curse of the saintly, the pious, the aged; of a parent or dying person; of those who have no human redress, like beggars, orphans, slaves; of strangers or guests who have been ill treated; all these are believed to have the power to make their wishes for good or ill come to fruition.

Essential for the fulfilment of a wish is intention, the force of ardently concentrated emotion, hope, belief, desire and purpose, all directed to one end. A deeply-felt wish, launched with full intention, whether of love or hate, has the power to heal or harm, cure or kill, bless or blight.

Wishes are thoughts, and if strongly enough conceived and projected, may become 'embodied', assuming the nature of thought-forms* which sooner or later alight somewhere. Wishes motivated by evil, spite, envy or greed, may fulfil their purpose but will always return to plague the sender. Folklore and fairy-tale repeatedly give warning of what can happen to those who make impetuous wishes, and the curious ways in which they are answered.

Books

See under will

WOMAN

Woman from earliest times has appeared to man as an enigma. She has been treated with suspicion and awe. She attracts and repels, is desired and feared, pursued and shunned, and in spite of physical intimacies continues to be a thing of mystery. She is not so much human as female, and remains in his eyes the *Ewig Weibliche* (German, 'eternal feminine'). 'Woman', said the German writer, Novalis (d. 1801), 'is man's goal.' A modern writer, Germaine Greer, speaking of woman, says, 'All she must contribute is her existence. She need achieve nothing, for she is the reward of achievement.'

Within herself she possesses certain transcendent qualities which she shares with the divine Mother Goddess. She embodies mystery through her fruitfulness. She is associated with nature and with the earth. Men in a number of primitive societies refuse to interfere with agriculture, believing it to be magically dependent on women. Because of her unique physiological experiences, like menstruation, defloration, conception, pregnancy, child-birth, lactation, she is responsive to the mysterious periodicities connected with the phases of the moon, the cycles of the months, the seasons of the year and the rhythms of nature.

She lives separate existences as virgin, wife, mother, widow or spinster, each with its own experience and power. As a mother she is one of the great primordial archetypes of humanity. From her womb a new creature is born, at her breasts it is nourished, by her hands it is guided. The man's function and identity were less evident in primitive communities. Matriarchal societies in which women are dominant reflect the supremacy of the mother.

Woman is superior to man in many ways. She has greater vitality; her resistance to disease, physical injury and major shocks is better than man's; girls, as a rule, are more precocious in their development than boys, do not succumb so easily to illness. Woman is more practical and down to earth, and some anthropologists think that rule by women preceded rule by men, and that the patriarchal system developed only when men settled down to a civilized life so as to leave women free to bring up the family.

Woman is the originator of families, the preserver of the established order and the perpetuator of traditions, which she imparts to her children. Through her the past is continued, not only in the physical life of her children, but in the respect for the traditional heritage that she instils into them. As the Great Goddess rules heaven, the woman rules the home.

It is the presence of women that lies at the source of most forms of totemism, exogamy, taboo, initiations, blood-rites, fertility rites and the mysteries. With woman are associated the ideas of the unconscious, for some instinctive and intuitive process seems to put her in touch, through some secret sympathy, with the very heart of things.

She symbolizes the wisdom of the community, and the old woman and *sage-femme* is the keeper of the tribal lore and often the source of tribal strength. She is priestess, prophetess, sibyl, medium, oracle, pythoness, witch. Skilled in herbs and balms she is the natural healer and nurse, first of her children, then of her hunter and warrior husband. Through her vagina man penetrates into her interior, and deep within her body the child is created. She therefore stands for the innerness of things, the place where secret and hidden things happen. In her womb* the great magical transformation takes place that changes sperm into men.

But there is an obverse side to her. She is the *femme fatale,* woman of destiny, drawing men to their doom and bringing woe to the people. She is therefore unlucky. Fishermen going out to sea, mariners before a voyage, miners going down a mine, consider it an ill omen if they should meet a woman before they set out. For the same reason many racing motorists do not like women in their pits.

She also epitomizes the fleshpots and the lust of concupiscence. She is the source of man's greatest pleasure, but is herself lust incarnate and sexually insatiable. In the misogynist view she is a symbol of sin and contamination; she is mistress, courtesan, whore. In varying contexts she is a siren, lamia, empusa, vampire, succubus, demoness, dakini, witch, sorceress, harpy. In the scheme of cosmic opposites woman represents the dark, negative and passive side.

Books

Alexander, W., *The History of Women from Earliest Antiquity,* Cannon, London, 1779.

Chapman, J. Dudley, *The Feminine Mind and Body,* Vision, London, and New York, 1967.

Deutsch, Helene, *The Psychology of Women,* Heinemann, London, 1946.

Farber, S. M. and Wilson, R. H. (eds), *The Potential of Women,* McGraw-Hill, New York, 1963.

Frieden, Betty, *The Feminine Mystique,* W. W. Norton, New York, 1963.

Greer, Germaine, *The Female Eunuch,* Granada, London, 1971.

Harding, Esther, *Woman's Mysteries: Ancient and Modern,* 2nd edn, New York, 1955.

Horney, Karen, *Feminine Psychology,* Routledge & Kegan Paul, London, 1967.

Kaberry, Phyllis, *Aboriginal Woman: Sacred and Profane,* Routledge & Kegan Paul, London, 1949.

Le Fort, Gertrude von, *The Eternal Woman,* E.T., Bruce, Milwaukee, 1954.

Montagu, Ashley, *The Natural Superiority of Women,* Allen & Unwin, London, 1954.

Thiselton-Dyer, Thomas, *Folklore of Women,* E. Stock, London, 1905.

Vaerting, M., *The Dominant Sex,* Allen & Unwin, London, 1923.

WOMB

Womb, a small pear-shaped organ in which the fertilized egg develops, is about three inches long in the non-pregnant state, but capable of growing large enough to house the full-grown foetus. Among the terms used in classical times for the womb was *hystera* by the Greeks, and *uterus* by the Romans, the latter term still current in medical circles. The term *matrix* came into use in later Roman times.

Some reincarnationists believe that before it is invested with a body the soul of man is free and fully alive, since it exists in the spiritual world, and when he is conceived in his mother's interior, his death begins. The womb is thus the symbol of the tomb. The womb is also the place of great magical transformation where sperm is changed into man, and as such it is an analogue of such transformation symbols as the oven, where bread is baked; the wheel, where clay is shaped into pottery; the loom, on which cloth is woven; and the vat in which grape juice is converted into wine.

For long the womb was regarded as an independent organism, a kind of animal within the female body hungry to bear children. The Book of Proverbs speaks of the grave and the womb being equally insatiable: they never say, 'We have had enough.' Plato in his *Timaeus* wrote that the womb was a creature yearning to be fertilized. If unfruitful for long it became restless and angry and left its proper place and wandered about the body, closing the passages for the air, stopping respiration, and causing anxiety, feelings of dread, and other symptoms of illness.

Hysteria (from the Greek *hystera*) was long thought to be due to the womb tearing itself loose from its anchorage and wandering in the female body. The Greek physician, Aretaeus (fl. AD 100), echoing the Platonic notion, likened the womb to an animal which when restive moved to various parts of the body, sometimes to the throat, then to the sides, then to the back, causing oppression in the lungs, heart, diaphragm, kidneys, liver and intestines, creating great distress in the woman and making her rave and scream. Even when his great successor, the physician Galen (d. AD 201), rejected the theory of the wandering womb which rages and struggles if unappeased, the belief persisted for centuries after his time. The cure, which was used till the late middle ages in Europe, consisted in exorcism and conjuration: 'I conjure thee, O womb, by the nine choirs of angels, to return to thy rightful place with gentleness.'

In many parts of Europe the womb-creature was believed to be shaped like a rat, toad, tortoise, or like a small oval pot with rib-like corrugations around it. In Brunswick and among the peasants of north Germany a new-born child was not placed near the mother for twenty-four hours, in case the womb tore at the mother's side to take possession of the child again. The womb was thought to be very susceptible to odours, delighting in pleasant ones and shrinking from evil smells. Hysterical seizures and uterine troubles were therefore often treated with fumigations: pleasant smelling incense to soothe the womb, unpleasant fumes of burnt feathers and foul smelling substances if it were recalcitrant.

The ancient Egyptians believed that in fertile women the womb was in free communication with the rest of the body, and one of the tests of a woman's ability to bear children was to insert some aromatic substance or even garlic into her vagina; if its smell appeared in her breath after a few hours she was fertile; if not, it was because the passage from the womb to the rest of the body was blocked, and this was a sign of her sterility. On the other hand, since conception blocks the womb, the woman, if not sterile, was diagnosed as pregnant.

In Bavaria the hungry uterus was offered small round morsels made of cat's grease, honey, nutmeg and other ingredients. It was believed that while the woman slept the womb-creature would emerge from the woman's mouth and partake of the fare and be appeased. Waxen, clay or metal votive figures in the presumed shape of the womb, such as a toad or tortoise, were hung on church altars after certain sicknesses resulting from disturbances of the womb.

Books

Ghalioungui, Paul, *Magic and Medical Science in Ancient Egypt*, Hodder & Stoughton, London, 1963.
Harding, Esther, *Woman's Mysteries: Ancient and Modern*, 2nd edn, New York, 1955.
Ploss, H. H. and Bartels, M. and P., *Woman* (ed. E. J. Dingwall), 3 vols, Heinemann, London, 1935.
Thiselton-Dyer, Thomas, *Folklore of Woman*, E. Stock, London, 1905.

XENOPHRENIA

(Gk. *xenos*, 'strange', *phrēn*, 'mind'), a comprehensive term applied to all those states in which the normal workaday consciousness is temporarily displaced or in abeyance, and a different kind of awareness supervenes. It covers every 'altered state of consciousness' (abbreviated ASC) in the human being. The term *dissociation*, formerly used to designate multiple personality and now largely obsolescent in psychological literature, is sometimes used as a substitute for xenophrenia. So is the term *trance*, in which a partial or complete cessation of physical consciousness occurs.

In xenophrenia it would seem that the fluctuating boundary between the conscious and unconscious mind is breached, and material from the unconscious filters into consciousness. One becomes oblivious of one's surroundings, brain memory becomes blurred or obliterated totally, and the mind opens out to another perspective. Normal awareness is lost at the point at which certain symptoms appear and the altered state takes place. The cause, onset, symptoms, duration and termination of xenophrenia vary considerably.

The transit between the waking (normal) and xenophrenic (altered) states of consciousness involves, as it were, a change of key or a shifting of gears.

The transition stages may be marked by (1) confusion of thought and dreamy states; (2) blackouts, inner darkness and unconsciousness without recall; and (3) the passage to the changed grade.

Xenophrenia includes both the substrata and the outer reaches of consciousness, when a person becomes sensitive to other 'deep in' and 'far out' dimensions. The mind can move 'downwards' and the level then reached could become pathological, resulting in depersonalization, 'possession' and insanity. It could revert to an atavistic level in the evolutionary scale, as when Dr Jekyll becomes Mr Hyde. Conversely, it could move 'upward' to achieve Objective or Cosmic Consciousness. All these could be interpreted as getting in touch with the excluded, alien or unknown portions of one's own inner self. But every altered state of consciousness provides a unique experience and possesses a near transcendent quality. William Dement, one of the pioneers in sleep research, described even the period of REMs (rapid eye movements), which accompany dreaming, as 'a special state of being'.

A xenophrenic state may give rise to such paranormal phenomena as precognition, clairvoyance, automatism, xenoglossis (speaking in strange tongues), allochiry (a displacement of tactile sensations), a disturbance of time-sense, delusions and hallucinations, and in some cases levitation. A person may develop analgesia, in which sensibility to pain disappears, wounds inflicted do not bleed, or else bleeding may occur without an inflicted wound (stigmata). There may be intense monoideism, in which a person is wrapt in deep contemplation, totally oblivious of what is happening around him.

The causes of xenophrenia are manifold, depending on a multitude of physical and mental factors. Many altered states are achieved by diminishing the effectiveness of the cortex and temporarily interfering with the circuits of the nervous system. Dissociation may occur as a result of injury or accident, a blow on the head, suffocation, partial strangulation, or carotid pressure. It may follow a brain tumour or glandular dysfunction, or occur during high fever, or in diseases like tuberculosis, syphilis, cancer, and mental and nervous disorders such as schizophrenia, hysteria, epilepsy, narcolepsy, migraine. It accompanies the dying condition.

Any overwhelming emotion, excitement, passion, such as terror, fear, shock, ecstasy, exhilaration, love, joy, rage, anger, jealousy, anxiety, panic, may trigger a sudden xenophrenic experience.

Again, monotonously repetitive activity of any kind creates a state of semi-somnolence conducive to xenophrenia. Prolonged chanting, singing, howling and ululation, and even repetitive prayers; playing with a fingering piece or a string of beads; continuous movement like whirling, dancing, swaying, swinging, can cause dissociation. The senses can be fatigued and lulled into a similar reaction by a number of methods. Thus, music, especially drumming, and rhythmic noise, work their effect through the ear; incense and perfume through the nose; staring steadily at something, flickering lights, watching a flame, scrying or looking at a bright surface, work through the eyes and optic nerves.

Furthermore, actual physical mortification of the flesh as in asceticism, fasting or starvation, thirst (Sioux Indians used this method), sensory deprivation, solitude, protracted continence, tend to alter the chemistry of the body and so cause dissociation. So do pain, torture, flagellation, prolonged deep breathing, violent exercise, exhaustion techniques, sexual excess, sleep deprivation.

Numerous experimental methods have been used to manipulate consciousness. For example, in electrical stimulation of the brain (ESB), hair-like electrodes are sunk into pre-selected spots in the brain, and electric currents passed down to produce a desired mental state. Electrical shocks may also be administered, as in electro-convulsive therapy (ECT) on psychiatric patients.

In what is euphemistically called chemical mysticism, toxins and other chemical agents are used to alter consciousness; these include alcohol, and a wide range of euphoriants, hallucinogens and psychedelics. Drugs are also introduced into the system by means of chemotrodes, tiny tubes through which chemicals are injected direct into the brain cells.

Both Aleister Crowley (d. 1947) and George Gurdjieff (d. 1949) used their own special methods to bring on dissociation through a kind of temporary derangement of the senses. Crowley made his pupils think backwards and then confusedly so that they were no longer aware of what they were doing, and were forced into a state of so-called 'unsanity'. Gurdjieff's method of 'dismantling the human machine' reduced a number of his pupils to physical wrecks. Today certain kinds of pop music deliberately employ compulsive insistent rhythms and a harsh broken beat to induce similar strange-minded states.

Two American researchers, R. E. L. Masters and his wife, Jean Houston, have invented what they call their Witches' Cradle, or Altered State of Consciousness Induction Device (ASCID). This ingenious contraption gets its name from the method allegedly used by witches to 'visit the devil'. They were said to suspend themselves in a large sack from a tree to swing about until they entered a state of dissociation. In the modern version the subject is blindfolded and strapped upright in a swing suspended from a universal joint and the gentle motion of his own body rocks him into a trance.

Depending on the type and degree of xenophrenia, the body may be rigid or inert, contorted or normal, cataleptic or mobile. Brain consciousness is never fully present. The person may be dimly aware of his surroundings in a state of semi-consciousness, or in a condition of complete oblivion; he may be sentient or insentient. There may be a total cessation of all outward mental and physical activity, so that he does not respond to external stimuli. He may return to consciousness in varying degrees of awareness of what he has experienced, or he may have no recollection at all.

Thus, there is no memory of what has taken place when a person emerges from a state of deep trance, unconsciousness, extreme drunkenness, catalepsy (as distinct from cataplexy, where the body is cataleptic but the mind remains conscious), epilepsy and narcolepsy. The latter is a nervous disease in which the patient has a sudden brief attack or irrepressible drowsiness, perhaps in the middle of dictating a letter, or while driving a car. Coming out of such profound xenophrenia he is often unable to move for several seconds after recovering.

In other forms of xenophrenia bodily movement is possible, but the workaday consciousness is absent and a deeper subliminal consciousness seems to take charge. This is found in somnambulism, automatism, certain kinds of hypnosis and even sleep. According to Tibetan belief, a momentary xenophrenia, of a high order, is attained by human beings for a fraction of an instant without any mystical exertion when they are (1) yawning, (2) falling asleep, (3) becoming unconscious, (4) having sexual intercourse, and (5) dying.

Possession, so called, involves the apparent taking over of the self by an intrusive entity. This we find in mediumistic trance, and in multiple personality. There are also cases where a person, unconscious of his surroundings, is completely engrossed in another sphere, for instance, in meditation, ecstasy, beatitude, inspiration, mystical rapture. Again, a person may retain a vague awareness of his surroundings, but cannot efficiently respond to the exigencies of everyday life; his movements are unco-ordinated and his speech slurred. This is found with those under the influence of drink or drugs, and in different degrees in infants, hysterics, the senile, the very weak and sick, and the insane.

In the xenophrenia of the dying person, the mind releases its hold on its earthly environment altogether. From the letter *theta,* the initial of the Greek word for death (*thanatos*) the term *theta consciousness* is derived. It is used for the form of awareness that is presumed to persist after the dissolution of the body.

Books

Braid, James, *Observations on Trance, or Human Hibernation*, London, 1850.
Cohen, Sidney, *The Beyond Within*, Atheneum, New York, 1965.
Farber, S. M. and Wilson, R. H. L., *Control of the Mind,* University of California Press, Berkeley, 1961.
King, C. Daly, *States of Human Consciousness*, University Books, New York, 1963.
Lausch, Erwin, *Manipulation,* Aiden Ellis Publishing Co., Nuffield, 1973.
Lilly, John C., *The Centre of the Cyclone*, Calder & Boyars, London, 1973.
Masters, R. E. L. and Houston, J., *The Varieties of Psychedelic Experience*, Blond, London, 1967.
Masters, Robert and Houston, Jean, *Mind Games*, Turnstone Press, London, 1973.
Payne, Buryl, *Getting There Without Drugs*, Wildwood House, London, 1974.
Prince, Raymond (ed.), *Trance and Possession States*, Bucke Memorial Society, Montreal, 1966.
Singer, J. L., *Daydreaming: An Introduction to the Experimental Study of Inner Experience*, Random House, New York, 1966.
Tart, Charles (ed.), *Altered States of Consciousness*, Wiley, New York, 1969.
Walker, Benjamin, *Beyond the Body*, Routledge & Kegan Paul, London, 1974.
Wavell, Stewart *et al.*, *Trances*, Allen & Unwin, London, 1966.
White, J. (ed.), *The Highest State of Consciousness*, Doubleday, New York, 1972.

Index

INDEX

INDEX

INDEX

INDEX

INDEX

INDEX

INDEX

INDEX